STATE TRANSFORMATIONS

Studies in Critical Social Sciences Book Series

Haymarket Books is proud to be working with Brill Academic Publishers (www.brill.nl) to republish the *Studies in Critical Social Sciences* book series in paperback editions. This peer-reviewed book series offers insights into our current reality by exploring the content and consequences of power relationships under capitalism, and by considering the spaces of opposition and resistance to these changes that have been defining our new age. Our full catalog of *SCSS* volumes can be viewed at https://www.haymarketbooks.org/series_collections/4-studies-in-critical-social-sciences.

STATE TRANSFORMATIONS

Classes, Strategy, Socialism

EDITED BY
GREG ALBO
STEPHEN MAHER
ALAN ZUEGE

Haymarket Books
Chicago, IL

First published in 2021 by Brill Academic Publishers, The Netherlands
© 2021 Koninklijke Brill NV, Leiden, The Netherlands

Published in paperback in 2022 by
Haymarket Books
P.O. Box 180165
Chicago, IL 60618
773-583-7884
www.haymarketbooks.org

ISBN: 978-1-64259-776-9

Distributed to the trade in the US through Consortium Book Sales and
Distribution (www.cbsd.com) and internationally through Ingram Publisher
Services International (www.ingramcontent.com).

This book was published with the generous support of Lannan Foundation and
Wallace Action Fund.

Special discounts are available for bulk purchases by organizations and
institutions. Please call 773-583-7884 or email info@haymarketbooks.org for more
information.

Cover design by Jamie Kerry and Ragina Johnson.

Printed in the United States.

10 9 8 7 6 5 4 3 2 1

Library of Congress Cataloging-in-Publication data is available.

Contents

PART 3

From Neoliberalism to Political Crisis

PART 4

Transforming Class Politics and the State

Acknowledgements

The idea for a book on state theory and the modalities of 'state transformations' was originally sparked by a two-day conference held at York University in October 2017, 'Transcending Pessimism, Reimagining Democracy', in honor of Leo Panitch's retirement from York. In December 2020, shortly after delivering the manuscript to our publisher, Leo tragically passed away after contracting Covid-19. Now, sadly, this book is not only in honor of Leo's retirement, but also in memory of Leo's intellectual legacy and lifetime of socialist activism. Leo was our teacher, our colleague, our friend, our comrade. His passing is a tremendous loss for socialists everywhere.

It is not possible to put together a conference and a volume of essays without the support and collective effort of a large array of people. The organization of the conference benefitted enormously from the practical and conceptual assistance of Frederick Peters, Saeed Rahnema, Kamilla Petrick, as well as the support of the staff in the Department of Politics at York University, in particular Carolyn Cross and Margo Barreto. We would also like to acknowledge the financial support for the conference from the Centre for Social Justice as well as the Department of Politics, Faculty of Liberal Arts and Professional Studies, and Office of the Vice-President at York.

In bringing this book to completion, several people provided us with invaluable advice and assistance, notably, Mathew Corbeil for his help with the bibliography and more, Jim Young for help with the index and more, David Fasenfest as the General Editor of the *Studies in Critical Social Science* Series at Brill, the Centre for Social Justice once again for financial aid, and Elaine Whittaker for allowing us to use her startling and transformative image for the book cover. Finally, we want to extend thanks to the vast network of Leo's friends and comrades who, in addition to the writers in this volume, contributed in one way or another to the conference and book – Scott Aquanno, Pat Armstrong, Amy Bartholomew, Dick Bryan, Avishai Ehrlich, Bryan Evans, Judy Hellman, Steve Hellman, Adam Hilton, Ursula Huws, Lorraine Minnite, Ananya Mukherjee-Reed, John Peters, Frances Fox Piven, Chris Roberts, Stephanie Ross, Byron Sheldrick, Sean Starrs, Bhaskar Sunkara Donald Swartz, Rosemary Warskett and Reg Whitaker.

The essays in this volume have many sources. Some were delivered initially as presentations to the York conference. Others were solicited for this volume. A few were published elsewhere in an earlier form and then substantially revised and extended for the volume. For this last group we would like to acknowledge the generous permissions to reproduce portions of the following essays: Ana Garcia e Caio Bugiato, "Repensando o Estado e Imperialismo nas

Relações Internacionais: as contribuições teóricas de Leo Panitch," *Revista de Estudos Internacionais*, 10:2, 2019; Sebnem Oguz, "Rethinking Globalization as Internationalization of Capital: Implications for Understanding State Restructuring," *Science & Society*, 79:3, July 2015; Charles Smith, et al. "Back-to-Work Legislation Roundtable," *Labour/Le Travail*, 86, Fall 2020; Bryan D. Palmer, "Leo Panitch: Political Passions and Socialist Sobriety," *Studies in Political Economy*, 98:3, 2017; Sam Gindin, "Socialism for Realists," *Catalyst*, 2:3, Fall 2018; Doug Henwood, "We Have No Choice But to Be Radical," *Jacobin*, July 30, 2020.

Figures and Tables

Figures

Tables

Notes on Contributors

Greg Albo
teaches political economy in the Department of Politics, York University, Toronto. He is co-editor of the annual *Socialist Register*, the most recent volume of which is *Beyond Digital Capitalism: New Ways of Living*. He also co-edited *Empire's Ally: Canada and the War in Afghanistan* and *Divided Province: Ontario Politics in the Age of Neoliberalism*.

Clyde W. Barrow
is Chair and Professor of Political Science at The University of Texas Rio Grande Valley. His most recent books are *The Dangerous Class: The Concept of the Lumpenproletariat* and *Toward a Critical Theory of States: The Poulantzas-Miliband Debate After Globalization*.

Caio Bugiato
is Adjunct Professor of Political Science and International Relations at Federal Rural University of Rio de Janeiro. He has recently published in *Revista de Estudos Internacionais*, *Critica Marxista*, and *Latin American Perspectives*.

Frank Deppe
is Professor of Political Science at Marburg University, Germany, and a member of the Scientific Council of the Rosa-Luxemburg-Foundation. His recent books include *Niccolo Machiavelli, Der Staat*, and *Revolution & Gegenrevolution*.

Ruth Felder
is an Assistant Teaching Professor in Political Science at Ontario Tech University, Canada. Her research focuses on the political economy of development in Latin America, and she has recently published in *Review of Radical Political Economics* and *Journal of Labour and Society*.

Ana Garcia
is Assistant Professor at the International Relations Institute of the Pontifical Catholic University of Rio de Janeiro, and the Graduate Program in Social Sciences at the Federal Rural University of Rio de Janeiro. She is co-editor of BRICS: *An Anti-Capitalist Critique*.

Sam Gindin
is former research director of the Canadian Auto Workers. He is co-author of *The Making of Global Capitalism: The Political Economy of American Empire*,

and most recently co-author of *The Socialist Challenge Today: Syriza, Corbyn, Sanders.*

Doug Henwood
is an economist, journalist, and broadcaster based in Brooklyn. He is author of *Wall Street: How It Works and for Whom* and *After the New Economy* and is currently working on a study of the rot of the American ruling class.

Martijn Konings
is Professor of Political Economy and Social Theory at the University of Sydney, Australia. His most recent books are *Capital and Time: For a New Critique of Neoliberal Reason*, and *The Asset Economy*.

Colin Leys
is Emeritus Professor of Political Studies at Queen's University, Canada, and Honorary Research Professor at Goldsmiths, University of London. His publications include *Market-Driven Politics* and, most recently, the co-authored book, *Searching for Socialism: The Project of the Labour New Left from Benn to Corbyn.*

Stephen Maher
is a Post-Doctoral Researcher at Ontario Tech University and an Associate at the York University Global Labour Research Centre. He is also Assistant Editor of the *Socialist Register*, and a co-author of *The Socialist Challenge Today: Syriza, Corbyn, Sanders.*

Sebnem Oguz
is Professor of Political Science at Baskent University, Ankara. She is a member of the *Socialist Register* editorial collective and the advisory board of *Praxis* and has published in *Science & Society* and the *Socialist Register.*

Bryan D. Palmer
is Professor Emeritus at Trent University, Canada and edited *Labour/Le Travail* for twenty years. His recent books include *Marxism and Historical Practice: Interventions and Appreciations* and *James P. Cannon and the Emergence of Trotskyism in the United States, 1928–1938.*

Dennis Pilon
is Associate Professor in the Department of Politics at York University, Toronto. He has recently published in the *Socialist Register* and *Labour/Le Travail* and is author of *Wrestling with Democracy: Voting Systems as Politics in the Twentieth-Century West.*

Larry Savage
is Professor of Labour Studies at Brock University, and President of the Canadian Association for Work & Labour Studies. He is the co-author of *Unions in Court: Organized Labour and the Charter of Rights and Freedoms.*

Charles Smith
is Associate Professor of Political Studies at St. Thomas More College, University of Saskatchewan, Canada. He is co-editor of *Labour/Le Travail* and co-author of *Unions in Court: Organized Labour and the Charter of Rights and Freedoms.*

Michalis Spourdalakis
teaches political sociology and serves as Dean of the School of Economics and Politics at the National and Kapodistrian University of Athens, Greece. He is a member of the Executive of the Nicos Poulantzas Institute and author of *The Rise of the Greek Socialist Party.*

Hilary Wainwright
is an editor of *Red Pepper* magazine. She is a Fellow of the Transnational Institute, and an Honorary Associate of the Institute of Development Studies, Sussex University. She is author of *Arguments for a New Left* and, most recently, *A New Politics from the Left.*

Alan Zuege
is Assistant Editor of the *Socialist Register* and co-editor of the *Socialist Register Classics* book series with Haymarket Books. He has also co-edited *Phases of Capitalist Development*; *Value and the World Economy Today*; and *The Globalization Decade.*

Introduction: State Transformations

Greg Albo, Stephen Maher and Alan Zuege

For activists and organizers in the English-speaking world, socialism has again emerged as the preeminent banner around which the political energies of the left are to be consolidated. After having shied away from this moniker as a result of the long shadow cast by the horrors of Stalinism and the repression of the Cold War, the rising tide of climate catastrophe and the social devastation wrought by decades of neoliberal restructuring have made clear the hollowness of once-popular slogans like 'changing the world without taking power', conceptions of the left as a 'movement of movements', and vague suspicions of 'grand narratives'. Indeed, a range of efforts at renewing mass socialist politics, of decidedly mixed success, have recently surfaced around the world, starting in Europe with a variety of political formations from Syriza in Greece to Die Linke in Germany and Podemos in Spain. This renewed interest also emerged notably around the campaigns of Bernie Sanders in the US and Jeremy Corbyn in the UK, both running *within* political parties which had long successfully deflected political challenges from the radical left. Despite the significant dilemmas this presented, these campaigns appeared to represent a new opening for the left to contest political power within the state, while raising the profile of socialist ideas.

Refreshingly, this new generation of activists, especially around Momentum in the UK and the Democratic Socialists of America in the US, has not defined itself in relation to the events of 1917 in Russia, inspirational though these certainly remain. And yet, an alternative seemed elusive. All too often, this led to the identification of socialism with the New Deal, or with European social democracy. Moreover, at the same time as socialism burst onto the scene in the Global North, inspirational efforts to develop a 'twenty-first century socialism' in the Global South – especially the Latin American 'Pink Tide' – appeared to flounder. The fundamental dilemma faced by the left everywhere, it seemed, was navigating a course between the impasses of social democratic politics, on the one hand, while getting beyond the limited politics of street protest, on the other. Faced with multiple, overlapping crises, how can the left build organizational forms able to serve as the fulcrum of working-class formation and revolutionary political agency, which can transform the capitalist state, rather than being transformed *by* it?

These impasses, and the ongoing disorganization of left forces, therefore only reinforces the need to revisit the relationships of class-party-state and

return to the critique of social democracy, articulated in the 1980s as neoliberalism was just getting underway, and before its utter capitulation through
the 'Third Way'.[1] The technocratic and top-down structure of social democratic
parties had long led them to turn away from the kind of cultivation of working-
class capacities and democratic engagement that would be necessary to move
beyond capitalism. Together with the longstanding marginalization of socialist
ideas as 'unrealistic', this meant that when crisis struck in the 1970s, these parties had little capacity to chart a course out of it – or even to effectively resist
the ruling class neoliberal onslaught. They were revealed more as vehicles for
accommodating workers to a new capitalist reality, than building the forces for
a transition to something better. What is needed, therefore, is not a return to
social democracy's failed politics of class compromise, but rather the creation
of a different kind of party – the discovery of which is one of the central tasks
of the budding socialist movement.

A return to the questions of class-party-state today must nevertheless confront the new political realities resulting from the relentless assault on working classes and the radical redesign of capitalist states through four decades
of neoliberal globalization. This is not to imply resignation or withdrawal into
the political ether of 'global civil society', however, for an alternative understanding of globalization and the state places the national political scene
firmly at the center of the struggle against global capitalism. Still, the task
of rebuilding left organizations and working-class politics confronts a new
configuration of imperialism and an enduring legacy of neoliberalism that,
for all the diverse socialist formations that are taking root today, is embedded
in the institutional materiality of the capitalist states they confront.[2] At the
level of theory, what is needed is a Marxist alternative to conventional political science and prevailing pluralist accounts of government institutions, on
the one hand, and vulgar Marxist reductions of the state, its institutions, and
its interventions to so many instruments deployed by the capitalist classes,
on the other – one which takes the capitalist state seriously as proper object
of theory as well as a strategic terrain for politics. While mainstream political
science has been unable to grasp the impact of the systemic drives of the
capitalist system on political institutions, conventional Marxist theories of
imperialism have failed to fully account for the different phases of imperialism and the unique nature of the global capitalist system that has taken shape
since World War II – founded upon the free movement of capital all around

---

1 For a sampling, see: Therborn (1978); London-Edinburgh Weekend Return Group (1980);
   Panitch (1986a); Miliband, Liebman, Saville and Panitch (1986); Williams (1989).
2 See for example the discussions in Panitch, Albo and Chibber (2011).

the world protected by a common set of global rules internalized in national state institutions and practices. What is needed, then, is a Marxist social science that does not divorce the state from the process of globalization, but rather examines how states have remained central actors in the drama of globalization.

All of these themes run through the essays compiled in the present volume – sometimes in the foreground, sometimes in the background, but always present, and always motivating the analysis. If the search for a socialist politics appropriate to our times, which has its historical roots in the politics of the New Left of the 1960s and 1970s, has yet to yield the concrete political forms necessary to reverse the decline of working-class power and decomposition of left forces, the intellectual openness that it demands and reinforces has nevertheless remained a point of light in dark times. The book's title, 'State Transformations', reflects many of the key themes found in the comparative study of contemporary states: the neoliberal restructuring of capitalist states, the changing economic and political architecture of imperialism, and the prospects of structural reform and democratic transformation in the direction of a very different kind of state. The subtitle, 'Classes, Strategy, Socialism', further speaks to the characteristic features of the interventions within state theory that are collected here: grounded in concrete analysis of the balance of forces, rooted in a class politics conceived in the broadest sense, and oriented to the strategic possibilities for socialist advance.

While the volume seeks to contribute to the study of these major transformations of political structures in recent decades, and to insist on the continued salience of class analysis to the study of the capitalist state, it also seeks to honor a major contributor to state theory, Leo Panitch, upon his retirement from his teaching post in the Department of Politics at York University, and now also in his memory upon his passing in December 2020. The volume does not seek to look back at Panitch's career or to catalogue his ideas, but rather to build upon the distinctive approaches and themes raised in his work, and especially to consider how they might inform a renewed research agenda in state theory and strategic orientations for a left again moving forward. The essays compiled here constitute a 'state of the discipline' of sorts in relation to Marxist approaches to the study of comparative politics and political economy. Each of the authors was touched, mentored, befriended, or inspired – mostly in some combination – by Leo Panitch. They have each made cutting-edge of their respective areas of study. In this vein, more than simply honoring Panitch – or, perhaps better, *by doing so* – the present volume seeks to take a modest step toward addressing what Panitch himself identified as the 'impoverishment of state theory'.

The volume is organized into four parts, each consisting of essays addressing a different thematic area: state theory and capitalist democracy; imperialist restructuring and global capitalism; from neoliberalism to political crisis;
and transforming class politics and the state. In the first part, on state theory
and capitalist democracy, essays by Clyde Barrow and Martijn Konings examine the trajectory of Marxist state theory from the 1970s to today, and point
out some ways to carry this theory forward in the context of the impasse it
confronts today.[3] Barrow traces Panitch's distinctive contributions to state
theory, first in transcending the deadlocked debate between Ralph Miliband
and Nicos Poulantzas in the 1970s, then carrying these insights forward in
his ground-breaking analysis of corporatism and the internationalized neoliberal state. Far from presaging a post-capitalist transition, Panitch saw corporatism as a means for disciplining the working class – which only became
more direct with the decline of these institutions with the shift 'from consent
to coercion' over the neoliberal period. Nor was globalization synonymous
with the usurpation of the state. Rather, what was at stake in the post-crisis
restructuring of the 1990s was the concentration of state power in those apparatuses which organized the internationalization of capital, alongside the
rollback of apparatuses focused predominantly on the domestic well-being
of the working class.

Konings illustrates how this has come hand-in-glove with the entrenchment
of neoliberal reason within the social institutions of capitalist democracy. As
he shows, it is the power of this ideology, with its tendency toward scapegoating and conspiracy theory, rather than the absolute autonomy of the capitalist
state which accounts for the fundamentalist thinking that culminated in the
presidency of Donald Trump. It is this, perhaps above all else, which forms
the ideational core of American republicanism – and which helps to channel oppositional or anti-establishment impulses in pro-market directions that
only serve to reinforce the very neoliberal structures that are at the root of
the dissatisfaction in the first place. Rather than framing the political conflict
as one of neoliberalism versus democracy, Konings argues, we need to understand how neoliberalism is constitutive of contemporary capitalist democracy – as well as the radical democratic movements and struggles that contest
its boundaries and institutional forms.

Similarly, Dennis Pilon and Larry Savage assess the possibilities for reviving class politics today, in the context of the decline of working-class identification with social democratic parties – as these have been overtaken by

---

3   Elaborated in the context of global finance in: Panitch and Konings (2009).

distinctly middle-class forces.[4] In their shift to the Third Way, such parties have moved away from representing working-class interests and have focused instead on a politics of identity and inclusion. In this way, Pilon and Savage point to the crucial role of the party in working-class formation. Far from simply disorganizing the working class, social democratic parties have constituted a particular form of working-class politics, albeit one which is constrained by the limits of capitalist social relations and thus bounded by the pressures of profitability and competitiveness as crucial foundations of its legitimacy – including financing social democratic programs. If workers drifted away from the working-class politics espoused by social democratic parties as these came increasingly under the sway of middle-class, technocratic, and professional forces, Pilon and Savage address themselves to the promise, and potential pitfalls, of the current revival of working-class politics around a new generation of political leaders like Alexandria Ocasio-Cortez, and the ongoing struggles of Momentum within and against the UK Labour Party.

In Part 2 of the volume, on imperialist restructuring and global capitalism, chapters by Sebnem Oguz, Ana Garcia and Caio Bugiato, and Ruth Felder deepen the exploration of the international conjuncture in which capitalist states and capitalist democracies are now situated. These complementary essays start from a shared understanding that the internationalization of capital is inextricably interwoven with the internationalization of the state – that state theory and imperialist theory are now inseparable. The chapters draw upon the distinct conceptual threads first developed by Nicos Poulantzas, who in the early 1970s had already discerned that the "internationalization of capital neither suppresses nor by-passes the nation states" – threads powerfully extended and developed in the work of Leo Panitch and Sam Gindin to escape the theoretical cul-de-sac of 'states versus markets', grasping the process of globalization as "a development not external to states but internal to them."[5] To this extent, nation-states are not declining or retreating but rather reorganizing in the course of mediating the expanded reproduction of capital, serving as key nodal points in the constitution and reproduction of global capitalism while taking charge of the management of 'domestic' class struggles.

In the twenty-first century context of global capitalism, these theoretical underpinnings are crucial for advancing state theory along what Barrow suggests was an empirical-historical 'road not traveled', one that might have

---

4 See the surveys of contemporary class politics and class formation in Panitch, Albo and Chibber (2013) and Panitch and Albo (2014).
5 Poulantzas (1975: 73); Panitch and Gindin (2005a: 142).

avoided "twenty years of wandering through an intellectual wilderness." It opens up concrete study of particular social formations differentially inserted into global capitalist relations and the "development of theoretically informed analyses of actual states situated in their own specific contexts of historical class formation, class struggle, and state organization." This approach further carves a path through the very different intellectual wilderness of 'globaliza-tion theory', overrun with vague abstractions and wild hyperboles of a bor-derless world economy, network society, stateless Empire, or transnational state – notions which have sewn both theoretical confusion and political disorientation. An alternative approach restores the capitalist state to the foreground, as a proper object of both theoretical development and political contestation in the period of neoliberal globalization.

Oguz begins the second part with her tour de force through the history of globalization and imperialism theory. After surveying the field of neoclassical, neo-institutionalist, and classical Marxist approaches to the internationaliza-tion of capital, she identifies a pivotal turning point marked by the interventions of Robin Murray and Nicos Poulantzas, which allowed for a reconceptualiza-tion of the underlying problematic through the lens of a differential 'space of capital' and 'space of the state'. Garcia and Bugiato complement this analysis in their review of International Relations theory, arguing that Marxism must take up a position *within* International Relations, one that not only transcends the traditional realism/idealism divide but also provides a necessary alterna-tive to established critical schools of neo-Gramscian and world-systems the-ory. An approach drawing on Poulantzas and Panitch in particular, they argue, can uniquely grasp the reconfigurations of imperialism through the course of capitalist development as well as account for the incorporation of rising states and regions within an increasingly integrated, American-led global capitalism.

Both Oguz's and Garcia and Bugiato's essays challenge the Lenin-Bukharin tradition as well as modern revivals of the classical model of inter-imperial rivalry. While showing appreciation for the significant contributions made by neo-Gramscian theory to international political economy, the essays critique the tendency in these works toward a globalism that treats states as 'transmis-sion belts' rather than political mediations in the globalization process. The chapters also expressly reject Michael Hardt and Antonio Negri's popular the-sis of a decentered and deterritorialized Empire as well as William Robinson's alternative conception of an organized, class-conscious transnational bour-geoisie that has 'broken free' of nation-states to constitute a global state appa-ratus. Oguz concludes by mapping out the major theoretical positions in the imperialism debate and making her own forceful case for a 're-territorialized' approach capable of theorizing the non-coincidence between the 'spaces' of capital and the state, within a framework for analyzing the restructuring of states as they internalize the contradictory demands of unevenly internationalized capitals. Garcia and Bugiato, meanwhile, extend their analysis using Panitch and Gindin's thesis of American 'informal empire' to contextualize the ascendance of China and other BRICS countries, which in turn have given rise to new imperialist dynamics within 'South-South' relations.

Ruth Felder's chapter employs many of the conceptual insights outlined in the preceding two chapters in her sustained study of political struggles and capitalist state restructuring associated with the rise and fall of Latin America's 'Pink Tide' governments, focusing on the case of Argentina. It is precisely the kind of theoretically informed, concrete investigation of historical class struggles and changing state forms that Barrow hoped might mark a path beyond the escalating abstractions of earlier state theory. Felder traces the emergence of Latin American 'neo-developmentalism' in the early 2000s as a response to the limits of neoliberalism, and charts its evolution and mutation under successive economic, political, and ideological conjunctures. Her study demonstrates that the capitalist state in Latin America, far from a simple 'transmission belt' or instrument of a 'comprador' bourgeoisie, remains a site for political contestation among contradictory capitalist groupings and antagonistic class forces which decisively shape the direction of social and economic policy within the constraints of international accumulation.

If the short-lived Latin American 'Pink Tide' showed the vulnerability of neoliberalism in subordinate links of the imperialist chain, the twin crises of the 'Great Recession' and 'Coronacrisis' a few years later would pose a more serious test of the crisis-management capacities of leading capitalist states and a more fundamental political challenge to the neoliberal globalized order itself. Part 3 of the book, 'from neoliberalism to political crisis', takes measure of the growing contradictions of capitalist states and liberal democracy over the past two decades in the European Union, United Kingdom, United States, and Canada. While the new imperialist configuration that crystallized over the last quarter of the twentieth century confirmed a crucial role for 'effective' capitalist states, above all the American state, in authoring globalization, securing the rights of capital worldwide, and containing class struggles at 'home', the reconstitution of political hegemony and state forms also exposed new cracks and fissures. As Poulantzas presciently observed, well beyond the "permanent instability" of bourgeois hegemony in the face of perpetual class struggle, "certain major contradictions within the state are now located between its economic role and its role in maintaining order and organizing consent" – and the capitalist state's current contradictory place in the reproduction of neoliberal globalization has only intensified this role as an "accelerator of the generic elements of political crisis and the generating force of that crisis itself."[6] The response of neoliberal states to these sharpening contradictions has also confirmed Gramsci's much earlier warning that capitalist hegemony is ever protected by the "armour of coercion."[7] With staggering economic inequality, growing social polarization, and a deepening crisis of political representation, as an array of reactionary social forces have moved into the political vacuum, neoliberal states have increasingly uncovered the authoritarian impulse underpinning the 'free economy and strong state' couplet.

While earlier parts of the book exposed how prevailing theoretical approaches – both critical and mainstream – tended to marginalize the political terrain of the nation-state and reduce the capitalist state's role in neoliberal globalization to its economic apparatus, Part 3 opens with Frank Deppe's stinging critique of the social democratic vision of a progressive, 'post-national' path to globalization, and a reminder of the capitalist state's vital ideological and repressive functions amidst the 'rebirth of nationalism and the crisis of the European Union'. Jürgen Habermas serves here as the symbol of a wider naïveté on the center-left that Europe could provide the model of a more 'rational', legally ordered 'cosmopolitan democracy' defined by world citizenship, one that might bring finally to a close a long and at times barbarous historical chapter of national chauvinism and inter-state violence. For many like-minded thinkers, such a model could be materially supported by a revival of corporatist economic arrangements paving the way for a progressive, 'high road' to international competition, allowing welfare states and global capitalism to co-exist. Set against this social democratic fantasy, Deppe chronicles the political nightmare that has instead materialized. Far from opening up a new 'post-national constellation', as Habermas hoped, it is something more akin to 'post-democracy' that has emerged across parts of Europe. Far from realizing the original utopian vision of a 'United States of Europe', Deppe shows how the neoliberal form of integration and the escalating political crises brought in its wake have instead spawned a very different set of political 'models': of authoritarian populism, repressive state formations, and new right variants of 'corporatism' appealing to nationalism to bind workers to 'their' company and state in international competition. By 2020, amidst the ongoing imposition of disciplinary austerity on Greece, a political standoff in negotiations over 'Brexit', and ruthless suppression of the so-called 'immigration crisis', the abject failure of the EU's response to the spreading Covid-19 pandemic came to

---

6   Poulantzas (1978c: 168, 212).
7   Gramsci (1971: 263).

be recognized by even many ardent proponents as the final nail in the coffin of 'Social Europe', if not an existential threat to the union itself.

The 'success' of capitalist classes in imposing privatization, welfare cuts, and regulatory liberalization not only exposed an increasingly brittle political hegemony but also a selectively weakened state administrative apparatus, ill-equipped to handle the biggest social, economic, and political crises of the last half-century. Colin Leys sets the historical stage in the UK: "loss of the empire, followed by exposure of the UK economy to global market forces after 1980, and the accompanying conversion of the political elite into agents of these forces, had exposed the inherited political structure to stresses it was increasingly unable to withstand." He poses the question of whether layers of contradictions historically embedded in the UK political field have condensed into a Gramscian 'general crisis of the state', in which social classes detach from their traditional political parties opening the way to growing social instability and potentially to political violence. Leys canvasses the disparate responses emerging from social democracy and the far right, and he probes the inability of a crumbling party system and ineffective constitutional state form to re-organize and re-unify the dominant classes in the face of a multifold crisis stretching from the global recession to Brexit and the pandemic.

In a parallel snapshot of the condition of the American ruling class, Doug Henwood shows how decades of crisis-management of an unstable financialized accumulation had taken a toll on the political and economic structures of neoliberal reproduction: the 'Coronacrisis', he argues, "hit a system that had been structurally weakened because of the systemic rot – the erosion of state capacity, declining health among a lot of the population, increasing financial fragility, inequality, precarity, and the rest." Henwood tracks this ruling-class 'rot' through its expression in both the Democratic and Republican parties, while further developing his thesis of a re-composition of the US power bloc amidst the consolidation of a capitalist network of corporate asset-strippers, extractive capital, and dark money groups around Donald Trump and his now firmly entrenched political faction.[8] The contemporary rot of the political establishment is contrasted with "the mid-20th century ruling class, which planned the postwar American imperial order with foresight and skill"; its most conspicuous legacy instead a threadbare infrastructure of healthcare, social services, economic planning, and emergency preparedness that was put on tragic, even pathetic, display when the pandemic struck.

---

8   Compare Henwood (2018) and Panitch and Gindin (2018b) for points of convergence, and divergence, on Trumpism and the reshaping of the American ruling class.

Charles Smith picks up the analysis of neoliberalism's increasing turn to coercion with a focus on the legal mechanisms of working-class incorporation and control within capitalist democracy. He explores the unique trajectory of neoliberalism in Canada through the lens of 'industrial legality', drawing on the work of Leo Panitch and Donald Swartz, looking at the ways the state channels workplace conflict into officially sanctioned, juridified forms. In particular he takes up the influential thesis of a 'permanent exceptionalism' – characterizing the increasing government resort to ad-hoc back-to-work legislation to limit the power of labor – which Smith confirms has all but become the new norm in Canadian state management of industrial conflict. As such it has become a leading weapon in the neoliberal state's arsenal of coercive discipline and Canadian capital has come to rely on it to maintain competitiveness. After a long and costly history of legal struggle, Canadian unions recently won minimal constitutional recognition of the right to strike, but Smith's essay asks to what extent the victory is a pyrrhic one, as the courts have applied the precedent haphazardly and the threat of state intervention remains unabated, with governments ever ready to invoke the neoliberal lexicon of national interest, economic sacrifice, and global constraints to justify 'emergency' back-to-work legislation. In this way Smith's survey of the labor law landscape rekindles the debate around the implications of legal strategy on working-class politics and organization, as well as the wider dilemmas of operating inside the politico-legal forms of the capitalist state.

A complete catalogue of neoliberal state restructuring in terms of policies and national cases could fill several volumes. It is hard to identify any part of the world or any part of the state apparatuses that has been untouched. An underlying theme of Panitch's writing on globalization and the 'new imperialism' was the difficulty of disentangling neoliberalism, from globalization or from Americanization, in state economic policies. This is not a story of a global victory of neoliberal 'ideas' resulting in the erasure of national and local difference, but of a gradual internalization of 'foreign' – and especially American – capital within national power blocs and a widespread adoption of international legal, policy, and regulatory norms within national policy regimes under the tutelage of American-led international institutions. The successes of this 'liberalization' project since the 1980s established a new phase of accumulation for the world's ruling classes. And it was matched by the inability of working-class movements to recover from the defeats of the 1970s – to form alternative class strategies that could move beyond 'competitive corporatism' and roll back the neoliberal policy agenda. On the one hand, social democratic parties accommodated themselves to neoliberalism through the Third Way and rid themselves of commitments to the postwar Keynesian welfare state;

and on the other hand, the varied reform efforts of Perestroika in the Soviet Union and East Bloc proved incapable of overcoming the combined contradictions of statist command economies and one-party political systems, and they dissolved into varieties of neoliberal 'shock therapy'.

This context of working-class defeat and decline of the political vehicles for socialist aspirations in the twentieth century is the starting point of our fourth and final part on 'transforming class politics and the state'. The New Left's various attempts to form an alternate more democratic, more participatory path through the impasse of social democracy and the end of authoritarian communism animates Hilary Wainwright's contribution. In this, Wainwright shares with Panitch an interest in the organized efforts at remaking the British Labour Party – from Tony Benn to Jeremy Corbyn – and opening up political space for experiments in popular democracy at the nexus of movement, party, and state. For Wainwright the struggle for popular control over production, whether outside the state producing commodities or inside producing social services, is also an endeavor to reclaim the knowledge and experiences of workers against skill-stripping technological changes and organizational hierarchies designed for social control and capitalist accumulation. The formative struggle at Lucas Aerospace in the 1970s, in the face of mass layoffs and job redesign, is illustrative here of the possibility for 'human-centered systems' that could inform 'alternative plans for socially useful production'. Wainwright traces a number of political experiments in popular planning that are at once struggles of social need against market valuations in solidarity economies and political efforts to rebuild the left through collaborations between left governments, state workers, and the activist citizenship of social movements. Indeed, for Wainwright the impulse toward popular control is again emerging in the struggle over "post-pandemic capitalism" in the form of new experiments in social provisioning and community-building that are less 'in and against the state' and more 'outside the state'.

Wainwright's contribution to socialist strategy pivots on a transformative politics being able to build and mobilize popular knowledges for a participatory administration from industrial plants to state agencies. Her studies have paid particular attention to the ways socialist parties must prioritize political development of their membership (but not exclusively) as much as their functioning as parliamentary machinations. It is just such a re-consideration of socialist 'parties of a new kind' that preoccupies Michalis Spourdalakis in his discussion of the problems of party-building for the radical left. He begins with an excursus on conventional theories of political parties – conceived in terms of an 'electoral market', as interest brokers, or as vehicles of political socialization and integration. All these theories suffer from the simplistic and

impoverished notion that society is little more than a combination of independent individuals. Thus, Spourdalakis argues they lead naturally to skepticism
about "whether the concept of class is still applicable to the conflict groups
of post-capitalist societies." These are views of parties that have often found
their way into the electoral calculations of social democratic parties as well
as parties of the right. But if the "material existence of any social class is the
result of its political organization," Spourdalakis argues, the parties of the left
can also suffer a reductionism of the party to the class. There is a need for
a 'relative autonomy' of the socialist party from its class base to form a clarity of its orientation, its functions of forming strategy and tactics, that is, the
socialist party's very existence as a democratic organization of class struggle
acting in the political scene that is not reducible to the complex class interests
the party represents. It is this necessary tension that needs to be navigated in
party-building on the radical left and in remaking the relationship between
movements and parties.

Spourdalakis underlines the significance of socialist political parties in
'making the class' through its organizing and strategic calculations. This recognition has become an integral part of an intense series of international debates
on the need to make-over the relationship of parties to working classes and
social movements. The challenge posed is whether left political parties can
re-balance their role as representative in parliament to function equally as
facilitators and coordinators of struggles outside parliament. But if the party-
movement relation is to form a creative and reinforcing dynamic, then a vision
of a democratic socialist alternative must become a mutual political reference
and a political program consolidated to guide immediate political struggles
and to serve as a point of continual political renewal and growth.

In the essays gathered in *Renewing Socialism* (2001), Panitch consistently
stressed the primacy of the political in any transition beyond capitalism, but
also as central to the constituent democratic institutions and practices of a
socialist society – from representative bodies to councils to the organs of economic planning. Such a process of radical democratization could be located
in struggles for 'structural reforms' or 'non-reformist reforms', in André Gorz's
phrasing, that do not limit themselves to demands consistent with capitalist
logic and needs such as struggles over work-time reduction or conversion of
industrial plants to socially useful production. This was a conception of socialist politics that Panitch often elaborated in collaboration with Sam Gindin.
And here Gindin offers an essay contending that an "institutionally-elaborated
alternative is now elemental to encourage social movements to press beyond
protest." Even if social ownership, workers' control, and democratic economic
planning are foundational to socialist society, "more systematic consideration

of socialism's possible functioning," Gindin suggests, is today "a requirement for reviving the receptivity to achievable utopias and the willful action to achieve them."

Part 4 ends with a contribution from the Marxist historian Bryan Palmer, a longtime colleague and comrade of Panitch within the Canadian left. Gindin's search for a plausible socialism and an organized socialist politics capable of taking and transforming state power, after decades of the erosion of working-class politics, was an animating feature of his joint writing with Panitch. While paying respect to Panitch's role as a leading public intellectual in Canada, it is this "socialist sobriety" that Palmer directs his attention toward. For Palmer, Panitch's writing was marked by an insistence on taking account of the politics of class struggle in its relation to class and state formation, in all its contradictions, and in particular to the global consolidation of the American empire – with its dominance over Canada – from the postwar period to neoliberalism. Here Palmer's long-standing differences in historical and political judgments emerge. For Panitch, it was impossible to disentangle socialist transformation from the terrain of the capitalist state. While the project of rebuilding the left requires grassroots capacity-building and educational projects across unions and social movements, particularly in a period of political reaction and left disorganization such as today, it also had to transform political structures requiring that it operates inside and outside the state. For Palmer this leads to a strategic map that is "overdetermined" by a "focus on the state" that needs to be matched by the leaps, audacities, and uncertainties of the streets. The "politics of possibility" for socialist advance in the twenty-first century, much like the entire history of the socialist movement, will be made as much in struggles in the streets as with struggles over the state.

Finally, the volume concludes with a postscript, which picks up where Palmer left off as well as recounts the original inspiration for this project, a tribute to Leo's intellectual and political contributions. Leo's career was committed to developing a critical political science of the state, building on a legacy stretching from Antonio Gramsci to Ralph Miliband and beyond. This was a commitment Leo shared with his colleagues and students – understanding the economic and institutional foundations of political power in terms of the most advanced research; taking those lessons into unions, movements, and parties; and, in turn, bringing more learning back into the classroom. This was and is a critical political science that could not avoid pointing to the enormous costs that modern capitalism has imposed on the world's working classes and the earth's ecology. It is fitting, then, to end the introduction to a volume in memory of Leo with the conclusion from his monumental study (in collaboration with Gindin), *The Making of Global Capitalism* (2012), that is, in substance, the point of departure for the essays that follow: "Yet the gap that exists between the stubborn realities of capitalism and the revolutionary spirit so manifest in public squares around the world which inspired the occupations in the US itself teaches a sobering lesson. It is not in fact possible to change the world without taking power. ... Whether called socialism or not, today's revived demands for social justice and genuine democracy could only be realized through ... a fundamental shift of political power, entailing fundamental changes in state as well as class structures."[9]

9   Panitch and Gindin (2012: 340).

PART 1

State Theory and Capitalist Democracy

∵

CHAPTER 1

From the Canadian State to the Making of Global Capitalism

Clyde W. Barrow

In 1976, the Poulantzas-Miliband debate (1969–1976) on Marxist state theory had just reached its conclusion in what appeared to be a profoundly disappointing stalemate between the world's two most renowned Marxist theorists of the state.[1] The exchange between Nicos Poulantzas and Ralph Miliband was a paradigmatic event as it set in motion a broader 'state debate' that seemed to fracture Marxist political theory into warring schools of thought.[2] The Poulantzas-Miliband debate echoed widely across the 1970s, and following their initial exchange in 1969–70, political theorists around the world quickly lined up around the question of whether Miliband's 'instrumentalism' or Poulantzas' 'structuralism' could rightly claim to be *the* Marxist theory of the state.[3]

A notable exception to this polarization appeared a year after the conclusion of the Poulantzas-Miliband debate when Leo Panitch, a young Canadian political scientist at Carleton University, pointed the way beyond this impasse in a book entitled *The Canadian State: Political Economy and Political Power* (1977a). The publisher called the book "a powerful collection of essays," and while reviewers who were generally skeptical of Marxism did not fully agree with this assessment, they did agree that the 15-chapter book displayed a remarkable "thematic consistency,"[4] primarily due to Leo Panitch's introductory essay which integrated the works of Ralph Miliband (1969), Nicos Poulantzas (1973), and James O'Connor (1973) into "a coherent perspective" on

---

1   Miliband (1970; 1973); Poulantzas (1969, 1976a); Laclau (1975). For a summary of the Poulantzas-Miliband debate, see, Barrow (2002; 2016: chs. 1–2).
2   Jessop (1982); Carnoy (1984); Alford and Friedland (1985); Barrow (1993).
3   Clarke (1991). Miliband never identified himself as an instrumentalist and Poulantzas rejected the structuralist label. These were analytical terms applied to them by others who summarized the debate after the fact, see, particularly Gold, Lo and Wright (1975a; 1975b). Poulantzas (1976a: 63–64) correctly dismissed these terms "as an utterly mistaken way of situating the discussion."
4   Grayson (1979: 651).

the state.[5] At the time, Miliband, Poulantzas, and O'Connor were indisputably the three leading state theorists in the world, although their works were generally presented as mutually exclusive theories of the state.[6] Panitch's success in blending these theoretical works into "a coherent perspective" was praised as "a signal contribution," to Marxist political theory.[7] The book quickly sold several thousand copies and on the fortieth anniversary of its publication, *The Canadian State* was still being described as "a remarkably influential collection of essays."[8] While most of the chapters in this book focused on political developments in Canada, Panitch emphasized that the Canadian state was not the only object of analysis, but instead the book's focus was on the Canadian state *in capitalist society* and, in this respect, the Canadian state shared many of the same institutional features and policy challenges as other states in other capitalist societies. Panitch was quick to remind scholars that even though the Poulantzas-Miliband debate had contributed to a renewed interest in Marxist state theory, the debate itself was also an effect of the changing material foundations of capitalist societies or what Miliband had called "the Western system of power."[9]

This Western system of power was the Keynesian Welfare State (KWS) that had emerged in some form in every Western liberal democracy after World War II. This state form was based on the simultaneous regulation of private business, the strengthening of labor unions, and the expansion of public health, education, and welfare programs.[10] The KWS included government-sponsored health insurance and medical coverage for citizens, government-sponsored old-age pensions, unemployment insurance, industrial accident insurance, cash assistance for the poor, the construction of publicly owned housing, expanded access to public education and higher education, protection of the right to collective bargaining, public ownership of basic resource extraction and common carrier industries (i.e., coal, oil, aviation, railways), and the regulation of business to protect workers, consumers, citizens, and the environment against negative externalities.

---

5   Manzer (1978: 405). Panitch (1996: 83) later included Claus Offe in this pantheon. O'Connor and Offe were often placed in a 'Hegelian' school of state theory, because of their emphasis on the contradictions of capitalism as opposed to its equilibrium and stabilization.

6   Gold, Lo and Wright (1975a; 1975b).

7   Manzer (1978: 405–06).

8   "Symposium" (2017: 175).

9   Miliband (1969).

10   Gough (1979).

However, by the early 1970s, the cumulative fiscal effect of these policies was being manifested in a long-term trend for government expenditures and national debt to increase as a percentage of gross domestic product in all of the advanced industrial democracies.[11] While the KWS was initiated in different capitalist countries at different times, at different paces, through different policies, and with differing aggregate effects on wealth and income inequality, there was no doubt that by the late 1960s the invisible hand of the market was being replaced by the visible hand of the state.[12] Nevertheless, Panitch was among a handful of early critics to argue that a second notable feature of advanced capitalist societies had been "the marked failure of social democracy in the post-war period" despite the emergence of the KWS.[13] While others hailed the KWS as a decisive advance for social democracy, Panitch concluded that the decades-long rise of the British Labour Party, the German and Swedish Social-Democratic parties, and the French and Italian Communist parties had failed to "effect fundamental changes in the social order."[14] In fact, the rise of the KWS had exposed a fundamental contradiction "between the formal political equality of liberal democracy and the socio-economic inequality of capitalist society." This continuing contradiction meant that "the connections between state and class structure" were not just an intellectual puzzle for political theorists, but an imperative political challenge for the left.

Finally, while the upheavals of the 1960s had largely come to an end by the early 1970s, the advanced industrial societies had nevertheless entered a decade of rising industrial class conflict (e.g., strikes) on a level not seen since the Great Depression.[15] The renewal of open industrial conflict was challenging the long-term viability of the Western elite consensus on the Keynesian welfare state as labor unrest and the growing costs of the KWS created a profit squeeze for capitalist enterprises (i.e., a falling rate of profit).[16] Panitch was

---

11   O'Connor (1973).

12   Graham (1976).

13   Panitch (1977a: vii).

14   Panitch (1977a: vii).

15   Hibbs (1976). Panitch (1986a: 201–02) was acutely aware of the fact that "in the early 1970s official strikes became more common and a significant radicalization was seen in both the industrial and political programmes of the union movements." Elsewhere, Panitch and Swartz (1988: 29) observe that the heightened degree of industrial conflict during the 1960s and 1970s "reflected both greater militancy on the part of workers" and "more determined resistance by capital and the state, in light of the deepening economic crisis."

16   Bell (1960); Glyn and Sutcliffe (1972).

cautious about the outcome of this industrial militancy, which he suggested "might have immediate radical consequences," but he also feared that it might become the "basis for the development of conservatizing corporatist structures."[17] Leftist scholars such as Panitch, and even conservative scholars attached to the ruling class,[18] both clearly recognized that the renewal of class conflict in the 1970s signaled a crisis of the Keynesian welfare state. Indeed, both sides recognized that the crisis of the 1970s had exposed the "big tradeoff" between efficiency (capital accumulation) and equality (legitimation) and this big trade-off raised deeper questions about the compatibility of capitalism and democracy.[19]

This crisis of liberal capitalism was the historical backdrop that led Panitch to the conclusion that "renewed interest in a Marxist theory of the state reflects a sense that the concepts and theories of modern political science, and the hypotheses that are derived from them to appropriate reality, are incapable of even addressing, let alone explaining, many of the major political questions of our time."[20] Yet, for this reason, Panitch chastised radical scholars for spending too much intellectual energy on the critique of mainstream social science, when it had already been exposed as deficient by political events.[21] To the extent that radical scholars focused their efforts on critiques of mainstream social science, they were addressing political problems defined by capitalist elites (e.g., governability) or abstract intellectual puzzles defined by bourgeois intellectuals (e.g., system boundaries).[22] In this respect, Panitch argued that radical scholars were often reproducing the intellectual hegemony of bourgeois social science by engaging with it "to the detriment of developing and applying new theory."[23] Consequently, Panitch's contribution to *The Canadian State* was an essay that sought to identify the alternative framework for a Marxist theory of the state and to explore some of the requisites of such a theory in light of the impasse left behind by the Poulantzas-Miliband debate.

---

17   Panitch (1977a: 23).
18   Crozier, Huntington and Watanuki (1975).
19   Bowles and Gintis (1982; 1987); Okun (1975).
20   Panitch (1977a: vii). See, Barrow (2017) and Kesselman (1982) on the intellectual ferment in political science during this time.
21   Barrow (2017: 438–41).
22   The Marxist debate on conducting immanent critiques of bourgeois social science versus the development of an alternative theoretical framework is discussed in Barrow (2016: chs. 1–2).
23   Panitch (1977a: viii).

1   State Theory and Historical Materialism

Panitch sought to anchor the theory of the state in his reading of Karl Marx, although he recognized that Marx's writings did not provide a "systematic examination of the state to match his work on the capitalist mode of production itself."[24] He followed closely in Ralph Miliband's footsteps in concluding that despite the later contributions of V.I. Lenin (1974) and Antonio Gramsci (1971), the Marxist theory of the state remained underdeveloped and that more work was necessary after the apparent fragmentation of state theory into so-called instrumentalist,[25] structuralist,[26] and then Hegelian (or systems-analytic)[27] schools of thought.[28]

In his lead essay for *The Canadian State,* Panitch postulates that a fully developed theory of the state in capitalist society must meet at least three basic requirements:

> It must clearly delimit the complex of institutions that go to make up the state. It must demonstrate concretely, rather than just define abstractly, the linkages between the state and the system of class inequality in the society, particularly its ties to the dominant social class. And it must specify so far as possible the functions of the state under the capitalist mode of production.[29]

Panitch was the only state theorist at the time (and perhaps for two decades) who argued that each of the three approaches – represented by Ralph Miliband, Nicos Poulantzas, and James O'Connor – had each made a contribution to answering one of these questions. Rather than seeing their works as incompatible, or as warring schools of thought, Panitch suggested that the insights of each theorist should be integrated into concrete analyses of actually existing states and their political development.

Panitch argued that the first requisite for a Marxist theory of the state was to provide a clear definition of the state, including a description of its internal

---

24   Panitch (1977a: 4).
25   Miliband (1969).
26   Poulantzas (1973).
27   O'Connor (1973).
28   This typology was first superimposed on Marxist state theory as a result of the highly influential essay by Gold, Lo and Wright (1975a; 1975b), but it was generally adopted by others in presenting the intellectual history of state theory (Jessop 1977; Jessop 1982; Carnoy 1984; Barrow 1993).
29   Panitch (1977a: 5).

organization and its sociological boundaries. Panitch again followed Miliband's
lead in defining the state as:

> ... a complex of institutions, including government, but also including
> the bureaucracy (embodied in the civil service as well as in public cor-
> porations, central banks, regulatory commissions, etc.), the military, the
> judiciary, representative assemblies, and (very importantly for Canada)
> what Miliband called the sub-central levels of government, this is, pro-
> vincial executives, legislatures, bureaucracies, and municipal govern-
> ment institutions.[30]

This definition of the state has three significant implications for a theoretical
analysis of the capitalist state. First, this definition explicitly draws a theoretically important distinction between government and the state. Miliband had
earlier chastised liberal pluralists and parliamentary socialists for their mistaken belief that "the assumption of governmental power is equivalent to the
acquisition of state power."[31] Miliband understood that the accession to governmental power at various points in the twentieth century by liberal, labor,
and social democratic *governments* was accompanied by their simultaneous
failure to conquer *state power* in its diverse forms and places within a more
expansive state system. The fact that a socialist government might control the
commanding heights of the parliamentary and executive branches of government, whether by election or revolution, did not automatically entail its
control of the military, the police, the intelligence agencies, the civil service,
the legal system, the sub-national governments, regulatory agencies, public
corporations, etc. Thus, Panitch notes that one reason for clearly delineating
the institutions of the state is that "it leads us away from assuming, as social
democrats consistently do, that election to governmental power is equivalent
to the acquisition of state power."[32]

A second important element of this definition of the state is the distinction
between the state system and the political and ideological systems. Panitch
observes that an equally important aspect of this definition of the state is
"what it leaves out. It leaves out political parties, the privately-owned media,
the church, pressure groups."[33] Panitch considered these institutions part of
the political and ideological systems and while they "no doubt form part of

---

30   Panitch (1977a: 6). Cf. Miliband (1969: 49).
31   Miliband (1969: 49–50).
32   Panitch (1977a: 7).
33   Panitch (1977a: 6).

the system of power in a liberal-democratic capitalist society ... they remain autonomous from the state" (except in the case of fascism).[34] Thus, Panitch (like Miliband) rejected Poulantzas' and Althusser's claim that institutions such as churches, the educational system, political parties, the press, radio, television, publishing, the family, etc. should all be brought within the realm of state theory as components of an ideological state apparatus.[35] This difference in how one defines the institutional boundaries of the state was more than an analytical quibble, because it is the definitional basis for drawing a distinction between state power and class power.[36] Panitch's point was that state power is not the only form, nor the only site, of ruling class domination, but it is the autonomy of the political and ideological systems *from* the state that opens theoretical spaces for "political and industrial expression through the voluntary organizations of the working class."[37]

Finally, by defining the state as a complex of institutions, Panitch was calling attention to the fact that the state system in capitalist societies is a vast and sprawling network of political institutions loosely coordinated, if at all, through mechanisms that sometimes provide only a tenuous cohesion. These fractures in the state, as well as the uneven development of its various sub-apparatuses, also provide openings for the non-dominant classes to capture parts of the state. It is the sprawling diffuseness of the modern capitalist state that allows it to be what Poulantzas called an arena of class struggle.[38] Importantly, this means that the conquest of state power by the working class is never an all or nothing proposition, because it is -- in the Gramscian phrase -- a war of position and a war of maneuver -- waged on many fronts, in many trenches, with shifting lines of battle, where victories and defeats occur side by side on the same day.[39] The conquest of state power is never absolute; it is never uncontested; and it is never complete, because it is an on-going and contingent *political* struggle. Panitch's definition of the state effectively mandates an analysis and understanding of state power that refers to particular historical circumstances and to institutional configurations that may vary widely from one capitalist society to another, and where over time class hegemony may shift in one direction or another within the same society.

---

34   Panitch (1977a: 6–7).
35   Althusser (1971); Miliband (1973: 87, 88 fn. 7 Chapter 1).
36   Barrow, Wetherly and Burnham (2008: 10–12).
37   Panitch (1977a: 7).
38   Poulantzas (1973: 115).
39   Gramsci (1971: 108–10, 229–35).

The second requisite for a Marxist theory of the state is that it "demonstrate concretely" the nexus between state and capital; that is, what makes the state "capitalist" as opposed to merely a state? Panitch draws on Volume 3 of *Capital* to point out that states perform "common activities arising from the nature of all communities, and the specific functions arising from the antithesis between the government and the mass of the people."[40] This means that all states perform a coordinating role that Poulantzas identified as the general function of the state.[41] Panitch argues that this general maintenance function "is undertaken apart from specific class interests, although of course framed within the boundaries set by the mode of production, and the relations of production of a given society."[42] Panitch identified this general function as a "repressive function" common to all states and, therefore, requiring a repressive state apparatus. In this respect, the general function of the state is consistent with Weber's definition of the state as "a human community that (successfully) claims the *monopoly of the legitimate use of physical force* within a given territory."[43]

The repressive function of the state secures the economic and social dominance of the ruling class simply by maintaining social stability and ensuring the extended reproduction of the mode of production in which a particular ruling class is dominant. At the same time, Panitch argues that this general maintenance function implies a certain degree of relative autonomy from the ruling class.[44] The state normally uses repression against subaltern classes to maintain law and order, but during periods of mass social upheaval the state may find that it can more efficiently restore order by making concessions to subaltern classes even if these concessions come at the short-term expense of the ruling class.[45]

However, as Panitch observes, this general function of the state is always "framed within the boundaries set by the mode of production, and the relations of production of a given society."[46] Consequently, it is always necessary to specify those structural constraints in terms of a specific mode of production. In the case of a state in a capitalist society, one must be able to identify the types of structural constraints that make the state a *capitalist* state. Panitch

---

40   Panitch (1977a: 4). See Marx (1998: 382).
41   Poulantzas (1973: 44–45, 47 fn. 8 Chapter 1).
42   Panitch (1977a: 4).
43   Weber (1946: 78, 82–83). Panitch (1977a: 8) explicitly identifies "a *coercive function*, that is, the use by the state of its monopoly over the legitimate use of force to maintain or impose social order."
44   Panitch (1977a: 4–5).
45   Cf. Moore (1966); Skocpol (1979; 1980); Sanders (1999).
46   Panitch (1977a: 4).

recognized that *Political Power and Social Classes* by Nicos Poulantzas was having a substantial impact on state theory at this time, precisely because of its argument that "the state's activities on behalf of the capitalist class are determined by deep structural relations rather than by similar class backgrounds and social positions of state personnel and businessmen."[47] While Panitch did not dispute this claim, his main concern was that Poulantzas:

> ... tends to remove from the theory of the state a concrete empirical and historical orientation. By establishing by definition the relationship between the state and bourgeoisie, one leaves out the central question, to be determined empirically in each instance, of the *extent* to which the state is acting on behalf of the dominant class.[48]

Panitch accepted Poulantzas' general theoretical claim regarding the importance of structural constraints, but he questioned Poulantzas' articulation of this principle as too abstract and overly deterministic. Indeed, Panitch viewed Poulantzas' theoretical claim as "a rather academic point" when applied to Canada (or the United States), because "the relationship between the first post-confederation cabinets and the financial bourgeoisie and the railway entrepreneurs was not only close – they were often the same people."[49] In other words, it might well be the case that states would act on behalf of the capitalist class without any close personal ties between them, but this claim was beside the point if in fact such ties did exist empirically and historically. Moreover, Poulantzas never specified any structural limits to state action within the capitalist mode of production, nor did he explain how these constraints worked in practice.

In contrast, Miliband had actually given significant attention to the problem of structural constraints,[50] but this analysis was completely overlooked in the heated fury of the Poulantzas-Miliband debate, evidently even by Panitch, who failed to elaborate on this point in his 1977 introductory essay. It may have been the case that Miliband's concept of structural constraint was theoretically underdeveloped, but Miliband had explicitly introduced the principle of business confidence and structural constraint – he even uses those terms – as

---

47   Panitch (1977a: 7).
48   Panitch (1977a: 8).
49   Panitch (1977a: 11). The same was true of the United States as documented empirically and historically by the corporate-liberal historians (Kolko, 1963; Weinstein, 1968) and by the power structure theorists (Mills 1956; Domhoff 1967; 1978).
50   Barrow (2016: 90–94).

factors facilitating a natural alliance between state and capital, regardless of who *governs,* because the state is dependent on capital investment for economic growth and tax revenue. The latter are necessary to the kws's political legitimacy, because its legitimacy is dependent on its ability to deliver needed public services and, especially, to ensure gainful employment for the working class. Thus, Miliband understood that this structural constraint is fundamentally important to ensuring that the state in capitalist society "functions" as a capitalist state.

However, what was also lost in the fog of the Poulantzas-Miliband debate were significant contributions by Ernest Mandel (1971), Amy Beth Bridges (1974), Claus Offe (1975), and Michael H. Best and William Connolly (1976) that met Panitch's demand for historical and empirical specificity.[51] In her early critique of Poulantzas, Bridges identified two constraint mechanisms that were later widely adopted by state theorists, mainly through the works of Fred Block (1977) and Charles Lindblom (1982). Bridges' main theoretical claim was that the state functions in the interests of the capitalist class, because the state's own fiscal solvency and legitimacy is immediately dependent on the overall performance of the economy, where investment and employment decisions are controlled by capitalists.[52] Offe (1975) elegantly codified these state-capital relationships as the dependency principle.

Finally, the third requisite for a Marxist theory of the state was that it "must specify the functions of the state in a capitalist mode of production."[53] Panitch identifies the coercive or repressive function of the state with its general maintenance function, but he drew on James O'Connor's *The Fiscal Crisis of the State* (1973) to identify two additional state functions that are historically specific to the liberal-democratic state in a capitalist mode of production: accumulation and legitimation. Following O'Connor, Panitch argues that "the state must try

---

51   Bridges' contribution was published in *Politics & Society*, which had been founded in 1970 by a group of political scientists affiliated with the newly established (1967) Caucus for a New Political Science. Outside of a few US academic leftists in political science, it is not likely that many people noticed the article when it was first published in 1974. Offe's (1975) contribution was published as a chapter in an obscure edited book, while Best's and Connolly's book (1976) was released by a small press with limited circulation only one year prior to Panitch's essay. Block's (1977) contribution appeared in the same year as Panitch's essay.

52   Marx (1979 [1852]: 191) observes in *The Eighteenth Brumaire of Louis Bonaparte* that "taxes are the source of life for the bureaucracy, the army, the priests and the court, in short, for the whole apparatus of the executive power. Strong government and heavy taxes are identical."

53   Panitch (1977a: 5).

to maintain or create the conditions in which profitable capital accumulation is possible. However, the state also must try to maintain or create the conditions for social harmony."[54] To promote capital accumulation, the state must promote a favorable business climate, but to promote democratic legitimacy, the state must pursue a variety of policies that undermine business confidence over the long-term. Panitch explicitly links the legitimation function with concrete state activities that are generally opposed by capitalist elites, such as welfare entitlements, anti-trust legislation, redistributive income taxation, union protections, and governmental consultation with labor representatives regarding economic and labor market policies.[55]

The necessity of simultaneously fulfilling mutually contradictory functions sets an outer boundary for the policy options available to state elites when confronted with economic or political crises. A capitalist state that blatantly exercises its repressive function to promote capital accumulation at the clear expense of the working classes undermines the basis of its loyalty and support, i.e., its legitimacy. However, the crisis of the KWS certainly raised the question of the possibility that the existing state form might be reconstituted in non-liberal and non-democratic ways that would allow it to continue promoting capital accumulation, while evading the restraints and restrictions of democratic legitimation. Thus, absent a strong socialist movement and the penetration of the state by working class parties, Panitch seemed to agree with Poulantzas that fascism and dictatorship are ever-present tendencies of the modern capitalist state.[56]

A major reason why Panitch was able to integrate three approaches that others saw as mutually exclusive theories was because he considered Marxism an empirical and historical social science, rather than an abstract philosophy.[57] One will never find an extended disquisition on epistemology or methodology in Panitch's work on political economy and the state. While Panitch agreed with Poulantzas that Marxism is a form of structural functionalism, he was more influenced on this subject by the historian Eric J. Hobsbawm than by Poulantzas.[58] Hobsbawm considered Marxism a distinct and unique form of

---

54   Panitch (1977a: 8).
55   Panitch (1977a: 19).
56   Poulantzas (1974a; 1976b).
57   Panitch (2002: 101) later wrote that "students who look back to Miliband and Poulantzas today for guidance ... would do well to pay less attention to the polemic between them (and the many caricatural commentaries on it) over 'instrumentalism' and 'structuralism'. They would also do well not to take too seriously the epistemologically ill-informed and rather hysterical charges of functionalism against Marxist state theory that came to be heard in the 1980s."
58   Panitch (1977a: 9).

structural functionalism as compared to its mainstream variants, which heavily influenced Poulantzas.[59]

First, according to Hobsbawm, Marxism "insists on a hierarchy of social phenomena (e.g., 'basis' and 'superstructure'), and second, on the existence within any society of internal tensions ("contradictions") which counteract the tendency of the system to maintain itself as a going concern."[60] The various sub-systems of the capitalist system are neither autonomous, nor co-equal in their effect on capitalist development. In addition, the inherent contradictions of capitalism (e.g., class antagonism) generate a constant cycle of crisis, disequilibrium, and political response to crisis. This means that a Marxist theory of the state must be able to conceptualize how the state develops and changes as it responds to periodic crises of accumulation and, consequently, Marxism is a *historical,* as well as an empirical, social science.

However, historical and empirical analysis does not render theory irrelevant. Insofar as one can identify structures and functions of the capitalist state, it is implicit that there are commonalities among individual states that allow one to conceptualize political or state forms (e.g., Keynesian Welfare State). However, Panitch observes that "the exercise of the various state functions is by no means uniform in all periods and in all societies, and the size and prominence of any one of the three state functions [repression, accumulation, legitimation] must be examined in light of the 'empirically given circumstances' of a particular society."[61] Consequently, Panitch insists that any theoretical analysis of a capitalist state must be done "not in an ahistoric way but in relation to the way the state's organization, its functions, and its linkages with society vary with the changes in the capitalist mode of production itself, and also vary with the specific conditions of a given social formation."[62]

Panitch anchored this claim in Volume 3 of *Capital*, where Marx states that:

> The specific economic form, in which unpaid surplus labour is pumped out of direct producers, determines the relationship of rulers and ruled, as it grows directly out of production itself and, in turn, reacts upon it as a determining element. Upon this, however, is founded the entire formation of the economic community which grows up out of the production

59   Hobsbawm (1968: 46); Barrow (2016: 11–12).
60   Offe (1984: 132) defines a contradiction as "the tendency inherent within a specific mode of production to destroy those very preconditions on which its survival depends." See, also Habermas (1970) and Barrow (1993: ch. 4).
61   Panitch (1977a: 9).
62   Panitch (1977a: 5–6).

relations themselves, thereby simultaneously its specific political form. It is always the direct relationship of the owners of the conditions of production to the direct producers – a relation always naturally corresponding to a definite stage in the development of the methods of labour and thereby its social productivity – which reveals the innermost secret, the hidden basis of the entire social structure, and with it the political form of the relation of sovereignty and dependence, in short, the corresponding specific form of the state. This does not prevent the same economic basis – the same from the standpoint of its main conditions – due to innumerable different empirical circumstances, natural environment, racial relations, external historical influences, etc., from showing infinite variations and gradations in appearance, which can be ascertained only by analysis of the empirically given circumstances.[63]

A theoretically informed analysis of state development and public policy must be attuned to the specific configuration of individual state apparatuses within this form (e.g., the high degree of decentralization in Canadian federalism as compared to the high degree of centralization in Mexican federalism or the existence of parliamentary vs. presidential systems). It must also be attuned to the level of capitalist development in different social formations and the extent to which structural constraints set the boundaries of state policy (e.g., the level of state debt, dependence on foreign direct investment, the degree of democratization). An individual state's ability to balance accumulation and legitimation will also depend on the relative class capacities of workers and capitalists.[64] A strong capitalist class and a weak working class may allow a state to pursue accumulation at the expense of legitimation for an indefinite length of time. Thus, theoretical concepts about state forms (structures) and state functions may guide the analysis of individual capitalist states, but such abstractions can never substitute for an empirical, institutional, and historical analysis of actually existing capitalist states. The other essays in *The Canadian State* were designed to exemplify this methodological approach by actually

---

63   Marx (1998 [1894]: 777–78). Similarly, in *The German Ideology,* where Marx and Engels (1976a [1846]: 31) first worked out the principles and method of historical materialism they state: "the premises from which we begin are not arbitrary ones, not dogmas, but real premises from which abstraction can only be made in the imagination. They are the real individuals, their activity, and the material conditions of their life, both those which they find already existing and those produced by their activity." The word "empirical" appears 72 times in *The German Ideology* usually in references to empirical relations, empirical conditions, empirical reality, and empirical existence.

64   Lembcke (1988).

analyzing a capitalist state through the lens of Marxist state theory. Soon after its publication, Panitch could observe with some satisfaction that other state theorists were also moving "beyond the abstract formalism and high level of generality that tended to characterize earlier work" on the capitalist state.[65] Panitch singled out the more recent work of two individuals in particular – Goran Therborn (1978) and Nicos Poulantzas (1978c) – whose newest books on the state "explicitly concerned themselves with tracing and delineating the changing patterns of bourgeois-democratic rule in the monopoly capitalist era."[66]

2   From Consent to Coercion

In *The Canadian State,* Panitch had warned that the industrial militancy of the 1970s might become the "basis for the development of conservatizing corporatist structures."[67] He followed up on this concern with articles that appeared in the most widely read Marxist journals, including *The Socialist Register, Politics & Society, New Left Review, Monthly Review,* and *Capital and Class,* as well as more mainstream journals, such as *Comparative Political Studies, Political Studies,* and the *British Journal of Sociology.*[68] Panitch observed that the previous decade of Marxist state theory had "considerably enhanced our understanding of the operation of the capitalist state."[69] However, he also concluded that state theorists had woefully neglected "the complex and contradictory relationship between the trades unions and the capitalist state" in their quest to understand the state-capital nexus.[70]

Michel Aglietta's *A Theory of Capitalist Regulation* (1979) simultaneously pointed to this lacuna in Marxist state theory, although he left it to others such as Panitch to fill that theoretical gap. Aglietta insisted that "the wage-relation" was the cornerstone of the capitalist mode of production, because it is the basis of economic exploitation and therefore a necessary requisite of capital accumulation. This meant that establishing and policing the wage-relation in capitalism was a critical element of the state's general maintenance function and its specific function of maintaining the conditions necessary for capital

---

65   Panitch (1986a: 187).
66   Panitch (1986a: 187).
67   Panitch (1977a: 23).
68   These essays were collected and published as a book in Panitch (1986).
69   Panitch (1986a: x).
70   Panitch (1986a: x).

accumulation. Significantly, Aglietta's analysis was building on Poulantzas' earlier claim that "the function of the state primarily concerns the economic level, and particularly the labour process, the productivity of labour."[71]

In following Poulantzas' lead, Aglietta argued that a Marxist theory of the state must account for the state-labor connection in advanced capitalism, because it was an integral part of the functioning of the KWS. Whereas Marxists had devoted considerable attention to documenting and analyzing the state-capital nexus, whether in terms of the personal connections between capitalists and state personnel or in terms of the structural power of capital – virtually no attention had been paid to the integration of trade unions into the structure of the capitalist state. By the mid-1980s, Panitch concurred that:

> Marxist theorizations of the capitalist state in the past decade have only tangentially noted, and have largely failed to address systematically, one of the most significant political developments pertaining to the working class in the modern period: the emergence within the democratic capitalist state of new political structures which articulate trade unions with state administration and business associations in a broad range of economic policy-making.[72]

Panitch was among the leading critics of the new corporatist paradigm, which he defined as "*a political structure within advanced capitalism which integrates organized socio-economic producer groups through a system of representation and co-operative mutual interaction at the leadership level and of mobilization and social control at the mass level.*"[73] Panitch identified a complex of corporatist policies and institutions as "the main political structures which social democratic governments have sponsored as a means of accommodating the trade-union movement to the capitalist state,"[74] but for this reason he criticized corporatism as "a system of state-structured class collaboration" that was "a danger to working class organizations."[75]

---

71 Poulantzas (1978c: 17; 1973: 52). Aglietta (1979: 32) observes that "the state thus develops by penetrating civil society and profoundly restructuring it. This penetration and restructuring show that *the state forms part of the very existence of the wage relation.*"

72 Panitch (1986: 187).

73 Panitch (1986a: 136); cf. Schmitter and Lehmbruch (1979); Lehmbruch and Schmitter (1982).

74 Panitch (1986a: ix).

75 Panitch (1986a: 209).

The ostensible purpose of corporatist institutions was to stabilize capitalist economies by mitigating industrial conflict with class compromise. However, corporatist relations were systematically destabilized by the first Arab Oil Embargo (1973), a Great Recession (1974–75), and nearly a decade of stagflation that culminated in the Volcker Shock of 1981.[76] While these historical events brought the political weaknesses of corporatism to the surface, Panitch viewed corporatism as structurally unstable, because it did not fundamentally alter the wage-relation as the structural basis of class antagonism between workers and capitalists. Panitch quickly recognized, as he had earlier feared, that "the immediate response of the state to these developments was in most cases a coercive one, designed to weaken the union movement in general or a particular sector of it."[77]

In an omen of things to come, the Swedish Social Democrats were ousted from power in two consecutive elections (1976, 1979) and, in retrospect, this event was signaling a crisis of the corporatist institutions and policies that were an integral component of the KWS. In the United States, newly elected President Ronald Reagan (1980), leading energized corporate elites, openly waged a new class war against workers and the poor by slashing social welfare entitlements and raising regressive payroll taxes to cover a looming deficit in the Social Security system.[78] In 1981, Reagan terminated 11,000 air traffic controllers in a move that *The New York Times* would later describe as "the strike that busted unions" in the United States.[79] Prime Minister Margaret Thatcher emulated Reagan by defeating the 1984–85 miner's strike in the United Kingdom, which the BBC described as a defeat that "managed to destroy the power of the trade unions for almost a generation."[80]

In *The Assault on Trade Union Freedoms*, Leo Panitch and Donald Swartz analyzed parallel events in Canada to conclude that governments in Western capitalist societies were now actively dismantling corporatist institutions and replacing them with a "strong state and free market."[81] The strong state described by Panitch and Swartz was first strengthening its capacity for the clandestine surveillance of domestic opponents. Panitch and Swartz pointed out that "fundamental issues" concerning the nature of liberal democracy were

---

76   Eckstein (1978).
77   Panitch (1986: 201).
78   Piven and Cloward (1982); Edsall (1984).
79   McCartin (2011). Union density in the United States subsequently fell from 20.1% of the workforce in 1983 to 10.5% in 2018 (US Bureau of Labor Statistics 2019).
80   Wilenius (2004).
81   Panitch and Swartz (1988: 68).

coming to the fore in many capitalist states with the discovery that police and intelligence agencies were routinely spying on peace groups, radical political parties, and trade unions.[82] Capitalist states were also employing repressive tactics openly and more frequently as documented by a "rising number of incidents over the past few years where police confronted groups of workers protesting the attacks on their freedom of association."[83]

Panitch and Swartz considered the shift in state policy significant enough to identify it as a new era marking the end of corporatism and the illusion of social democracy. As they described it: "The era we have entered marks a return, albeit in quite different conditions, to the state and capital relying more openly on coercion – on force and on fear – to secure that subordination."[84] The KWS had relied on the socialization system – culture, ideology, and education – as well as redistributive policies to legitimate its role in capital accumulation, but ironically in an era described by mainstream political scientists as a "rollback" of the state, Panitch was arguing that "the promotion of the free market yields not less state but a more coercive state."[85] In fact, as capitalist states rolled back or dismantled key structures of the KWS, those same states were preparing for renewed class war – domestically and abroad – by strengthening their repressive and surveillance apparatuses.

3   The Impoverishment of State Theory

Despite the increasing influence of Marxist state theory within academia during the 1960s and 1970s, Panitch had warned left-wing scholars to "cautiously avoid the illusion that by virtue of its strength alone a Marxist theory of the state will gain prominence. The rise and fall of theories is not merely the product of intellectual competition with the most fruitful coming out on top."[86] Panitch predicted that the continuing rise (or fall) of Marxist state theory would depend on its relationship (or disconnect) with the working class, because a social base is "the *sine qua non* for the sustenance of any body of ideas."[87] A quarter-century after he issued this warning, Panitch reminisced that "I do not think I realized when that was written just how little time we

---

82   Panitch and Swartz (1988: 9).
83   Panitch and Swartz (1988: 10).
84   Panitch and Swartz (1988: 15–16).
85   Panitch (1993: 9).
86   Panitch (1977a: x).
87   Panitch (1977a: x).

had, how contingent the further development of the Marxist theory of the state would be on immediately favorable political conditions."[88] The intellectual and political conditions that had generated interest in the Marxist theory of the state quickly dissipated over the next two decades and the result was what Panitch described as "a remarkable impoverishment of state theory" during the 1980s and 1990s.[89] As Panitch observes: "By the beginning of the 1980s, a strong reaction to the new Marxist state theory set in and it soon became quite unfashionable" in academic circles.[90] Ironically, scholarly interest in state theory began to wane just as states in the capitalist societies were strengthening their domestic and international coercive capabilities as a response to the crisis of the Keynesian Welfare State.

There were few theoretical advances in state theory during this time as many radical scholars simply drifted into new areas of research. Bob Jessop's (2002) strategic-relational approach to state theory received significant attention during this time, but it was primarily a refinement and highly complex modification of "the later" Poulantzas (1978c).[91] The other exception to the turn away from state theory was the rise of the new institutionalism and state autonomy theory. The new institutionalism in political science and sociology provided the methodological platform for advancing a new state autonomy theory that conceptualized the state purely as an organization that attempts "to extend coercive control and political authority over particular territories and the people residing within them."[92] A fundamental thesis of state autonomy theory was that in pursuing this political objective (i.e., coercive control) state managers act as self-interested maximizers whose main interest is to enhance their own institutional power, prestige, and wealth. Thus, state autonomy theorists argued that states are not only decision-making organizations, but autonomous organizational actors that must be considered real historical subjects in relation to social classes.[93]

The aim of this research strategy was to avoid what its proponents considered "the dead end of metatheory" by focusing on the analytically limited task of constructing empirical generalizations based on comparative historical

---

88   Panitch (2002: 92).
89   Panitch (2002: 93).
90   Panitch (2002: 92).
91   Poulantzas (1978c).
92   Skocpol and Amenta (1986: 131); Hall and Ikenberry (1989: 1–2); Orren and Skowronek 1986); Poggi (1990: 19–33). The new institutionalism was closely associated with *Studies in American Political Development, Politics and Society,* and the *Journal of Policy History.*
93   Block (1980); March and Olsen (1984); Zucker (1987).

case studies of policy formation and state institutional development.[94] The adherents of the new institutionalism were a diverse set of scholars with wide-ranging substantive concerns, but they nevertheless shared the theoretical goal of establishing the "possible autonomy of the state" in capitalist societies in order to demonstrate that state organizations and elites (i.e., the state apparatus) "might under certain circumstances act against the long-run economic interests of a dominant class, or act to create a new mode of production."[95] The new institutionalists' main argument was that state theory needed to incorporate a historical and organizational analysis of state institutions (i.e., the state apparatus), but this was hardly an original insight as the same point had already been made by Miliband (1969) and even more strongly by Panitch and his co-authors in *The Canadian State* (1977a).

Nevertheless, in *The State in Capitalist Society*, Miliband had conceded that the state "is a nebulous entity" and he had even gone so far as to suggest that the state "is not a thing, that it does not, as such, exist."[96] Instead, the state, as Miliband conceived it, is merely an analytic reference point that "stands for ... a number of particular institutions which, together, constitute its reality, and which interact as parts of what may be called the state system." This observation posed "the problem of state cohesion," which was one of the many issues broached in the Poulantzas-Miliband debate. What gives the state unity? What constitutes 'stateness'?

Fred Block, Claus Offe, and Charles Lindblom introduced concepts such as business confidence, the dependency principle, and the privileged position of business to explain the functional coherence of state policy in promoting capital accumulation, but this answer only explains what makes the state a *capitalist* state; it does not answer the prior question of what allows the state to act with strength and organizational cohesion, i.e., its capacity to act as a state? The one theoretically significant contribution of the new institutionalists of the 1980s and 1990s was to provide some direction in answering this question. The most useful concept of state capacities was formulated by Stephen Skowronek, while Richard Bensel developed a comparative taxonomy of state strength that built on Skowronek's earlier work.[97]

94   Skocpol (1987).
95   Evans, Rueschemeyer and Skocpol (1985: 348); Skocpol (1973: 18); Skocpol (1979: 28); Stepan (1978); Nordlinger (1981); Bensel (1990).
96   Miliband (1969: 48–50).
97   Skowronek (1982: 19–31); Bensel (1990).

Nevertheless, the impact of state autonomy theory on Marxist state theory was limited and the new institutionalism itself never generated an actual
theory of the state.[98] Their work was at best useful in better understanding
how state apparatuses organize state capacities within a mode of production
and how those institutions further narrow the policy options available to state
elites, but even on these terms, Panitch dismissed the approach as one that
quickly and clearly reached a dead end. Panitch correctly criticized state autonomy theory for not pursuing "an investigation of the modalities of class power
within the state apparatuses and the role these apparatuses play in sustaining
and reinforcing the economic and social power of financial capital" inside the
state.[99] Despite its allegedly comparative historical approach to state theory,
Panitch also rejected state autonomy theory as "a discourse that empties the
categories of state and market of historical and comparative specificity," due
to the "abstractness and generality" of its basic thesis.[100] Panitch also observed
that it was a great historical irony that state autonomy theory rose to prominence in the 1980s "at the very time when the structural power of capital and
the strategic and ideological reach of capitalist classes has become perhaps
never more nakedly visible."[101] In this context, Panitch wryly concluded that
"rarely has an academic theory been less apposite to its time than the one that
asserted state autonomy against the theory of the capitalist state."[102] In fact,
the new institutionalism and state autonomy theory rapidly degenerated into
a vacuous non-theory and, consequently, its leading proponents stumbled
their way back to the old pluralist paradigm as they attempted to grapple with
the relation between the state and civil society.[103]

The abandonment of grand theory during the 1980s took place within the
context of a more widespread intellectual disillusionment with grand scale
meta-narratives, such as Marxist theory, and their attendant transformational
political projects.[104] The shift from Marxist to Post-Marxist to post-structuralist
and post-modernist theory shifted analysis away from macroscopic to micro-
scopic forms of power and, therefore, to the multiple "technologies of power"
such as language, family, interpersonal relationships, culture, leisure and

---

98   Barrow (1993: ch. 5).
99   Panitch (2002: 95). Domhoff (1990; 1996) developed this line of argument with theoretical
      vigor and supported it with a wealth of empirical and historical data.
100   Panitch (2002: 94).
101   Panitch (2002: 92).
102   Panitch (1996: 83).
103   Domhoff (1996: ch. 8).
104   Lyotard (1984).

entertainment, and the configurations of repressed desire.[105] In place of socialist revolution, the "new philosopher" Bernard Henri-Levy called for "a provisional politics, a small-scale program, which some of us think can only be precarious, uncertain, and circumstantial – in a word, a matter of feeling."[106]

In this effort to identify the "polymorphous techniques of power" the concept of the state became merely the effect of a discursive practice (political theory) that concealed power more than it revealed it.[107] Timothy Mitchell's influential application of Foucauldian analysis to state theory concluded that "focusing on the state as essentially a phenomenon of decision making or policy is inadequate," because the state is "an effect of detailed processes of spatial organization, temporal arrangement, functional specification, and supervision and surveillance, which create the appearance of a world fundamentally divided into state and society."[108] Consequently, he argued, "the state should not be taken as a free-standing entity, whether an agent, instrument, organization or structure, located apart from and opposed to another entity called society." The state was effectively dissolved back into civil society as a merely conceptual or analytic distinction in an otherwise unbroken panoply of space and time. The result, as Panitch lamented, was that the previous "advances made in Marxist state theory were swept away as part of the general post-Marxist, poststructuralist, postmodernist trend."[109] Panitch was one of the few prominent theorists who continued to emphasize "the continuing salience of class struggle" within and against the capitalist state amidst the rise of new social movement theory and identity politics.[110]

Finally, the 1990s was the decade when "globalization" became a common buzzword among scholars in numerous fields. The cottage industry in globalization sparked a renewal of political economy, but in its initial stage globalization theory continued to push state theory into the background.[111] Indeed, there was a never-ending litany of books and articles on the crisis of the nation-state, the eclipse of the state, the retreat of the state, and even the end of the nation-state.[112] The central theme in these eulogies was that nation-states had

---

105   Foucault (1972: 12); Deleuze and Guattari (1987). Jessop (1991: 91) echoes the sentiment that the 1980s was marked by a shift "of attention from the state and class struggle to the micro-physics of power and the problems of identity formation."

106   Henri-Levy (1977: 68).

107   Foucault (1980: 11).

108   Mitchell (1991: 95).

109   Panitch (2002: 92); cf. Sim (2001).

110   Panitch (1986a: ix); Boggs (1986); Laclau and Mouffe (1985).

111   Barrow and Keck (2017).

112   Poggi (1990); Evans (1997); Strange (1996); Ohmae (1990).

lost control of their national economies, currencies, territorial boundaries, and even their cultures and languages and that macroscopic forms of power were shifting from the nation-state to the global market, transnational corporations, and globalized channels of communication.[113] Why study an institution in retreat or one in the twilight of its sovereignty?[114] Panitch concluded that it was in the study of globalization that "the impoverishment of state theory may be most readily recognized and lamented."[115]

4   Globalization and the State

America's defeat in the Vietnam War (1973), two Arab Oil Embargos (1973, 1979), a Great Recession (1974–75), a decade of stagflation, the Volcker Shock (1981), and a two-decades long productivity paradox combined to convince many scholars that America was in decline.[116] The United States would either be displaced by new world powers, such as China and the European Union,[117] or US decline would lead to the emergence of a genuinely new multi-polar world order governed by international norms and treaties that would supersede the declining nation-state.[118] Panitch self-identified two essays – "Globalization and the State" (1994) and "Rethinking the Role of the State" (1996) – as pivotal works in his own return to state theory.[119] Panitch observed that in these two essays he first:

> ... contested the widespread notion that capital has 'bypassed' or 'escaped' or 'diminished' the power of the state. I have argued that this notion ... fails to see that globalization is a process that takes place under the aegis of states and is in many ways authored by states. But it will not advance our understanding very much if we merely assert the continuing importance of states amid globalization, while failing to explore the determining patterns of state action in our era. To properly make sense

---

113   Castells (1997).
114   Wriston (1992).
115   Panitch (2002: 95–96).
116   Arrighi (2005).
117   Arrighi, Mamashita and Selden (2003); Meyer-Larson (2000).
118   Hardt and Negri (2000).
119   Panitch (2002: 97–98).

of globalization, we cannot do without many of the tools of analysis of Marxist state theory.[120]

Indeed, in a series of articles published from 1994 to 2005, Panitch continued to emphasize that even in the midst of globalization the Marxist theory of the state remained salient and "the study of the capitalist state today must still meet the three requisites" outlined in *The Canadian State* and as developed by subsequent theorists.[121] While Panitch leaned heavily on Ralph Miliband in *The Canadian State*, he increasingly turned to Poulantzas in the 1990s and 2000s, but it was the empirical-historical Poulantzas of *Fascism and Dictatorship* (1974), *Classes in Contemporary Capitalism* (1978b) and *State, Power, Socialism* (1980), rather than the "structural abstractionist" *Political Power and Social Classes* (1973).[122]

First, in response to the Greek and various Latin American coups d'état, Poulantzas had temporarily turned his attention to an analysis of exceptional states, such as Nazi Germany and Fascist Italy. Poulantzas claimed that as the "sharpness of class struggle" intensified inside the advanced industrial countries during the 1970s, it was not only accelerating a world-wide crisis of imperialism, as manifested in the Vietnam debacle and other anti-colonial struggles, it was putting fascism back on the political agenda as a possible political response by the capitalist class.[123] The state's response to popular upheavals in the United States, Germany, Mexico, Japan, and elsewhere was growing increasingly violent, while many governments in the United States and Europe were expanding the use of covert domestic surveillance and the subversion of foreign governments as anti-insurgent political strategies.[124] By the 1990s, Poulantzas' work on fascism and dictatorship now seemed to provide an explanation for developments that Panitch had earlier chronicled as the collapse of corporatism.

Second, in *Classes and Contemporary Capitalism*, Poulantzas argued that capital had also begun to reestablish and reconstitute the basis of its political and economic power in response to these events; first, in individual nations, and then on a global scale. Poulantzas warned that the political and ideological conditions for a new American imperialism were being put in place "by establishing relations of production characteristic of American monopoly

---

120   Panitch (2002: 98).
121   Panitch (2002: 100).
122   Panitch (1996: 88–89).
123   Poulantzas (1974a: 11).
124   US Congress (1976).

capital and its domination actually inside the other metropolises."[125] While
fascism had appeared as a realistic political strategy for capital, the major
defeats for the working class and other popular movements were not generally
being inflicted by direct political repression, but through economic reforms
that were reconstituting the social relations of production inside national
social formations.

In *State, Power, Socialism*, Poulantzas deepened this argument by observ-
ing that in the stage of competitive capitalism, and even in the early phases
of monopoly capitalism, "the State's strictly economic functions were *subordinated*, though not reduced, especially to its repressive and ideological functions."[126] The State was mainly involved in "organizing the socio-political space
of capital accumulation" by establishing its political and material conditions
within specific territories, i.e., nations. However, while others were bemoaning
an emerging crisis of the welfare states in the 1970s, Poulantzas was already
theorizing this development as the beginning of the transition to a new form
of capitalist state. According to Poulantzas: "the State's present role in the
economy alters the political space as a whole, economic functions henceforth
occupy the *dominant place* within the State ... *The totality of operations of the
State are currently being reorganized in relation to its economic role*."[127] The state
was now actively responding to the sharpening of domestic class struggle, and
to the crisis of imperialism, by managing these contradictions with new strategies and policies designed to reconstitute the relations of production, the
division of labor, the reproduction of labor-power, and the extraction of surplus value.

While the state's social welfare responsibilities were being curtailed as part
of the transition to this new state form, Poulantzas observed that its economic
functions were simultaneously increasing to such an extent that one could
now theoretically identify a specialized *state economic apparatus* in addition

---

125   Poulantzas (1975: 47). The internalization of American capitalism within a foreign national
        social formation was symbolized in France amid media fanfare and culture shock over
        the opening of the first McDonald's on the Champs-Élysées in 1972. There are now more
        than 1,200 McDonald's in France, including locations at the Louvre and Sorbonne, two
        on the Champs-Élysées, and several more across the French Riviera. France has the most
        McDonald's locations per capita in Europe and the fourth-highest number per capita in
        the world (Wile, 2014). Similarly, Crothers (2010).
126   Poulantzas (1978c: 168).
127   Poulantzas (1978c: 167) argues that one concrete result of this strategy was that "a num-
        ber of previously 'marginal' fields (training of labour-power, town-planning, transport,
        health, the environment, etc.) are directly integrated, in an expanded and modified form,
        into the very space-process of the reproduction and valorization of capital."

to the repressive and ideological state apparatuses (e.g., the strengthening of central banks, finance and trade ministries, state labor exchanges, workforce retraining, regional economic development agencies, etc.). What was left of the welfare state was systematically being subordinated to the requirements of capital accumulation. Basic social services such as health, education, and welfare were no longer funded or measured for their ability to meet human needs, but were reconfigured and funded based on their return on social investment. Social welfare policy was fundamentally restructured to ensure that such policies facilitated capital accumulation, e.g., welfare became workfare and education was refocused on skills and workforce development, rather than citizenship. Healthcare was about extending and improving the productivity of human capital.[128] An essential aspect of this restructuring of the state form was that the responsibility for public policy was increasingly shifted away from the more "democratic" and representative institutions of the state apparatus into non-accountable and unelected fortresses insulated from public pressure and often directly controlled by capitalist elites (e.g., central banks and treasuries, national security councils, the World Trade Organization).

Panitch built on Poulantzas' observations to reassess the theory of the state in the context of economic globalization or what Poulantzas had more accurately labeled the internationalization of capital. However, in contrast to most globalization theorists, Panitch argued that the state was not declining; it was becoming more repressive and more attuned to the requirements of capital accumulation, and all at the expense of democratic institutions. In his 1994 essay on "Globalisation and the State," Panitch directly challenged globalization theorists with his counter-thesis that "globalisation both is authored by states and is primarily about reorganising, rather than by-passing, states."[129] He argued that "capitalist globalisation is a process that takes place in, through, and under the aegis of states; it is encoded by them and in important respects even authored by them; and it involves a shift in power relations within states."[130] For this reason, Panitch criticized globalization theory as "a false counterposition between globalising capital and the power of states."[131] He pointed out that "not only is the world still very much composed of states ... capitalism has not escaped the state but rather that the state has, as always, been a fundamental constitutive element in the very process of extension of capitalism in our

---

128   Becker (1993).
129   Panitch (1994: 63).
130   Panitch (1994: 64).
131   Panitch (1994: 68).

time."[132] Thus, Panitch concludes in "Rethinking the Role of the State" that "the nature of state intervention has changed considerably," but this does not mean that the role of the state has diminished in capitalist societies.[133]

Because of his earlier work on the collapse of corporatism and the rise of neoliberalism, Panitch was acutely aware of the fact that the role of the state in capitalism had not diminished during the previous decade even though the nature of state intervention in the economy and society had changed considerably. Panitch observed that "far from witnessing a by-passing of the state by a global capitalism, what we see are very active states and highly politicised sets of capitalist classes."[134] Panitch also emphasized that an important aspect of reconstituting the state form globally was "the constitutionalizing" of neoliberalism. Panitch suggested that capitalist states were "the authors of a regime which defines and guarantees, through international treaties with constitutional effect, the global and domestic rights of capital."[135]

Ian Robinson had articulated the same concept in his analysis of the North American Free Trade Agreement (NAFTA) by noting that such treaties, including the WTO, go far beyond the effort to merely liberalize trade between nations, or to construct an international division of labor, as previously characterized the world capitalist system.[136] These new treaties prohibited discrimination between national and foreign-owned corporations (so-called national treatment) and even created new corporate property rights such as guarantees of intellectual property rights, the repatriation of profits, and extended patent protection, among others. In this respect, a plethora of new trade treaties did far more than merely liberalize trade between countries; they instead functioned "as an economic constitution, setting the basic rules governing the private property rights that all governments must respect and the types of economic policies that all governments must eschew."[137] The private property rights established and protected by these treaties typically went well beyond those previously established in most countries, although they frequently mirrored US property and contract law, which effectively extended Fifth and Fourteenth Amendment protections to virtually the entire globe, with those rights enforced, accordingly, by the American state. Thus, what was needed, according to Panitch, was new historical and empirical research on

---

132   Panitch (1994: 87).
133   Panitch (1996: 85).
134   Panitch (1994, 63).
135   Panitch (1994, 64).
136   Cf. Wallerstein (1979).
137   Robinson (1993: 2).

the changing hierarchy of state apparatuses and how these apparatuses operated within the structural constraints of global capitalism.[138]

Importantly, however, Panitch rejected the claims of mainstream apolo-
gists, who promoted globalization as a "new world order" governed by international law, human rights, and liberal-democratic norms.[139] Panitch countered
the claim that globalization is a multilateral process unfolding among equal
nations and equal states and instead argued that it is the political and economic
form of a new imperialism that institutionalizes the hegemony and reproduction of American capital on an ever-extending (global) scale. Panitch insisted
that "states, and above all the world's most powerful state, have played an
active and often crucial role in making globalization happen."[140] Globalization
was not just globalization; it was a peculiarly American form of non-territorial
informal empire, built on the financialization of global capitalism.[141]

Panitch was again building on insights gleaned from Poulantzas' prescient
essay on "The Internationalization of Capitalist Relations and the Nation
State,"[142] who according to Panitch, wrote at a time "when a new era of imperialism was being born."[143] Panitch argues that Poulantzas' most significant contribution to the globalization debate was his recognition:

> (i) that when multinational capital penetrates a host social formation,
> it arrives not merely as abstract 'direct foreign investment', but as a
> transformative social force within the country; (ii) that the interaction
> of foreign capital with domestic capital leads to the dissolution of the
> national bourgeoisie as a coherent concentration of class interests; (iii)
> but far from losing importance, the host state actually becomes respon-
> sible for taking charge of the complex relations of international capital
> to the domestic bourgeoisie, in the context of class struggles and political
> and ideological forms which remain distinctively national even as they
> express themselves within a world conjuncture.[144]

Panitch suggested that "these elements still provide the conceptual building
blocks we need to develop a theory of globalization."[145] Poulantzas had traced

---

138   Panitch (1994: 72).
139   For example, Fukayama (1992).
140   Panitch (2000b: 5).
141   Panitch and Gindin (2004a; 2004b; 2004c); Panitch and Konings (2009).
142   Poulantzas (1975: 37–88).
143   Panitch (2000b: 9).
144   Panitch (2000b: 8–9).
145   Panitch (2000b: 9).

the contours of "a new type of non-territorial imperialism, implanted and maintained not through direct rule by the metropolis, nor even through political subordination of a neo-colonial type, but rather through the 'induced reproduction of the form of the dominant imperialist power within each national formation and its state'." Moreover, a unique and significant characteristic of this new imperialism was the ability of American capital and the American state to integrate other major capitalist powers, such as the European Union, Great Britain, Japan, Canada, and Australia into its hegemonic project as junior partners.

Thus, in contrast to both Marxist and International Relations theorists, who prophesied the decline of American power, Panitch remained impressed by "the American capacity to manage the radical restructuring of global capitalism in forms that reproduced their imperial dominance."[146] Rather than seeing the International Monetary Fund, the World Bank, and World Trade Organization as the beginnings of a transnational state,[147] Panitch argued that the US enjoys such pre-eminence in these institutions that they serve instead as "the international mediators of US hegemony."[148] By the early to mid-2000s, Panitch had staked out a controversial position on the state that challenged both mainstream globalization theory and Marxist theories of an emerging transnational capitalist class and transnational state.

5   American Empire and the Making of Global Capitalism[149]

The final step in this theoretical development was to document the actual making of global capitalism, including the building of an American Empire. This task was undertaken in Leo Panitch and Sam Gindin's magisterial book, *The Making of Global Capitalism: The Political Economy of American Empire* (2012), which is designed to empirically document Panitch's earlier claim that states are the principal agents of globalization. In this work, Panitch and Gindin historically and empirically link the internationalization of state policy to the problem of the reproduction of capital on an expanded scale, while linking globalization to a theory of capitalist economic development.[150]

---

146   Panitch (2000b: 13–14); also, Panitch and Gindin (2005b).
147   Robinson (2004); Sklair (2001).
148   Domhoff (1990: 153–86).
149   This section appeared previously as part of an article by Barrow and Keck (2017).
150   See Marx (1996 [1885]: Part II, ch. 27 and Part III, chs. 20–21).

In *The Making of Global Capitalism,* Panitch and Gindin document how states, particularly the United States, built global capitalism after World War II. The book stands in sharp theoretical contrast to most globalization theorists, who emphasize the inexorable unfolding of globalization in ways that allegedly by-pass states or render them powerless. In contrast to the globalization theorists, Panitch and Gindin suggest that "continuing competition and class conflict, and the contradictions to which they gave rise, not only determined but were also determined by the actions of capitalist states."[151] Panitch and Gindin provide a historical and empirical analysis of the emergence of global capitalism that demonstrates how early globalization theorists were mistaken in their "notion that, in going global, capitalist markets were escaping, by-passing, or diminishing the state."[152] They argue that by "showing that the making of global capitalism cannot be understood in these terms," historically, their book transcends the false dichotomy between nation-states and global markets and reestablished the functional relationship between states and capitalism.[153]

Panitch and Gindin define globalization as "the geographic extension of competitive markets, a process dependent on the removal of state barriers to this, and the overcoming of distance through technology."[154] In their account of globalization, Panitch and Gindin document how "the American state has played an exceptional role in the creation of a fully global capitalism and in coordinating its management, as well as restructuring other states to those ends."[155] Thus, what makes the American state distinctive (i.e., exceptional) within the global political economy is "its vital role in managing and superintending capitalism on a worldwide plane." Another notable feature of the book is that it does not avoid words like "capitalism" and "empire" in favor of polite euphemisms, and this directness leads Panitch and Gindin to the conclusion that if one reviews the actual history of globalization it becomes clear that most globalization theorists (and new institutionalists) have been "wildly erroneous" in designating "the American state as 'weak'."[156]

The opening sentence of *The Making of Global Capitalism* makes clear that it is a book "about globalization *and* the state." Indeed, the explicit purpose of the book is to show "that the spread of capitalist markets, values and

---

151   Panitch and Gindin (2012: vii).
152   Panitch and Gindin (2012: 1).
153   Panitch and Gindin (2012, 1).
154   Panitch and Gindin (2012: 3).
155   Panitch and Gindin (2012: 1).
156   Panitch and Gindin (2012: 16).

social relationships around the world, far from being an inevitable outcome of inherently expansionist economic tendencies, has depended on the agency of states – and of one state in particular: America."[157] Moreover, Panitch and Gindin seek to demonstrate that "the relationship between the American state and the changing dynamics of production and finance was inscribed in the very process that came to be known as globalization."[158] However, the book's theoretical argument also differs from that of many international relations realists by arguing that in constructing America's "quite distinctive imperial state, the Pentagon and CIA have been much less important to the process of capitalist globalization than the US Treasury and Federal Reserve."[159] The most unique and impressive characteristic of *The Making of Global Capitalism* is that it documents this process in meticulous detail over 456 pages as opposed to merely asserting its theoretical claims as dogmatic propositions.

Panitch and Gindin describe the making of global capitalism as a series of policy responses to economic or financial crises, or to political contradictions (i.e., class struggle) that required a periodic restructuring of the fundamental institutions that organize the world's capitalist economies. Partly by design, and partly by happenstance, world leaders and the states they governed largely initiated the process of globalization as we know it today at the end of World War II. Panitch and Gindin acknowledge that capitalism was in some ways always "global," or at least worldwide, particularly by the end of the nineteenth century when Great Britain ruled an empire where the sun never set.[160] However, inter-imperialist rivalries, the pursuit of territory and protectionism eventually brought this early globalization process to an end in two World Wars and a Great Depression.

However, prior to both world wars, the United States had already emerged as a major exporter of capital as its major banks and industrial corporations expanded internationally in search of new and more economic opportunities for profit. American capital was multinational capital even before the outbreak of World War I, but it often found itself blocked and hindered outside the Western hemisphere by the closed door and protectionist policies of the existing imperial powers. Thus, the United States emerged as an early proponent of global trade liberalization, the national treatment of foreign direct investment, and the security of loans to foreign countries and creditors. However, despite its early policy of gunboat diplomacy, it was only in the crucible of the

---

157   Panitch and Gindin (2012: vii).
158   Panitch and Gindin (2012: vii).
159   Panitch and Gindin (2012: vii).
160   Panitch and Gindin (2012: 6); Wallerstein (1979; 1982).

Great Depression and World War II "that the American state developed sufficient institutional capacity to take the helm in a project for making capitalism
global."[161] Both events led to massive efforts at state-building, which strengthened the US state's economic, ideological, and repressive apparatuses.[162]

Thus, while the old imperialist powers – Great Britain, France, Germany,
The Netherlands, Belgium, Italy, and Japan – emerged from the Second World
War in a severely weakened condition – economically, politically, and militar-
ily – the United States emerged as the pre-eminent world power, at least in
the capitalist First World due to its military capabilities, the size of its economy, and the depth and liquidity of its financial markets. Panitch and Gindin
argue that the earlier globalizing tendencies of capitalism[163] were revived by
the United States after 1945 as "the capitalist states of Europe and Japan were
restructured under the aegis of the American state."[164] Thus, following World
War II, Panitch and Gindin observe that "the American state, in the very process of supporting the export of capital and the expansion of multinational
corporations, increasingly took responsibility for creating the political and
juridical conditions for the general extension and reproduction of capitalism
internationally."[165]

However, Panitch and Gindin conclude that a major difference between
American leadership and British leadership of the world capitalist economy was that during the Pax Britannica "the densest imperial networks and
institutional linkages" ran North to South "between imperial states and their

---

161   Panitch and Gindin (2012: 7).
162   Waddell (2001: 3–4) poignantly challenges the new institutionalists' focus on domestic
      welfare policies because it "leads to inadequate and misleading assessments of 'feeble' US
      national capabilities compared with the welfare states of Western Europe. US national
      governance, after all, is not only defined by its welfare state but also by a powerful and
      encompassing national security 'warfare' state that rivals European welfare states in its
      commitment of societal resources."
163   In *The Communist Manifesto*, Marx and Engels (1976b [1848]: 488) observe that: "The bour-
      geoisie has through its exploitation of the world market given a cosmopolitan character
      to production and consumption in every country ... it has drawn from the feet of indus-
      try the national ground on which it stood. All old-established national industries have
      been destroyed or are daily being destroyed. They are dislodged by new industries, whose
      introduction becomes a life or death question for all civilized nations, by industries that
      no longer work up indigenous raw material, but raw material drawn from the remotest
      zones; industries whose products are consumed, not only at home, but in every quarter
      of the globe." Marx's and Engel's description of globalization is not that of an inexorable
      technologically determined process, but an account of what the capitalist class has done
      "through its exploitation of the world-market."
164   Panitch and Gindin (2012: 2).
165   Panitch and Gindin (2012: 6).

formal or informal colonies."[166] In contrast, under US leadership the densest economic networks and institutional linkages were constructed "between the United States and the other major capitalist states."[167] Moreover, these asymmetrical linkages, where the United States asserted the preeminence of its currency, wealth, legal institutions, and military power, were institutionalized in the Bretton Woods agreement (1944), the United Nations Security Council (1946), the General Agreement on Tariffs and Trade (1947), the International Bank of Settlements (World Bank), the International Monetary Fund, and the North Atlantic Treaty Organization (NATO). These new institutions allowed the United States to build an informal empire by "integrating all the other capitalist powers into an effective system of coordination under its aegis."[168]

Panitch and Gindin (2012, 10) also emphasize that another unprecedented aspect of the informal American empire "was the extent to which US governments supported the revival of potential economic competitors – through low-interest loans, direct grants, technological assistance, and favorable trading relations – so they could sell their products to the US." Importantly, this set a pattern "for the economic integration of all the leading capitalist countries" that continues to this day and that gave those competitors a vested interest in the economic growth and strength of the United States, because the US became an important lender to those countries' industries and a key market for their exports.[169] The development of GATT into the WTO facilitated a transition from soft integration based on lower tariffs and more trade to hard integration based on cross-border networks of production and service delivery.[170] This process was asymmetrically deepened with regional agreements such as the European Union and the North American Free Trade Agreement.

Panitch and Gindin argue that the dollar crisis of the 1970s, which led to the end of Bretton Woods "was ultimately due to the contradictions produced by the success of the 'golden age' in producing near full employment by the 1960s."[171] The global financial system was essentially undone by the

---

166   Panitch and Gindin (2012: 7).
167   Panitch and Gindin (2012: 7).
168   Panitch and Gindin (2012: 8).
169   Chang (2003: 250–51) documents that even today "the bulk of FDI occurs among the developed countries; only a handful of developing countries take part in the transnational investment story. For example, in 1989, the Group of Five (G5) economies alone received 75% of world FDI. By comparison, between 1983 and 1989, only 19.7% of world FDI went to developing countries. ... Moreover, even within the developing world, FDI is highly concentrated among a few countries." For another excellent historical and theoretical account of this process, see Domhoff (1990: chs. 5–6).
170   Panitch and Gindin (2012: 10).
171   Panitch and Gindin (2012: 13).

contradictions of its success. The success of the Bretton Woods golden age led to growing worker militancy in the advanced capitalist countries, rising expectations for continued increases in social welfare spending, and assertions of economic nationalism in the Third World, which all "combined to deepen 'the crisis of the dollar.'"[172] However, Panitch and Gindin observe that the "institutional infrastructure for the internationalization of the state built by the US, Europe, and Japan in trying to save Bretton Woods would lead in the 1970s to the creation of the G7, and would be crucially important in guiding the passage of international capitalism through the crisis."[173] (including an IMF bailout of Great Britain and the development of the IMF's fiscal austerity model for addressing national balance of payment crises). Importantly, Panitch and Gindin conclude that "it was only when class discipline was eventually imposed inside the advanced capitalist countries [i.e., the Volcker shock] that an exit from the crisis of the 1970s was found."[174]

The Volcker shock, as well as the election of neoliberal "conservatives" to executive office in Great Britain (Thatcher), Germany (Kohl), and the United States (Reagan) set in motion the current neoliberal phase of globalization, but Panitch and Gindin argue that to peg the beginnings of globalization at this time (as many scholars do):

> ... misses the continuities between their prescriptions for free markets and the long-term goals already articulated by the American state at the time of the relaunching of global capitalism in the postwar era ... Neoliberalism involved not only the restructuring of institutions to ensure that the anti-inflation parameter was enforced, but also the removal of barriers to competition in all markets, and especially in the labor market. Breaking the inflationary spiral [of the 1970s] involved, above all, disciplining labor.[175]

In this respect, neoliberalism and neoliberal globalization "was essentially a *political* response to the democratic gains that had been previously achieved by working classes and which had become, from capital's perspective, barriers

---

172   Panitch and Gindin (2012: 14).
173   Panitch and Gindin (2012: 14).
174   Panitch and Gindin (2012: 14).
175   Panitch and Gindin (2012: 15). For a brief history of GATT and WTO that illuminates the continuity of objectives from 1947 in the first Geneva Round of GATT negotiations to the Uruguay Round (1987–1994) culminating in the creation of the WTO, see, Barrow, Didou-Aupetit and Mallea (2003: 6–10).

to accumulation."[176] The G7 emerged as the chief vehicle for forging consensus among finance ministries and heads of state, while the World Bank re-emerged as the major coordinating agency for central bankers. Meanwhile, Panitch and Gindin argue "the IMF became the vehicle for imposing neoliberal 'structural adjustments' on Third World economies."[177] By the turn of the millennium, Panitch and Gindin observe that "all the elements of 'globalization' – the transformations in the global division of labor, the development of competitive networks of production, and a new financial architecture to facilitate accelerated financialization – were implicated both in the US economy's continuing centrality in global capitalism and in the successful integration into it of the huge and fast-growing Chinese economy."[178]

The Making of Global Capitalism was published just as the world was barely emerging from the first great crisis of the twenty-first century so the political response to it, as well as the role of any new international institutions, was far from clear at the time of its publication. However, Panitch and Gindin observe that because of its economic and political integration, the political fault lines of global capitalism now "run within states rather than between them" – between globalized elites and localized masses. Panitch and Gindin observe that these new lines of cleavage, which were either unanticipated by globalization theorists or dismissed by them, is "replete with implications for the American empire's capacity to sustain global capitalism in the twenty-first century."[179] The intensification of domestic conflict in the globalizing metropolises is particularly significant as these states have been the political leaders and military enforcers of neoliberal globalization since the end of World War II.

6   Conclusion: Toward a New Kind of State

The Canadian State catapulted Leo Panitch to international prominence in the late 1970s, and, had Marxist state theorists followed his lead, they might have avoided twenty years of wandering through an intellectual wilderness. The book called for the development of theoretically informed analyses of actual states situated in their own specific contexts of historical class formation, class struggle, and state organization. However, this theoretical concern

---

176   Panitch and Gindin (2012: 15).
177   Panitch and Gindin (2012: 17).
178   Panitch and Gindin (2012: 19).
179   Panitch and Gindin (2012: 21).

was quickly displaced by the rise of neoliberalism in the 1980s, which openly declared its intent to roll back the Keynesian Welfare State (KWS) and to reestablish "free markets" and "limited government."[180] This new political context led Panitch to shift his focus from the theory of the state per se to the instability of corporatist structures, which were critical to the functioning of the Keynesian Welfare State. Finally, when confronted with a triumphant Washington Consensus in the 1990s, Panitch returned to the theory of the state to argue that the process of neoliberal globalization was best understood as the consolidation of an informal empire under the hegemony of the American state.[181] This last phase of his theoretical development culminated in a *magnum opus,* which was co-authored by Sam Gindin, and published as *The Making of Global Capitalism: The Political Economy of American Empire* (2012).

Panitch's theory of the capitalist state has challenged other political economists and state theorists in four major ways.[182] First, although his work was heavily influenced by the writings of Ralph Miliband and Nicos Poulantzas, he was never caught up in the Poulantzas-Miliband debate of the 1970s. Instead, he was perhaps the first state theorist to suggest that the entire 1970s state debate had generated a caricature of Miliband and Poulantzas that both theorists rejected as vulgarizations of their work.[183] In contrast to the general trajectory of the state debate during this time, Panitch rejected the endless quibbling about epistemology and methodology and instead preferred to build on the work of previous state theorists by using their insights to analyze actually existing states in capitalist societies.

Second, when Panitch shifted his attention to the dismantling of the Keynesian Welfare State in the 1980s, which included the collapse of corporatist structures based on voluntary class compromise, he never described these political developments as a decline of the state. In contrast, Panitch was one of the few political economists to recognize that even as it retreated from the provision of public goods and services, including the privatization of state-owned industries, the state was simultaneously strengthening its repressive and coercive apparatus as part of its strategy to weaken trade unions, break strikes, quell citizen protest, and discipline recalcitrant nations that resisted the imposition of a neoliberal world order. Thus, as Ellen Wood would observe,

---

180   Friedman (1962).
181   Palmer (2017: 326).
182   Keucheyan (2013: 96–99).
183   Panitch (1977a: 4); Barrow (2016: chs. 4–5).

globalization has certainly been marked by a withdrawal of the state from its social welfare and ameliorative functions and, for most observers, "this has perhaps more than anything else created an impression of the state's decline," but they missed the fact that this retreat was often being imposed on recalcitrant populations through repression and coercion.[184]

Third, as key capitalist states strengthened their repressive apparatuses in the 1980s and 1990s, Panitch recognized that they were also building a more powerful state economic apparatus that shifted macro-economic management from fiscal policy to monetary policy.[185] Monetary policy was used to aggressively reduce inflation (e.g., the Volcker Shock), while fiscal policy became a form of global austerity – mostly targeting health, education, and welfare spending to pay for reductions in corporate taxes and to lower marginal income tax rates on the wealthy. This shift in macro-economic policy was not only a new form of class war; it laid the groundwork for the financialization of capitalist economies, while removing macro-economic policy from elected legislatures to "independent" central banks and treasuries (i.e., international investment bankers and bond holders). Finally, while many state theorists, political economists, and international relations theorists were wringing their hands about American decline during this time, Panitch saw the emergence of neoliberalism in the 1980s, and globalization in the 1990s, as a transfusion that reinvigorated the American state and its ability to continue superintending global capital well into the twenty-first century.

The political fault lines opened up by the Great Recession have offered some hope for a renewal of socialism as even in the United States "democratic socialism" has been catapulted back onto the national political agenda in a way not seen since the first two decades of the twentieth century.[186] Panitch long argued that the rise of neoliberalism creates both the possibility and the necessity of renewing socialism as well as the necessity of building a different kind of (democratic) state to reverse the authoritarian trajectory of neoliberalism.[187] Nevertheless, in many of his more "political" writings, Panitch expressed distress at how little resistance the left has offered to the new right's assault on the welfare state and its confident declaration that "there is no alternative" to neoliberalism.[188] On the one hand, much of this acquiescence has

---

184   Wood (2003: 140).
185   Panitch and Swartz (1988: 32).
186   Albo, Gindin and Panitch (2010); Barrow (2019: 3–10).
187   Panitch (1993; 2001).
188   Panitch (2001: 12).

been institutionalized in the electoral strategies and policy programs of the traditional social-democratic parties, whose entrenched party elites have vigorously blocked the emergence of a radical socialist alternative within those parties.[189] At the same time, Panitch pointed out that there is no shortage of blueprints for socialism.[190] Yet, what is missing from these blueprints is "the establishment of the political means of realizing them, i.e., the creation of new political institutions which would mobilize and educate [workers and citizens] not only for economic democracy but also for a transformation of conventional modes of representation and administration within the state."[191]

In this respect, Panitch suggested that the on-going crisis of the capitalist system has also brought the contradictions of social democratic parties into focus. In a follow up to Miliband's *Parliamentary Socialism*, Panitch and Colin Leys document how the internal life of the social democratic parties has undergone "a serious decline as a result of their integration into the institutions of 'managed capitalism'."[192] The main problem, according to Panitch and Leys, is that "when the socialist vision gives way to the pragmatic management of capitalism, there is little scope or need for a party-based 'counter-hegemonic' community."[193] This means that local party organizations are reduced to centers of electoral mobilization, but party organizations cease to play a role as "centres of education and mobilization, oriented to an alternative way of life." Panitch and Leys argue that the larger purpose of a socialist party should be "to create a new popular base for democratic socialism" and not just to compete in elections.[194] Democratic socialism is more than a political party and more than elections; it must be a broad-based social movement. It must be a social movement, because "socialism" involves more than a conquest of state power; it must penetrate the private sector and civil society to create an entirely new mode of production. For as Marx and Engels describe it in *The German Ideology*:

This mode of production must not be considered simply as being the reproduction of the physical existence of the individuals. Rather it is a definite form of activity of these individuals, a definite form of expressing

---

189   Panitch and Leys (2001).
190   For example, Carnoy and Shearer (1980); Bowles, Gordon and Weisskopf (1984); Ollman (1998).
191   Panitch (1993: 7).
192   Panitch and Leys (2001: 6).
193   Panitch and Leys (2001: 6).
194   Panitch and Leys (2001: 4).

their life, a definite mode of life on their part. As individuals express their life, so they are.[195]

Panitch and Leys contend that a significant component of a new socialist state would be the public ownership of a large share of the financial sector and the development of new models of public enterprise.[196] In fact, out of pure necessity, and much as Marx predicted, the United States, Great Britain, and other capitalist states did nationalize large swaths of the financial sector during the global financial crisis of 2008–2010 and, yet, rather than taking this opportunity to build a different type of state, and to redefine the nature of the state's relationship to capital and workers, neoliberal governments (including Barack Obama) moved as quickly as possible to return trillions of dollars in nationalized financial and industrial assets to the same corporate pirates who had pillaged and nearly destroyed the global economy. The same pattern is being reenacted in the United States a second time under the Trump Administration. Thus, socialism does not only seem possible, it increasingly seems to be a necessity, but the left does not have the mass popular base or the organizational capacity to implement or sustain a socialist program.

These problems were explored at length in a 1993 essay by Leo Panitch entitled "A Different Kind of State." Panitch suggests that the solution to the political and economic crisis of liberal democracies lies not in privatizing the public sector, as neoliberals have done, but in further democratizing the state. Panitch proposes political reforms that are designed to build on the gains of liberal democracy, which has "attenuated, even though it has certainly not done away with, the relations of domination and subordination among people that are inscribed in terms of class, status, gender, and race."[197] The main limitation of liberal democracy, according to Panitch, is that liberal rights have an "individualist bias" often to the detriment of collective rights. Thus, Panitch considers the welfare state and the winning of welfare rights to be a significant advance beyond classical liberalism (i.e., neoliberalism), because it "established the potential for all to have the minimum resources that would make liberal and citizenship rights something more than the purely formal entities they had been for considerable sections of the population for considerable periods of their lives."[198] The welfare state is worth defending and even expanding, and its loss is a significant step backward for all workers and ordinary citizens. The

---

195   Marx and Engels (1976a: 31).
196   Panitch and Leys (2001: 12).
197   Panitch (1993: 5).
198   Panitch (1993: 5–6).

current Covid-19 pandemic has almost made a universal basic income a main-stream conversation.

Nevertheless, Panitch argues that a purely liberal conception of rights also imposes "limits and constraints on our citizenship rights," because liberal rights are "usually cast in the form of 'freedom from' rather than 'freedom to': that is the negative freedom of not being made to do something as opposed to the positive freedom necessary for full human development."[199] Importantly, for Panitch "both aspects of freedom need to be applied not only to the state, but to business enterprises in the private sector, whose legal status of corporate individuality belies their essentially public nature."[200] However, given the recent history of nationalizations, which have yielded nothing but the social-ization of debt and toxic assets, Panitch argues that "only far more democra-tized public institutions will ever have the creativity and the popular strength necessary to democratize the private sector. *The real issue of our time is not less state versus more state, but rather a different kind of state. ...* We need to shake the bureaucratic model to its foundations" and this includes democratizing the judicial system.[201]

While Panitch considered liberal bills of rights an important aspect of lib-eral democracy, he accurately observed that in practice bills of rights often have the "effect of increasing the importance of an undemocratically struc-tured legal and judicial apparatus within the political system. The result may be a legalization and justification, rather than a democratization, of politics and administration" as liberals are now discovering in the United States, where a reactionary US Senate majority is loading up the federal judiciary with con-servative judicial activists, who are already waging a judicial campaign to roll back democratic achievements of previous decades and who will act as a bul-wark against any democratic initiatives going forward.[202]

While there is much cause for pessimism, Panitch nevertheless suggests that "the massive anticapitalist protests from Seattle to Prague to Quebec that captured the world's attention at the beginning of the new millennium attest to the fact that the spirit of revolution ... is hardly a thing of the past."[203] Yet, at the same time, Panitch presciently warned that "it is through crises that

---

199   Panitch (1993: 6); cf. Berlin (1969).
200   Panitch (1993: 6); Barrow (2001) discusses how corporations analytically fall within the public sphere of government and governance even if one relies on the concepts of main-stream political science.
201   Panitch (1993: 6, 10).
202   Panitch (1993: 11).
203   Panitch (2001: 1).

capitalism has historically tended to recover its dynamism," but "where and when it is unable to do so, and where no viable socialist alternative, or at least few means of democratic defense exist, the consequences are always appalling."[204] And, on that note, I conclude this critical review by suggesting that the authoritarian trajectory of political development identified by Panitch as early as the 1980s is currently unfolding in two ways that signal a profound crisis for both global capitalism and liberal democracy.

First, a main conclusion of *The Making of Global Capitalism* is that political fault lines now "run within states rather than between them" – between globalized elites and localized masses. Whether this development provides an opening for socialist renewal depends on whether socialists can mobilize popular discontent against "global elites" to protect the welfare state, democratize the state, and socialize (not necessarily nationalize) key sectors of the means of production. While the grassroots democratic socialist movement led by Senator Bernie Sanders has offered a glimpse of hope, his campaign has twice been deflected by the same machinations of "parliamentary socialism" analyzed first by Ralph Miliband and then by Leo Panitch and Colin Leys in their books on this topic. Social Democratic parties continue to be impervious to radical democratic reform as they consistently seek the support of so-called "moderate" (i.e., center-right) voters, rather than make a single policy concession to the socialist left.

Consequently, rather than a vibrant socialist renewal, quite the opposite has happened as right-wing populists gain political power by offering illiberal and anti-globalist solutions to the economic problems of a decomposing working class. The election of Donald J. Trump as US President, England's Brexit and the subsequent election of Boris Johnson, political developments in Eastern Europe (e.g., Hungary, Poland, Serbia), and the rise of right-wing parties in Western Europe stand as evidence that it is the right-wing that is mobilizing popular discontent against global capitalism and the results, as Panitch suggested, will be appalling if not reversed in the near future. Furthermore, right-wing populists who have captured state power have been able to disorganize the global elite networks that sustain global capitalism much faster and to a much greater degree than once thought possible by most political analysts.

On January 20, 2017, Donald J. Trump, a billionaire New York real estate investor was inaugurated as the forty-fifth President of the United States. The fact that Donald Trump was unlike any other candidate for the office has been apparent since he announced his bid for the US Presidency in January of 2016

---

204   Panitch (2001: 7–8).

by descending on a gold escalator in his famous Trump Tower to announce his bid for the US Presidency. Donald Trump promised to "Make America Great Again" and, throughout his campaign and inaugural speech, he painted a dystopian portrait of the United States as a broken country, while repeatedly declaring that: "I alone can fix it." His fixes include the construction of a 2000-mile-long "big, beautiful wall" to stop illegal immigration from Latin America. He promised to reverse the new global world order that had ostensibly destroyed the American working class by imposing tariffs to discourage imports and "bring good jobs back to America." Trump promised to withdraw the United States from international treaties on trade, climate, and security because they "cost too much money" and "destroy American jobs." Many of his ideas were not only not 'politically correct' in American politics, but were unconstitutional or illegal, but as Trump recently said: "radical judges invent laws that Congress never passed" so those alleged laws, and judicial interpretations of the US Constitution, have no binding effect on him as President.[205]

While Trump (like Boris Johnson) has been portrayed as a clown in the mainstream media, his big, beautiful wall is under construction despite opposition from the US House of Representatives and despite illegal transfers of funds from military and other accounts to pay for it. Thousands of immigrant women and children seeking political asylum from violence at home are now caged in "detention centers" – some call them concentration camps – where they lack basic sanitary facilities, health care, and adequate food and water. Donald Trump has unilaterally imposed 25% tariffs on goods imported from China, Europe, and Japan, among others, and has disrupted the global trading system to an enormous degree. He has withdrawn the United States from the Paris Climate Accords and the Trans-Pacific Partnership, while forcing Canada and Mexico to renegotiate the North American Free Trade Agreement. Trump has openly cast doubt on the United States' willingness to abide by Article 5 of NATO, the cornerstone of the alliance, while publicly insulting allies and demanding that European nations contribute more troops and money to NATO. Meanwhile, he heaps praise on dictators such as Vladimir Putin and Kim Jong Il. As if emulating his new-found "friends," Trump routinely violates the law and the US Constitution despite being impeached as he is assisted by appointed cronies and the backstop of a Republican majority in the US Senate that now openly voices its contempt for the working class and democracy.

If, as Poulantzas suggests, one of the primary roles of the state is to organize the capitalist class, then the United States, acting as the superintendent

---

205   Trump (2019).

of global capitalism is now failing to fulfill the basic maintenance function of a capitalist state. The United States is now a state that is not willing to act in the interests of capital as a (global) whole, because as Trump says, the United States has been victimized by "bad deals" with its NATO allies, NAFTA partners, and the WTO.[206] As Panitch and Gindin recently observed: "Trump has not only led the attack on free trade but at the same time overseen the erosion of institutional capacities essential to managing the global capitalist economy."[207]

This scenario raises the question of what happens to the liberal democracies, and even to global capitalism, absent a strong socialist movement? The rise of authoritarianism has been a clear and present danger since the emergence of neoliberalism in the 1980s. However, in the long historical past, such threats were largely rebuffed by the power of the American state. The United States intervened against the absolutist powers in World War I. It blocked the rise of Nazism and fascism in World War II, and it challenged Communist totalitarianism with the Cold War (1945–1993). While the United States was supported by its liberal democratic Western allies, the US state largely underwrote the costs of sustaining and reproducing capitalism, and sometimes liberal democracy, on an ever-expanding global scale. What happens if the United States itself becomes a threat to the world order it created in its own image, and if the network of global alliances and international institutions built to sustain that world order continue to fray and come apart at the seams?

Nicole Aschoff recently pointed out that Donald Trump's policies and rhetoric have "created a deep crisis of legitimacy for the dominant ideas guiding global capitalism."[208] Indeed, recent developments in the United Kingdom, the United States, and elsewhere may even "mark the end of neoliberalism's heyday" and "the emergence of a competing vision of capitalism" that is pessimistic, xenophobic, racist, and misogynist and held together by escalating domestic state violence, surveillance, incarceration, and cultural isolation of perceived enemies of the new order.[209] The intensification of domestic conflict in the globalizing metropolises is particularly significant as these states have been the political leaders and military enforcers of neoliberal globalization since the end of World War II. The American and British states, in particular, have been the architects and underwriters of global capitalism, so if they withdraw from a world of their own making, it will certainly constitute a political crisis of *global* capitalism, as well as a crisis of democracy, but it most assuredly does not presage a decline of the state.

---

206   Farber (2018).
207   Panitch and Gindin (2018b: 15).
208   Aschoff (2017).
209   Barrow (2017: ch. 7).

CHAPTER 2

Beyond the Impasse of State Theory

Martijn Konings

What light could Marxist state theory possibly shed on a world that has produced the US Presidency of Donald Trump? What is left to uncover or demystify that is not already painfully, glaringly obvious? We can't even approach this as a matter of right-wing elites having tried but failed to hide their schemes, yet being accommodated by a passive public. In some respects, the situation is the opposite: many attributes of power that Marxist state theory would have assumed elites have an interest in hiding from public scrutiny are either not considered worth covering up or indeed positively advertised to whip up support in the electoral arena.

This situation presents an unfamiliar challenge to critical approaches in state theory, which are set up to interrogate the extent to which the exercise of political power works according to the ideals of democratic legitimacy or if it is in fact driven by something else. In Marxist state theory, that something else is of course capital. Trump defies this schema in very obvious ways. At this point, key factions of capital may have made some kind of peace with his rule; but many expected from Hillary Clinton (and now expect from Joe Biden) very similar accommodations but without being required to deal with the constant disruptions to business-as-usual arising from Trump's unpredictable and erratic provocations at home and overseas. In that sense, Trump is strangely autonomous – almost entirely a circus unto himself, his actions ostensibly driven far more by a particularly potent personality disorder than by strategic readings of the political landscape.

At the same time, it would be extremely naïve to think that the Trump presidency somehow validates the kind of disconnect of politics from capital that was depicted in the 'state autonomy' literature.[1] This approach attained extraordinary scholarly traction during the last two decades of the previous century, and it continues to legitimate the widespread tendency to think of the role of the state in formal institutional terms. As administrations of the time made clear just how beholden political power was to the rule of capital, neo-Weberian scholars reinterpreted the past through historical sociologies

---

1 Skocpol (1985).

of state-building that stressed the principal autonomy of bureaucratic institutions and rejected the Marxist focus on capitalism as blinkered and reductionist. What Marxists called neoliberalism and viewed as driven by the interests of capital, these scholars thought of as failures of state-building. From such a perspective, Trump appears as the conclusion of a decades-long decline of state capacity. If such a take hews closely to how Trump's progressive contenders like Hillary Clinton would view the current situation, that also hints at its superficiality.

A 'state autonomy' perspective is patently powerless to make sense of the Trump phenomenon: even as Trump is clearly not part of any rational principal-agent relationship that could be approached in instrumental or functional terms, he is nonetheless emphatically a symbol, a mere manifestation of contradictions located elsewhere that were in operation well before they could express themselves in such strange public spectacles. So, what do we make of this paradox: on the one hand, a political project unhinged and untethered; on the other hand, this very irrationality being so emphatically nothing but a symptom of something deeper? Marxist state theory has a particular concept to refer to such a paradoxical situation – 'relative autonomy', meant to highlight the fact that while the political sphere has its own rationality, this independence is not to be taken literally and always remains tied to the capitalist society over which the state presides. Unfortunately, this notion of relative autonomy has typically been elaborated through a structuralist theoretical lens that approaches the concept as primarily descriptive, as positively representing an objective reality. In that way, it suppresses the paradoxical character of the process it refers to.

If the structuralist 'relative autonomy' problematic was not always unproductive, at this point Marxist theory seems to have become caught in a series of formalistic solutions to the problem, increasingly allowing for the sui generis nature of political struggles while also insisting that these are ultimately, in a 'last instance' way, tied to the reproduction of capitalist power. This chapter will propose a different approach, oriented not to a quantitative rebalancing of the lines of causal determination, but to a more qualitative reconsideration of how the nature of politics changes with the rise of capitalism. Here a reconceptualization of ideology is pertinent. Marxist state theory has become less and less confident in using this concept, laying the basis for its almost complete rejection in post-Marxist theory, but it remains critical to an understanding of our times. This chapter reviews key currents in Marxist state theory and related critical approaches in order to chart a path out of this impasse and point towards a more productive elaboration of the state's paradoxical relative autonomy.

1   Structuralist Antinomies

Poulantzas' work is widely seen as a central point of reference in modern Marxist thinking about the state, and it provides a useful starting point for the discussion here. Recognizing that the state possesses an institutional framework separate from the economy, Poulantzas sought to articulate the mode in which capitalist class domination is present within it. His conceptual framework was provided by Althusserian structuralism, which views societies as composed of economic, political and ideological levels. Taking issue with an overly rigid separation of such levels, Poulantzas argued that relations of production are not 'economic' in any strict sense, but always involve political and ideological aspects.[2] The capitalist state possesses a materiality of its own, but this should not be seen as a genuine autonomy or independence, as indicating an external relation between capital and state. Rather, the state's autonomy is relative to the balance of class forces, which "express themselves, in a necessarily specific form, *within the State itself.*"[3] The state's institutional field is selective, biased in favor of capital.

Poulantzas contrasts his own approach with both the 'instrumentalist' conception of state action and theories that 'derive' the capitalist state from the economic logic of capital. It is, however, not clear that Poulantzas' conception of the state is, or can be, as distinct from the theories he criticizes as he himself believes. For if it is the case that production relations are present in the state in a *specific* mode (i.e., in a way that cannot be deduced from capital's economic logic), then it still has to be shown why and how the political field is carved out in favor of capital (rather than being neutral, or selective in favor of the subordinate classes). Tellingly, Poulantzas' less-abstract discussions of the state's personnel and the economic functions of the state frequently draw on the insights of those instrumentalist theories that he is at pains to criticize. Meanwhile, the main *theoretical* reason advanced for the fact that contradictions are generally resolved in favor of the bourgeoisie is that it is the 'function' of the state to maintain the unity of capitalist society.

The relevance of these considerations is borne out by the uses to which Poulantzas' work has been put. Authors such as Hirsch and Jessop, who have tried to build on and refine Poulantzas' state theory and integrate it with regulation theory, have tended to stretch the concept of relative autonomy to its limit.[4] The struggles that are waged on the political and ideological level are

---

2   Poulantzas (1975: 17).

3   Poulantzas (1978c: 132).

4   Hirsch (1995); Jessop (1990).

seen to be ever more independent from economic logics, yet those struggles seem ever less capable of doing anything other than reproducing the structures of capital. Put differently, the political and ideological levels become more independent, but in the last instance this increased autonomy is entirely functional to the reproduction of the rule of capital and attendant class relations. For instance, Jessop faults Poulantzas for his residual structural-functionalism and his lack of appreciation for the "political indeterminacy of the institutional structure of the state."[5] Poulantzas, it is claimed, stresses too much the state's "'structural selectivity' and leaves little room for the influence of political struggle on class domination."[6] Jessop proposes to remedy this with a greater emphasis on the strategic capacities of actors vying for hegemony on the field of the state, i.e., by allowing for a higher degree of voluntarism. However, to the extent that Jessop strips Poulantzas' understanding of the state's selectivity of its residual structural-functionalism, it also becomes a more arbitrary notion.

Seen from this perspective, the state derivation school in fact pointed in some useful directions.[7] Poulantzas' characterization of this approach as "an attempt to 'derive', or let us say deduce, the particular institutions of the capitalist State from the 'economic categories' of capital accumulation"[8] may be valid for some of the contributions to the debate, but it is not very accurate with respect to others. The latter precisely rejected the possibility of deducing 'particular institutions' from the economic logic of capital but rather claimed that the *form* of the state needs to be grounded in the historically specific nature of capital: the separation of state and society was to be seen as itself the process whereby capitalist class relations are constituted.

This insight might have been the starting point for a fruitful redirection of analytical efforts, pointing away from the introduction of ever more pluralism (in order to avoid the charge of reductionism) and towards an alternative way of articulating the nature of the state's relationship to society. But unfortunately the state derivation debate itself is hardly helpful here, for it did not go much beyond Holloway and Picciotto's rather perfunctory call for "an understanding of the state based on the dialectic of the form and content of class struggle."[9] Those who have tried to continue or revive this tradition in more recent years have largely ignored this injunction,[10] rendering the approach

---

5   Jessop (1990: 69).
6   Jessop (1990: 69).
7   For a key selection of contributions to the state derivation debate, see Holloway and
        Picciotto (1978a).
8   Poulantzas (1978c: 51).
9   Holloway and Picciotto (1978b: 30).
10   For example, Bonefeld (1992); Clarke (1991).

formalistic and its analytical grip on the concrete relations between capitalist relations and state institutions tenuous.[11] And, perhaps more serious and telling, insofar as they do undertake more historically and empirically oriented investigations, their accounts end up drawing on and looking rather like the regulationist theories that they are so critical of.

Not only, then, is the derivationist conceptual framework too abstract – in which case we could simply proceed to undertake concrete investigations on the basis of it. The inability of its proponents to descend to more concrete levels of analysis is very much bound up with a deep-seated theoretical ambiguity. Part of the problem is hinted at by the ring of implausibility which attaches to the notion that political, ideological, and economic relations need to be conceived as 'forms of manifestation' of capitalist production relations. The crucial point that the institutional form of the state is already constitutive of capitalist relations of production, is rendered somewhat irrelevant if one fails to specify how such 'forms' differ from the 'levels' of Althusserian structuralism. In other words, the regulationist combination of structural-functionalism and pluralism is replaced with a ubiquity of form-determinations which ends up producing similar dilemmas and difficulties (since these forms are all seen as manifestations of the same underlying class content). How, then, can we put the form-based critique of Poulantzas' structuralism to more productive use?

2   Beyond Structuralism

Although it is hard to disagree with the arguments that Poulantzas directs against his own stylized version of instrumentalism, it is interesting to note that while Miliband never spelt out his conception of relative autonomy in any great theoretical detail, when it came to the interpretation of historical developments his understanding of it seemed to give rise to fewer dilemmas than Poulantzas'. Whatever the theoretical silences and problems in what is usually regarded as his most important contribution to state theory, *The State in Capitalist Society* (1969), to anyone acquainted with the analysis of the selectivity embedded in the structures of state institutions in *Parliamentary Socialism* (1961) the charge of 'instrumentalism' cannot but seem simplistic. In Miliband's approach, the autonomy of the state is relativized not so much by capitalists' capacity to capture key positions in the state's apparatuses, but rather by the general outlook and practical disposition of actors operating on

---

11   Barrow (1993: 98).

the institutional field of the state. This work also paid much greater attention to the institutional specifics of twentieth-century democracy, and the way its dynamics expressed not just the purely *political* but also the *economic* integration of the working classes. Parliamentary democracy was understood not as an arena that served to provide post-hoc legitimation for an already constituted capitalist economy, but as the place where such economic structures were reshaped.

Miliband did not really do justice to the conceptual implications of his work. Nor were those who have adopted a broadly Milibandian mode of enquiry in their work particularly keen to return to the abstract theoretical questions that Poulantzas and Miliband debated. Discouraged by the aridity and conceptual acrobatics that increasingly came to characterize the work that went under the banner of 'state theory', they focused primarily on producing conceptually informed and politically illuminating historical work.[12] This was hardly the work of historians who tell us everything about nothing, but of critical social scientists whose conceptual awareness allowed them to recognize the developments, actors, and institutions that should occupy a central place in the writing of history. The fruitful contributions of these authors contrasted starkly with the products of those who ventured into history from a more committed structuralist or form-structuralist perspective. The former became involved with the writing of epochalist histories of the post-WWII order that were rather similar to more mainstream institutionalist accounts of this transformation.[13] The latter produced historical readings of the rise and fall of the Keynesian era that differed in very few respects from the structuralist and regulationist approaches they criticized.[14]

In part owing to this fruitfulness of Milibandian sensibilities in clarifying historical processes, recent years have seen a revaluation of his work.[15] Yet it is not clear that these contributions have really captured the significance of Miliband's work in a way that would immunize it from some predictable concerns. Barrow and Wetherly suggest that the charge of instrumentalism rests on misreadings of Miliband's work, and they argue for the continued relevance of approaches that seek to articulate – but do not try to collapse the distinction between – capitalist class power and state power.[16] While this point has considerable validity within the conceptual parameters of traditional Marxist

---

12   For example, Coates (1989); Panitch and Leys (1997).
13   Hirsch (1995); Jessop (2002).
14   Clarke (1988); Bonefeld (1993).
15   See, in particular, the contributions to Wetherly, Barrow and Burnham (2008).
16   Barrow (2008); Wetherly (2008).

theory, its effect is of course also to reinstate the central dilemma of such per-spectives – i.e., how exactly to articulate capital and state without recourse to functionalist explanations. Indeed, approaching Miliband's contribution in this defensive way entails the risk that we might end up supplying yet another formulaic solution to what is a substantive theoretical problem. Similarly, Burnham suggests that we conceptualize Miliband's approach through a form-theoretical perspective.[17] But the problem here is the same as the one high-lighted in the previous section, i.e., that it has never been quite clear what it means to think of the state's separation from society as a determination of its form rather than its structure or substance.

What Miliband's work shows us is that the problem of the state is at its core a problem of ideology. That is not to deny that public authority possesses its own materiality, but rather to argue that any such institutional autonomy is itself produced through distinctions that are at the heart of how modern power operates. To draw a distinction between state and capital is not merely to describe a pre-existing state of affairs, but it is to participate in the construc-tion of an institutional configuration in which certain kinds of relationships are seen to be non-political even though they involve power and control. The separation of state and capital is part of a political discourse that produces social effects.[18] This entails an important shift in our understanding of ide-ology: instead of being another level, existing alongside the political and the economic realms, the workings of ideology should be conceived as prior to, and productive of, capitalist power, including its appearance through differ-entiated spheres of life. If this point was hardly recognized by Miliband the theorist, it was precisely in this respect that his historically oriented writings contributed most. And it is here that the notion of 'form' (so central to the der-ivationist framework) acquires a fuller meaning: if it is to play a useful role in thinking the state in a critical way, it needs to draw attention to the ideological dimension of social constitution.

This argument – that the ideological separation of the political and the eco-nomic is prior to, and should be seen as the very way in which capitalist rule takes shape – has often been associated with the theoretical contributions of Political Marxism. According to Wood, pre-capitalist societies were character-ized by a fusion of political and economic power: relations of production were organized under political auspices and directly backed up by force. In capi-talist society this changes because of the constitutional delimitation of state

---

17 Burnham (2008).
18 Cf. Abrams (1988); Bratsis (2002); Mitchell (1999).

authority: individual property rights serve to limit the reach of the state and guarantee its holder a sphere of public non-interference. The birth and development of capitalism is a process whereby power loses its explicitly political character and becomes privatized and embedded in a sphere of seemingly depoliticized, 'economic' interactions.[19] This approach is in keeping with the point I made earlier about ideology: it views ideology not as external legitimation of a reality already in place, but as something that attends the constitution of social relations in a direct way. In other words, Political Marxism provides a more rigorous way of following through on form-theoretical work on the state. It does not start out from the existence of capitalist class relations and then retrofit the empirical-institutional forms of capitalist society around them (as 'forms of appearance' of a presumably foundational relationship). Instead, it theorizes the specific rationality of capitalist class conflicts as fully shaped by the institutional transformation of property and the ideological separation of the political and the economic.

However, Political Marxism tends to view this constitution of a private sphere defined by private property relations as a one-off event, or at least something that, once set in motion, maintains its momentum. The fact that the role of the state has increased rather than decreased with the development of modern capitalism appears as something of a mystery. In this sense it puts *too* much faith in the materiality of ideology, its direct, practical embodiment in social practices and relations. And as a consequence, the political sphere is once again consigned to a largely superstructural status. It is as if the political dimension is fully pre-empted by the ideological separation of an economic sphere and the way this hides relations of power as seemingly non-political relations of production and exchange – if the dynamics of the political sphere can proceed relatively freely, it is because they are essentially inconsequential, pre-defined to be harmless.

This is of course a strange endpoint for a theory that began by assigning explanatory priority to the political dimension. The issue here is that, despite the turn towards a more materialist notion of ideology in the sense that it is seen to attach more closely to practices, the notion of ideology that Political Marxism uses is still very conventional in a key aspect: ideology is seen in terms of conceptual templates or interpretative frameworks that serve to obscure the nature of underlying social relations and so allow them to persist. However, the distinctiveness of modern ideology consists in the fact that it does not primarily work through such obfuscation. That may be a useful way to think

---

19   Wood (1995).

about pre-modern ideology and its appeal to transcendent, other-worldly symbols of authority. Of course, to some extent this view of the past reflects our own inability to relate to it, leading us to exaggerate the extent to which people would have believed literally and naively. But in that capacity, it none-theless serves to underline something distinctive about how modern ideology works: that it is not reliant for its efficacy on cognitive misdirection or on peo-ple's willingness to believe in literal and unquestioning ways.

3   Resituating Capital

It is useful here to engage with post-Marxist work, which has sought to eman-cipate issues of discourse, ideology, and knowledge from any notion that they serve to legitimate or obscure a deeper reality that powerful interests need to remain unacknowledged. They place much greater emphasis on the auton-omy of the political and the ideological dimensions, doing so not in terms of *relative* autonomy but in terms of *actual* autonomy, stressing not ideological misrecognition but instead the productiveness of political symbolism. Within the field of state theory, no doubt the most well-known contribution is from Laclau and Mouffe, which proposed a notion of discursive hegemony produc-tion that strips the concept of any residual economic determinations and pres-ents a pluralist understanding of power that seemed always particularly poorly attuned to the neoliberal counter-offensive amidst which it was formulated.[20] But the Laclau and Mouffe book was so purposely a polemically charged inter-vention into the debates outlined here – and in many ways merely presented the logical poststructuralist resolution of the structuralist antinomies that I have outlined – that its use for reorienting the debate and reconfiguring its parameters is in fact quite limited.

A more useful interlocutor here is Lefort, whose emphasis on the auton-omy of the political developed in a less antagonistic relationship to state-theoretical debates.[21] Indeed, the notion of capital hardly featured in his work at all. For Lefort, the defining feature of modernity was the opening up of 'the political', humanity's emerging awareness that it was making its own history, and that the institutions in which humans lived were not governed by external authorities or transcendent laws. His central concern was to explain why this shift, and the consequent need to justify authority with reference to the secular

---

20   Laclau and Mouffe (1985).
21   Lefort (1988).

interest of 'the people', did not entail a process of progressive democratization but was marked by the recurrent re-emergence of totalitarianism and authoritarianism. Why does a society that is born from the cancellation of monarchical power – i.e., a republic – constantly give rise to new forms of authority that the people experience as oppressive?

Lefort views Machiavelli as the first thinker to clearly articulate this opening up of the 'the political' and, as Marchart argues, his work can be read as a philosophical reflection on modernity understood as a "Machiavellian moment."[22] The Machiavellian moment is a phrase introduced by Pocock's famous book, which uncovered a modern republican tradition of thinking about authority that had its origins in Renaissance Italy and subsequently migrated to the Anglo-American world.[23] Pocock's re-reading of the rise of the Anglo-American world challenged the tendency to view the development of England and America in terms of Lockean liberalism, and his interpretation became the basis of a republican paradigm that no longer interpreted the political development of the United States through the lens of possessive individualism and private property, but rather in terms of civic virtue and a shared commitment to preventing concentrations of political power. This was an important impetus behind the more general revival of republican thought in political theory, which looks to this tradition as an alternative to neoliberalism's reassertion of the rule of capital.[24]

In this way, republicanism has come to be appropriated as a forgotten political tradition. As a left-of-center political argument, this has of course never been all that powerful – and indeed entirely ignores the fact that neoliberalism has always and very successfully staked its *own* claim to the republican tradition and that this has been central to its success. And that tells us something about the status of republicanism, and in particular the fact that it has remained alive and well into the present – just emphatically not in the guise imagined by progressive republicanism. So, while the engagement with post-Marxist theories of the internal contradictions of the political is useful as a way to reset our thinking, it is certainly not possible to keep capital out of this story without it becoming incoherent. Indeed, merely positing this kind of republicanism as an alternative to capitalism implies some common point of reference that needs to be acknowledged.

This is where we need to shift our attention. Instead of a primary focus on situating the state in relation to a capitalist structure we assume we understand,

---

22   Lefort (2012); Marchart (2007).

23   Pocock (1975).

24   Pettit (1997); Sandel (1998).

we need to examine the preconceptions that such an exercise brings to our understanding of capital. In almost all state-theoretical narratives, capital features in a specific capacity – as what Hegel termed a "bad infinity,"[25] an irrational, self-referential movement that has no end or purpose other than its own self-continuation and self-augmentation. This image of capital has been central to the critique of capitalism since Marx, but it has also found tremendous traction in more left-of-center critical perspectives (in contemporary debates, it is most prominently represented by Polanyi's notion of 'disembedding').[26] As such it is the image of capital employed even by those (like Polanyi and his followers) who challenge the very assumption of capital's centrality. This critique of capital as bad infinity rehearses a pre-modern, religiously driven critique of capital as a movement whose self-referentiality rivals God's power over creation. Its deployment in modern times is, most notably in Marx's work, meant to highlight the irrational element in a putatively modern and rational age. But there is still something awkward about this repurposing of a pre-modern critique of capital – above all, it fails to register how our relationship to capital *changes* with the transition to modernity.[27]

A re-examination of the republican problematic allows us to bring the problem into sharper focus. The republican reading of American history makes too little of something that was already suggested by Pocock's own book: the fact that republicanism underwent a much more significant ideological reconfiguration as it migrated from Italy to the Anglo-American world than with its initial recovery during the renaissance.[28] The re-appropriation of Roman Republicanism in Renaissance Italy may have been highly creative, driven by a wish to repurpose it for a world that was more deeply aware of historical time and secular contingency. But a key line of continuity consisted in its deeply undemocratic character, the fact that its recovery was driven not by a sense of its democratic potential but precisely by the fact that it could provide a basis for oligarchic rule.[29] These elite interests certainly included mercantile elites far more prominently than before, but this was still very much a pre-capitalist world where trade and commerce were deeply bound up with politically constituted property and war making. Any hopes that 'doux commerce' would be the vehicle for a comprehensive pacification of civil society would have been purely notional and aspirational at this point.

---

25   McNally (2003); Harvey (2018a).
26   Polanyi (1944).
27   Konings (2018).
28   Kennedy (2009).
29   Pangle (1988).

Prevailing conceptions of capital were similarly still deeply shaped by the
church's critique of capital: for all their advantages, commerce and trade were
seen as always corrosive of order, prone to disembedding themselves from their
proper domain.[30] It was only later on, in the Enlightenment and in particular
its Scottish incarnation, and in the context of more rapid domestic capitalist
development, that this critique of capital begins to change. Key here was the
emergence of a conception of capital, money, and trade as 'neutral' institutions, mere instruments for the coordination of secular life that allowed for the
creation of wealth and material progress. Prior to this, such a notion had been
unthinkable: even when the use of money had been tolerated and its corrosive
effects contained, it was never seen as in-principle neutral, and it was never
above suspicion. Smith's work has become such a central point of reference
in the modern social sciences because it expressed the re-conceptualization
of capital not as a threat to divine order but as a specifically secular source of
order – 'capital' becomes 'the market'.[31]

This implies a very significant shift in our relationship to capital – which
appears less and less as a bad infinity, and increasingly as a benevolent univer-
sality, a way of organizing society that has tremendous capacity for inclusion,
in principle capable of accommodating any number and variety of secular
interests – a distinctly, modern form of community. And this shift in thinking
about capital was key to the reconfiguration of republicanism, giving it its dis-
tinctively modern economic focus.[32] The central image here is that of the 'market' as a flat, decentralized way of organizing society that is non-exclusionary
and systematically counteracts concentrations of power. Modern republicanism, premised on the civilizing effects of commercial interaction and distributed property as checks on corruption, looks to the market as a foundation of
civil society and as a bulwark against monarchical concentrations of power. It
was only in the Anglo-American context that republicanism acquired 'democratic' credentials in the way that we might nowadays understand it. In that
sense, it took the rise of capitalism to activate the democratic potential of
republicanism.[33]

The market has always been the most potent ideological image of capital –
as we, neoliberal subjects, know all too well. But the logic at work here only
becomes comprehensible if we distance ourselves from a traditional notion
of ideology, one that views it as a way of depicting something in a misleading

30   Le Goff (1988).
31   Smith (1999 [1776]).
32   MacGilvray (2011).
33   Konings (2015).

way and thereby facilitating its undetected existence. The connection between ideology and practice is more immediate than that suggests, situated at the level of intuitive apprehension more than conceptual reflection. This theoretical point has often been taken to point in the direction of a re-conceptualization of ideology in terms of embodiment and lived experience, which may yet turn out to provide new resources for critique but has more often than not become associated with the poststructuralist retreat from critique. There is, however, another way to approach the issue.

Such an approach is indicated by Vogl's reflections on how, with the rise of modernity, "theodicy" was transformed into "oikodicy."[34] Theodicy was the theological endeavor of reconciling the omnipotence and benevolence of God with the existence of human misery and misfortune. With the rise of modern capitalism, this logic shifted towards economic phenomena: oikodicy as conceived by Vogl refers to the logic whereby moderns continuously reinvent a rich panoply of rationalizations for why the market has not delivered the inclusive and just social order that we expect of it (here we encounter ideology in its role of 'excuses, excuses', as analyzed in Dean).[35] The critique of capital does not disappear; instead, the context in which it works increasingly serves to harness that critique to its expanded reproduction, conferring on capitalism its characteristic infuriating resilience. The expression of critique now comes to be attended by an implicit baseline notion that, in its very innermost structure and when operating properly, society is organized as a republican market, an innocuous institution that privileges no one in particular and instead rewards effort and merit in politically neutral and impartial ways. When moderns criticize capital for its disembedding tendencies, they typically do so by adopting the standpoint of the market. This reflects a distinctly modern fantasy of institutional neutrality, the belief that we can have institutions that are dynamic, productive of tremendous wealth, but also impartial, passively representative of our interests and identities.

This shift in the nature of ideology was at the heart of Lefort's thinking. His central objective was to explain why the decline of external, transcendent legitimations of authority did not result in transparently democratic self-determination. His starting point here was to emphasize the logical impossibility of direct democratic self-determination, which would require an impossible act of self-referential signification. 'The people' cannot represent itself as such: it cannot observe itself from a disembodied, external point of view and

---

34   Vogl (2014).
35   Dean (2009).

consequently its self-observation is marked by a moment of "occlusion." This original non-coincidence of the people with itself opens the door to "occultation," discursive strategies to suppress the awareness of this founding paradox and to project an imaginary coherence of sovereign authority. Lefort emphatically did not view this as a return to pre-modern forms of authority but precisely as the operation of a specifically modern form of ideology, which works not by asking for positive endorsement of symbols soaked in religion and myth but through inducing active participation in covering up our awareness of the groundlessness of any authority.

Reflecting the time in which he was writing and the disillusionment among critical thinkers with the turn taken by the communist countries claiming to govern in the name of the people, Lefort himself was entirely focused on how this ideological logic manifested itself in the context of totalitarianism. But for our purposes here it is critical to note that the distinctiveness of occultation as a modern phenomenon has always been particularly apparent in the logic of capitalism, and in particular in neoliberalism as the renewal of its foundational market fantasy. After all, a true moment of foundational occlusion occurs in the Smithian reconception of 'capital' as 'market': in its Smithian origins, the gap between 'capital' and the 'market' is almost imperceptible, a crack in a mirror that is only visible when observed from very specific angles. But the consequences of this are far-reaching: from now on, the problems of capital are conceptualized as a corruption of its true form of the market. No one reading Smith can fail to appreciate the plausibility of his descriptions of the benevolent social effects of commerce and trade, and that very element of plausibility leads us to forever search for ways to recapture such foundational innocence. The oppressions and exclusions of capital never appear as its necessary preconditions or effects, but only ever as the imperfections of the market, its corruption by external forces or indeed its insufficient reach.

The logic of occultation is centrifugal: the edifice of rationalizations forever expands in order to ensure we don't confront its founding contradiction. This institutes a dynamic of relative autonomy, but not one that we can hope to capture in terms of a functional logic. The dynamic is driven not by the needs of capital accumulation understood in a rational way, but by the need to suppress awareness of an original blind spot and to invent new rhetorical techniques to that end. Ideology works not by giving us actual reasons for adopting particular practices, but through the construction of a smokescreen of rationalizations that allow us to persist with practices that we experience as problematic. That smokescreen certainly has a cognitive dimension, but our engagement is affective and libidinal, sustained by our enjoyment of what it offers. As occultation works not through reasons but through constant post-hoc rationalizations, there is something inexhaustible and relentless about it, as neoliberalism and Trump in particular have made abundantly clear. The waning efficacy of external, transcendent legitimations of authority does not result in a more rational public sphere but in an ideological logic of legitimation that is far more florid, dynamic, and expansive than the more literal ideological legitimations of an earlier time.

We are unlikely to ever uncover a deep-structural principle that will allow us to specify the logic of relative autonomy in terms of a set of causal determinations. In that sense, there are only 'instrumental' uses of the state, interests and identities that seek a certain kind of political representation and forge particular alliances in pursuit of their objectives. However, such political interactions are oriented by an image of capital that has much greater moral appeal and regulative capacity than is typically acknowledged and that is consequently much more capable of inflecting political dynamics than its critics recognize. The fact that the logic of capitalist integration is undergirded by an affectively charged image of the market has of course become particularly apparent with the rise of neoliberalism. But the analysis of the 'excuses, excuses' logic of capitalist legitimation offered in this chapter is certainly not meant to suggest that nothing can ever get better, that all forms of critique and resistance are doomed to failure or that they all become incorporated into the logic of capitalist legitimation in a uniform or predictable way – the development of twentieth-century capitalism provides plenty of evidence to the contrary. But it does mean that there is no resistance to capital that simply limits its reach without becoming part of it, without transforming and legitimating it from within, instituting its own 'oikodicy'.

The persistent tendency of progressive commentators to view mid-twentieth century order in terms of a 'balance' between capitalist and democratic principles serves to obscure the extent to which this was a process of incorporation rather than a rational settlement or a conscious compromise.[36] Marxist perspectives have often criticized Rawlsian, Keynesian and similar social-democratic perspectives on social justice and institutional solidarity for being insufficiently radical, but they have generally not accounted for the profound ways in which such conceptions are indebted, at their very core, to a distinctly capitalist rationality. In this way they have tended to maintain the great smokescreen that still hangs over our view of the postwar period, and that has left progressives so poorly prepared to diagnose the pro-market offensive of the right.

---

36   Panitch (1985).

4   Conclusion: Neoliberalism and the State

The market, imagined as a decentralized coordination mechanism that ensures that people get what they deserve and works to prevent illegitimate concentrations of power, induces a certain fanaticism that breaks out of the bounds of civilized public debate. Unable to see its own limitations, neoliberal reason can only understand the failure of its core fantasy as the result of corruption by an external force. This is the distinctive way in which a mentality that takes itself to be rational and secular – answering to no higher authority than the welfare of the people itself – tends toward conspiracy thinking and scapegoating. Every piece of evidence demonstrating that the world doesn't resemble a free market comes to serve as yet so much more evidence of the depth of corruption and therefore only serves to reinforce the need to 'drain the swamp'. Of course, Trump-style theatrics often appear far removed from any actual economic issues, but that is precisely the point – his key strength is the disavowal of all responsibility for any existing problems and the unconditional commitment to blaming others, above all minorities and the progressives who coddle them, so engendering something like a centrifugal dynamic of hatred. To progressives this project seems highly uncivilized, but to the many Americans who support Trump this uncompromising stance seems like a highly principled unconditional refusal to accommodate himself to existing political realities. There is considerable truth to Steve Bannon's conviction that Trump is a modern-day Andrew Jackson, working to restore the republican promise of the American polity with a single-minded commitment to the ruthless subordination and eradication of those standing in the way of its realization.

Progressive critics have had persistent difficulty relating to the moral and affective charge at the heart of neoliberalism and the claim to political community that has afforded the project. That is one of the reasons that the field of neoliberalism studies has become more and more focused on right-wing stealth strategies that bypass the democratic process.[37] However, the 'neoliberalism versus democracy' formula simplifies the problem in a way that is unhelpful and poorly attuned to the degree to which neoliberalism has shaped the world of actually existing democracy. This is what motivated the engagement with post-Marxist thinking in this chapter, which provides a powerful reminder of the dark side of democracy itself. And bringing capital back into that story allows us to understand the degree to which popular sentiment and

---

37   Mirowski (2013); Brown (2015).

democratic dynamics are not just limited by capital as a material constraint but in fact thoroughly shaped by its ideological force.

The main problem is not that progressivism too must operate on the republican terrain – for all intents and purposes, it constitutes the political horizon of modernity, and the Bernie Sanders campaigns of recent years demonstrate the possibility of appealing to a very similar set of traditions in a politically radical and non-exclusionary way. The problem is that the progressive mainstream so persistently refuses to acknowledge the way in which neoliberal thought has already staked its claim to this legacy and has done so successfully. Instead, we are treated to an endless exercise of polite criticism and neutral fact-checking that is entirely unable to engage with the reasons why people vote for someone like Trump and in this way, it ends up merely adding fuel to the fire of anti-elitism. The disconnect has rarely been more apparent than in the utter inability of progressive intelligentsia to get a handle on the support for Trump in 2016.

A sober perspective on the role of progressivism and social democracy in the making of neoliberalism is perhaps the most significant legacy of the Milibandian perspective – not interested in declarations about what such political projects intend or profess to be about, it has always focused more closely on how they actually work to effect an integration of the population into the capitalist system.[38] And that has allowed it to see that, as the contradictions of such integration have become apparent over the past decades, these projects are more and more relegated to playing the role of provocateurs in a neoliberal morality play. Contemporary democracy is fully a capitalist democracy – not because the political system is inconsequential or superstructural or because it has been captured or sidelined, but because it has evolved hand-in-hand with the incorporation of the working classes into capitalism and because it is now the terrain on which the limits of that incorporation are playing themselves out.

---

38   Panitch and Gindin (2012).

CHAPTER 3

Working-Class Politics Matters

Identity, Class, Parties

Dennis Pilon and Larry Savage

... the possibility of realizing a socialist project cannot conceivably do without working class identity, consciousness and politics forming its mass base and organizational core. This is not only because of the potential size of a collectivity that draws upon those who occupy subordinate positions in productive relations, but ... because of the centrality of such a collectivity to the constitutive principle of the whole social order. If the issue is in fact social transformation, the supercession of capitalism as a system, then the mobilization of the working class's potential range and power is the key organizational and ideological condition.

LEO PANITCH, *Working Class Politics in Crisis*[1]

∴

Today the term 'working class' often appears anachronistic when it surfaces in contemporary public and political discourse, almost as if someone is deliberately attempting to conjure up the 'olden days' of coal mines, bread lines, and Great Depression-era unemployment. In fact, it is rarely used by media commentators, government bodies, or public figures, who much prefer to characterize the great mass of people as belonging to the 'middle class', with perhaps a passing reference to the rich and poor as notable but not terribly significant demographic bookends. Perhaps more surprisingly, the term working class has also been largely excised from the language, discourse, and print/web copy of most left or progressive political parties. It would follow then that any call for a return to a working-class politics might strike people as nonsensical. How can a politics be working class if no such group appears to exist or self-identify

---

1   Panitch (1986a: 16).

as working class? Indeed, both popular and academic commentators would argue that this is precisely why left parties have dumped the label – they are simply mirroring changes in the broader society that downplay the importance of class, disowns the label 'working class' as pejorative, and accepts the view that 'everyone is middle class now'.

Despite such views, terms like working class and the idea of a working-class politics remain crucial to any left political project concerned about capitalism and its effects. After all, the claimed demise of the working class is almost as old as the left itself and it remains as inaccurate today as it ever was. Indeed, the 'end of class' thesis is both empirically false and strategically catastrophic for those who seek to alter the class-based inequalities of modern societies. By contrast, utilizing any number of broad measures and definitions of class, it is clearly evident that a working class is very real and that cultivating its political awareness and power is essential to securing any lasting political changes that touch on class. Thus, there is the absolute need for a reinvigorated working-class politics. In what follows, this chapter will seek to draw upon and develop Leo Panitch's various insights about working-class politics, namely that it is essential to the broader left project, that it must be self-emancipatory and furthered by the working class itself, and that it must develop a balance between a dynamic broad-based organizational capacity in civil society and the creation of structures and institutions capable of taking on and transforming the capitalist state.[2] And, perhaps most importantly, it must do this by contributing to a distinctive working-class formation that can anchor such a project.[3] This will be accomplished by delving into some of the reasons why this project of self-emancipation is so challenging as well as examining how some contemporary left party candidates and activists are attempting to engage the working class in a way that could encourage more working-class politics.

The chapter will take up the problem of working-class politics by exploring debates over the key role of the working class in 20th century left politics, the state of the working class and working-class politics in this new century, and the necessary and potential links between a working-class politics and more state-focused left projects.

---

2 Panitch addresses these themes throughout his published work. For a few illustrative examples, see Panitch (1986a); Panitch and Gindin (2016); and Panitch (2018).

3 On the necessity of working-class politics being not merely 'class-focused' but 'class-rooted', i.e. contributing to working class formation, see Panitch and Gindin (2016); and Panitch and Gindin (2006a).

1   The Role of the Working Class in Twentieth-Century Left Politics

A call for working-class politics begs the questions of why the working class particularly should be the focus of a progressive politics. Of course, for many on the left, it is simply obvious that workers and their needs should be the priority. But others question why this should be a matter of faith, alternatively arguing that other classes are more important, that the working class has changed into something else over time, or that issues and identities beyond class should now take priority. But if we take up the question historically, there were concrete reasons why the left focused on the working class, and those reasons can still be marshalled to address concerns about the alleged 'privileging' of class in the present.

In the nineteenth century, many radicals and socialists focused their attention on the working class as a reaction to its material deprivation, particularly miserable living and working conditions. The focus then resulted from a normative commitment, rooted in a values-based judgement about the injustice of such conditions and the need to ameliorate them. While agreeing with such normative assessments, Karl Marx and Friedrich Engels argued that the centrality of the working class to their understanding of left politics was more the product of analytical rigor than simply morality.[4] In their analysis of the inner workings of capitalism, only the working class had an objective interest in and power to transform capitalism into something else. This was so for a number of reasons. First, as a totalizing system of social reproduction, capitalism put the working class at the center of the process of materially reproducing the society. This meant that the working class was strategically placed to disrupt the production process and prevent capitalists from gaining their profits, either by suspending work or redirecting resources elsewhere. Second, as the largest social class by far, the actions of workers could be decisive in terms of sustaining or challenging capitalist social relations. Finally, because social relations under capitalism were necessarily and unavoidably antagonistic, workers had no choice but to confront the social conditions of their exploitation. Only the working class had both the potential power to act and an unavoidable need to act.

But such potential did not determine how the working class might respond. This is where politics came in. Marx and Engels argued that the working class was uniquely – but only potentially – open to challenging capitalism as it was

---

4   For a summary of Marx and Engels' views on the key role of working class in socialist struggle, see Draper (2018). The rest of the discussion here draws insights from Panitch (1986a: 16–19, 51–2, 220); Wood (1986: 12–15, 92, 189); and Mulhern (1984).

the only class not to profit by exploiting another class and, thus, had no necessary interest in sustaining such social relations. Of course, they recognized
that workers might choose to focus only on their particular immediate interests (i.e. their local job conditions, pay, benefits) rather than their universal
ones (i.e. in changing the system as a whole). This is why they called for a mass
political party that could help shape this potentiality into a concrete possibility, what they referred to as 'shaping the proletariat into a class'.[5] So while the
objective position of the working class left it potentially open to and capable of
collectively responding to economic conditions, in Marx and Engels' view, only
an explicitly working-class politics could bring workers together as a class and
turn them into a force that could effectively challenge their exploitation and
those in power responsible for it.

The historical development of mass left political parties in the late nineteenth and early twentieth century largely confirmed Marx and Engels' analysis of what would be required to carry out working-class politics, that is, mass
involvement in politics by the working class themselves as minimum condition.
As the historian Geoff Eley recounts, the German Social Democratic party of
the late nineteenth century both organized the working class into politics and
was run by working-class people themselves.[6] The 'mass party' model invented
by the political left could challenge the more privileged political forces of their
societies precisely because of their 'mass' nature, which saw them raise small
amounts of money from a great many sources, staff these parties with working
people themselves, and involve the membership in developing policy, running
for office, and doing the outreach work necessary to compete in elections. The
party's efforts were so successful that it became the model for working-class
political organizing across Europe. Variants of the mass party approach took
root in Anglo-American countries as well, often building out of or amalgam-
ating pre-existing political groups, faith communities, cooperative societies,
and trade unions.[7] The working-class character of such parties was crucially
important, acting both as a reflection of working-class people that helped
draw them to the party as well as an anchor keeping such parties linked to their
needs and ways of understanding the world. However, subtle changes in the
1960s would begin to alter this dynamic. As Gerassimos Moschonas notes, the
postwar baby boom created a situation where a huge cohort of young people
came of political age in the 1960s but had few opportunities to engage in conventional politics, given the closed and highly elitist nature of most western

---

5   Marx and Engels (2012: ch. 2).
6   Eley (2002).
7   For the United Kingdom experience, as an example, see Bullock (2017).

political party systems. As the only parties with open membership rules and
fairly democratic internal decision-making, left parties (understood here primarily as social democratic and labor parties) became a pole of attraction for
youth across the class divide. Over time, this contributed to what Moschonas
has called a 'middle class-ization' of the left, with such parties seeing leaders
and representatives from working-class backgrounds eventually replaced by
those from more middle-class circumstances.[8]

At the same time as middle-class youth began to embrace left parties, academics provided research claiming to demonstrate a marked decline in subjective class identifications as well as more concrete class differences. From
the early 1960s on, a variety of academic works emerged proclaiming an 'end
of class', ranging from sociological studies of self-identifications across a
continuum of class locations, to ethnographic work on the 'underclass' and
'under-privileged', to behavioral studies of voter attitudes, voting patterns, and
elections results.[9] In different ways, all claimed that formerly working-class
identifications were giving way to more middle-class ones, in line, they argued,
with the increasing prosperity and upward class mobility accompanying the
postwar period. Election studies particularly claimed to find little in the way of
'class voting' going on in elections, arguing that voters were more influenced
by family, religion or short-term pocket-book issues.[10] Despite challenges by
scholars whose research was more firmly rooted in class analysis and working-
class studies, the mainstream academic consensus that class had ceased to be
the defining cleavage in western politics and society was bolstered by dominant cultural characterizations of the west as both classless and defined by a
merit-based class mobility. More recent cultural scholars have taken a different
approach to displacing class as the central category of social analysis, arguing
against what they call the 'privileging' of class.[11] For them, other markers of
social identity – such as gender, race, sexuality, etc. – had overtaken class as
the most important marker of oppression, which should thus constitute the
focus of left organizing and advocacy. Indeed, for these scholars and activists,

---

8   Moschonas (2002: 120–21, 130–1, 221). Of course, Moschonas is primarily talking about the
     social democratic left in Europe, to which one could add the various labor parties in the
     Anglosphere. The pattern might well be very different in the Western European Communist
     parties, which tended to have more strict rules and conditions for membership.

9   See Clark, Lipset and Rempel (1993); and Clark (2003).

10   These debates are reviewed critically in Evans (1999).

11   For an emblematic and highly influential statement of this position see Laclau and
     Mouffe (1985). For rebuttals that point out the problematic class divisions that define
     Laclau and Mouffe's new, non-working-class leadership for the left, see Wood (1986) and
     Burgmann (2005).

the working class was part of the problem, enjoying privilege and helping to regulate and enforce dominant identities.

Despite these attempts to erase, redefine or displace the working class from its central role in left politics, Marxists have typically remained more steadfast in resisting such claims and challenging the assumptions and evidence behind them. Panitch, particularly, has argued against the conflation of working-class politics with simply electing left, labor or socialist governments.[12] Limiting an analysis of working-class politics to left-wing election results or self-identifications of class in voter surveys tells us very little about how the working class engages in politics. Instead, to advance a genuine study of working-class politics and class formation, we need to examine more critically who we think constitutes the working class, their historic and potential impact, and the barriers to their self-identification, political development, and concrete engagement with conventional politics.

2   The State of Working-Class Politics in the New Millennium

Classes, then, are still with us. In the conventional narrative, post-WWII economic development across western countries led to an erosion of class boundaries and a flattening of class differences. The rich and poor remain, but they are vastly outnumbered, we are told, by a broad middle class that encompasses most everyone in real terms. Such claims are seldom backed up by compelling facts. Utilizing a fairly basic understanding of class defined by income and wealth, the data show that the broad class structure of the prewar era remained largely intact throughout the postwar period. Living standards of the poor and working classes did improve after WWII but this did not significantly erode the divisions amongst classes themselves. A rising tide may lift all boats but it doesn't convert a dinghy into a yacht. And the appearance of class mobility created by the postwar economic boom largely evaporated with the beginning of the downturn from the 1970s on. Contra these 'end of class' and 'we are all middle class now' claims, Marxist class theorist Erik Olin Wright, for one, argued in 2015 that:

> ... class remains a significant and sometimes powerful determinant of many aspects of social life. Class boundaries, especially the property boundary, continue to constitute real barriers in people's lives;

---

12   Panitch (1992).

inequalities in the distribution of capital assets continue to have real consequences for material interests; capitalist firms continue to face the problem of extracting labor effort from non-owning employees; and class location continues to have a real, if variable, impact on individual subjectivities.[13]

Setting aside debates about the reality of class, some argue that, regardless of class location, 'class' neither defines who people think they are, nor motivates them to vote in specific and predictable ways. Scholars focused on 'class voting' allow that class position (defined variously by income, residential neighborhood and/or education) once did impact voting decisions as evident in the historic vote for socialist and labor parties, but they argue that its influence has declined over time to the point where now class factors are deemed much less significant. Researchers studying some western countries, such as the US and Canada, claim the class vote was never a strong factor to begin with as evidenced by the lack of strong (or any) socialist or labor parties.[14] Relying heavily on quantitative behavioral methods, this body of research often highlights the failure of respondents to self-identify in class terms, and points to a lack of fit between researchers' criteria for measuring class and any strong discernible voting patterns for ostensibly 'class' parties. Critics argue that such 'end of class' conclusions rely on faulty and narrow definitions of class, as well as the use of inappropriate methodologies to study class, and thus fail to convincingly demonstrate that class no longer shapes society, social identity, or influences politics.[15]

Two key points emerge from the latter research. First, the 'end of class' work tends to mistake the shift from an industrial to post-industrial workforce for a breakdown in class divisions. As Wright notes, such researchers "seem to be mistaking the increasing complexity of class relations in contemporary class societies with the dissolution of class altogether."[16] By contrast, a wealth of research demonstrates that while the content and style of work is changing, its essential class character is not.[17] The quantitative bias of the 'end of class' work is partly responsible for these problems, as nuances of identity as a lived experience can seldom be effectively captured through surveys, and is better

---

13   Wright (2015: 155).
14   Neiuwbeerta and Ultee (1999).
15   See Andersen (1984); Evans (2000); Oesch (2008); and Van Der Waal, Achterberg and Houtman (2007).
16   Wright (2015: 155).
17   See Yates (2007).

served via qualitative ethnographic or depth interview techniques.[18] Second, the failure of voters to vote 'class' in ways recognizable to the 'end of class' researchers may have more to do with a lack of clear 'class' options on the ballot than any disinclination to vote class. For example, examining British evidence from the 1980s into the new millennium, Geoffrey Evans and James Tilly argue that class voting hasn't so much declined, but rather the opportunities to vote class have declined. For them, a "supply-side constriction in the choices presented to voters, rather than the weakening of class divisions, accounts for the declining political relevance of redistributive values and the class basis of party choice."[19]

The inability of voters to 'choose' class also lines up with a broader problem of 'classed people' being able to 'see' class, particularly public, media, and cultural representations of their class reality, a problem then only compounded by the shift away from explicit class appeals from left parties and the lack of locally rooted visible working-class formations. Communication and culture scholars have long noted the middle- and upper-class biases of popular culture in film and television, where the overwhelming representations of everyday life showcase a one-dimensional world of upper middle class and wealthy lifestyles and consumption.[20] But media scholars also underline the absence of the working class from more serious cultural artefacts such as newspapers and broadcast news.[21] This cultural invisibility is mirrored politically as well, with few working-class people visible as leaders or representatives of political parties. Even labor and socialist parties have witnessed a dramatic decline in the number of elected officials that come from working-class backgrounds. For instance, where the British Labour Party could once that claim 72 percent of its representatives came from manual working-class background between 1918 and 1935, that percent had slipped to just 11 percent by 1979. Utilizing a union background as proxy, the figure was 15 percent for Labour MPs in 2015.[22] Studies of membership in and activism within political parties by class demonstrates a strong bias toward the professional middle classes with much lower participation from the working class.[23] This decline in working-class visibility and

---

18   For a general discussion of these problems, see Pilon (2019; 2015). For a concrete example of more sophisticated ways to research working class identity methodologically, see Skeggs, Thumim and Wood (2008).

19   Evans and Tilley (2012: 963).

20   See Holtzman and Sharpe (2015).

21   See Heider (2004).

22   See Bothwick, Ellingworth, Bell and Mackenzie (1991: 713–17); and Hunter and Holden (2015).

23   Carnes (2016).

involvement with left political parties has coincided with a decline in working-class participation in elections as voters too. From averages of 70–80 percent voter turnout across western countries in the decades immediately following WWII, the percentages slipped to a range more like 50–65 percent from the 1980s on. While academics tend to focus on low youth turnout as key, a more critical reading of the data provides clear evidence of a strong class dimension to the decline in overall voter participation. For instance, one study focusing on low turnout by youth nonetheless noted that youth attending post-secondary institutions had seen an increase in turnout over the period under study (1968–2000). The problem was that increases in turnout by that group of youth were erased by a more dramatic decline in voter turnout amongst youth not attending post-secondary institutions.[24] Given what we know about the classed aspects of those who typically do and do not attend post-secondary institutions, this would seem to be clear evidence of a class impact on voter turnout.

The fact that working-class people are increasingly missing from electoral politics is not merely a problem of inclusion, meaning that it would be normatively preferable to have them participate. A host of research suggests that a lack of working-class involvement in politics has concrete and consistent effects on demonstrable political outcomes. Most broadly, it affects the character and depth of welfare states, with greater social and economic equality as well as a more robust array of social supports present in countries with higher levels of working-class political engagement. This is because the presence of working-class people in politics helps anchor left parties to their needs and issues. As Jonas Pontusson and David Rueda argue, an increase in economic inequality alone is not enough to assure that left parties move left economically. Here their evidence from late twentieth century Western Europe shows that the mobilization of low-income voters is crucial to making that happen.[25] Thus the bottom line is that left parties cannot deliver progressive economic

---

24   For a critical review of this literature, see Pilon (2015).
25   Pontusson and Rueda (2010). And, by contrast, where working class voting power is weak, so are the social programs and even access to the political system itself. See Hill and Leighley (1992); Carnes (2013); Gilens (2013); Carnes (2012); Larcinese (2007); Avery and Peffley (2005). Ironically, where middle class voters dominate (and working-class voters are fewer or absent) the results are not even very good for the middle class either, as such electoral conditions weaken their ability to demand and secure universal programs, leaving them facing more burdensome, direct economic costs for services in health, education and home care. For work that underlines the social impact of different welfare states, see Scruggs and Allan (2006).

policies on the basis of middle-class votes alone – they need the working class to do it.

All this raises a central question: why has working-class participation in politics, electoral or otherwise, declined over the past fifty years? The reasons are complex and multi-faceted, but not impossible to unravel, particularly if researchers have an interest in specific challenges facing working-class people in modern capitalist societies. Many researchers focus on changes in voter preferences, i.e., a decline in public interest in being involved in political party activity, either as party members or volunteers. Some relate this to the emergence of welfare states from the 1960s that have had the effect of reducing public reliance on direct support from parties or political machines. Others credit a shift in public attitudes favoring a post-material politics focused on social or lifestyle issues (e.g., gender, sexuality) over economic ones (e.g., wages, benefits). Either way, researchers connect these trends to changes in political party mobilization efforts, seeing parties move away from direct forms of voter contact to more mediated approaches to finding out what voters want (e.g., polling) and communicating what the party will do (e.g., advertising).[26] While there is some truth to these claims, they do not help us understand why working-class voters specifically have dropped out of politics at a greater rate and in larger numbers than other classes of voters. Here we need to attend to those factors that differentiate working-class engagement with politics from other classes.

Election scholars and popular commentators tend to talk about voters in universal and highly individualist terms. Even where they do note differences in political engagement, they tend to ignore or simply 'not see' class in terms of its impact on politics and election outcomes. For instance, researchers do note differences in political engagement by levels of education. Voters with some post-secondary education participate more, on average, than voters with only a high school education or less. For them, this is simply a matter of information, with the former group participating more because they have more, and the latter participating less because they have less.[27] But education scholars point out that post-secondary educational attainment is a very 'classed' accomplishment, with those that go and those that do not divided broadly (though not exclusively) along a middle-class/working-class dividing line.[28] And differences in participation levels are not merely a matter of differences

---

26 Lees-Marshment (2001).

27 For an illustrative treatment of the relationship between education and voting, see Tossutti (2019).

28 For a broad overview of the class implications of secondary education, see Whitty (2001).

in informational resources, but a much more complex process involving dominant cultures of participation and differential levels of social entitlement.

French sociologist Pierre Bourdieu notes that class privilege in capitalist
society is not merely about money and property and control over work. It
manifests culturally as a form of what he calls 'social capital' where the upper
and middle classes cultivate particular ways of talking and acting and refer-
encing social reality that are then recognized as culturally superior in more
supposedly neutral economic and academic spaces.[29] The ability to 'perform'
this sort of learned class privilege then reinforces the considerable economic
privileges they already enjoy, buttressing their control of social spaces in ways
characterized as resulting from merit rather than class privilege. Working-class
people generally lack such class training or the confidence to perform it and, as
such, are left out, either because they fail to be recognized or included by such
middle-class gatekeepers, or because they exclude themselves when they recognize their lack of fit with such institutionalized spaces. Elections and political
activity have increasingly become such an institutionalized space, defined by
a middle class and elite focus on 'being knowledgeable'. Even though research
shows middle-class people to be no better informed than working-class people, middle-class social capital translates into a sense of entitlement that
operates regardless of any actual ability to demonstrate political knowledge.
Meanwhile, working-class people tend to opt out of political activity, either
believing they are not worthy (because they are not knowledgeable enough) or
because the environment is simply too foreign to their experience – they lack
the requisite dominant social capital.[30]

The politics of class has not always played out this way. Indeed, the twentieth century was defined and decisively shaped by the entry of the working class
into mass politics in western countries. This was accomplished by working-
class movements and political parties that directly mobilized working people into political activity, drawing from pre-existing and visible working-class
communities and social formations.[31] Part of this involved issues of identity.

---

29   For a general introduction to these ideas, see Bourdieu (1994).
30   Such views are supported by research that demonstrates a link between welfare states
      that reinforce structural rather than individualistic understandings of inequality and
      greater participation by poor and working-class groups. See Lister (2007).
31   Research highlights the uneven impact of education on voter turnout, noting the role
      of working-class parties instead, at least until recently. See Gallego (2010). Upsurges in
      broad-based social movement activity have also acted as a spur to greater working class
      electoral participation. See Winders (1999). And conventional research on voter turnout
      continues to highlight the effectiveness of direct forms of voter contact with less commit-
      ted voters. See Niven (2004).

Working-class politics spoke with a working-class accent, about working-class issues, by people who were recognizably working class, in working-class neighborhoods.[32] As noted above, left parties of various stripes increasingly were taken over by the middle and upper classes from the 1960s on. By various measures, the percentage of people from working-class backgrounds elected by political parties across western countries is minimal and research shows that the absence of representatives from the working class has a clear impact on policy.[33]

But it is not merely being present that makes a difference in working-class politics, it also matters what happens when working people engage with politics. The best practices historically offered working people transformational opportunities, chances to discover something about themselves, their class and their potential. This is why the move towards the professionalization, moderation, and modernization of left parties, and the move away from active recruitment and participation of working people into left parties, has been so devastating for working-class politics. Without active mobilization around working-class identity, working-class people lack the social capital and sense of entitlement to demand political representation and policy on their own terms. And without them, left parties will not actively pursue policies to address working-class needs or be able to act on more vague progressive promises to a more easily mobilized middle-class electorate even if they manage to gain power.

3 The Necessary Links between Working-Class Politics and State-Focused Left Projects

A genuine working-class politics requires an active, mobilized working-class base, one that helps to develop the capacities of working-class people to speak for themselves, rather than simply vote or defer to others. There is both a moral and practical reason to undertake this kind of deep political organizing in working-class communities even though many left party operatives argue that the practical thing to do is to eschew this approach altogether. That's because left parties must always confront the logic of the electoral game. How left parties best position themselves to win votes while maintaining a set or core ideological principles and positions is a matter of strategy. As Adam Przeworksi

---

32   Recounted in depth in Eley (2002).
33   Pilon (2015).

and John Sprague put it, "Leaders of socialist parties must repeatedly decide whether or not to seek electoral success at the cost, or at least the risk, of diluting class lines and consequently diminishing the salience of class as a motive for the political behavior of workers themselves."[34] Though critics argue that Przeworksi and Sprague's take on the 'dilemma of electoral socialism' is too zero sum (and that it is possible to avoid it through more effective mobilization), it is undeniable that many left parties have understood the challenges this way.[35]

The supra-class electoral strategies adopted by many left parties in advanced capitalist democracies in the 1970s and 1980s were designed to broaden their appeal to the middle class in order to build an electoral coalition more reliably capable of winning elections.[36] By pursuing this strategy, left parties that had initially emerged as vehicles to organize the working class in the electoral arena were now, whether consciously or unconsciously, beginning the work of disorganizing the working class. These processes were sustained over several decades by declining working-class influence in left parties as a result of a continued influx of middle-class technocrats into key positions in party apparatuses. Having all but lost their respective working-class anchors amid a crisis in social democratic electoralism in the 1990s, the decision of many left parties in advanced capitalist democracies to double-down on strategies of modernization and moderation was based, in part, on a mistaken belief that adapting to neoliberal political imperatives was the only viable alternative to traditional social democracy.[37]

The 'modern' and 'moderate' strategies and organizational changes of left parties in the realms of political branding, campaign marketing, and voter outreach only further diluted their class appeal, and thus their relevance as vehicles of working-class politics. Increasingly, polling and focus group data has shaped left parties' (and all parties') political orientations.[38] In advanced capitalist democracies, there has been a shift from what Jennifer Lees-Marshment calls "sales-oriented" parties – which attempt to find the most effective ways to communicate their ideological principles and policy positions to voters – towards "market-oriented" parties, which use polling and focus groups

---

34   Przeworksi and Sprague (1986: 3).

35   For a critique of the narrow axiomatic assumptions embedded in Przeworksi and Sprague's analysis, see Sainsbury (1990).

36   Przeworksi and Sprague (1986).

37   Panitch and Leys (2001).

38   Lees-Marshment (2001); Ormrod (2006).

to uncover the policy preferences of segments of the electorate and then craft campaign commitments that will likely resonate with those groups.[39]

Rachel Gibson and Andrea Römmele argue that left parties initially demonstrated resistance to brand-centered or market-oriented political marketing strategies on the basis of ideology.[40] Jared Wesley and Mike Moyes explain that "the challenge is complicated for left-wing parties ... in that the principles held by certain party members are often antithetical to the market-based approach to the economy, politics, and campaigning."[41] However, since the turn of the century, left parties in advanced capitalist democracies have, to varying degrees, embraced the very same political marketing strategies deployed by their liberal and conservative counterparts.

In the Canadian context, David McGrane argues that between 2000 and 2015 the social democratic Federal New Democratic Party (NDP) transformed itself into a market-oriented party through the twin processes of moderation and modernization. McGrane makes the case that the NDP's political market orientation "was excessively geared toward party members and key external stakeholders – unions – and only superficially toward voters or competitors ... an important part of the party's moderation and modernization was becoming more voter and competitor oriented and less stakeholder and member oriented."[42] That meant altering policy positions that were considered too left-wing, and, in the words of Susan Delacourt, transforming NDP platforms into "simple, easy-to-understand promises, limited in scope and ambition, in part to reassure anyone nervous about the NDP's reputation for favouring sweeping social change."[43] Longtime party operative Michael Balagus explained that, "traditional NDP politics relies a lot on confrontation. It relies a lot on class. And when you do that, the tent gets smaller and smaller. I think by being more inclusive, by working with the business community ... By working with labour, by working and also broadening the tent, [you have] ... a very successful formula."[44] However, the NDP's embrace of a political marketing orientation has seemingly extended beyond a supra-class effort to simply broaden the tent. After the 2008 general election, Delacourt argues that the NDP began to imitate and replicate the top-down and micro-targeted political marketing strategies of the ruling Conservative Party. "Like the Conservatives, they would come

---

39   Lees-Marshment (2001).
40   Gibson and Römmele (2001).
41   Wesley and Moyes (2014: 76).
42   McGrane (2019: 7).
43   Delacourt (2013: 164).
44   Balagus, as cited in Wesley and Moyes (2014: 76).

to see the voters as beleaguered consumers with very personalized complaints, whether it was credit-card rates or not being able to find a family doctor. The NDP would shed its reputation for being solely the voice of groups – students, unions, and protesters – and get far more precise about talking to voters as individuals."[45]

As part of a survey of the literature on voter efficacy, Royce Koop argues that potential negative impacts of "market-oriented" political marketing include a risk that parties become unresponsive to citizens that fall outside of strategically selected segments of the electorate, thus fueling cynicism about politics and politicians. That's because "citizens with high degrees of efficacy are optimistic about their own utility in politics, whereas citizens with low levels of efficacy feel hopeless in this respect."[46] Working-class non-voters who tune out elections or people who have "dropped out" because they don't see their interests represented are almost certain to be overlooked by parties slicing and dicing the electorate in pursuit of the most efficient bang for their marketing buck. Of course, not having parties reach out to these voters only reinforces their tendency towards non-participation. The implications of this finding for working-class constituencies abandoned by left parties in pursuit of more efficiently targeted middle-class votes is significant.

The tendency of left parties to reach out to potential middle-class allies in an effort to become more electorally viable is certainly not new, but the degree to which they have diluted class appeals in the neoliberal era in order to accomplish this has rendered many left parties virtually indistinguishable from their bourgeois counterparts. It is increasingly clear that a desire to make peace with capital in order to inoculate conservative working-class voters and capitalists themselves against the belief that a left government will fundamentally restructure the economy and society is a key electoral goal of left parties. Overall, an overreliance on formal market intelligence has seemingly transformed some left parties into ideologically incoherent weathervanes in search of individualized 'consumer-citizens'. This strategic gamble has come at the expense of a focus on politically organizing and mobilizing the working class itself.

This dynamic is also in evidence at the level of policy development and internal party affairs, where the use of polling and focus groups to determine party platforms has undermined the role of rank-and-file party members in shaping parties' priorities and ideological perspectives. The substitution of

---

45   Delacourt (2013: 162).
46   Koop (2012: 224).

rank-and-file party democracy with political marketing techniques has further marginalized working-class activists from 'modern' and 'moderate' left parties and, as a result, may well hamper the ability of left parties to increase the efficacy of working-class voters based on a coherent set of class-based policy prescriptions.[47] Over time, working-class political mobilization that is not rooted in deep organizing and engagement results in an atrophied and demobilized base, whose sole job it is to show up every few years to vote for 'their' party, even when that party has become ideologically unrecognizable. Because left parties are less connected to the organized working class than ever before, they have a diminished capacity to organize voters through their unions. By replacing policy conventions and party conferences with various kinds of formal market intelligence to determine the party's aims and objective serves to further alienate and demobilize activists and volunteers and reduces their stake in the party as a vehicle for working-class politics. While left parties continue to have 'ground games' where volunteers or paid staff contact voters on the doorstep or over the telephone, the parameters of the game have narrowed, focusing primarily on identifying voting intentions rather than learning about the issues people care about, or what might motivate them to get more involved. In short, modern ground games do very little to build the base and efforts to 'get out the vote' are designed not to increase voter turnout overall, but rather to suppress it amongst competitors.[48]

Overall, the concentration of power in the hands of a small handful of professional party strategists has dramatically shifted the center of power in left parties. These shifts, which occurred at different times in different national contexts, represent, in the first instance, a strategic response to the modernization of campaign techniques by bourgeois parties competing for power. In short, left parties adopted strategies of moderation and modernization to keep up with their competitors, even if that meant diluting the salience of class by competing on the terrain of individualized 'consumer-citizens'. Modernization also helped to sustain and build the professional cadre of the party, which increasingly saw its role as indispensable, thus justifying even greater centralization of power and an even more reduced role for left party members and activists. Finally, modernization and centralization have helped produce a vicious circle to justify continuing with this approach, even when it fails to produce electoral victories. Party strategists are well aware that centralization and modernization has significantly reduced the role of party members, but

---

47   Koop (2012: 227).
48   Meslin (2019).

reason they cannot switch to a grassroots distributed volunteer model of campaigning because years of centralization and modernization have hollowed out the base.

This dismal outlook has not gone uncontested. In fact, a number of inspired left candidates and movements have effectively challenged their own parties to rethink working-class political organizing and mobilization. A big part of this push has been the recognition that moderation and modernization need not be two sides of the same coin for left parties or candidates. There is nothing inherently moderate about the distributed leadership volunteer tactics or social media engagement and digital communications strategies that are increasingly viewed as key to mounting successful grassroots campaigns.[49] In fact, several left parties and candidates have proven themselves very adept at adapting these modern technologies to support their grassroots left-wing political campaigns.

The explicitly democratic socialist campaigns of Bernie Sanders and Alexandria Ocasio-Cortez in the US and the British Labour Party's 2017 campaign under the leadership of Jeremy Corbyn all effectively demonstrated how the use of modern campaign technologies and political marketing strategies, including the use of digital campaign networks, apps, and databases, can be used to activate the base, recruit and mobilize volunteers, target traditionally disaffected segments of the electorate, reinforce a clear ideological perspective, and successfully deliver voters to the polls.[50] While most parties and candidates use digital technologies to bolster campaign outreach efforts and amplify campaign themes, the challenge for left candidates is to use them in a way that does not relegate working-class voters and activists to the role of passive cheerleader. Instead, digital technologies must be harnessed in a way that meaningfully and democratically engages working-class voters as part of a broader class-based political project.

Using grassroots organizing and mobilizing strategies, Democratic congresswoman Alexandria Ocasio-Cortez (AOC) won her New York City-area Congressional seat after upsetting a long-time Democratic incumbent in a 2018 primary. Despite outspending AOC by a margin of 18 to 1, her corporate-backed opponent could not withstand the grassroots challenge mounted by AOC and her army of volunteers who used a voter contact app developed in the final weeks of the campaign that helped push her over the finish line. The Reach app, which permitted volunteers to canvass contacts remotely through

---

49   Price (2017).
50   Vizard (2015); Richardson (2016); Penney (2017: 402); Nickelsburg (2019); Green (2019); Ries (2019); Martinez (2019).

text messages and upload results into the campaign database, reportedly helped turn out identified voters at higher rates than conventional canvassing methods.[51] AOC easily sailed to election in the general election later that year and has since skyrocketed to prominence in US politics where she is using her impressive social media following to help push her party and her country decisively to the left on everything from taxation, to immigration, to workers' rights and climate change.

Like AOC, US Senator and self-described socialist Bernie Sanders has proven adept at merging visual branding and authenticity with campaign technology and advanced voter identification tools to build a class-based grassroots political movement. Sanders' 2016 'dark horse' campaign combined an unprecedented reliance on digital tools with a big organizing model and apps like Hustle and Slack to facilitate rapid mobilization and voter follow up, and to recruit volunteers into assuming greater roles and responsibilities in the campaign.[52] Moreover, as Penney notes, while "the 'official' Sanders organization built applications to transform supporters into a tightly controlled distribution network for its social media messaging, this was complemented by 'unofficial' grassroots networks that circulated more informal and culturally oriented appeals."[53]

Building on the unexpected level of support Sanders received in 2016, his 2020 presidential campaign focused primarily on attracting votes from disaffected working-class, racialized, and young people – key demographics who are routinely counted on by elites to not show up at the polls. The campaign's refined distributed grassroots voter contact model, facilitated in the 2020 campaign through a new app called BERN, allowed volunteers to track their outreach to friends, family, neighbors, and co-workers as part of a decentralized database for use by Sanders' national campaign.[54] The strategy, combined with impressive and sustained fundraising tallies, helped propel Sanders into frontrunner status in the first few Democratic primary contests before his establishment opponents coalesced around former Vice-President Joe Biden in an effort to stall his momentum.[55] The combination of billionaire-backed attack ads, anti-socialist media hysteria, and the Sanders campaign's inability to effectively connect with older Black voters ultimately short-circuited his second presidential bid.[56] Sanders, however, remains one of the most popular

51   Nickelsburg (2019); Green (2019).
52   Price (2017: 74).
53   Penney (2017: 402).
54   Ries (2019).
55   Pramuk (2020).
56   Harris (2020).

national figures in US politics and his campaigns have clearly pushed the political terrain to the left and laid the groundwork for sustained organizing and movement building.

Like Sanders, former UK Labour Party leader Jeremy Corbyn relied heavily on rank-and-file activists to build and sustain support for the promotion of an explicitly class-based politics. After winning the party leadership in 2015 on an anti-austerity platform as a 'dark horse' candidate, Corbyn weathered a challenge to his leadership from the Labour Party old guard in 2016 before exceeding all expectations in the 2017 UK election that followed by increasing his party's share of the vote by 9.6 points to 40 percent, thus denying the governing Tories a majority. 'Corbynmania' helped to drive up voter turnout to 68.8 percent – the highest participation rate since the 1997 general election. Voter turnout increased the most among voters aged 18–24 and 25–34, with both groups seeing roughly 10 points increases in participation rates.[57] The Labour Party's anti-austerity manifesto, *For the Many, not the Few*, clearly resonated with working-class voters, who had begun to abandon the party in record numbers in the aftermath of Tony Blair's third way approach to government and public policy. Corbyn's campaign was greatly assisted by Momentum, a pro-Corbyn left-wing tendency within the British Labour Party committed to grassroots engagement. Its viral campaign videos and "unseat campaign," designed to flood Conservative marginal electoral districts with pro-Corbyn foot canvassers, proved incredibly effective at organizing and mobilizing working-class voters to get involved.[58]

However, the Labour Party's subsequent 2019 campaign defeat clearly demonstrates the limits of digital campaign techniques in the absence of gains in substantively rebuilding working-class communities and the capacities of working-class people to engage directly in politics and resist the 'dirty tricks' politics of their enemies. While many of the same digital strategies from 2017 were used in the 2019 campaign, Parliamentary Labour Party disputes over Brexit forced Corbyn to uncomfortably commit during the campaign to a second referendum after another round of negotiations with the European Union. This strategic fumble alienated working-class Leave supporters within the party and undermined Corbyn's efforts to transcend the Brexit debate by uniting working-class voters around a radical manifesto focused on wealth redistribution and democratization of the economy. Consequently, Corbyn was lambasted by the media (and some in his own party) as both a preposterous

---

57   Dempsey and Loft (2019).
58   Doherty (2019).

fence-sitter and a reckless socialist bent on bankrupting the country.[59] At the same time Corbyn and the Labour Party were subjected to a relentless, ongoing smear campaign on a host of issues in the press (particularly unfounded claims of anti-semitism), aided by anti-Corbyn forces working against him in Labour's head office and opportunistic defections of right-wing Labour MPs to other parties (which were also given lavish media attention).[60] Nor did the attacks end with Labour's defeat, as media pundits have worked hard to shape the narrative of the election since then as "Labour's worst defeat since 1935," despite the fact that Labour's 2019 popular vote was higher than the result for the party in 2015 and 2010 under different, more centrist leadership.[61] The contrast in results for the Labour Party between 2017 and 2019 speaks to the limitation of campaign technologies in the absence of an energized and democratically-engaged membership base able to overcome cleavages designed to disorganize working-class voters.

Despite Labour's electoral defeat in 2019, what Corbyn, AOC, and Sanders, all share in common is a political authenticity that carries with it a certain working-class appeal. They are all unapologetically left-wing and did not come to embrace their socialist politics overnight through focus groups or shifts in public opinion. For Corbyn, Ocasio-Cortez, Sanders, and others on the left who are challenging third way politics, the goal is not to simply mobilize a nominally progressive segment of the electorate to vote, but rather to build a transformational working-class politics sustained by a movement of working-class people demanding structural change. Moreover, the candidacies of Corbyn, AOC, and Sanders demonstrate the potential for left parties to use authenticity and plain language storytelling to weave radical ideas into campaign communications and voter engagement strategies. Their campaigns, for example, have become instrumental in driving support for public ownership, universal social programs, workers' rights, and taxing the wealthy – policy ideas that had become toxic in the neoliberal era. In this way, these and other left-wing challengers to social democratic party establishments have succeeded in rekindling the socialist imagination of working-class voters by eschewing moderation while simultaneously embracing modern campaign techniques to better engage and connect with the working class.

---

59   Panitch and Leys (2020: 243).

60   On media bias, see MacLeod (2019); Kennard (2019); and a variety of academic reports from the Media Reform Coalition. For evidence of opposition to Corbyn within Labour's head office, see Panitch and Leys (2020).

61   For a taste of the 'worst defeat' headlines, see Gardner (2019); and for some counterevidence, see Beckett (2019).

4   Self-Transformation and Working-Class Politics

> In the sense of those people who are unpropertied workers and
> who are not involved in the supervision of collective labour, there is
> indeed a working class majority in all advanced capitalist countries
> and the first task of a socialist party ought to be the nourishment of
> an understanding and consciousness of the existence and potential
> of this working class majority. The socialist potential of such iden-
> tity, while by no means foreordained, lies in the sense of collective
> power as well as the sense of collective deprivation which an under-
> standing of the centrality of class relations to the whole social order
> entails.
>
> LEO PANITCH, *Working Class Politics in Crisis*[62]

The working class is real and increasingly exists as an untapped resource for the
left. Ironically, whether the left sees itself as a revolutionary force, a democratic
socialist movement, or merely 'liberals in a hurry', evidence from a century of
political struggle across western countries suggests that none of these efforts
can succeed without mobilized support from the working class. Thus, all roads,
it would appear, lead back to the necessity of working-class politics defined
by the active participation and leadership of the working class itself. We have
sketched out why that is so, some of the challenges involved in pursuing it, as
well as concrete examples of how it might actually be done. Of course, on the
latter point, some eyebrows might be raised that an investigation of working-
class politics would focus so much attention on the voter mobilization efforts
of left parties and candidates. After all, Panitch often complained of this very
reductionism – that analysts would simply judge working-class politics by the
number of votes for labor, socialist, or vaguely defined progressive parties. But
our purpose here was not to laud left candidates who could mobilize working-
class voters as some kind of end in itself, but rather to underline that left parties must come up with ways of connecting with and involving working-class
people if they are to have any hope of pursuing a genuine working-class politics. Thus, effective organization and mobilization of the working class is the
crucial first step in advancing working-class politics, whether to vote, to march
in the streets, or take power more directly.

    Of course, Panitch had little time for the trite dualism that pits electoral poli-
tics against protests and demonstrations, preferring instead to link a mobilized

---

62   Panitch (1986a: 52.).

and engaged working-class politics to campaigns to occupy and transform the state, and by extension the social relations it authorizes and enforces. But for a left party government to pursue such a radical course requires that a mobilized working class understand itself and its key role in defending a transformative politics. So, organization and mobilization are key, but the kinds of organization and mobilization are also crucial. If the past three decades are anything to go by, attempting to reach working-class people through a largely undifferentiated 'call out' of some kind of universal voter doesn't work very well. Even mainstream scholars now increasingly highlight how connecting with working-class people on the basis of their distinct identity is pretty important in motivating them to participate in politics.[63] Yet the point for the left is not merely to reflect working-class concerns as they may be presently understood, but to help shape such understandings. To do that the left has to engage better with who working class people are, and how they understand themselves and their problems. As Marcus Green and Peter Ives note, drawing from Gramsci, the transformation of the working class into a political force requires knowledge and engagement with the 'common sense' of their experience. Left leadership cannot simply impose a correct political line on the masses, but instead must create openings for self-transformation so that the working class might see their experience and understandings in new ways.[64]

---

63   Gest (2018: 146–55). It is also telling that even conventional behavioral work can sometimes uncover strong support for 'working class' as a self-description of American identity, with one study finding 47 percent of respondents in the US prepared to accept the term. See Jacobs (2012).

64   Green and Ives (2009).

PART 2

Imperialist Restructuring and Global Capitalism

∴

CHAPTER 4

Globalization as Internationalization of Capital

Understanding Imperialism and State Restructuring

Sebnem Oguz

The process of globalization[1] has brought significant changes within state apparatuses.[2] The main problematic of this chapter is how to understand the contradictory nature of these changes. This involves two inter-related theoretical questions.

The first is straightforward: why is state restructuring in response to globalization a contradictory process? This chapter will argue that the keyword in answering this question is the internationalization of capital. This process has been mystified under the rubric of 'globalization', which obscures these contradictions. In that sense, 'globalization' is an ideological term that needs to be demystified. In contrast, the term 'internationalization of capital' implies, first of all, that the 'national' level still matters, both in the sense that national spaces are still relevant for capital accumulation, and that international capital accumulation cannot proceed without nation-states; and second, that it is primarily capital, foremost as a social relation but also as specific form of value and property claims, that is internationally mobile in the so-called globalization process. In this framework, it can be argued that the main reason why the current restructuring of states is a contradictory process is that the internationalization of capital, which intensifies the conflicts among different sections of capital and their demands on the state, leads to intra-state conflicts over major economic policies.

The second question concerns the state: does the internationalization of capital also necessitate the internationalization of political-administrative processes? Broadly speaking, there are two main theoretical camps on this question. On the one side, a wide range of approaches has become popular, especially in the context of the expansion of capitalism on a world scale following the collapse of the Soviet bloc. These approaches tend to theorize

---

1 This chapter is a revised and extended version of Oguz (2015).
2 For the purposes of this chapter, I limit the definition of globalization to the rather narrow economic realm. However, this should not be taken as the subsumption of all other realms into economics.

globalization as the increasing deterritorialization of social relations, whereby not only economic, but also political-administrative processes have become internationalized. They thus tend to treat both the space of capital accumulation and the space of state action as global. Accordingly, they focus exclusively on the global scale and cannot explain the contradictions of state restructuring within specific social formations. Usually, the political implication of these approaches is a kind of progressive liberalism based on an abstract internationalism.

A major challenge to these approaches has come from different versions of institutionalist approaches, which argue that both economic and political processes are still primarily national. These approaches theorize globalization as increased competition among national blocs of capitals supported by their own states. Although these approaches form an alternative to the completely deterritorialized approaches, their understanding of territoriality is also problematic, as it assumes a correspondence between the space of capital accumulation and the space of state action, reducing the contradictions of internationalization to rivalry among national blocs of capitals and states. Politically, these approaches tend to legitimize left nationalist positions based on protectionist policies.

In brief, what is problematic about both camps is the assumption of compatibility between the space of capital accumulation and the space of state action, whether at the global or national level. This makes it impossible to explain the contradictions of international accumulation as reflected within specific social formations and to develop class-based political alternatives. In this chapter, I aim to offer an alternative to both approaches through a close reading of the major works in the Marxist tradition. Following Dick Bryan,[3] I will argue that the main element of such an alternative is a differentiated conception of space, that is, a differentiation between the space of capital accumulation and the space within which the conditions of accumulation are secured. The distinction between these two kinds of spaces, which I will briefly call the 'space of capital' and the 'space of the state', is crucial for the purposes of this study, as the whole debate around globalization and state has been marked by confusion of the two spaces, either treating both as national or both as international. To the contrary, this chapter will argue that the 'space of capital' is distinct, although not separate, from the 'space of the state'. The space of capital accumulation is, in its inner logic, international, while the space of state action, in its institutional matrix and political essence, is mainly

---

3   Bryan (1995: 51).

national. Accordingly, the main contradiction of internationalization arises from the contradiction between the internationality of accumulation and the nationality of the state. In what follows, I will critically examine the literature in this regard. After a discussion of the dominant approaches, I will suggest an alternative.

Theoretical discussions of the internationalization of capital and state are not new. The literature on this issue flourished in the 1970s in response to the new phase of internationalization of capital through the spread of transnational corporations (TNCs) in the postwar era. Mainstream research on the subject has followed two traditions since then: neoclassical economics and neo-institutionalist theory. While the neoclassical approach regards the internationalization of capital as a process that can best proceed with minimal state interference, the neo-institutionalist approach emphasizes the role of states as institutional actors regulating this process. Both approaches treat the state and the internationalization of capital as identities operating in separate social spheres and forms, with independent agencies and causal relations. Therefore, they cannot explain the contradictions of the process of internationalization as reflected within state apparatuses. The elements of an alternative approach can be found within the Marxist literature.

1   Mainstream Approaches to the Internationalization of Capital and the State

According to neoclassical theory, TNCs act as efficient allocators of resources internationally so as to maximize capital efficiency and in this process world welfare. There are three versions of neoclassical views:[4] capital flow models which regard foreign direct investment (FDI) as simply a capital flow which increases the stock of capital in the host country;[5] product cycle theories which emphasize technology transfer and the importance of TNCs in providing access to overseas markets for Third World exports;[6] and internalization theories which regard TNCs as a way of bypassing imperfections in external markets.[7] The political implication of all three approaches is that the state should not intervene with respect to international investment except to provide a more favorable environment for foreign investors. The neoclassical framework

4   For a good overview of this literature see Jenkins (1987).
5   Meier (1972).
6   Vernon (1971).
7   Caves (1982); Dunning (1981).

has served as the theoretical justification for the neoliberal policies proposed by the IMF and World Bank until its neo-institutionalist turn in the late 1990s.

The neo-institutionalist critiques of neoclassical theories on this issue have followed two main lines. The first is based on Stephen Hymer's view of the impact of TNCs in the 1970s. In response to neoclassical writers like Raymond Vernon, Hymer emphasized the oligopolistic nature of TNCs, with the implication that there is a need for state control of TNCs, especially in the areas of transfer pricing and restrictive business practices.[8] Thus, for Hymer, host states should actively intervene in bargaining with TNCs in order to ensure that a greater share of economic monopoly rents accrue to the host country. The state, moreover, should give preferential treatment to national capital.[9] This approach has guided the theoretical framework for United Nations Conference on Trade and Development (UNCTAD) policies, which stress the adverse consequences of foreign capital for developing countries and advocate an active role for host states in negotiating investment terms with TNCs.[10]

A second theoretical strain within neo-institutionalism has emerged as a reaction to the structuralist Marxist theories of state in the 1970s, and the concept of relative autonomy of the state from capital. In *Bringing the State Back In*, writers like Peter Evans and Theda Skocpol criticized previous state theory for being society-centered and neglecting the autonomy and organizational possibilities of the state for developmental purposes.[11] As Paul Cammack points out, what was involved here was the assimilation of Marxist state theory into a non-Marxist framework in two steps: the replacement of 'class' with 'society' and then the counterposition of 'society' to the 'state', thus dissolving the class dynamics that underlined both.[12] Building on such analysis, neo-institutionalist writers like Robert Wade, Linda Weiss, Paul Hirst, and Grahame Thompson emphasized the autonomy of states in the economy, arguing that the world economy is more 'international' than 'global', and that there is scope for state actions to boost the productivity of firms operating within their territory.[13]

Throughout the 1980s and 1990s, the neo-institutionalist approach was regarded by many on the left as an alternative to neoliberalism. It provided the

---

8   Hymer (1979).
9   Jenkins (1987).
10   See Kozul-Wright (1995), and Kozul-Wright and Rowthorn (1998) for the UNCTAD position in the globalization context.
11   Evans and Skocpol (1985).
12   Cammack (1989).
13   Wade (1996); Weiss (1997); Hirst and Thompson (1996).

theoretical basis for social democratic alternatives in the advanced capitalist countries, and also informed the national-developmentalist alternatives in the Third World, with its emphasis on the role of the state in strengthening the bargaining power of developing countries in a global economy.

When neoliberal theory and practice faced a serious crisis in the late 1990s, neoliberal theorists often turned towards neo-institutionalists' analytical tools and concepts to identify more clearly the institutional contexts for their own framework. These positions formed a revised neoliberal orthodoxy. As a result, the neo-institutionalist perspective lost much of its status as an alternative to neoliberalism and became an adjunct to neoliberalism and its emphasis on the efficiency of markets and the state role in supporting institutions for contracts and exchange.

It should be noted that the convergence between the neoclassical and neo-institutionalist theories was a dual process. As the 1990s progressed, both neo-classical and neo-institutionalist theories faced theoretical limitations and increasingly turned to some of the other's propositions. This was not surprising given the theoretical affinity between the two on the primacy of market efficiency and the separation of state and market into distinct social spheres. On the one hand, much of neoliberal theory (as with Joseph Stiglitz and Douglass North) increasingly integrated institutions as a foundation for market regulation. On the other hand, neo-institutionalists increasingly embraced the notion of the efficiency and dynamism (as with Peter Evans, John Zysman, and others) of embedded markets with appropriate social dimensions. The convergence between neoclassical and neo-institutionalist approaches led to a revised neoliberal synthesis that found its most clear political expression in the advanced capitalist countries in 'Third Way' social democracy, and in the Third World in the new development orthodoxy of the World Bank. Leo Panitch rightfully called this process, in both theory and policy, 'the social democratization of global capitalism'.[14] The elements of an alternative approach challenging this revised neoliberal synthesis, rests, therefore, with the Marxist literature. That's where I would like to turn now.

---

14   "More than it likes to admit," Panitch (2000: 7) argued, "this critique of neoliberalism has much in common with the cynical idealism of the Third Way and the World Bank's current project of building a 'post-Washington Consensus' – globalization with a social-democratic face."

2   Marxist Approaches to the Internationalization of Capital and the State

Marx's views on the internationalization of capital are most clearly articulated in the *Communist Manifesto, Grundrisse* and *Capital.* In the *Manifesto*, Marx and Engels discuss the internationalization of capital in the early phases of capitalism marked by the spatial expansion of capitalist social relations into non-capitalist social formations, treating the formation of a world market and the modern state as related processes. However, the concept of space in the *Manifesto* is problematic, mainly because it is too universalistic, neglecting the importance of territorial differentiation.[15] In the *Grundrisse,* on the other hand, Marx discusses the internationalization of capital as part of the circulation process of capital. He argues that "a precondition of production based on capital is the production of a constantly widening sphere of circulation."[16] He then goes on to the formulation that "circulation proceeds in space and time."[17] On one side, capital tries to tear down every spatial barrier to exchange, and conquer the whole earth for its market; on the other side, to annihilate this space with time, i.e., to reduce to a minimum the time spent in motion from one place to another.[18] This is the most sophisticated treatment by Marx of the temporal and spatial dimensions of the expansion of capital in the same piece of writing. The same could not be argued for the discussion of the issue in the second volume of *Capital.* The main concern of Marx here is to unravel the inner dialectic of capitalism considered as a closed system, so it doesn't involve any spatial dimension.[19] What is clearly lacking in both the *Grundrisse* and the second volume of *Capital,* however, is the role of the state. As Marx's views on the internationalization of capital were mostly shaped in the context of the expansion of capitalism into non-capitalist formations rather than the movement of capital among capitalist formations, he discussed the role of the state mostly in repressive rather than economic terms. Thus, although Marx provided significant insights for the analysis of the historical and spatial dynamics of the internationalization of capital in different parts of his work, and touched upon the role of the state in other parts, he never brought all these together in the same theoretical framework. Therefore, on the question

---

15   Harvey (2001: 278).
16   Marx (1993: 407).
17   Marx (1993: 533).
18   Marx (1993: 539).
19   Harvey (2001: 308); Bryan (1995: 70).

of how Marx would view the distinction between the space of capital and the space of state, it is difficult to make a definitive judgment.

The discussion on the internationalization of capital and the state took a new route in the context of the imperialism debates at the end of the 19th century. The inter-imperial rivalries of the late 19th century "forced Marxists to confront directly the dynamic relations between inner and outer transformations" of capitalist accumulation.[20] Thus, different from Marx's writings, the classical imperialism debate had a distinct spatial flavor from the beginning, as well as a more direct preoccupation with the question of the state. This could be most clearly seen in the writings of Bukharin and Lenin. In *Imperialism and World Economy*,[21] Bukharin explained the rapid growth of the world economy by the unusual uneven development of the productive forces of world capitalism accompanied by the export of capital. He argued that through the "transfusion of capital from one 'national' sphere into the other, there grows the intertwining of 'national capitals'; there proceeds the 'internationalization' of capital."[22] However, he argued, the same process also sharpens the conflicts among various 'national' groups of the bourgeoisie, so a reverse tendency towards the nationalization of capitalist interests begins.[23] In this process, the entire national economy turns into "one gigantic combined enterprise under the tutelage of the financial kings and the capitalist state, an enterprise which monopolizes the national market."[24] As such, Bukharin's analysis ignored the tendency of big corporations to compete all over the world, rather than uniting to face foreign competition.[25] Thus it led to the misleading conclusion that competition is suppressed within national boundaries. On the other hand, his emphasis on the tendency for nationalization of capital led him to problematize the concept of the state in relation to capital more comprehensively than other classical theorists of imperialism. In the process of competition among state capitalist trusts, Bukharin argued, the state begins to play a very large part and becomes more than ever before an "executive committee of the ruling classes."[26] So paradoxically, his conception of the capitalist class as an entity united by finance capital on a national basis led him to theorize the state as a direct instrument of big capital with no inner contradictions.

---

20   Harvey (2001: 308).
21   Bukharin (1975 [1915]).
22   Quoted in Radice (1975: 26).
23   Quoted in Radice (1975: 29).
24   Quoted in Radice (1975: 30–31).
25   Brewer (1990: 114).
26   Radice (1975: 123).

In *Imperialism, the Highest Stage of Capitalism* (1917), Lenin basically followed Bukharin to emphasize the historical tendencies for monopolization,
the formation of finance capital, and the export of capital as the major factors
leading to the formation of national blocs of centralized capital and intense
national rivalries among them. In that sense, the main strength of Lenin's
approach was its historical dimension. However, his analysis was precisely
problematic on those terms. Like Bukharin, Lenin also took for granted the
division of the world on the basis of national blocs of capital, and gave no
answer to the question why a "country" should be a relevant unit of analysis in this context.[27] Thus, the whole line of argument by Bukharin and Lenin
on competing national blocs of capital was marked by failure to differentiate
between the 'space of capital' and the 'space of the state'. They treated both
of these spaces as national, so they saw the only contradiction of the internationalization of capital as a rivalry among national blocs of capital/state, with
no inherent contradictions in the international accumulation process itself.[28]

When the debate on the internationalization of capital reemerged in the
early 1970s, the main concern was how the postwar proliferation of transnational corporations (TNCs), as well as the rise of Europe and Japan as new centers of accumulation, affected the balance between the 'internationalization'
and 'nationalization' of capital as reflected in the state form. In this context,
Ernest Mandel and Bob Rowthorn represented the Lenin-Bukharin line of
argument.[29] Mandel argued that the international amalgamation of capitals
inside Europe had reached a considerable degree so as to challenge the hegemony of the United States and also affect the state form in Europe. "The growth
of capital interpenetration inside the Common Market, the appearance of
large amalgamated banking and industrial units which are not mainly the
property of any national capitalist class," Mandel argued, "represent the material infrastructure for the emergence of supranational state-power organs."[30]

According to Mandel, the interpenetration of national capitals within
Europe would necessarily be accompanied by the transfer of state power to the
supra-national level, mainly because only a supra-national state could respond
to a general recession through European-wide policy instruments like a single currency or taxation system.[31] For Mandel, the state aimed "to guarantee
directly the profits of the dominant sectors of the big bourgeoisie."[32] In the

27   Brewer (1990: 123).
28   Bryan (1995: 51).
29   Mandel (1967; 1970); Rowthorn (1971).
30   Mandel (1967: 31).
31   Mandel (1967: 33).
32   Mandel (1970: 51).

European case, this implied that only a supra-national state could guarantee the profits of the "big European concerns" by "generating the necessary purchasing power, keeping up employment while continuing to limit redundancies to a 'reasonable' volume and to sell the major part of their output."[33] Thus, Mandel's conception of an emerging European state as the instrument of big European capital was a reformulation of Bukharin's instrumentalist theory of state at the regional level. Mandel also argued that the process of European integration would mean enhanced inter-imperial rivalry between the US and Europe. As such, his approach differed from that of Lenin and Bukharin only in the sense that he defined the competing state-capital blocs in regional rather than national terms. The problem essentially remained the same: a failure to differentiate between the 'space of capital' and the 'space of the state' by defining both spaces as regional.

Rowthorn agreed with Mandel on the growing challenge of European and Japanese capital to American hegemony.[34] The only difference lay in his emphasis on foreign direct investment by the Europeans and Japanese, in contrast to Mandel's emphasis on exports. Rowthorn was preoccupied with the question of the relationship between internationalizing capitals and the state. He discussed this in terms of the relationship between the "strength of capital" and the "autonomy of a state *vis-a-vis* other states." Rowthorn argued that there is no correspondence between the strength of capital and the autonomy of the state in a specific country. For instance, the weakness of the British state should be explained by the very strength of the cosmopolitan activities of British capital, which undermined its domestic economy. This led to a situation in which many British companies conducted a larger part of their business in areas where the British state had no control. If, as in the case of internationalizing British capital, the state power available to capital was not commensurate with its needs, there were two main courses of action. The state could ally itself or even merge with other states, thereby placing greater state power at the disposal of its capital. Alternatively, capital could change its nationality.[35] Rowthorn then argued that "alliances or mergers of states are likely to be of more immediate significance in view of the growing unity of the Common Market and Britain's application for membership."[36] Thus, he reached the same conclusion as Mandel: a European capital supported by a European state in rivalry with US capital supported by its own state. He even

33   Mandel (1970: 97).
34   Rowthorn (1971: 45).
35   Rowthorn (1971: 49).
36   Rowthorn (1971: 49).

went further than Mandel to add that this new bloc of European capital with its European state would act as a "nationalist" force.[37]

Thus, on the question of what institutions would take care of the needs of the internationalizing capitals if not their own national states, Rowthorn posed two possibilities: a supra-national state aligned with the capitals operating in its region, or a total shift in the nationality of these capitals. Rowthorn overlooked a third alternative: the possibility that 'host' nation-states could assume responsibility for the foreign capitals operating within their territories. This third alternative, which can be called the 'internalization' alternative, was neglected by both Mandel and Rowthorn. In brief, Mandel and Rowthorn posed the right question of who would oversee the expanded reproduction of internationalizing capitals in the new post-war economy, but their answer of 'supra-national states' was deeply problematic, as they reformulated Bukharin's and Lenin's conception of 'national blocs of state/capital' as 'regional blocs of state/capital', thereby reducing the contradictions of internationalization to rivalry among regional blocs of capitals/states.

3   New Departure Points: Murray, Poulantzas and Palloix

When Robin Murray posed the same question in 1971, he gave a quite different answer. Murray contended that the rapid postwar expansion of TNCs had led to a "territorial non-coincidence" between internationalizing capitals and their domestic states, which was reflected as a contradiction in the state form.[38] "In the process of capitalist production and reproduction," Murray argued, "the state has certain economic functions which it will always perform ... In tracing the territorial expansion of individual capitals, one of the central points at issue will be what institutions perform these structural economic functions for the expanded capitals."[39] He identified six primary functions of the capitalist state: "guaranteeing of private property rights, economic liberalization, economic orchestration, input provision, intervention for social consensus, and the management of the external relations of a capitalist system."[40] In the new era of internationalization of capital after 1945, he argued, these functions may be performed by different agents: the domestic state, foreign state structures, the accumulating capital itself, or the existing state bodies in cooperation with

---

37   Rowthorn (1971: 50).
38   Murray (1971: 85).
39   Murray (1971: 87).
40   Murray (1971: 88–93).

each other. Thus, "there was no necessary link between a capital and its state in the area of extension, that capital was rather a political opportunist."[41]

Murray's analysis was criticized for implying a weakening of the national state as a result of the internationalization of capital.[42] Murray indeed argued that the internationalization of capital often leads to a decrease in the power of nation-states; however, this was not an automatic outcome of his analysis. The whole point about his argument on the 'political opportunism' of capital was that the decline of the nation-states was only one of the historical possibilities and not the only logical outcome. In other words, for Murray, the relationship between internationalizing capital and state was contingent, taking different forms depending on various factors such as "the degree of productive centralization, stage of overseas company development, forms of international flow, degree of dependence on state partiality and the strength of foreign competition."[43] This contingency was both a strength and a weakness of his analysis. It was a strength because, in contrast to Mandel and Rowthorn who saw the supra-national state as the main actor to perform public functions for internationalizing capitals, Murray argued that it was only one of the possible actors. And through his emphasis on the territorial non-coincidence between internationalizing capitals and the state, Murray paved the way for a discussion of the differentiation between the space of capital and the space of the state. In this sense, Murray's contribution led to a new departure in the theories of the internationalization of capital.

Yet, Murray left the question of the relationship between state and international capital too contingent – even ambiguous – by arguing that necessary extra-market functions for international capital could be performed by all sorts of institutions. It was precisely this problem that Poulantzas decisively tackled. Poulantzas argued that "the current internationalization of capital neither suppresses nor bypasses the national states."[44] According to Poulantzas, "the reproduction of capital as a social relation is not simply located in the 'moments' of the cycle: productive capital – commodity capital – money capital, but rather in the reproduction of social classes and of the class struggle."[45] In that sense, "the economic functions of the state are in fact expressions of its overall political role in exploitation and class domination; they are by their nature articulated with its repressive and ideological roles in the field of class

---

41   Murray (1971: 109).
42   See Warren (1975 [1971]); Fine and Harris (1979); and Radice (1984).
43   Murray (1971: 100–102).
44   Poulantzas (1974b: 73).
45   Poulantzas (1974b: 97).

struggle of a social formation."[46] Thus, in terms of Murray's question as to which institutions would assume responsibility for the public functions necessary for the reproduction of international capital, Poulantzas gave a decisive answer: these functions had to be internalized by the nation-states themselves.

> It is impossible to separate the various interventions of the state and their aspects, in such a way as to envisage the possibility of an effective transfer of its 'economic functions' to supranational or super-state apparatuses, while the national state would retain only a repressive or ideological role. ... at the very most, there is sometimes a delegation in the exercise of these functions. In fact, by looking in this direction, one loses sight of the real tendencies at work: the internalized transformations of the national state itself, aimed at taking charge of the internalization of public functions on capital's behalf.[47]

In this way, he resolved the ambiguity in Murray's analysis by arguing that even when the space of capital is international, the space of the state has to remain national.

From another angle, Christian Palloix also departed from Murray's analyses. Palloix's main concern was criticizing the approaches that exclusively focused on TNCs. Against these approaches, he argued that the TNCs are only one part of broader processes of the internationalization of capital. Palloix thus took up the study of the internationalization of capital based on Marx's analysis of the circuits of capital in Volume 2 of *Capital.* Using Marx's analysis that the circuit of capital goes through three stages – money, commodity, and production – Palloix argued that the circuit of commodity-capital has operated internationally from the very beginnings of capitalism, whereas the internationalization of the money-capital circuit and that of productive capital are more recent phenomena. Palloix, moreover, argued that the role of the state has been continuous, but varied during the different phases of internationalization, depending upon what the internationalization of capital implied for the management of the law of value by the state.[48] "In the historical development of the internationalization of capital," he argued, "the nation-state will, with increasing seriousness, internally consider its external reality, insofar as certain parts of the state – some more than others – will submit to the international situation."[49]

---

46   Poulantzas (1974b: 81).
47   Poulantzas (1974b: 81).
48   Palloix (1977: 12).
49   Palloix (1977: 13).

So, while the internationalization of certain parts of the state is barely visible in the earlier phase of internationalization of commodity capital, the nature of the state apparatus is profoundly changed in the latter phase of internationalization of money-capital and of productive-capital. In the earlier phase, the state attempts to establish a commercial network by reflecting the international law of value on the national law of value.[50] In the latter phase, however, "certain parts of the state must reflect the increasingly urgent necessity for international standards – as expressions of the international law of value – in the structure of national production and trade for capital whose self-expansion occurs in the international arena."[51] Thus, "the state becomes hierarchical as a result of the predominance of the monetary sanction, reflecting internationalization." Palloix was thus quite clearly on the side of theories that differentiated between the space of capital and the space of the state, and he problematized the 'internalization' of public functions of international capital by nation-states. He made three important contributions to this line of thinking. First, by differentiating between the histories of internationalization of each circuit of capital, he added a historical dimension to the debate. Second, he explained the specificity of the latest phase of internationalization as the pre-eminent role of the money form as the expression of international value. This theme was taken up by Bryan in his analysis of the distinctiveness of the recent internationalization of capital as the subjection of all national calculations to international standards.[52] Lastly, through his discussion of the varying role of the state in each phase of internationalization of the circuit of capital, Palloix was able to identify the nature of the restructuring of the state in the recent phase: the reordering of the internal hierarchy of the state apparatus and increasing contradictions within the state reflecting the requirements of monetary sanction. This was a theme shared by Poulantzas and revived in the globalization context by Robert Cox, Leo Panitch, and others.[53]

4   Deterritorialization of State and Capital

When the debate on the internationalization of capital and state re-emerged in the context of globalization in the late 1980s, the main context was the expansion of capitalist relations of production to all parts of the world following

---

50   Palloix (1977: 13).
51   Palloix (1977: 14).
52   Bryan (1995).
53   Poulantzas (1974b); Cox (1987); Panitch (1994).

the collapse of the Soviet bloc. This gave rise to conceptual approaches that tended to theorize internationalization as an increasing deterritorialization of social relations. The internalization problematic of the post-Murray debate was increasingly replaced by analyses that focused exclusively on the global level. This can be most clearly seen in neo-Gramscian approaches, which have increasingly shifted to a deterritorialized approach to the internationalization of capital and the state in the course of their development since Cox's initial work in 1987.

In *Production, Power, and World Order* Cox argues that the postwar world order is characterized by the 'internationalization of production', that is, location of different components of production in different territorial jurisdictions;[54] and the 'internationalization of state', a process whereby national state structures are adjusted to the exigencies of the world economy in response to external pressures and realignments of internal power relations.[55] Thus Cox has an 'internalization' problematic in the sense that he focuses on the mechanisms by which the internationalization process is managed by national state structures, e.g., through restructuring of the hierarchy of agencies within governments and prioritization of those agencies that act as links between the world economy and the national economy.[56] Thus, Cox takes the national level quite seriously as the space of state action for the reproduction of the conditions of accumulation. However, Cox gives primacy to the 'world order' as the explanatory factor in understanding changes in national state structures[57] and argues that the "state becomes a transmission belt from the global to the national economy."[58] As Panitch argued, Cox's 'outside-in' orientation to the internationalization of state is limited at this point. The notion of the state as a transmission belt from the global to the national economy "is not only too formal in its distinction between global and national economy, but also too 'top-down' in its expression of power relations."[59] This conception of the state does not allow for an analysis of how nation-states *mediate* the conflicts among different sections of capital within a social formation. This limitation can only be overcome if the role of states is conceived not only as *internalization* of the reproduction of international capital accumulation but also its *mediation* with national social forces. In Panitch's words, "the role of states remains one

---

54   Cox (1987: 109, 244).
55   Cox (1987: 253).
56   Cox (1987: 228).
57   Cox (1987: 109).
58   Cox (1992: 27).
59   Panitch (1994: 71).

not only of internalizing but also of mediating adherence to the untrammelled logic of international capitalist competition within its own domain."[60] This is exactly the point where Poulantzian analyses differ from neo-Gramscian ones.

Among neo-Gramscian approaches that have followed from Cox's work, William Robinson offers a rather nuanced version of the deterritorialization thesis. Robinson argues that economic globalization has led to transnational class formation and the emergence of a transnational state (TNS), which is increasingly able to absorb the nation-state within its larger structure.[61] Robinson's thesis has been taken up by other authors and sparked significant debates.[62] The formation of "a transnational capitalist class (TCC), which exercises its class power through an incipient transnational state apparatus" forms the backbone of this thesis.[63] The TCC exercises its class power through two channels: "a dense network of supranational institutions and relationships that increasingly bypass formal states and that should be conceived of as an emergent transnational state" and "the utilization of national governments as territorially bound juridical units (the inter-state system), which are transformed into transmission belts and filtering devices, but also into proactive instruments for advancing the agenda of global capitalism."[64] According to Robinson, this thesis does not suggest that "there are no longer national and regional capitals" but rather "the TCC has established itself as a class group without a national identity and in competition with nationally based capitals."[65] Thus, he argues that contingents of the TCC struggle with nationally based capitals to insert each country into global circuits of accumulation using the state apparatus as a site of struggle; and that this dialectical process between national contingents and global political/economic actors with both the state and the market as sites of struggle constitutes a central transformative process in modern capitalism. In that sense, Robinson's thesis does not break with the 'internalization' problematic of Cox's initial work. The problem, however, starts with his conception of nation-states as "transmission belts and filtering devices."

As with Cox, Robinson's conception of the state does not allow for an analysis of how nation-states *mediate* the conflicts between the TCC and other sections of capital within a social formation. Also, the conception of supranational

---

60   Panitch (1994: 71–72).
61   Robinson (2001: 158).
62   For example, in the volumes of *Science & Society* from 1999–2002.
63   Robinson and Harris (2000: 27).
64   Burbach and Robinson (1999: 35).
65   Robinson (2005: 318).

institutions as parts of a transnational capitalist *state* trivializes the concept of state itself, as it reduces the state to an economic apparatus, disregarding its repressive and ideological functions. Therefore, as William Tabb argues, it is much better to see supranational institutions as global governance institutions rather than parts of a transnational capitalist *state*.[66] Furthermore, although there is no question about the empirical validity of the argument on the TCC as a fraction of capital, the same cannot be said for the argument on the formation of a TNS. As a typical example, the whole process of European integration shows that the TCC's push for political integration has never been as whole-hearted as its push for economic integration, as full political integration would deprive it of the opportunity to take advantage of regionally differentiated control mechanisms over labor. In Tabb's words, "TCC who are seen as pushing for the formation of a TNS have not done very well lately."[67] The rejection of the European Union Constitution in 2005, and the loss of momentum in the political integration of European states since then, is a good example in this regard.

Other neo-Gramscian approaches that have followed from Cox's work have distanced their foci of analysis further away from the internal dynamics of specific social formations. Instead they have focused almost exclusively on the supra-national level. In this context, the concept of civil society has come forward as a major conceptual focus besides the state and capital. This preoccupation with civil society, however, has meant a further digression away from analysis of states in relation to capital, and a further deterritorialization of the debate. This can be most clearly seen in what has come to be known as the Amsterdam International Political Economy project, specifically in Kees van der Pijl's concept of transnational 'state/civil society complexes'. van der Pijl uses Cox's 'state/civil society complexes' to identify two forms of state in relation to transnational class formation: Lockean and Hobbesian.[68] The Lockean state/civil society complex has its origins in post-1688 Revolution England, where the self-regulation of a property-owning civil society and the separation of public and private spheres was guaranteed by the state. The Hobbesian state/civil society complex, on the other hand, is characterized by the suspension of the differentiation between state and society in favor of a 'state class', with the prototype being France in the 17th and 18th centuries.[69] Internationalization of capital, van der Pijl argues, has been accompanied by the internationalization of the Lockean state/civil society complex, through a constant expansion

---

66   Tabb (2009: 45).
67   Tabb (2009: 45).
68   van der Pijl (1998).
69   van der Pijl (1998: 78).

of the "Lockean heartland" absorbing the "Hobbesian contender states." It does not evolve as "an economic process in a fixed landscape of sovereign states" but it is "an aspect of a process of expansion of the state/society complex in which capital crystallized under what proved to be the most favorable conditions."[70] In that sense, it can be argued that van der Pijl sees both the space of capital and the space of the state as transnational – in the form of a transnational state/civil society complex. He argues that a "denationalized, total capital on a world scale" is governed by "international quasi-state structures" based on Lockean foundations absorbing the challenges of the Hobbesian perspective.[71]

   Michael Hardt and Antonio Negri converge with van der Pijl on an overlap in the transnationality of the space of capital and the space of the state. They argue that sovereignty has taken a new form, composed of a series of national and supranational organisms united under a single logic rule, which they call 'Empire'.[72] What we are witnessing is a qualitative passage "from imperialism to Empire and from the nation-state to the political regulation of the global market."[73] According to Hardt and Negri, "economic geography and political geography are destabilized in such a way that the boundaries among the various zones are themselves fluid and mobile. As a result, the entire world market tends to be the only coherent domain for the effective application of capitalist management and command."[74] This process requires the formation of 'a global quasi-state' as the new political form of command.[75] Hardt and Negri have the most extremely deterritorialized approach to capital as well. Following Deleuze and Guattari, they argue that capital operates on the plane of *immanence*, "through a generalized decoding of fluxes, a massive deterritorialization, and then through conjunctions of these deterritorialized and decoded fluxes."[76] The functioning of capital, they argue, is "deterritorializing and immanent in three primary aspects that Marx himself analysed":[77] separation of populations from territories in the processes of primitive accumulation, reduction of all forms of value to money, and the immanence of laws by which capital functions to the very functioning of capital. Therefore "capital tends toward a smooth space defined by uncoded flows, flexibility, continual

70   van der Pijl (1998: 83).
71   van der Pijl (1998: 77–8).
72   Hardt and Negri (2001: xii).
73   Hardt and Negri (2001: 237).
74   Hardt and Negri (2001: 254).
75   Hardt and Negri (2001: 255).
76   Hardt and Negri (2001: 326).
77   Hardt and Negri (2001: 326).

modulation, and tendential equalization."[78] Modern sovereignty, on the other hand, operates on the plane of *transcendence,* through the "striation of the social field." As such, "transcendence of modern sovereignty conflicts with the immanence of capital."[79]

This contradiction between the "smoothness" of the space of capital and "striation" of the space of sovereignty has been mediated by civil society for one historical period but not anymore. The withering away of civil society through the decline of the labor unions involves the "smoothing of the striation of modern social space" and sovereignty itself becomes immanent like capital.[80] The space of sovereignty becomes smooth and thus completely compatible with the space of capital. There are two problems with Hardt and Negri's argument. First, even their own emphasis on the privileged position of the United States is enough to show that the space of sovereignty has not been that much 'smoothened'. Second, the completely deterritorialized concept of capital implied by the concept of immanence is problematic, as it primarily refers to money capital, and even money capital is not totally deterritorialized. For example, if a bank holds the mortgage debt on much of the infrastructural investment within a territory, then it undermines the quality of its own debt if it sends all surplus money capital to wherever the rate of profit is highest. In order to realize the value of the debt it already holds, it may be forced to make additional investments within a territory at a lower rate of profit.[81] Furthermore, whatever the degree of dominance of the money form in the current context, it is still *only one* of the forms of capital. This is a point equally missed by John Holloway.

According to Holloway, the capitalist state necessarily takes the form of the nation-state because exploitation and coercion are separated in capitalism, and the nation-state serves the "decomposition of global social relations" as a crucial element in the fragmentation of opposition to capitalist domination, in the decomposition of labor as a class.[82] Thus for Holloway, "there is a basic territorial non-coincidence between the state and the society to which it relates."[83] In terms of the distinction between the space of capital and the space of the state, then, Holloway makes a strong case. The problems start when Holloway makes a contrast between the mobility of capital and the immobility of the

---

78   Hardt and Negri (2001: 327).
79   Hardt and Negri (2001: 327).
80   Hardt and Negri (2001: 332).
81   Harvey (1999: 421).
82   Holloway (1994: 31).
83   Holloway (1994: 32).

state. "The contrast between the spatial liberation of the process of exploitation (mediated through the flow of capital as money), on the one hand, and the
spatial definition of coercion (expressed in the existence of national states), on
the other," he argues, "is expressed as a contrast between the mobility of capital and the immobility of the state."[84] In this framework, Holloway criticizes
approaches that treat capital "as though it could be understood in terms of
its personal, institutional or local attachment, instead of seeing these attach-
ments as transitory moments in the incessant flow of capital."[85] Thus, Holloway
sees all "immobile" forms of capital (like productive capital) as "transitory" and
therefore irrelevant for the analysis of the relation between global capital and
the nation-state. He only takes into consideration the money form of capital
because "the absolute contingency of space is epitomized in the existence of
capital as money."[86] In this context, Holloway argues that the relation between
global capital and the national state can be imagined through the metaphor
of nation-states as "reservoirs seeking competitively to attract and retain the
maximum amount of water from a powerful and largely uncontrollable river"
of global capital.[87] In this understanding, global capital cannot be tied down
to any particular part of the world. This deterritorialized concept of capital,
coupled with a concept of nation-state whose role is reduced to a "reservoir,"
which cannot control but only respond to the unstoppable movement of capital, forms the limits of Holloway's approach.

The problem with this approach, as with Hardt and Negri, is the treatment
of the space of capital only in terms of the flows of money capital. The theorization of money capital as 'the global capital' leads to a totally deterritorialized
concept of capital ('immanent' in the case of Hardt and Negri, and 'a-spatial' in
the case of Holloway). The exclusive focus on money capital leads to the misleading view that all capital is mobile, and the main contradiction is between
the mobility of capital and immobility of the state. When the entire process of
the circulation of capital is taken into consideration, however, it becomes clear
that the real tension is "between fixity and motion in the circulation of capital,
between concentration and dispersal, between local commitment and global
concerns," which puts "immense strains upon the organizational capacities of
capitalism."[88] In other words, it is wrong to see capital as totally mobile and
free from spatial bounds because "a portion of the total social capital has to be

---

84   Holloway (1994: 33).
85   Holloway (1994: 34).
86   Holloway (1994: 31).
87   Holloway (1994: 38).
88   Harvey (1999: 422).

rendered immobile in order to give the remaining capital greater flexibility of movement."[89] The understanding that much of capital still remains territorially based also means that financialization can be overstressed in current Marxist discussions of capitalist crisis. The exclusive focus on the mobility of money capital as if other fractions of capital no longer exist, moreover, leads to an inability to explain the contradictions within capital in the process of internationalization. Thus, what we need is not only a territorialized concept of state but also a territorialized concept of capital.

5   Towards a Re-territorialized Approach to Capital and the State

The conceptual tools of a territorialized approach to state and capital in the context of globalization can be found in the works of Dick Bryan, Konstantinos Tsoukalas, Greg Albo, and Leo Panitch and Sam Gindin, who all emphasize in their own ways the non-coincidence between the space of capital and the space of the state, and how this non-coincidence is reflected as a contradiction within each national state. In what follows, I will draw upon their arguments to discuss why territoriality is still important in the globalization debate.

The territoriality of capital basically means that production and accordingly exploitation always take place in specific territories. As Albo points out, "the appropriation and production of value and commodities through the exploitation of labor takes place in spatially specific places of production; but the circulation of commodities and the distribution of value in exchange flows is potentially not bounded to any particular place."[90] The places of production "are constituted by the specific territorially-embedded conflictual social property relations of capitalism."[91] The contemporary internationalization of markets, in this context, is "a contradictory 'space of flows' between these 'spaces of production'."[92] The increasingly vast division of the stages of material production over different national spaces does not run against this argument, as territoriality here does not necessarily refer to a single national space. It rather refers to the locality of production itself, whether it is divided among a plurality of national spaces or not. In Bryan's words, "capital exerts its presence within the state by its locality, not by its nationality of ownership."[93] In

---

89   Harvey (1999: 419).
90   Albo (2003: 6).
91   Albo (1997: 8).
92   Albo (1997: 8).
93   Bryan (1992: 332).

the same vein, Tsoukalas argues that economic activities do not take place in a "trans-territorial class vacuum." Exploitation always takes place "within the territories of specific societies organized as sovereign states."[94] Accumulation can take different organizational forms but its operationalization, by definition, remains domestic.

The territoriality of the state, on the other hand, means that the conditions of exploitation are still reproduced at the national level, where social classes are reproduced, and political domination is located. In this context, against conceptions that look for the reproduction of the accumulation process at the supra-national level, Tsoukalas follows Poulantzas in arguing that "the overall responsibility for reproducing internal class relations and equilibria resides with national states" because "social coherence, systems of exploitation and class conflicts remain purely internal affairs."[95] "On the material level," he argues, "deregulation, labor fragmentation, productivity and profit maximization can only be ensured within a juridically-given territorial context. In this sense, far from dispensing with national states' functions and services, the extended reproduction of the accumulation of international capital is totally dependent on their constant intervention."[96] Tsoukalas thus revives Poulantzas' basic argument that the economic functions of the state are not just some technical tasks that can be separated from its political functions and transferred to the supra-national level. "The political and ideological cohesion of social formations, still materialized only by and through states," he argues, "provides the basis for reproducing the (interchangeable) coherent socio-economic and legal environments necessary for any productive organization."[97] In the same vein, Albo argues that "the social practices of capitalism have historically been compartmentalized within the territorial domain of nation-states which have provided a common currency, legal structure, class formation and social institutions, and which interact as part of a world market."[98] In that sense, the role of the nation-state in reproducing the overall conditions of class domination has not declined with globalization. In Panitch's words, "global class interpenetrations and contradictions need to be understood in the context of the nation-state's continuing central role in organizing, sanctioning and legitimizing class domination within capitalism."[99]

---

94   Tsoukalas (1999: 58).
95   Tsoukalas (1999: 61–62).
96   Tsoukalas (1999: 67).
97   Tsoukalas (1999: 67).
98   Albo (2003: 7).
99   Panitch (1994: 67).

TABLE 4.1   Space of capital and space of the state in Marxist theory

	Space of capital	Space of the state
Hardt and Negri	deterritorialized	deterritorialized
Holloway	deterritorialized	territorialized
Tsoukalas, Albo, Panitch & Gindin	territorialized	territorialized

Thus, in contrast to Hardt and Negri, who treat both state and capital as deterritorialized, and Holloway, who treats the state as territorialized but capital as deterritorialized, Tsoukalas, Albo, Panitch and Gindin treat both spaces as territorialized. Their positions are summarized in Table 4.1.

The next question concerns how to understand the contradictions of internationalization as reflected within capital and state in this process.

6   Contradictions within Capital and State in the Process of Internationalization

The contradictions within capital in the recent internationalization process can be explained by two main factors. First, the contradiction between the internationality of capital accumulation and the nationality of the state is expressed within the capitalist class of each social formation as the incompatibility of different demands on the state. In Tsoukalas' words, "the contradictions and antagonisms of international capital are now directly present within national socioeconomic formations;" thus "it is now even more true that the contradictions between fractions of capital within national states are 'internationalized'."[100] The second factor is related to the nature of the recent internationalization process. Globally integrated capital markets have brought the whole spectrum of monetary policy into the division between capitals.[101] The conflicts associated with state regulation of the money system are more complex than those associated with tariff and trade policy. The dilemma for individual states in this context is that many state policies advantage one part

100   Tsoukalas (1999: 59–60).
101   Bryan (1995: 84).

of capital, but penalize another.[102] The only policy that can please all parts of capital at the same time is the assault on labor. That is why globalization can only proceed in the political context of neoliberalism.

How are we, then, to formulate the divisions within capital in the recent process of internationalization? What we are looking for here is a conceptualization that refers specifically to the contradictions in the recent process of internationalization, involving the spatial dimension as well as the role of the state. Bryan's framework is quite helpful at this point. He suggests a division based on the four forms of international integration in terms of different spatial combinations of production, realization, and reproduction: the national circuit, the global circuit, the investment-constrained circuit, and the market-constrained circuit. Each of the different phases in the circuit of capital involves the impact of state policy, and thus is a basis for divisions among individual capitals over state policy.[103]

National capital is the capital that produces, sells, and reinvests in the same national space. It is small scale (not large enough to reproduce internationally) and likely to be concentrated in import-competing or naturally protected industries. Global capital produces within a nation-state, but it can sell on global markets and reinvest beyond the borders. Its realization and reproduction is located according to international conditions of profitability. Investment-constrained capital can sell on global markets but cannot consider international production. It is integrated into international accumulation at the level of exchange, but not production. It consists of smaller-scale capital that produces exportable commodities but is not large enough to undertake production internationally. The lifting of capital controls in the 1980s reduced the importance of this form of accumulation; these capitals also shifted into the global circuit as they either outgrew protected investment opportunities or such opportunities dried up. Finally, market-constrained capital can invest internationally, but can only sell within national markets. (See Table 4.2.)

Each of the different phases in the circuit of capital involves the impact of state policy, and thus the basis for division between individual capitals over state policy.[104] Each of the four fractions of capital described above benefit from different kinds of state policies. For instance, tariff and exchange rate policies are the central concern for market-constrained capital: "these policies form a critical divide between different sorts of TNCs in their expectations of

---

102   Bryan (1995: 5).
103   Bryan (1995: 88).
104   Bryan (1995: 88).

TABLE 4.2   Circuits of capital and international accumulation

	Production (C..P..C′)	Realization (C′-M′)	Reproduction (M′-C′)
National	National	National	National
Investment-constrained	National	International	National
Market-constrained	National	National	International
Global	National	International	International

SOURCE: BRYAN (1995).

Note: C..P..C′: production of commodities;
C′-M′: realization of commodities through the act of exchange; and
M′-C′: reproduction of capital (allocation of revenue to new production).

nation state policies."[105] Controls on imports of commodities and money capital, as well as the impact of monetary policy on the exchange rate, determine the size and fortunes of each. The internationalization of capital has reduced capital in the investment-constrained circuit, but capital in the national and market-constrained circuits still exert significant influence in the policy formation of nation-states. The exchange rate remains a major irresolvable conflict between capitals engaged in different forms of accumulation.[106]

The main strength of Bryan's scheme is that it is defined with reference to the state, so it can contribute to explaining the contradictions of state policy. Each form of accumulation is reliant on state intervention for its relative prominence within the national spaces of accumulation, "because interventions which advance one form of accumulation inevitably retard another."[107] In sum, Bryan's analysis of the four types of capital producing within the same territory, but having differing sites of realization and reproduction, is very helpful for understanding the contradictions within capital in each social formation. Since Bryan focuses on the types of accumulation involving a process of production within the nation concerned, and production here is equated only with the existence of a labor process, it is possible in this framework to explain the contradictions within an internal capitalist class divided according

105   Bryan (1995: 91).
106   Bryan (1995: 92–93).
107   Bryan (1995: 98).

to its differential forms of integration with the processes of international accumulation. The next question concerns how these contradictions are reflected within the state apparatuses.

The contradictions of international accumulation are reflected within national states as increasing divisions over economic policies, as states have to internalize and mediate the conflicting demands of unevenly internationalized capitals operating within their territories. The main mechanism of internalization is the change in the internal hierarchy of states, whereby the executive branch is re-ordered to augment the role of agencies dealing with capital accumulation in general and economic internationalization in particular.[108] The major mechanism of mediation, on the other hand, is what Poulantzas identified as the rise of 'authoritarian statism'.[109] Poulantzas did not specifically refer to the internationalization of capital when he used the concept of authoritarian statism. Rather he used it to define the new state form that emerged to contain the specific contradictions of capitalism in the late 1970s. As such, the concept has its own specificities. However, as Bob Jessop points out, the core tendencies associated with authoritarian statism – the decline of the political scene, the growing autonomy of the executive, and the political role assumed by the state administration – have become even more relevant today.[110] There are both historical and theoretical grounds for this. Historically, the tendencies described by Poulantzas are grounded in the process of internationalization of capital under the dominance of the United States, which forms the beginning of globalization.[111] And theoretically, authoritarian statism refers to the management of capitalist contradictions directly by the state apparatus rather than mediations of the political scene. In that sense, it is still relevant for understanding the state restructuring in response to the ongoing internationalization of capital, because the increasing contradictions induced by internationalization tend to be managed directly by the executive branch of the state rather than via the political scene.[112] The next question concerns the implication of this argument for understanding the current form of imperialism.

---

108   Palloix (1977); Poulantzas (1978c); Cox (1987); Panitch (1994); Albo (2002).
109   Poulantzas (1978c).
110   Jessop (2011).
111   Kannankulam (2003).
112   Panitch (1994); Tsoukalas (1999); Albo (2002); Jessop (2006); Kannankulam (2003); Essex (2007).

7   Understanding Imperialism Today

The argument that nation-states continue to play key roles in managing capitals – even when these are global in their reach – have important implications for understanding the current form of imperialism At this point, it
is necessary to revisit the conceptual relationship between capitalism and
imperialism. Capitalist societies differ from previous ones by the formal separation of the economic and political spheres. This means that management
of the contradictions of the accumulation process is not undertaken by capitalists themselves, but by the nation-states under whose jurisdiction they
operate. In this framework, imperialism can be defined with reference to the
power relationships among nation-states which are each responsible for the
management of the international accumulation process within their own
territories. In that sense, imperialism does not reveal itself in the accumulation process as such, but in the geopolitical sphere of power relationships
among nation-states, which is relatively autonomous from the international
accumulation process. The internalization of the management of the international accumulation process by nation-states means that the contradictions of imperialism are displaced into the class contradictions internal to
each social formation. Therefore, as Panitch and Gindin argue, theories of
imperialism cannot be isolated from theories of internationalization of capital and the state.[113]

Imperialism has taken different forms in successive stages of the internationalization of capital. In the late 19th century, when internationalization of
capital was quite limited (mainly based on the flows of commodity-capital and
money capital rather than productive capital), contradictions of internationalization were displaced into inter-imperial rivalry. In that sense, Lenin's and
Bukharin's argument on competing national blocs of capital was grounded in
a real historical process. The problem with theories of inter-imperial rivalry in
the postwar era, however, has been "their elevation of a conjunctural moment
of inter-imperial rivalry to an immutable law of capitalist globalization."[114]
This is the case, for instance, with Mandel and Rowthorn's thesis on inter-
imperial rivalry between Europe and the US in the postwar context, or with
Alex Callinicos' more nuanced reformulation of the inter-imperial rivalry thesis in the globalization context, which emphasizes interdependence as well
as rivalry between Europe, the United States, and East Asia.[115] These theses

113   Panitch and Gindin (2005b).
114   Panitch and Gindin (2005b: 5).
115   Callinicos (2009).

ignore the qualitative break in the pattern of international capital flows in the postwar era, i.e., the acceleration of internationalization of productive capital through the expansion of US multinational corporations.[116] This forms a radical break with the inter-imperial rivalries of the previous period, because, as Poulantzas has forcefully argued, when multinational capital penetrates a host social formation, it arrives not merely as abstract 'direct foreign investment', but as a transformative social force within the country; and leads to the induced reproduction of the form of the dominant imperialist power within each social formation.[117] As Panitch and Gindin argue:

> this is not to say that such states became mere replicas of the US, given the variety of social structures or institutional and cultural traditions within them. Instead, what emerged was a dynamic combination that reflected the interaction of American penetration and dominance with the particularities of each nation-state. Nor did they become merely passive actors in the American empire; relative autonomy operated in relation to the internationalization of the state as well, reflecting the balance of social forces and political initiatives in each state.[118]

Thus the position of Marxists on the relationship between the space of capital and space of state have implications for their understanding of imperialism too. These positions are summarized in Table 4.3.

With the internationalization of all circuits of capital in the 1970s, and their expansion into the former Soviet bloc since the 1990s, imperialism is now more than ever an internal affair of each social formation, the specific form of which depends on the class forces involved in the international accumulation taking place within their territory. This argument also means that the position of a nation-state within the imperialist chain can change more rapidly than in the past, in line with the rapidly changing patterns of international capital flows. The recent attempts of the Turkish state to assume a sub-imperialist role in the Middle East through 'neo-Ottomanism' is a good example in this regard, as it shows the changing needs of the newly growing and internationalizing capital groups in Turkey. Even the United States as the most powerful state in the imperialist chain is not exempt from the effects of these changes – not because of the rivalry of other rising powers such as Russia or China, but because of the rapidly changing character of international accumulation itself. In this

---

116   Panitch (2000b).
117   Poulantzas (1974b).
118   Panitch and Gindin (2005b: 108).

TABLE 4.3   Marxist approaches to the relationship between space of capital and space of the
             state: Implications for imperialism theories

	Space of capital	Space of the state	Relation between the two spaces	Implications for imperialism theory
Lenin, Bukharin, Neo-institutionalist approaches	National	National	Congruent	Contradiction displaced into inter-imperial rivalry
Mandel, Rowthorn, Callinicos	Regional	Regional	Tendentially congruent	Contradiction displaced into new forms of inter-imperial rivalry between regional blocs
Robinson, van der Pijl, Hardt & Negri	International	International	Tendentially compatible at the international level	Contradiction displaced into global civil society vs. global state in tendential formation
Poulantzas, Tsoukalas, Bryan, Albo, Panitch & Gindin	International	National	Contingent contradiction between territorial states and global capital flows	Contradictions displaced into class contradictions internal to each social formation, with induced reproduction of the form of the dominant imperialist power within each state

context, the concept of 'empire' – with its connotations of a stable world order which is hard to reverse – might be too static for analyzing the contradictions of this process, as well as the ongoing struggles against it.[119] So the concept

---

119   It should be noted, however, that there are differences in the connotations of the specific uses of the concept of 'empire' in terms of the main problematic of this chapter.

of imperialism remains as a more powerful tool for analyzing the changing character of the power relationships among nation-states in response to international accumulation.

8   Conclusion

This chapter has been motivated by the attempt to formulate an alternative to the left-nationalist and progressive liberal positions that have dominated the analyses of globalization and the state over the past two decades. The key question, in this context, is whether economic globalization also necessitates political globalization. Many progressive liberals, including social democrats and some Marxists, argue that not only economic, but also political processes have become globalized. They do not engage with the contradictions of state restructuring within specific social formations. In contrast, left-nationalists – with a similar ideological diversification – treat both economic and political processes as primarily national. They do not engage with the contradictions of the international accumulation process itself.

This chapter has argued that there is a third alternative: even when economic processes are internationalized, their administration remains primarily a national affair. There are a number of theoretical and historical reasons for this. At the most abstract level, the capitalist state necessarily takes the form of the nation-state because exploitation and coercion are separated in capitalist societies, and the nation-state serves the fragmentation of opposition to capitalism. As the capitalist state is inherently bound up with national identity and nationalist ideology, and their reproduction, the 'objective' need for a transnational state runs up against an immanent limitation: state power, to remain legitimate and therefore serve the needs of national or transnational capital, requires a basis for its hegemonic power over its subaltern population, and that power requires the existence of an 'other', a hostile exterior. And historically, this is even truer in the neoliberal era, as the normative loyalty to the

---

For instance, Panitch and Gindin's concept of 'American empire' implies a distinction between the space of state and space of capital, by defining imperialism at the state level. They argue that "the US imperial order involves ruling with and through other states, themselves relatively autonomous from the imperial center" (2005b: 122). Robinson's concept of "empire of global capital" (2005: 325), on the other hand, implies a non-differentiated space, where imperialism is defined at the level of accumulation rather than state level, therefore trivializing the concept of imperialism by blurring its difference from global capitalism.

state is increasingly attached to political myths, national symbols, and rituals of participation rather than socio-economic resource allocations, as in the previous period. This means that the legitimation function of states, which can only be accomplished through the ideological, cultural, linguistic, historical context of a national setting, comes to the fore. The concept of a transnational capitalist state misses this point by reducing the state to an economic apparatus and disregarding its repressive and ideological functions.

This alternative can explain the contradictions of state restructuring within specific social formations without falling into the pitfalls of either abstract internationalism or nationalism. It has also the political potential, therefore, to move beyond both liberalism and nationalism and their particular units of analysis in their conceptions of the internationalization of capital and the state. This is particularly important for socialist alternatives, as the left is torn between progressive liberalism and left-nationalism, and is suffering from both organizational weakness and ideological disorientation. The belief of many progressive liberals, for instance, that European integration will bring a cosmopolitan democracy stems from the assumption of a territorial coincidence between European capital and its supranational state. Similarly, the belief of left-nationalists in the protectionist alternatives stems from their assumption of a territorial coincidence between national states and their capitals. When we posit that there is, in fact, a necessary territorial non-correspondence between the reproductive logic of capital to internationalize and the institutional and territorial specificity of the state, however, it can be seen that protectionism only serves the agenda of globally expanding capitalists in their struggle for an increased share of the world market, a process that Albo has called 'progressive competitiveness'.[120]

The conceptual emphasis on the very material foundations of the territorial non-correspondence between capital and the state is a necessary underpinning to the making of a socialist alternative today. It implies that the territorial state is still available as a target of oppositional struggles, even if capital is internationalized. The internalization of the management of the international accumulation process by nation-states means that contradictions of imperialism are also displaced into the class contradictions internal to each social formation. This implies that anti-imperialist struggles are now much more part of the anti-capitalist struggles at home, rather than cross-class national alliances against externally defined global forces. The increasing concentration of power in the national state apparatuses through authoritarian statism to

120   Albo (1997).

resolve all these contradictions means that the left has now a very clear target and political terrain. In fact, the shift in the worldwide protests from the global to the national scale, i.e., from the anti-globalization protests of the late 1990s against supranational institutions like WTO, to the national uprisings of the 2010s sparked by the Tahrir Square protests are strong signals of hope in this direction.

CHAPTER 5

The State and Imperialism in International Relations Theory

Ana Garcia and Caio Bugiato

In the past few decades,[1] many have contributed to International Relations (IR) theory with different Marxist-based analyses of the world order.[2] Despite the differences among these analyses, they fulfill a pedagogical gap: IR students should learn, from the beginning, that Marx himself had thought about issues of war and diplomacy in the nineteenth century; that questions about the nature of imperialism at the beginning of the twentieth century were at the heart of the ontological 'first debate' in IR theory between realists and idealists; and that the state is not a coherent unit with a 'national interest,' which relates to others in a conflictual manner within an anarchic realm. Rather, the state is a much more complex space of class relations, and the international realm is historically constituted by the uneven development of capitalist social relations. This chapter argues that Leo Panitch's analysis of the internationalization of the state, American informal empire, and the 'making of global capitalism' should be read, also, as International Relations theory. Historical materialism led Panitch to develop theories and concepts grounded in economic and political dynamics in historical concrete realities. We consider that Panitch's critical thinking occupies a unique place in the field of International Relations, which has been mainly averse to Marxism, and, given such uniqueness, his contributions and interventions to the debates must be known by those interested in IR issues.

Considering Panitch as an International Relations theorist implies a profound discussion of the role and the functions of the state (and its agencies) in their relations with market actors (banks and businesses), as well as rethinking the nature of the current imperialist configuration and mechanisms of domination, which are unlike those of the nineteenth century. In order to understand this, one must consider the processes of internationalization of the state,

---

1   This chapter is a revised and extended version of Garcia and Bugiato (2019).

2   There is a large list of authors who would fit this proposition. We may quote Adam Morton, Alex Callinicos, Andreas Bieler, Bastiaan van Apeldoorn, Brenno Teschke, Ellen Meiksins Wood, Justin Rosenberg, Kees van der Pijl, William Robinson, Stephen Gill, among others.

of production and finance, as well as of the integration of Europe, Japan, and later China into the American informal empire. Nicos Poulantzas' theory of the capitalist state underpins Panitch's (and Gindin's) theoretical formulations. Therefore, in this chapter we will seek to explain the theory of the capitalist state and its internationalization, the construction of the American informal empire, and its contributions to current reflections on the ascension of emerging powers, such as the BRICS and particularly China.

1   The Capitalist State and Its Internationalization

Nicos Poulantzas's analysis of the capitalist state and imperialist relations between the United States and postwar Europe had a great influence on Panitch's theorizing. At the core of Poulantzas's theory were his profound reflections on the relationship between the state and social classes. He understood the capitalist state as a factor of cohesion within a social formation (state/society) crossed by class struggles. This structure of class domination was elucidated by the concept of power bloc. The power bloc comprises the contradictory unity of bourgeois class fractions around general objectives – referring to the maintenance of capitalist relations of production – which does not eliminate the particular objectives of each fraction within the bloc. This unity is guaranteed by the common interest of the fractions in governing the state directly or indirectly.[3]

Poulantzas argued against an 'instrumentalist' view of the state. The nature of the capitalist state is not reducible to the relationship between the individuals and groups that constitute its apparatus. It is a strategic field of relations, a space of material condensation of the relationship between social forces and class fractions. It is able to unify the power bloc by maintaining a relative autonomy from the various class fractions with their particular interests. This autonomy is constitutive of the capitalist state, reflecting the separation between the institutional materiality of the state and the relations of production.[4]

In Poulantzas's theory of imperialism,[5] the power bloc cannot be apprehended on a purely national level, but rather only in a complex international system of capitalist states, in which each takes charge of the interests of national and foreign capital in particular social formations. This international reproduction of capital entails the penetration of foreign capital into other

---

3   Poulantzas (1977).
4   Poulantzas (1978c: 127).
5   Poulantzas (1978a).

social formations, a process that the Poulantzas calls the internalized and induced reproduction of capital – with a tendency to embrace every corner of the world.

Poulantzas directs his analysis of imperialism to the relationship between the central (and not just the central and peripheral) countries, which is reflected in Panitch's analysis of the American empire. According to Poulantzas,[6] the induced reproduction of American monopolistic capitalism within other metropolises meant the expanded reproduction of the political and ideological conditions of the development of American imperialism. European states and others were themselves in charge of the interests of imperialist capital within their own national formation.

Panitch and Gindin drew on Poulantzas' theory to understand present day globalization and imperialism. They did so in three different dimensions.[7] The first concerned the relationship with the production process. The separation of the political from the economic within capitalism involved a distancing of the state from the organization of production, investment, and the appropriation of surplus value. In turn, it maintained the juridical, regulatory and infrastructural framework necessary for the production process to occur, as well as the capacity to police capital-labor relations, manage the macro-economy, and act as the lender of last resort. According to Panitch and Gindin, the role of the capitalist state is not merely reactive. Rather, states have developed sophisticated mechanisms for promoting and orchestrating capital accumulation. Thus, the relative autonomy of the capitalist state does not mean being autonomous from capitalist classes or the economy, but rather having the capacity to act on behalf of the system as a whole (autonomy), while their dependence on the success of overall accumulation for their own legitimacy and reproduction nevertheless leaves those capacities bounded (relative).[8]

The second dimension is the form of political rule. The separation of state from society within capitalism entails a constitutional distancing of political rule from the class structure. The establishment of the rule of law as a liberal political framework for property owners at home, as well as the establishment (or imposition through military intervention) of liberal democracy around the world as the modal form of the capitalist state in the postwar period, exemplifies this.

Finally, the third dimension concerns the national and territorial form of the capitalist state, and the deepening economic ties within a particular

---

6 Poulantzas (1978a).
7 Panitch and Gindin (2005b).
8 Panitch and Gindin (2005b: 2).

territory. Capitalist imperialism meant the spatial extension of the law of value and capitalist social relations, through a process in which the territorial state and its liberal-democratic form were universalized and inscribed into international institutions and international law in the mid-twentieth century. This process, however, took the form of an informal imperialism, within which particular states took responsibility for creating the political and juridical conditions for the general extension and reproduction of capitalism at an international level.[9]

In a 1994 essay, Panitch criticizes Robert W. Cox's reading of the "internationalization of the State,"[10] which would imply a collection of hierarchical changes in the state apparatus (greater power for bureaucratic agencies connected with international finance and trade, subordinating others connected to social sectors), in a way that better meets the pressures of the world market.[11] Panitch argues that, while Cox sees the process of internationalization of the state as being determined from the "outside-in," Poulantzas sees state transformations as arising from contradictory internal formations, i.e., conflicts between fractions of the bourgeoisie and workers. According to Panitch this results not merely in a straightforward change in hierarchy, but rather a transformation in the nature of the very agencies connected to labor and to social services. As he put it, "Ministries of labour, health and welfare are perhaps not so much being subordinated as themselves being restructured" to accommodate the logic of capital accumulation.[12]

In this sense, globalization is not simply the result of market forces. On the contrary, national states – and the American state in particular – are central to the construction of global capitalism, with its role of maintaining property rights, supervising contracts, stabilizing currency, etc. According to Panitch and Gindin, the 'internationalization of the state' means the process through which states encourage and support capitalists in carrying out activities beyond their own borders, always maintaining, however, a national dimension in the processes of capitalist internationalization. Moreover, as the interaction

---

9   Panitch and Gindin (2005b: 2–3).

10   Cox (1987).

11   Cox sees the process of internationalization of the state as based on three elements: the formation of a consensus about the 'needs' and requirements of the world economy; the hierarchically structured participation of the dominant classes in the United States, Europe, and Japan in the formation of this international consensus; structural adjustments within the States to better internalize external pressure on national economies. Within this process, accountability moves from domestic structures to the notion of "international obligations." (Cox, 1987: 254).

12   Panitch (1994: 72).

with foreign capital affects domestic social forces, this in turn contributes to generating that combination of inside and outside pressures through which states come to accept a certain responsibility for reproducing capitalism internationally.[13]

In this way, capitalist states (both central and peripheral) take responsibility for promoting the accumulation of capital, and by doing so contribute to the administration of the international capitalist order managed by the United States. This must be understood in terms of the 'relative autonomy' of the capitalist state, which has the autonomous capacity to act on behalf of the system as a whole, without disconnecting from capitalist classes.[14]

From this perspective, the American state did not dictate this to other states but, instead, introduced parameters within which other states would define their course of action.[15] In the process of supporting the export of capital and the expansion of its multinationals, the American state assumed an imperialistic and policing role, with growing responsibility in the creation of political and juridical conditions for the extension and reproduction of capitalism at an international level. The internationalization of the American state was not easy. It required the development of the capacities of state agencies to promote American products around the world, lowering its commercial tariffs and those of other states as well as policing commercial and investment regimes in order to guarantee the free circulation and accumulation of capital around the world – not only American capital. Panitch and Gindin stress the active role of different state agencies, such as the Judiciary, the Treasury, the Federal Reserve, and other executive departments.[16]

The expansion of American multinationals was a fundamental ingredient in the construction of its imperial role. The 'internationalization of production' gathered pace in the 1920s, but it was essentially in the 1950s with the reconstruction of the European economies that multinational corporations became not only economic, but essential political players. They fostered the construction of institutional, juridical, and economic institutions of European integration in order to circulate and operate in the region. This involved national treatment of foreign investors, free repatriation of profit, a unified regime of exchange and tariffs, as well as labor laws that favored capital, both American and European. According to Panitch and Gindin, the very conception of the European firm started to emulate the US corporate model. Thus,

---

13   Panitch and Gindin (2012: 4).
14   Panitch and Gindin (2012: 4).
15   Panitch and Gindin (2012: 8).
16   Panitch and Gindin (2012: 31–35).

strong ties were formed between American and European capitalists, in a process seen as the "Canadianization" of Europe.[17]

Finally, another crucial aspect in the construction of global capitalism was the 'internationalization of finance', linked to the processes of internationalization of the American state and production. The growing integration of the City of London with the American financial market originated with the Eurodollar market, which led to the continuous process of ending capital controls and restructuring banking regulations. Panitch and Gindin sustain that the London Eurodollar market was complementary (and not competitive or threatening) to Wall Street, as American and New York investment banks were investing more and dominating that market. In the 1960s, the growth of the American financial sector had already assumed international dimensions, with American practices and institutions appearing in the integration and expansion of financial markets around the world. The triad Treasury-Fed-Wall Street, and with them the Treasury's securities market, became increasingly central to global financial operations linked to the domestic US financial market. Thus, the regulatory regime established after the 1929 crisis[18] blurred the international expansion of US banks along with non-financial multinational corporations with the development of the unregulated Eurodollar market, extending the reach of American financial operations well beyond its borders.[19]

The result of all this was that the expansion of markets and capitalist social relations depended on states, in particular the US state. The United States developed the interest and the capacity to superintend the construction of capitalism globally. However, they did not do this alone but through a high level of integration between advanced capitalist states, and later also China. The management of capitalist globalization relied on interstate commitment, particularly connections through G7 (and later the G20), that, at times of crisis, managed to avoid protectionism and to strengthen the role of the United States as lender of last resort.

---

17   Panitch and Gindin (2012: 113–115).
18   The *Glass-Steagall Act* came into force after the 1929 crisis with the aim of separating commercial banking activities from investment banking. The former dealt with the general public's current accounting, while the latter was able to carry out risky operations overseas without directly impacting people's bank accounts. This legislation was gradually deconstructed through pressure from American banks.
19   Panitch and Gindin (2012: 117–22).

2   Rethinking Imperialism as American Informal Empire

The internationalization of the state, of production, and of finance constituted what Panitch and Gindin call "informal empire." They are critical of classical theories of imperialism, such as those of Hobson and Lenin. In their discussion with the classics, Panitch and Gindin maintained that a new theory of imperialism must transcend the theory of inter-imperial rivalry.[20] In their focus on the 'stages' of capitalism, classical scholars failed to pay sufficient attention to the spatial dimension of the internationalization of capital. Furthermore, they had elevated a "conjunctural moment of inter-imperial rivalry to an immutable law of capitalist globalization."[21] Capital exportation was not founded on over-accumulation of capital in the metropolises, but on the accelerated pressures of competition and opportunities elsewhere, along with the strategies and emerging capacities arising from developing capitalism that spurred and eased international expansion at the end of the nineteenth century.[22]

Hence, there would not have been an exhaustion of consumer possibilities in the central countries. New prospects of internal accumulation were introduced through technological development and unequal competition. Imperialism proved not to be a unilateral movement of capitalist expansion "inside-out," but a two-way one of deepening capitalist relations at home and spreading capital abroad. Therefore, although outward capital expansion means that a certain degree of monopolization has been reached at a domestic level, it does not mean that the monopolies and conglomerations have saturated the possibilities of accumulation.[23]

Panitch and Gindin state that the relationship between imperialism and capitalism must be understood through an extension of theory of the capitalist state, and not as a derivation of theories of economic stages and crises. In their words,

> When states pave the way for their national capital's expansion abroad, or even when they follow and manage that expansion, this can only be understood in terms of these states' relatively autonomous role in maintaining social order and securing conditions for capital accumulation.[24]

---

20   Panitch and Gindin (2004b).
21   Panitch and Gindin (2004b: 5).
22   Panitch and Gindin (2006: 25).
23   Panitch and Gindin (2006).
24   Panitch and Gindin (2004b: 7).

In the phase of imperialism under the domination of the US, a new theory is required to explain "what made plausible the American state's insistence that it was not imperialistic, and how this was put into practice and institutionalized; and conversely, what today makes implausible the American state's insistence that it is not imperialistic ..."[25] Panitch and Gindin, therefore, highlight the need to analyze imperialism historically and socially in relation to transformations in capitalism.

According to Panitch and Gindin, imperial networks and institutional liaisons, which were formerly related to the North-South relationship (formal, colonial empires), started to be established between the US and the main capitalist countries, in particular in Europe, in the period following the Second World War. Hence, the "American informal empire" is marked by the capacity of the US to penetrate and coordinate other leading capitalist states. The dynamism of American capitalism (and its worldwide appeal) combined with a universal language of the ideology of liberal democracy supported the capacity of the informal empire to go beyond former empire.[26] In building modern multinational corporations, with direct foreign investment in production and services, the American informal empire proved more capable of penetrating other social formations, even in more developed economies.

Curiously, the US presented itself as anti-imperialist and supported processes of decolonization in the 20th century. At the same time, the United States claimed the right to intervene against other sovereign states and withheld interpretation of international rules and norms.[27] According to Panitch and Gindin: "only the American state could arrogate to itself the right to intervene against the sovereignty of other states (which it repeatedly did around the world), and only the American state reserved for itself the 'sovereign' right to reject international norms and laws when necessary. It is in this sense that only the American state was actively 'imperialistic'.[28] This reflection is evident in the frank statement of the ex-Secretary of State of the Bill Clinton

---

25   Panitch and Gindin (2004b: 4).
26   Informal empires are formed by means of economic and cultural penetration in other states, supported by political and military coordination with independent governments. In the view of the authors, the principal factor that determined the change in the expansion of formal empires, after 1880, was England's incapacity to incorporate the emerging capitalist powers of Germany, the US, and Japan into its "imperialism of free trade" (Panitch and Gindin, 2004b: 8).
27   Panitch and Gindin (2012: 12).
28   Panitch and Gindin (2004b: 16).

administration, Madeleine Albright, "If we have to use force, it is because we are America. We are the indispensable nation."[29]

Panitch and Gindin's analysis differs from critical theories based on Gramscian International Relations (such as Robert Cox) in arguing that the US did not have to incorporate the demands of subordinate classes in other states into the construction of its empire. The American informal empire was hegemonic in terms of other states and capitalist classes, however even with all the cultural and economic penetration of the US into other societies, this never became the "direct transfer of popular loyalty" of other populations to the American state. Active consent to the domination of the informal empire was mediated by the legitimacy that other states retained or established on behalf of any particular project of the American state, through the capitalist classes in these other countries. In this way, the world capitalist order was organized and regulated through the reconstruction of other states' bureaucratic, coercive, juridical institutions and practices to secure the accumulation of capital everywhere – and thus with territorial occupation no longer a foundation of the imperial strategy.[30]

In this sense, Panitch and Gindin seek to dismantle another common-sense notion within Marxism (classical and contemporary) as well as realism in International Relations: the expectation of a resurgence of inter-imperial rivalry (or of revisionist powers in the case of realism). The rise of Japan in the 1980s, and the rise of China in the 2000s, brought this discussion to the fore. In Panitch and Gindin's view, these analyses fail to perceive the depth of the incorporation of other advanced capitalist states into the new American empire. Contrary to inter-imperialist rivalry, the US supported the revival of its economic competitors through loans, aid, and favorable trading conditions. The growing flows of investment from Europe and Japan into the US, and vice versa, lent support to the profound integration of global production networks.[31]

The pace of Europe's integration into the American informal empire quickened with a succession of regional integration agreements. Panitch and Gindin argue that European integration followed financial liberalization and the pressure of business associations, both European and American. Within this context, the scope for trade union demands was limited. From the outset, monetary integration was accompanied by the removal of capital controls, reinforcing the commitment of European states to fiscal rules (defined in the

---

29   Panitch and Gindin (2004b: 3).
30   Panitch and Gindin (2004b: 32).
31   Panitch and Gindin (2012: 10).

Maastricht Treaty), and strengthening European financial markets within guidelines set down by the US. The integration of Europe into the American informal empire is also apparent in the emulation of American practices by European businesses and banks, accentuating financial and industrial link-ages. American banks and businesses played a central role in mergers and acquisitions in Europe, driving integration and encouraging the development of a European common market. This was not a one-way street, with an increasing flow of investment and trade from Europe to the US.[32]

The emergence of Japan as a powerhouse has also been subject to the various forms of integration into global capitalism driven by the US. According to Panitch and Gindin, the 1970s financial crisis spurred Japan's financial integration into global circles. It controlled inflation more quickly and its workers' organizations were less militant than those of Europe and the US. Japanese businesses increased their investment in manufacturing sectors, increasing productivity and the levels of exploitation of workers. Banks, in turn, underwent a rapid process of internationalization and actively bought bonds overseas, in particular US Treasury bonds. This increased Japan's dependency on the US financial market. In the 1980s, the US was the main importer of Japanese products, such as cars, putting the US automobile sector under pressure and leading to mass lay-offs of workers. Panitch and Gindin claim that Japan never showed any interest in substituting the dollar with the yen, and far less in taking responsibility for global financial leadership. In the 1990s, Japan, as a member of G7, lived through the worst contradictions associated with the realization of global capitalism, and the possibility of it substituting the US as the hegemonic power was no longer being discussed.[33]

3   Other Perspectives on Current Imperialism and Global Rivalry

It is worth noting that others within the Marxist tradition in International Relations have sustained the idea of an end of inter-imperial rivalry in the age of globalization and imperialism following the Cold War. Yet, they did so in an opposite manner to Panitch and Gindin's concept of informal empire. Authors such as Michael Hardt and Antonio Negri and William Robinson argue, in general terms, that global capitalism is politically and economically organized along transnational (and not international) lines.[34] According to

---

32   Panitch and Gindin (2012: 196).
33   Panitch and Gindin (2012: 203–11).
34   Hardt and Negri (2000); Robinson (2004).

this view, internal bourgeoisies and national states would be extinct; instead, a transnational capitalist class would be globally unified, and operate through supra-national entities (such as international organizations) that would usurp the sovereignty and authority of particular populations and territories from nation-states. For this reason, imperialist disputes and geopolitical rivalries would have ended, as the inter-state system would gradually integrate into an 'empire', or a transnational system.

Others take a different perspective and see a permanence of imperialist rivalry and the reproduction of imperialist practices in various parts of the world. They do not deny the centrality of the United States in imperial global capitalism, but bring new elements to the analyses. David Harvey claims that there were many types of empire not just one, and these many different imperialisms are defined not in rigid and abstract ways, but rather correspond to "realities on the ground."[35] He distinguishes the new imperialism by the continuous practice of primitive accumulation, which is based on violent practices of new and continuous expropriations: accumulation by dispossession.[36] For Harvey, capitalism faces constant crises of capital realization, which do not come from under-consumption but from over-accumulation of surplus. Over-accumulation in a given territorial system generates a capital surplus, which is displaced onto other territories – what Harvey calls a spatio-temporal fix. Thus, crises in capitalism would be long and comprehensive phases of devaluation and destruction of surplus capital that cannot be profitably absorbed.

Harvey argues that, in order to identify what is new in the "new imperialism," it is necessary to "follow the capital surpluses and look for the geographical and territorially-based practices that attach to their absorption or devaluation."[37] For Harvey, we live in a world where the problem of absorbing the surplus is more acute than ever, and imperialist practices are beginning to emerge in East and Southwest Asia. In this region, China is "looking to search out ways to dispose of its own capital surpluses by re-asserting a very ancient logic of its own conception of territorial power."[38] Harvey argues that an accurate understanding of imperialism must go beyond the traditional notion of North-South domination and look at a series of imperialist practices dispersed through an unequal geography of distribution of the capital surplus.

---

35   Harvey (2018).
36   Harvey (2003).
37   Harvey (2007: 70).
38   Harvey (2007: 70).

In a different direction, Alex Callinicos defends the permanence of geopolitical global rivalry after the Cold War.[39] For him, imperialism is a specific form of systemic political domination that is broad, expansionist, and produces differences and inequalities. Imperialist capitalism is constituted by the intersection of two forms of competition: economic and geopolitical. Callinicos argues that after the end of World War II the United States built a strategy of international power, seeking to deepen alliances with Western Europe and Japan: the so-called triad. In this sense, globalization would be a tacit, non-formal agreement between imperialist states in the contemporary world. Callinicos points out that the exercise of power by the triad states has come to rely on new instruments – international organizations – that allow domination not necessarily via direct military intervention and control of territories. NATO, the UN Security Council, the Marshall Plan, and the Bretton Woods Agreement have ensured that the United States leads this bloc of power, with allies in key regions of the globe, particularly Western Europe and East Asia. Above all, this alliance was intended to contain the progress of the USSR and China in their respective regions. The existence of the triad does not mean that there are no internal contradictions between these states. When conflicts intensify and possibilities for understanding or persuasion are exhausted, the use of force becomes imperative: the present world is not a concert of the great powers.

Harvey and Callinicos, each in their own way, understand that global capitalism is embedded in imperialist conflicts and geopolitical rivalries. Economic crises and the competitive logic of capitalism compel states and dominant classes to seek new forms of accumulation beyond their borders. This geopolitical competition would generate conflicts over territory, natural resources, influence over states and security, and at its extreme, armed conflict. Imperialism in the system of states in competition would denote instability in international relations and its historical propensity for war, while capitalism persists.

4   Contributions to an Analysis of the BRICS and the Rise of China

Panitch and Gindin analyze the rise of the current emerging powers, in particular China, in terms of their integration into American informal empire, and not as a challenge to it. This does not mean that economic competition between different centers of accumulation is non-existent. It is, however, mitigated by

---

39   Callinicos (2007; 2009).

the construction of global capitalism: through internationally integrated networks of production and trade, as well as the central position of the dollar and Treasury bonds in global financial flows, and the construction of institutional, juridical, and economic infrastructure of other national states in accordance with the American state's rules, guaranteeing that capital (foreign and domestic) accumulation is protected.

According to Panitch, the rise of the great economies of the 'Global South', that gained pace with the financial crises, particularly that of 2008, essentially further increased the US's imperial responsibilities.[40] The creation of the G20 as an initiative of the American Treasury during the Asian crisis in the 1990s has evidenced the need (and ability) for the American state to limit damage and manage the way out of crises with other economies. Neither China nor Russia have demonstrated any capacity or interest in taking on wide-ranging responsibilities for the management of global capitalism, as this would require even greater liberalization of their economies.[41] Therefore, the G20 was designed to lead the emerging economies to take responsibility in the new international financial architecture too, while legitimizing the continued role of the US as supervisor of an increasingly volatile global capitalism.[42]

Global financialization involved a new global division of labor, with the transfer of parts of manufacturing (hierarchically divided) to developing countries. The economic growth of China and of other countries in Eastern Asia was fundamentally due to the hierarchical expansion of world manufacturing, whose central players were, once again, US transnational corporations. According to Panitch and Gindin, this integrated network of production depends on the US consumer market (the growth and maintenance of which depend, in turn, on household debts), along with the outflow of US investments through the expansion of its multinationals and inflows from other countries into the American market. The latter systematically created challenges to the US balance of trade, stretching the ability of the American state to sustain global capitalism and manage domestic pressures.[43]

---

40   Panitch (2014; 2015).
41   Panitch (2014: 98).
42   Panitch (2015: 64).
43   Panitch and Gindin (2012: 283). An illustrative example of this integrated network of production and finance is the corporation Apple, which has transferred most of its manufacturing to China, yet sells its products at prices based on the American consumer market. Thus, it achieves very high profit margins through the exploitation of the Chinese workforce, while generating a trade deficit for the US economy (Panitch and Gindin, 2012: 291).

The beginning of the opening up of the Chinese economy in the 1970s coincided with a new stage in the American informal empire following the crisis in that period. The 'open door' policy opened the Chinese market and welcomed global capital by establishing a series of measures that were favorable to multinational corporations. The rise of China was driven, then, by the arrival of a considerable number of important foreign firms, mainly from the US, in sectors that are a source of knowledge and technology, setting up particularly in Hong Kong.[44] Foreign capital migrated to China for reasons that go beyond low salaries and infrastructure – this was essentially a question of trust in the Chinese state as protector and guarantor of their investments:

> Among the various reasons why foreign capitalists invested in China – a cheap labour force, the potentially massive domestic market, high quality public infrastructure in transportation, communications and education – *confidence that their investments would be protected by the state* was far from the least important.[45]

Thus, we come to a fundamental issue for Panitch: China has to be analyzed (and so the other BRICS) based on the theory of the capitalist state. In contesting Giovanni Arrighi's thesis in *Adam Smith in Beijing*[46] – in which he sustains the idea that the Chinese state played the role of 'invisible hand', using the market and free-competition as an instrument of economic development, thus fulfilling its own 'national interest' – Panitch reaffirms that, what is determinant of the capitalist state is its relationship with the dominant class *as a whole* and not with specific sectors, which may or may not compete with each other.[47] The specific mode of organization of the capitalist state, its function as guarantor of relationships of property, reproducer of capital-labor relations, and upholder of accumulation is incongruent with of Arrighi's fragile concept. For Panitch, the commodification of the workforce and the integration of workers into a society based on production and consumption through market relations, defines the nature of economic development in contemporary China.[48] In this scenario, it is difficult to accept the unproblematized notion of 'national interest' in a class society.[49]

---

44   Panitch and Gindin (2013: 149–50).
45   Panitch and Gindin (2013: 150, emphasis added).
46   Arrighi (2007).
47   Panitch (2010).
48   Panitch (2010: 84–85).
49   Panitch (2010: 83).

In this sense, Panitch disagreed with Arrighi on the US's loss of capacity to sustain its imperial power, as this would confuse temporary contradictions ('signs of crisis') with long-term structural contradictions. The flow of capital from Eastern Asia to the US, by increasing the trade deficit, also demonstrates its capacity to sustain the global circulation of capital. The US project was never to rule the world directly, nor to pass this task on to international institutions, but rather to conceive a project of global capitalism consistent with its attempt to make or maintain other states as capitalist, with institutions and bureaucratic, coercive, and juridical practices that would guarantee the accumulation of capital everywhere. The nature of the US as the capitalist empire of the twentieth century has been misunderstood by Arrighi – in his understanding, the US was frustrated in its search to build a 'global state' with direct territorial occupation and strict defense of US capital.[50] For Panitch, the material bases of the American informal empire were far from being exhausted.

5   Conclusion: Transcending Pessimism

In this chapter, we have outlined the contributions of Leo Panitch's theoretical framework to rethink categories that are central to International Relations, especially the state and imperialism. To this end, we investigated his discussion on the internationalization of the state, production, and finance that underpins what he came to call the American informal empire, and the integration of Europe, Japan, and later China into global capitalism.

The conception of the American informal empire built upon the penetration and coordination of other states to guarantee the reproduction of capitalist relations in each social formation, as well as at a global level, has been a major influence for our analyses of 'South-South' foreign direct investments (FDI) and the rise of BRICS. All BRICS countries are mainly recipients of FDI from US, European, and Japanese multinational corporations. The capitalist development of the BRICS took place, in the past few decades, by creating and facilitating conditions for accumulation of foreign capital within their territories, supported, among other mechanisms, by the framework of investment protection agreements for foreign capital to come and stay 'in'.[51] However, the other side of the coin is that the rise of the BRICS can also lead to new cycles of capital accumulation and to new expropriations in other countries and

---

50   Panitch (2010: 81–82).
51   Garcia (2017).

regions of the 'South'. As empirically discussed in different works,[52] the BRICS end up reproducing in 'South-South relations' the same logic of competition over natural resources, labor power, and market access that is imperialist in nature.[53] In Africa and Latin America, multinational corporations and states have developed competitive strategies and approaches, producing new power hierarchies within the 'South and East'.

We conclude by remarking that Leo Panitch was a declared socialist and internationalist. At the end of the twentieth century, and beginning of the twenty-first century, in the absence of concrete alternatives to capitalism, he stated that there is a need to transcend political pessimism and revive utopia. A socialist project in the twenty-first century must rethink the relationship between state and democracy, and be committed to the development of skills that enable the envisioning of utopian objectives. In this way, a socialist project must enhance different economic, social, environmental, gender, and living dimensions, maintaining a utopian vision and sensitivity.[54] Panitch was an intellectual who was dedicated to the struggles in the wider spheres of politics and in the 'small' spheres of everyday life. His intellectual formulations corresponded to his style of dealing with students, staff, and regular people in day-to-day life; yet another lesson to students of International Relations who dare to dream of changing the world.

---

52   Bond and Garcia (2018); Garcia and Kato (2020).
53   In contrast, Bugiato's analyzes of the Brazilian bourgeoisie and foreign policy claim that at least the Brazilian State cannot be considered imperialist (Bugiatio, 2014 and 2017).
54   Panitch (2001: 204–6).

CHAPTER 6

Bringing Class Back In

The State, the 'Pink Tide' and the Case of Argentina

Ruth Felder

The Latin American 'Pink Tide' of the 2000s brought about renewed debates about development strategies and the role of the state in development. In this context, an emerging Latin American 'neo-developmentalist' policy blueprint gave a central role to the state in renewing conditions for economic growth and reversing the dismal social indicators resulting from neoliberal reforms. The implementation of these neo-developmentalist policies was initially instrumental in fueling growth and improving the well-being of many Latin Americans. But by the turn of the decade, they gradually became less effective as the political consensus that had made them possible was waning. By mid-2010s, right-wing governments were coming to power in the region with the promise of putting an end to the Pink Tide's alleged 'policy mismanagement'. The decline of the neo-developmentalist policy blueprint raises questions about the role of the state in development and its capacity to overcome the protracted economic and social problems of the region.

The Pink Tide took several forms – supporting national control over resource extraction in Bolivia; the building of local bases of power and redistribution through 're-nationalization' of oil revenues in Venezuela; to more conventional forms of developmentalism combined with massive anti-poverty policies in Brazil and Argentina; and many others. The Argentinian case took still another course in struggle over the policy regime of the central economic apparatuses of the state, and conflict with creditors over sovereign debt. In this chapter, I will focus on the experience of Argentina to explore the scope and limitations of the neo-developmentalist policy blueprint. The country emerged as a highly successful case in the early 2000s only to become an example of the failure of neo-developmentalist policies to create conditions for sustainable growth by the end of the decade. This trajectory invites us to reflect about the reasons that account for the success or failure of development strategies and the policy orientations associated with them.

1   The Neo-developmentalist Alternative to Latin America's
      Development Impasse

Latin American neo-developmentalism emerged in the early 2000s as a
policy response to the limitations of neoliberalism and as a way for Latin
American economies, especially the middle-income economies of the region,
to transcend their subordinated position in the international division of labor.[1]
Briefly, the neo-developmentalists take distance from the neoliberal agenda
for liberalization and deregulation to focus on the role of the state in improving the competitiveness of domestic actors in a context of intensified global
competition.[2] Exchange and interest rate regulations, combined with synergies with transnationalized companies that are in a better position to expand
output, are expected to allow countries to catch up with developed economies.
Neo-developmentalism, with its emphasis on exports, is also different from the
classical Latin American developmentalism of the 1940s-1960s in its rejection
of the problems associated with the unequal terms of trade between center
and periphery.[3] Differences around the action of the state are especially telling. Neo-developmentalists argue for a state that supports markets rather than
replacing them, and that creates incentives for improving the efficiency and
competitiveness of private economic actors rather than protecting inefficient
and uncompetitive ones.[4]

    Latin American neo-developmentalism has not been free from contro-
versy. For some, the search for alternatives to neoliberal policies brought back
economic populism, including protectionism, intrusive regulations and irre-
sponsible distributive policies that were destined to fail.[5] This rejection of neo-
developmentalism has been politically productive to catalyzing opposition to
the Pink Tide, but its normative tone makes it ineffective to understand the
scope and limitations to neo-developmentalist experiences. More sympathetic
analysts and critics from the left have raised questions about the extent to
which the neo-developmentalist strategies were effectively leaving neoliberalism behind, the extent to which the focus on the state dismantles the core of

---

1   The systematic discussion of the meaning of development and the analysis of the origins,
    arguments and controversies around new-developmentalism are beyond the limits of this
    chapter. Here I only present a brief summary of some neo-developmentalist ideas to analyze
    the Argentinean case.
2   Boschi and Gaitán (2009).
3   Katz (2014).
4   Bresser Pereira (2013).
5   Edwards (2019).

the neoliberal agenda, and the problems associated with the juxtaposition of neoliberal and neo-developmentalist policies, among others.[6] The decline of neo-developmentalism has been associated with several causes, including the end of the commodity boom, the increasing lack of trust in governments by large sectors of the population of the countries, the effects of policy mistakes, and the absence of political will to push for change.[7] Without neglecting the effects of these factors, they do not suffice to explain why problems became critical when they did and why policy choices became gradually constrained.[8]

The changing balances of forces underlying the period of economic growth of the early 2000s, I will argue, led to the exacerbation of distributive disputes, eroded the capacity of the state to boost growth and manage conflict, and ultimately put limits to the economic sustainability and the political viability of the neo-developmentalist strategy.

Before moving on to discuss the case of Argentina, a few words about the neo-developmentalist state are in order. First, the neo-developmentalist state is a proactive state that engages in relations of power and cooperation with business with the purpose of aligning their action with its own strategic goals but is autonomous from them.[9] Second, the state is expected to be able to improve domestic competitiveness regardless of the initial position of the country.[10] Underlying these two premises is an overstatement of the capacities of the state and a neglect of the structural limitations to its action in seizing the benefits of global competition and managing class conflict.

This overstatement is closely linked with what Poulantzas characterizes as the state as a subject: a state that stands above society and has its own sources of power. From this point of view, development revolves around the will of the state but this will remains unexplained.[11] An interpretation of the recent Latin American experiences that transcends this limitation has to bring class back to the analysis of the state, as argued by Leo Panitch over numerous texts, and pays attention to the specific forms in which class relations and class struggles that express themselves within the sphere of the state.[12] A class perspective also makes it possible to move beyond abstract formulations about state capacities

---

6   See, for instance, Ban (2013); Morais and Saad Filho (2012); Ramírez Gallegos (2016).

7   Pereira (2020); Grugel and Riggiriozzi (2018); Webber (2019); Wylde (2018).

8   Rojas (2018).

9   Fine (2013).

10   Bruff and Ebenau (2014).

11   Poulantzas (2008).

12   For examples see: Panitch (2002; 2001).

as inherent to the neo-developmentalist state to identify the factors that affect the state's ability to create incentives for private actors and appropriate and allocate resources in different conjunctures. This is central to make sense of changes in the trajectories of the Latin American neo-developmentalist states, the Argentinean state among them, and the shift from a virtuous moment of robust growth, favorable social indicators and widespread consensus to the demise of new-developmentalism amidst an economic slowdown and a plateau in the improvement of social indicators. Before focusing on this shift in Argentina, I will briefly summarize the period of neoliberal reforms in the country, paying attention to the factors that created conditions for neo-developmentalist policies in the 2000s.

2 Neoliberal Reforms and Their Crisis

By the end of the 'lost decade' of the 1980s, which in the case of Argentina culminated in a hyperinflationary crisis in 1989, Carlos Menem (1989–99) won the presidential election and announced an ambitious plan for privatizing state-owned companies and liberalizing the economy as the way to reduce state spending, attract investments, and leave instability and stagnation definitively behind.[13] In addition to a broad range of institutional reforms, in 1991 the Argentinean peso was pegged to the US dollar to control inflation while the sovereign debt in arrears was restructured, thus allowing the country to regain access to international credit. By the mid-1990s, reforms, macroeconomic stabilization, and massive capital inflows created conditions for growth and resulted in some improvements in the extremely negative social consequences of hyperinflation. The recovery also catalyzed support from domestic and international investors and the International Financial Institutions (IFIs) and helped to make the costs of reforms socially tolerable. But the currency peg led to a gradual appreciation of the Argentinean peso, which, combined with trade liberalization, put the competitiveness of domestic manufacturing to the test, while the burden of sovereign debt was growing. By 1998, all this combined with international financial turmoil and the falling prices of Argentinean exports resulted in a long recession, rising unemployment, poverty, and growing social unrest. Declining economic performance also raised questions about the ability of the Argentinean state to meet its financial commitments, which triggered a rise in the country risk premium and augmented

---

13 I draw upon my primary research in the historical narrative that follows. See Felder (2013).

the costs of debt servicing. Thus, policymaking became increasingly contradictory, reflecting the tensions between the need to deepen austerity and reassure creditors and the need to allocate fiscal resources to de-escalate social conflict and address the demands of politicians and domestic economic actors who were withdrawing support for the government.

By 1999, the government focused on tightening austerity hoping it would boost the confidence of creditors and recreate conditions for growth. But austerity was more difficult to impose amidst rising social conflict and, at the same time, less effective for gaining the support of the IFIs and creditors, as it was now taken as evidence of the financial weakness of the Argentinean state. By 2001, capital flight was putting the domestic financial system on the brink of collapse. Unemployment and poverty were reaching unprecedented levels, while employed and unemployed workers and middle-class groups affected by austerity and recession were converging in demonstrations, strikes, road blockades, and riots. The government's attempt to further austerity aggravated social anger and ended in a social rebellion and a major political crisis, with President Fernando de la Rúa's (1999–2001) resignation and the appointment of Peronist Senator Adolfo Rodríguez Saá(2001) as the provisional president.

The political crisis opened a period of disputes about the desirable growth strategy for the country and the policies and institutional arrangements required to achieve it. As the following section will show, policy reorientations materialized through a conflict-ridden process in which the neo-developmentalist strategy took shape.

3   Hitting Bottom: Default, Devaluation, Stagnation and
       Political Crisis

In a context of the uncertainty about the future of the economy, intense social conflict and a serious legitimacy crisis of the early 2000s, the government was unable to allocate the costs of the crisis and create new conditions for growth. This inability was expressed in a succession of short-lived and erratic policies that would only gradually acquire a more defined direction.

In late 2001, Rodríguez Saá took power amidst disagreements between, on the one hand, some government officials, pundits, the IMF, and the US government who defended a deepening of austerity to regain access to international financial markets; and, on the other hand, those politicians, government officials, economists, and domestic business organizations who pushed for policy changes that would improve the competitiveness of domestic capital and help manage acute social conflict. Unable to mediate between these two options

and without resources to service the sovereign debt or access to credit to refi-
nance it, the government defaulted on part of this debt with the purpose of
renegotiating its terms. Amidst international distrust created by this decision,
acute fiscal hardship, social unrest, and lack of support from his own party,
Rodríguez Saá resigned one week after his appointment and was replaced by
Peronist Senator Eduardo Duhalde (2001–03).

One of Duhalde's first decisions was to abandon the currency peg and let
the peso depreciate, thus tipping the scale in favor of exporters and manufacturers producing for the domestic market, who would now enjoy a higher level
of protection from external competition, and against banks and the foreign
owners of public utilities, who saw the international value of their domestic
assets depreciate.[14] In addition, export duties on several commodities were
imposed and an 'economic emergency' was declared, granting the government
broad powers to introduce legal and institutional changes, allocate resources,
and cancel or postpone commitments in order to manage the immediate consequences of the crisis.

The devaluation of the peso triggered a resurgence of inflation, which had a
strong impact on the purchasing power of wage earners who, in a situation of
extraordinarily high unemployment, were in a weak position to demand wage
rises. Thus, the already high levels of poverty worsened, which combined with
the intense social unrest of the period, raised warnings about the governance
of the country and called for the rapid implementation of massive social assistance programs.[15]

In the second half of 2002, the government challenged IMF's preference for
a free-floating exchange rate regime and introduced exchange regulations that
succeeded in counteracting speculation. This in turn led to a fall in inflation,
which, combined with the more competitive exchange rate that followed the
devaluation, created better conditions for growth. Then, rising exports and an
incipient recovery of the domestic market started to reverse a long period of
recession.

The end of the period of acute economic crisis, however, did not solve the
multiple problems faced by the state during 2002. On the one hand, negotiations with the IMF were reaching a dead end, as it kept demanding an
overly ambitious reformist program to grant assistance and the government
was coming up against serious political obstacles to meeting these demands.
The absence of IMF's support made negotiations with private holders of the

---

14   Gaggero and Wainer (2004).
15   Logiudice (2011).

defaulted debt unfeasible and blocked access to international borrowing.[16] This lack of international credit and the government's efforts to regain access to it were important elements in the severity of the crisis. But the default would also be instrumental in the recovery as it gave the state some fiscal relief and, equally important, it freed economic policymaking from the need to issue political signals aimed at rolling over the debt.

In addition, macroeconomic stabilization did not immediately translate into political stability. On the contrary, social mobilization continued during most of 2002 and the government's attempts to control it through repression aggravated the political crisis and, ultimately, acted as a catalyst for Duhalde's resignation and the calling of an anticipated presidential election. Néstor Kirchner (2003–07), the governor of the southern province of Santa Cruz and the candidate fielded by Duhalde, became the president in May 2003.

In the following years, social mobilization would decline in a context of robust growth and the reconstitution of the legitimacy of the state. But the period of growth would also strengthen the political initiative of the capitalist fractions leading it, including their capacity to veto policies that affected their interests. These moments are the focus of the following two sections.

4   Up from the Ashes: Economic Recovery and the Making of the Post-neoliberal Consensus

Kirchner took power acknowledging the need to address the social and political consequences of the crisis of neoliberal reforms and the political limits to further austerity. He criticized the privileges of powerful economic actors and corporations and argued for a strategy of "growth with social inclusion" that reserved a central role for the state.[17] In the aftermath of the 2001 social uprising, Kirchner's challenges to the premises of neoliberalism was not only politically feasible, but central for rebuilding the legitimacy of state. Yet, the way out from the crisis not only required the rebuilding of the legitimacy of the state but also the reestablishment of conditions for capital accumulation.[18] This tension would inform economic policymaking in the following years.

When Kirchner assumed power, the economic recovery initiated in late 2002 was consolidating based on the competitive effects of the devaluation and rising international commodity prices that constituted the bulk of Argentina's

---

16   Damill, Frenkel and Rapetti (2005).
17   Kirchner (2003).
18   Piva (2018).

exports.[19] Trade balances became positive, and fiscal balances also improved with growing state revenues and spending. Gradually, unemployment dropped, and workers' incomes experienced some recovery. Wage increases and lower unemployment, combined with the implementation of comprehensive social assistance programs, gradually helped to reduce poverty.

As the economic recovery progressed, the government released its proposal for restructuring the defaulted sovereign debt. In 2005, over 70 percent of creditors accepted an average 55 percent reduction in the principal of the debt, lower interest rates, longer maturities, and a higher proportion of the debt denominated in Argentinean pesos.[20] After the restructuring, the government announced that it would not meet the demands of holdouts. In 2006, the government cancelled the IMF's assistance program by paying off Argentina's entire debt with the institution using Central Bank's foreign reserves. These measures alleviated the burden of debt servicing and gave the state more room to intervene in the economy in ways that would have been unfeasible in the context of an IMF assistance program. Negotiations with creditors and the IMF were also an opportunity for the government to garner domestic support by stressing the need to prioritize the most urgent predicaments of the population over the interests of international finance. In addition, the state actively manipulated the exchange rate to improve the competitiveness of Argentinean exports, set caps to the price of public utilities, expanded state spending and granted subsidies to diverse economic activities.

By the mid-2000s, social conflict was declining while social movements and organizations, especially the movements of unemployed workers, which had led massive social mobilizations in the late 1990s and early 2000s, were undergoing important changes. First, the fall of unemployment was leading to a reduction in the number of members in these organizations. Then, the reorientation of economic policies and the more open attitude of the Kirchner administration toward some of their demands led several organizations to turn their previous confrontational stance into moderate opposition or active support to the government. The government, at the same time, was seeking the support of the traditional union leadership – which has historically tended to defuse mobilization and conflict – rather than that of the unemployed workers' movements and other more progressive groups, including those that had been more clearly aligned with its policies since 2003.[21] The fall of unemployment and the revitalization of collective bargaining gave this union leadership

---

19   Costa, Kicillof and Nahón (2004).
20   Damill, Frenkel and Rapetti (2005).
21   Massetti (2010).

a renewed political relevance, and some unions in the most dynamic economic sectors obtained important wage rises for their workers. Workers' gains,
however, were unevenly distributed in a highly fragmented labor market with
a very large number of precarious and informal workers.[22]

This way out of the crisis, with vigorous growth rates, challenges to international finance, and improvements in several critical social indicators strengthened the appeal of the neo-developmentalist policy orientation. In this context,
Cristina Fernández de Kirchner (2007–15) won the 2007 presidential election
with 45 percent of the ballots, 22 percent ahead of her nearest challenger. But,
as the following sections will show, Fernández de Kirchner's tenure came along
with the gradual exhaustion of this virtuous phase, including the acceleration
of inflation, the deterioration of the positive fiscal and external balances, and
a plateau in job creation, among other changes. Underlying this decline, there
were changes in the balances of forces that gradually came against the economic and political limitations of the neo-developmentalist policies in an
international economic context that was taking a turn for the worse.

5   From Euphoria to Crisis

By the mid-2000s, inflation accelerated. The prices of Argentina's main agricultural commodity exports were rising, and these price increases were affecting
domestic food prices. In addition, the consumption boom was straining the
production capacity of the manufacturing sector. In the following years, the
sector – highly dependent on imports – would also show a growing external
deficit.[23]

In this context, maintaining conditions for economic growth and uphold-
ing consensus proved increasingly challenging for the government. After 2007,
rising inflation became compounded with a real exchange appreciation that –
intended to be an anti-inflationary tool – resulted in competitive losses for
domestic manufacturing.[24] Growth and job creation decelerated and the very
positive fiscal and external performance of the previous years deteriorated.

As the price of basic staples was steeply increasing, in March 2008 the government attempted to introduce a sliding-scale export duty on grain exports
that would fluctuate with changes in international prices. Its stated purpose
was to delink the domestic prices of foodstuffs from rising international prices

---

22   Felder and Patroni (2018).
23   Schorr (2012).
24   Campos, González and Sacavini (2010).

and alleviate inflationary pressures. The response from the country's main landowner organizations was a lockout that forced the government to set the project aside. The dispute between the state and landowners helped to catalyze a heterogeneous opposition force that gathered groups with very diverse and even contradictory interests and claims that ranged from the need to address persisting poverty to the need to abide by the rule of law, enforce fiscal and monetary discipline, avoid excessive state intervention in the economy, and recreate investors' trust. An indicator of the government's political fall-off was the poor performance of the incumbent party in the mid-term election of 2009 in which it lost 20 seats in the Congress Lower Chamber and 4 in the Senate.

While this domestic crisis was unfolding, the effects of the global crisis began to be felt in the country. The international prices of Argentina's main export commodities dropped from their peak in mid-2008 as international demand collapsed with economic growth coming to a sudden stop. Central Bank reserves fell, capital outflows intensified, and the deficit in the financial and capital account rose.

In this context, the government took pains to recover from its political crisis while protecting the economy from global turmoil and creating conditions to attract capital inflows and make up for the growing external imbalances. It let the US dollar appreciate, increased interest rates and, at the same time, expanded state spending and the lending of public banks.[25] In late 2008, it nationalized pension funds that had been partially privatized in the 1990s and created a sovereign investment fund whose resources were invested in infrastructure projects and in shares of large companies. These resources were also instrumental in the expansion of conditional cash transfer and workfare programs, which helped to manage social conflict and regain political support in a less dynamic labor market.

The government also decided to use foreign reserves to service the restructured sovereign debt while the Economy Ministry opened negotiations with the holdouts of the 2005 restructuring in order to regain access to international credit. In 2010, 67 percent of the holdouts accepted the new restructuring.[26] A remaining nine percent of holders refused the government's offer for the second time.[27]

By 2011, growth resumed, and Fernández de Kirchner was re-elected with 54 percent of the vote, 38 points ahead of the second candidate. But growth was now less vigorous than in the mid-2000s. Fiscal and trade balances were

---

25   Kulfas (2016).
26   Oficina Nacional de Crédito Público (2010).
27   Secretaría de Finanzas (2010).

deteriorating while inflation regained momentum, affecting workers' wage gains and exacerbating distributive clashes.

A primary expression of – and a catalyst for – the unravelling of neo-developmentalist policies was the acceleration of capital flight during the late 2000s and early 2010s.[28] After using large amounts of central bank reserves to make up for money outflows and prevent the devaluation of the peso during 2011, the government turned to gradually stricter exchange controls, required exporters to surrender their foreign currency earnings held in the country, and restricted both imports and the transfer of profits abroad.

By the second half of 2012, growth stalled. Even though this new slowdown helped to keep the current account deficit under control, central bank reserves kept falling. More problematically, inflation kept rising, thus intensifying the competitive losses of domestic manufacturing and exacerbating pressures for a major devaluation of the peso.

The government continued working to create better conditions for attracting investment and resume borrowing in international financial markets, but with meagre results. In 2012, these measures included expropriating 51 percent of the shares of the local oil company, controlled by Spain's Repsol since its privatization in the 1990s. This was intended to reverse falling national oil production and reduce the import of fuels and natural gas, which had been a factor in the country's deteriorating trade balance in the late 2000s.[29] In 2013, the government passed a bill granting important benefits to international investors in the oil sector and negotiated agreements with several transnational oil companies to develop shale oil and gas resources. Similarly, the government made efforts to create better conditions for agribusiness and mining through more favorable regulations and repression of those who raised concerns about the environmental impact of extractive activities or opposed land grabbing associated with these activities.[30] The government also took pains to address some of the unresolved effects of the 2001 crisis in order to regain access to international financial markets and boost investors' confidence. It abided by several adverse rulings by the World Bank's International Centre for the Settlement of Investment Disputes that it had previously challenged (a condition for signing an agreement with the World Bank to renew its assistance programs). The government also accepted to pay-off Argentina's outstanding debts to the Paris Club; compensate Repsol for the expropriation of the oil company; and, finally,

---

28   Gaggero and Rúa (2013).
29   Pérez Roig (2012).
30   GER-GEMSAL (2013).

agreed to open negotiations with creditor holdouts of the 2010 sovereign debt restructurings, turning back from its previous refusal to satisfy these demands.

When the trade balance became negative in 2013, the government prioritized the protection of the Central Bank's reserves over the supply of foreign currency to satisfy manufacturing's needs of imports, which further affected growth.[31] By early 2014, in the conjuncture of worsening trade balances and declining fiscal and macroeconomic performance, the decision of large crop exporters to reduce the surrender of dollars in the domestic exchange market led to a dramatic fall in foreign reserves and forced a thirty percent currency devaluation. This time, distributive disputes and high inflation rapidly eroded the competitive effects of the higher exchange rate. Shortly after, the government's plan to resume borrowing in international financial markets to make up for external imbalances was blocked by a US court decision requiring the country to settle with a holdout hedge fund that was demanding full payment of the defaulted debt bonds in its hands. The decision temporarily blocked payments to bondholders that had participated in the 2005 and 2010 debt restructurings, forcing the country into a technical default.[32]

Labor conflict was also spreading as job creation and workers' wage gains were languishing. By 2013, some of the leaders of the *Confederación General del Trabajo* (CGT, General Confederation of Labour) who had been aligned with the government since the mid-2000s, were taking distance from it, as the room for negotiating some benefits for unionized workers in exchange for social peace was narrowing.[33] In addition, shop-floor disputes over employment and wages and protests by informal and precarious workers became more frequent.

By the end of Cristina Kirchner's second term in office, the state became increasingly ineffective in managing the crisis, much less to address the structural causes of the economic imbalances. Meanwhile the post-neoliberal consensus of the mid 2000s was turning into anger over inflation, and suspicions of corruption and state's profligacy, among other problems. In this context, a political opposition from the right was consolidating on arguments about the need to abide by the rule of law, re-establish the confidence in the Argentinean economy, leave populism behind, and overcome divisions among Argentineans with synergies between state and markets, efficient management, and a less confrontational style of leadership.[34] Under the leadership of Mauricio Macri (2015–19), this opposition won the 2015 presidential election.

---

31 Kulfas and Matías (2016).
32 Cosentino, Isasa, Carreras Mayer, de Achával, Coretti and Dall'o (2017).
33 Patroni (2018).
34 Bohoslavsky and Morresi (2016).

Starting in late 2015, the new government took pains to make the country trustworthy for business by eliminating regulations and subsidies and resuming debt payments, among other decisions. To the chagrin of the government, the return to the neoliberal policy repertoire failed to deliver the expected results. Instead, inflation accelerated, foreign direct investments never materialized, and the level of Argentinian sovereign debt became unsustainable.

Likewise, the government's plan to 'leave populism behind' by limiting the capacity of the working class and other groups to mobilize and place demands onto the state failed. Moreover, intense social mobilization blocked most of the government's agenda for structural reforms.[35] Yet, none of these protests and struggles sufficed to reverse the exacerbation of the regressive distribution of wealth, and gradually metamorphosed into electoral disputes around Macri's bid for reelection. In late 2019, a broad coalition led by Alberto Fernández (2019–23) and Cristina Fernández de Kirchner defeated Macri and took power with a new iteration of the neo-developmentalist agenda, although this time with more business-friendly undertones. The new government faced the challenge of addressing an already serious economic crisis when the Covid-19 pandemic altered its policy priorities and raised new questions about the capacity of the state to overcome the crisis and recreate conditions for capital accumulation in a much more uncertain world.

6   The Illusions of Neo-developmentalism

The analysis of the Argentinean case shows that neo-developmentalism has been shaped by the specific historical, political, and ideological conjunctures of social mobilization and contestation over development strategies in the context of the crisis of neoliberalism. Moreover, neo-developmentalist policies institutionalized the struggles against neoliberalism of the late 1990s and early 2000s that has been characteristic of the Latin American Pink Tide. In Argentina, the economic recovery of the early 2000s helped to strengthen the anti-neoliberal consensus that had accompanied the 2001 crisis, which in turn contributed to legitimizing policy reorientation and shaped a post-neoliberal political moment. But the very ensemble of economic, political, and policy changes that was instrumental in setting political limits to the continuation of austerity, and made the neo-developmentalist policy innovation possible, resulted in changes in the balances of class forces that led to a gradual

---

35   Piva and Mosquera (2019).

exacerbation of distributive disputes that gradually came across the structural limitations of the Argentinean economy. Moreover, its protracted external restriction strengthened the political power of commodity exporters to veto distributive policies. Thus inflation accelerated, and the state became increasingly unable to manage distributive conflict amidst declining growth. In this context, the centrality of the state that had been effective during the virtuous stage of neo-developmentalism turned politically problematic as the failure to maintain conditions for "growth with social inclusion" was seen as the direct responsibility of the state.

The recent social trajectory of Argentina leaves no doubt about the role of the state in creating the economic and political conditions for addressing the crisis of neoliberal reforms. But the Argentine case also illustrates a dilemma that all the Pink Tide governments ran up against, that policy choices were shaped and constrained by changing balances of forces that was steadily eroding. This conclusion is in line with the theme of Leo Panitch and Sam Gindin on the role of the state – particularly of the economic policy apparatuses – of building neoliberal globalization and managing its contradictions between and within national states on the backs of historical defeats of working-class movements.[36] It draws attention to the illusion that the state can lead processes of social transformation in the absence of popular capacities to organize and struggle apart from the state and over the state.

Much of the most audacious challenges to the neoliberal policy blueprint developed in the context of crisis and ascent of struggles against the consequences of neoliberal reforms of the early 2000s. Underlying the economic recovery and the political normalization that followed the crisis there were momentous changes in the balances of class forces, including the strengthening of capitalist fractions with capacity to block policies that affected their interests. In this context, the state was unable to maintain the neo-developmentalist policy orientation, much less transcend the structural obstacles to development. This experience is a warning against the illusion that progressive governments will lead processes of social transformation in the absence of social forces able to make this change possible.

---

36   Panitch and Gindin (2012).

PART 3

From Neoliberalism to Political Crisis

∵

CHAPTER 7

The Rebirth of Nationalism and the Crisis of the European Union

Frank Deppe

During the German election campaign of 1998, the philosopher Jürgen Habermas met with soon-to-be Chancellor Gerhard Schröder and other leading Social Democrats in the Willy Brandt House of the Social Democratic Party (SPD) in Berlin. He gave a lecture entitled "The Postnational Constellation and the Future of Democracy" which outlined the basic challenges confronting a social democratic government in the early twenty-first century.[1] The modern nation-state characterized by mass democracy and welfare provision, with origins in the French Revolution of 1789, was an achievement of the European working-class movement and culminated in the Fordist configuration of Western capitalism after 1945. As the twentieth century came to a close, that state confronted the new realities of globalization, which for Habermas meant the "growing extent and intensification of traffic, communication and exchange beyond national boundaries."[2] Quoting Robert Cox, he asked: "Is economic globalization an uncontrollable, inflexible force to which liberal democracy is inevitably subordinate?"[3]

1 Globalization and the State

Habermas acknowledged that the forces unleashed by global market liberalization – the enhanced power of transnational corporations, the transfer of industrial production to the periphery of the world economy, and the rise of global financial markets – imposed new constraints on nation-states. Neoliberal ideology and politics enabled these global competitive pressures by replacing Keynesian policies with market-oriented, supply-side policies – deconstructing the welfare state, attacking the trade unions, and opening

---

1 Habermas (1998: 91ff). A version of the argument is also published in English (Habermas, 2001: ch. 4).
2 Habermas (1998: 101–2). See also Habermas (1999; 2001).
3 Habermas (1998: 104).

the way to "post-democracy."[4] Habermas's "rational" and progressive answer to neoliberal globalization was to propose "new forms of a postnational democracy": from democratic self-control within civil societies[5] to ("still distant") projects of "cosmopolitan democracy" approved by David Held and Ulrich Beck.[6] Meanwhile Manuel Castells proclaimed the "Rise of the Network Society" characterized "by widespread destructuring of organisations, delegitimation of institutions [including the national state], fading away of major social movements, and ephemeral cultural expressions."[7] *Governance* rather than (national) government became the frame of reference to analyze the new relationship between the global economy and global politics. New forms of agency came to the fore in these complementary analyses looking to break with neoliberal globalization. Institutions created by multilateral agreements (like the EU) were regarded as agents of transnational political management, while non-governmental organization (NGOs) seemed to be the new agents representing social movements within a global civil society.[8]

Most of these sociologists criticized the market radicalism of neoliberals and showed sympathies for the new social movements which came up in the 1970s and still shared the anti-state aversion of the radical movements of 1968. They were convinced that the nationalism which prepared and accompanied the world wars of the twentieth century had no chance to come back. European integration seemed to support this belief. It was a new (and quite unique) model of transnational multi-level politics which advances by transferring national sovereignty to the EU level.[9] It is creating "a common practice of democratic politics which is nourished and strengthened by a European civil society."[10] Thus, the next step on this path to a European Federal State is the engagement for "a social Europe which throws its weight into the cosmopolitan perspective."[11]

Habermas provided a response to the first phase of neoliberal globalization in his calls for a post-national cosmopolitan democracy and he still defends his idealistic concept of a liberal post-nationalism to this day. Neoliberal hardliners have always combined their transnational economic strategy of market liberalization with an aggressive class politics at home: to overturn the class

4   Crouch (2004); Deppe (2013).
5   Habermas (1998: 134).
6   Held (1995); Beck (1997).
7   Castells (2000: 3).
8   Held, McGrew, Goldblatt and Perraton (1999); Held and McGrew (2000).
9   Deppe, Felder and Tidow (2003).
10   Habermas (1998: 151).
11   Habermas (1998: 169).

compromise of the welfare state and to strengthen state apparatuses in the field of civil and military security. The social consequences of neoliberal politics (decay of infrastructure, social insecurity, poverty, crime, etc.) required not only more state control over individual citizens and institutions, by modern technologies of supervision, but also more financial resources for police, judiciary, secret services, prisons, and the repressive state apparatuses as a whole. In this sense, the social democratic response to neoliberal globalization offered by Habermas and others was both politically naïve and theoretically blind to the centrality of states in economic globalization, to the political reproduction of neoliberalism, and to the emergence of a hard right opposition as the dislocations of neoliberal globalization deepened.

For Stephen Gill, national politics became reorganized in the form of a "new constitutionalism" that enforced competitiveness as a primary goal. "Central ... to new constitutionalism is the imposition of discipline on public institutions, partly to prevent national interference with the property rights and entry and exit options of holders of mobile capital with regard to particular political jurisdiction."[12] At the same time, according to Bob Jessop, the state apparatuses and policy regime shifted from the "Keynesian Welfare National State" to the "Schumpeterian Postnational Workfare State," to functions connected to global competitiveness, open financial markets, austerity policies, and agencies responsible for security at home and abroad.[13] Analyzing global power structures one must of course pay attention to the fact that there exist differences between 'great powers' and small states.

For a more theoretically integrated view of globalization and national states, it is worth returning to Leo Panitch's essay written in 1994 entitled "Globalization and the State."[14] As a scholar of Ralph Miliband, Panitch critiques the Marxist debate on imperialism and the state for its preoccupation with the study of economic "laws." Prevailing Marxist approaches reduced the state to an apparatus of bourgeois class domination, underestimating the relative autonomy of the state as well as the relation of class forces reflected within the system of state apparatuses.[15] At the same time Panitch rejects the "premise that globalization is a process whereby capital limits, escapes and overtakes the nation state."[16] Almost twenty years later – after further study

---

12   Gill (2003: 132).
13   Jessop (2002).
14   Panitch (1994).
15   Poulantzas (1978b: 114ff).
16   Panitch (1994: 63).

and debate – Leo Panitch and Sam Gindin came to the following conclusion in their seminal study of *The Making of Global Capitalism*:

> In contrast with those who have emphasized the marginalization of states, our argument is that states need to be placed at the center of the search for an explanation of the making of global capitalism. The role of states in maintaining property rights, overseeing contracts, stabilizing currencies, reproducing class relations and containing crises has always been central to the operation of capitalism. ... The American state has played an exceptional role in the creation of a fully global capitalism and in coordinating its management, as well as restructuring other states to these ends.[17]

The twenty-first century is obviously characterized by deep transformations in world order and in the socio-economic and political structures of the developed capitalist countries of the West. This does not mean, as Panitch and Gindin argued in rejecting the thesis of Michael Hardt and Antonio Negri's "Empire," that the present world order is constituted by the loss of sovereignty of the national state.[18] This flattening of the world market and the state system into 'empire' is to lose sight of the continued relevance of socialist politics – and the pivot of political power – at the level of the national state. The relationship between the internationalization of capitalism (globalization), the imperial structures of world order, and the functions of the national state have to be studied thoroughly. It is a core aspect of Marxist analysis of imperialism and therefore of political strategies of the left. Many of the concepts developed at the end of the twentieth century – stressing the end or the erosion of national sovereignty as a consequence of globalization – are seriously confronted with the dominance of national and nationalist politics and ideologies in the struggle for world order. Just as important is the terrain of the national in constructing authoritarian nationalism as an ideology of national states and parties in providing a path to power. To Donald Trump and his followers – in Hungary, Poland, and many other states – 'liberal cosmopolitism' (often identified, with an implicit anti-semitism, with George Soros and his project of an 'open society') is their main enemy.

17 Panitch and Gindin (2012: 1).
18 Gindin and Panitch (2002).

2   European Integration and the 'United States of Europe'

In the early days of European integration after the Second World War, the utopia of the 'United States of Europe' – as a political and economic project – excited many young people. The European Federalists referred to social democratic and conservative traditions, represented by the followers of Count Richard Coudenhove-Kalergi and Otto von Habsburg.[19] The path to integration, however, followed a different direction: it started with sectoral economic cooperation (coal and steel, 1951) and by reducing customs (1958).[20] Political scientists such as Ernst B. Haas presented a neo-functionalist concept of a 'spill-over-process' to justify the agenda: starting with a customs' union that will – if successful – necessarily put the union of economic and monetary cooperation on the agenda. As trade linkages increased, transnational political cooperation might then evolve into a constitution of the United States of Europe. These initial treaties were proclaimed as the basis to overcome the nationalisms that had led the European states into two self-destructive world wars between 1914 and 1945.

The politics of integration, however, were always characterized by a specific combination of national and common interests between the allies. Transnational market liberalization was necessary for the reconstruction of the Western European economies after the war within the Bretton Woods framework of the American Empire.[21] Anticommunism united conservative and social democratic parties across the borders; the US-led North Atlantic Treaty Alliance (NATO) guaranteed security. For the World War II Allies, the policies of European integration policies were always directed towards the control of West Germany. And Germany – under the protection of the US and within NATO – recovered quickly and regained its position as the strongest (export-oriented) economy in Western Europe. Regaining prominence in international politics was of course a primary goal of the West German ruling class. From the beginning, cooperation between France and West Germany was the

---

19   In 1924, the Austrian philosopher and journalist Richard Coudenhove-Kalergi (1894–1972) published a book entitled *Pan-Europe*, in the same year he founded the 'Paneuropean Union' which until today proclaims the United States of Europe as their political goal. In Germany, since 1949 the programs of the governing parties have been committed to this goal. After the unification of Germany in 1991, and with the enlargement of the European Union (EU) from 6 in 1958 to now 28 member states, this goal was replaced by a concession to the institutional form of the EU and to stronger political cooperation within the EU.

20   Haas (1958).

21   Panitch and Gindin (2012: 96ff).

key for success and stability, and their centrality also constituted the hierarchy of power distribution within the European Economic Community (EEC), formed with the Treaty of Rome in 1958, and its institutions (and remained so in the EU). German Chancellor Konrad Adenauer and French President Charles de Gaulle pursued their respective national interests within this context. Even today, de Gaulle's 'L'Europe des patries' is the model of antifederalist pro-European conservatives. Britain, which joined the EEC in 1973, was always regarded as an 'unfriendly companion' because the right-wing of the conservatives and the left-wing of Labour – out of different motives – never accepted the liberal 'market philosophy' and the federalist perspective of European integration. British Prime Minister Margret Thatcher confessed proudly that she had successfully opposed the 'socialist projects' of Jacques Delors.

However, national governments within the EEC pursued specific strategies which were – in the case of France, Great Britain, Netherlands, Belgium – determined by their decline as colonial powers. They lost wars which ruined state finances and forced them into more dependence on the US. On the other side, national politics were affected by specific national constellations of class forces which shaped the 'Fordist class compromise', by strong political parties of the left and trade unions. Until the late 1970s, transnational market liberalization went together with expanded national state interventionism, with the stabilization of the 'national Keynesian welfare state' taking different institutional manifestations. The neo-functionalists advocating European integration never understood why national policy regimes and strategies acted as a brake to the 'spill-over' into political integration.

3   The Great Transformation and New Constitutionalism of the EU

The last quarter of the twentieth century opened a period of 'great transformation', not only in world order and politics, but also in the relationship between capital accumulation and state regulation enforced by economic globalization and the consolidation of neoliberal politics and ideology at the national level. With the formation of the EU in 1991, the character of the European project fundamentally changed: from market liberalization to market integration which, at the same time, transformed the existing structures of complementarity between European integration and national regulation.[22] The EU established a project of enlargement of an economic zone with free movement of goods,

---

22   Bieling and Deppe (2003).

workforce, capital and services (and now has 28 member states and more than 500 million inhabitants). At the same time, the first steps were taken to establish an EU regime of a common foreign policy, and of an economic policy controlling inflation, rates of exchange, national debt, and national fiscal policy. The guiding principles of fiscal policy became the reduction of inflation and fiscal austerity, both imposing the pressure of market competition and of neoliberal politics and ideology across the EU space. National governments had to implement the politics of privatization, market deregulation, and flexibility of labor markets thereby weakening trade unions all over Europe.[23] With the introduction of the Euro in 1999 in 19 of the member states, national sovereignty over monetary policies was transferred to the European Central Bank. The ECB was explicitly constructed as an institution independent from the European Commission, the 'Ecofin' Council of the national ministers of finance, and from national governments (who were represented by the governors of their national central banks).

The 'new constitutionalism' of the EU was governed by competition – from individual performance (such as education or jobs), to corporate performance in global markets, and from these on to national government policies.[24] The laws of global competition, mediated by the EU, formed a 'market democracy' that states had to adapt to. In Germany, the 'red-green' government led by Gerhard Schröder (Sozialdemokratische Partei Deutschlands – SPD) – after the impact of German unification and stagnation in the 1990s – quite successfully executed this new constitutionalism by deconstructing the national welfare state, imposing labor market flexibility, and opening for global finance in order to strengthen the position of German export industries. The weakness of the German unions guaranteed relatively low wages.[25] The Euro made German exports free from the former pressure of revaluation of the deutsche-mark. Astonishingly, since 2001 Germany's export surplus was continuously growing. In the following years, German politics was dominated by a coalition of interests to stabilize the cost advantages that the EU policy regime had for German 'export champions'.

In March 2000, the prime ministers of the then member states of the EU assembled in Lisbon for an extraordinary European Council summit to welcome the new millennium and chart a framework for development. Among the leaders were prominent social democrats: among them Tony Blair (UK),

---

23   Lehndorff, Dribbusch and Schulten (2017).
24   Gill (2003).
25   Deppe (2013).

Gerhard Schröder (Germany), Lionel Jospin (France), and Massimo d'Alema (Italy) who at home represented still strong social democratic parties which had accepted the ideology of a 'Third Way' including the market philosophy of neoliberalism.[26] Looking back over the past decade, they celebrated the end of state socialism set against the successful dynamics of European integration, drawing up the following balance-sheet:

- the expansion to Eastern and South Eastern Europe after the end of the Cold War; finally enlarging the Union from 15 to 28 member states in the years to come;
- the realization of the Common Market Programme – pushed by the French Socialist Jacques Delors who was president of the European Commission between 1985 and 1995;
- the Maastricht Treaty of 1992, which opened the way to common economic and monetary policies; and
- the introduction of the Euro common currency from 12 of the 15 member states and the establishment of the European Central Bank (ECB) in 2000.

Looking to the future, the Council proclaimed new goals for the Union. As the leading trade bloc in the world economy, the EU "must now become the most competitive and dynamic – science based – economic region in the world – a region which is capable to guarantee continuous economic growth together with more and better employment and greater social cohesion." To become a "global player" the EU must have: its own currency (established with the Euro) and offer dynamic EU-wide financial markets; constitutional reform to strengthen political cooperation within the EU-institutions; a common foreign policy to speaking with one voice in international politics; and formation of EU military capacities (apart from those of NATO). These were, for the EU member states, essential to the vision of a united Europe as a "global player" and major world power with its own place as a "global empire."[27] Social democratic leaders dreamt of a socially attractive and progressive union which could challenge its global competitors (US, China, Russia) in the world market but alongside high living standards, universal access to good education, top quality universities, stable democratic institutions, social security, and environmental politics.

---

26   Giddens (1998).
27   The quote and discussions of Lisbon here are drawn from Bieling (2010).

4   The Visions of Lisbon Disappear

In less than a decade later, the 'Great Financial Crisis' of 2008–10 opened a period of setbacks to the project of European integration.[28] Since the Second World War, European politics has time and again been confronted with economic crises with periods of 'euro-sclerosis' being followed by phases of 'euro-phoria'. These crises, however, were 'cathartic' insofar as they ultimately produced solutions that moved Europe towards closer cooperation, further market integration, and member enlargement.[29] Still today, the poor countries of the Balkans appeal for EU membership hoping to share the prosperity of the richer members, to take advantage of an open labor market (and the export of unemployment), and to receive subsidies from EU funds for agricultural and regional policies.

Now, for the first time, the politics of European integration are seriously confronted with the threat of failure and erosion. The centrifugal forces – articulated by nationalist governments as well as by political and class forces – seem to be stronger than common interests. The ambitious vision of Lisbon from 2000 has disappeared. Nationalisms of different kinds are gaining ground, as the EU is increasingly subject to popular disapproval in many countries. Both liberal and socialist internationalism are under attack from right-wing populism. The radical left, too, criticizes the EU as an instrument of transnational capitalist class dominance. The current orientation of European politics appears to be one of status-quo 'muddling through', while seeking to avert the danger of a major break-up and to sustain the economic advantages of the rich EU members (with Germany at the head of this group). Emotional appeals to the unity of 'Europe' invoke the ideological construct of a 'glorious history' of democracy, peace, and prosperity. The price of failure for European elites – not only in the bigger states within the Union, such as Germany and France – will be insignificance and dependency upon the great world powers, notably China and the US, at the level of global power politics in the twenty-first century. These elites also know that the EU – as an integral part of the American Empire – will be weakened by its decline. Crisis management dominates the agenda of national and European politics:

– In the South of Europe, the economic and financial crisis was intensified by the austerity regime of the EU imposed by Germany and its allies in the North. Greece, with its left-wing Syriza government led by Alexis Tsipras

---

28   Tooze (2018: 373ff).

29   In an early article analyzing the Post-Maastricht-crisis of the EU, I made a distinction between "crises of evolution" and "crises of existence" (Deppe 1993; Deppe 2017).

that had promised a break with neoliberal politics, was forced to accept conditions for financial help from the 'Troika' made up of the EU Commission, IMF, and the ECB. The policies of austerity devastated the country and imposed poverty upon large parts of the population. Many blamed the EU, and especially 'rich Germany' with its unflinching Chancellor Merkel, and ascribed to European elites a ruthless commitment to exploit and dominate the poor partners of the EU periphery and, most importantly, a desire to humiliate a left-wing government. The European left, in solidarity with a severely disadvantaged left-wing government in Greece, sharply criticized EU economic policies directed towards saving the financial sector in the interest of German banks.

- In 2015, the 'refugee crisis' destroyed the EU regime for handling migration and asylum (the 'Dublin Regulation') and sparked massive protest in several countries. The German government for a brief moment opted for 'open borders' while other governments of the EU closed their national borders, and since then have refused to take in refugees. It is not only the governments of Hungary and Poland that have done so; the government of Italy, led by a coalition of the right, has also opposed the EU migration policy and closed its southern harbors along the Mediterranean coast to refugees coming from North Africa. The 'refugee question' divides parties and states within the Union. The humanitarian crisis in the Mediterranean (notably in the refugee camps on several Greek islands) damages the image of the EU and its liberal claims to human rights and social justice.

- In June 2016, a majority of 52 percent in the UK voted in a national referendum for an exit from the EU, further confirmed by the results of the British general election of December 2019 and the victory of the Conservative Party under the leadership of Boris Johnson. Since then, 'Brexit' has opened a fissure in the political system in Britain itself. The EU, unable to offer a solution within the European treaty framework, fears the economic and financial consequences of Brexit and worries that the way is now open for other states to leave the EU. Indeed, exit from the EU is being encouraged by American right-wing nationalists – such as Steve Bannon and Donald Trump himself. Russian President Vladimir Putin seems to be pushing in the same direction, supporting right-wing nationalists in order to weaken the EU, which has imposed sanctions against Russia (after the annexation of Crimea), allowed NATO to expand to the Russian borders, and to move US troops and missiles into Poland.

- In October 2017, the regional parliament in Catalonia passed a motion supporting its independence from Spain. Since then, politics in Spain has been paralyzed by the confrontation between supporters and opponents of Catalonian independence dividing the left-wing and the right-wing conservative forces. General elections in November 2019 did not result in a clear majority; the left in Spain is deeply divided over the 'national question'. The left-populist party of Podemos has since joined the minority government of the PSOE (Partido Socialista Obrero Español) led by Pedro Sanchez, which depends upon Catalan votes and is confronted with strong right-wing nationalism in other parts of Spain.

Since 2000, after the EU's eastward enlargement and the introduction of the Euro, public opinion polls have revealed declining support for the EU especially in Western Europe. The referendum on a European Constitutional Treaty failed in France and the Netherlands in 2005. From then, the split between 'elites' supporting the European project and 'the common people' identifying European politics (and globalization) with social inequality and personal social insecurity has continuously deepened. In the metropolitan areas of Europe (such as London, Paris, Berlin, Frankfurt, Rhein-Main, Barcelona, Warsaw, and others), the majority of people with higher levels of education and income are 'pro-European'. In contrast, people in the countryside, in declining old-industrial regions of the EU – facing high levels of unemployment, rotting infrastructure, and the threat of precarious employment amidst cheap labor supply from eastern Europe and immigrants desperate for work from outside – support 'anti-European' forces.

The asymmetric structure in the distribution of economic and political power within the EU has been reinforced since the early 1990s by neoliberal market-centered policies, by the enlargement towards the East, and by the turn to austerity policy in the Euro-crisis of 2010. With the Maastricht Treaty in 1993 and the founding of the EU, and the introduction of the Euro in 2000, the socio-economic gap between the 'rich' and the 'poor' member states (especially in the east and south of Europe), and the gap between countries with a positive or a negative trade balance, has widened. Even France and Italy have declined relative to Germany. The EU economic and monetary regime has always been directed towards basic market freedoms and the control of inflation. This regime of austerity ('debt-brake') was pushed by the rich members of the union, with Germany as its most powerful advocate, as a policy mandate for joining the Eurozone. In particular, the governments of Germany, the Netherlands, Austria, and Finland took the position that public debt (as a consequence of welfare politics) and a lack of competitiveness (which is connected to the level of wages and social benefits) are the main determinants of national crises. These countries have had considerable current account surpluses and their financial systems have a strong position as international creditors across the

EU. The protection of their national banking systems was a central motive for organizing EU and ECB assistance to debtor states. In the case of crisis management *vis-à-vis* Greece, financial aid was combined with structural adjustment 'reforms' such as privatization, pensions, and wage reduction by the Troika. The 'Troika Plan' was pushed ahead despite a national referendum in Greece rejecting the 'bailout' and the national election victory of Syriza in 2015. The German government, with the rigid Wolfgang Schäuble as Minister of Finance, insisted upon the subjugation of the Syriza government through the terms of EU support. Syriza lost support from their own voters, humiliated by political demands of the 'rich brothers' in the North of the EU. In 2019 the conservative party New Democracy came back into power.

EU crisis management after 2011 prevented a financial breakdown, but also exacerbated the regional divisions between and within states. It is impossible to disentangle the negative popular image of the EU from this management, and nationalist propaganda by right-wing populist parties have exploited it. The left, moreover, is divided between fundamental criticism that supports exit strategies from the EU, and a pro-European position which demands institutional reforms that break with austerity policies and allow space for greater social justice and democracy within the Union. In 2015, the refugee crisis intensified these cleavages between border countries of the EU in the South (especially Greece and Italy) and the richer countries in the North. The 'Dublin-Regime', the regulatory agreement on how to register and distribute refugees within the EU, collapsed. Chancellor Merkel opened German borders for more than two million migrants in 2015. In stark contrast, the so-called 'Visegrád-States' of Eastern Europe refused any immigrants from Syria (and the Global South in general). They justified their position with resort to extreme nationalist arguments, including the ideological trope of the need for war against Islam which threatened the Christian Occident. In the richer Northern states, as with Germany, the Netherlands, and Britain, the refugee crisis also unleashed right-wing populist parties and movements which reject the EU and defend national identities and a strong national state.

5   Nationalism and Racism as Answers to the Decline of Neoliberal Hegemony

After the financial crash and the refugee crisis, a wave of right-wing populism and nationalism has changed the political landscape of Europe. In Hungary and Poland, these forces are in government. They not only oppose further European political integration, but also restrain democracy and civil rights at home. Nationalism is combined with an ideological stew of Catholicism, anti-liberalism, and anti-socialism; and this nationalism has always been connected to a strong national state offering security against enemies from within and outside.[30] The primacy of national interest – 'make our country great again' in echoes of Trumpism – dominates this nationalist ideology as well as opposition to transnational political integration and open borders. In France, the Front National became the strongest party of the opposition. In Austria and Italy, parties of authoritarian nationalism have been part of governing coalitions and are still among the strongest parties in these countries. The forces of the political left, in contrast, are strong supporters of European integration, but they have entered a period of defeat and erosion. The communist parties, for instance in France and Italy, largely disappeared after the end of the Soviet Union; social democracy is in the midst of a serious crisis from electoral declines in key countries such as Italy, France, Germany, and the Netherlands, although there are exceptions in Britain, Spain, Portugal, and Denmark. Parties of a new European left are still fledgling and in a minority position where they have gained some electoral and movement presence.[31]

At the beginning of the new century, the post-national cosmopolitan perspective was dominant within the EU. However, nationalist politics and ideologies were still present in different contexts. Conservative national parties – many of them in government after the war and central agents of integration policies – always represented large parts of the population. They supported conservative political values of family, religion, national culture, and history, and a powerful state. Fiercely anti-communist, they stood at the front line of the ideological battles of the Cold War. Of course, the articulation of conservative values was influenced by national traditions, especially in the countries that had colonial empires, as with France, Britain, Belgium, Spain, and Portugal. In France, the Front National and the French 'new right' slowly expanded their political presence since 1970, taking advantage of the crisis of the traditional working-class left. In West Germany after the Second World War, the Christian Democratic Party under Adenauer represented the majority of a generation which had trusted in the 'Führer' and his regime until the 8th of May 1945. Angela Merkel modernized the Christian Democrats by opening them to coalitions with the SPD and the Greens and by supporting – in accordance with

---

30   The political philosophy of Carl Schmitt – one of the most important intellectual supporters of German fascism – still serves as a point of reference for the New Right in Europe. After the end of communism, liberalism is the main enemy. See: Deppe (2016: 157–206); Weiß (2017).

31   Deppe (2020).

policies of German capital – liberal positions with respect to migration. But from the beginning of the twenty-first century, sociologists began registering that about 20 percent of the German electorate agreed with elements of the far right anti-liberal, anti-democratic, and nationalistic ideology.[32] Confronted with the risks of social decline as a consequence of the economic crisis and globalization, these views spread and became a focus of social aggression, especially against Muslim migrants.

After the end of the Soviet Union (and of Yugoslavia), many countries in Eastern and South-Eastern Europe joined the EU (and NATO) to protect their national sovereignty against Russia. At the same time, right-wing parties and governments began to glorify nationalist traditions and heroes from the pre-communist era (for instance Józef Piłsudski in Poland and Miklós Horthy in Hungary). In Western European countries, portions of the white working class (often in countries with legacies of strong communist or social democratic mass parties now in decline) were suspicious of migrant workers, most often as competitors in the labor market, and they felt distant from their culture and religions. Yet, in France for instance, they also accepted the internationalism of their national communist party and supported anti-imperialist movements in the Third World.[33]

There is a sense in which the laws of global competition and this new nationalism have generated a new kind of corporatism: corporations, communities, and countries are engaged in a permanent transnational struggle for the 'survival of the fittest' that binds workers to 'their company' and 'their state'. Within the EU, nationalist sentiments are further inflamed by conservative media and parties when poor and mismanaged countries (such as Greece or Italy) need help and support from the richer countries (like Germany or Austria). Then right-wing mass media blame the 'lazy Greeks' for high pensions and immense state deficits, and many Germans – from all class strata – frankly claim that 'we should no longer be the paymaster of Europe'.

The geopolitical struggle for a new world order was opened with the end of the Soviet Union; it has been accompanied by a revival of assertive nationalist politics and ideology. Indeed, the politics of the American Empire itself is based upon the ideology of the unique – even exceptionalist – role of the US in modern history. All presidents before (and after) Trump have been equally committed to keeping America 'Number One'. Both Russia's recovery under Putin and China's advancement since its opening to the capitalist market have

---

32   Heitmeyer (2018).

33   In his *Return to Reims*, Didier Eribon (2016) illustrates this contradiction in the case of his own family.

been accompanied by massive nationalist propaganda at the center of state ideology. The conservative governments of their neighbors in Asia, notably Japan and India, as well as in Eastern Europe, also pursue nationalist politics.

Within the EU, the rebirth of nationalism was able to profit from cultural and political resources which were never extinguished or even exhausted. With the fractures in the neoliberal cycle of hegemony, however, the contradictions specific to global financial capitalism turned back – reflexively – toward national politics.

First, global capitalism produces contradictions which create mass popular feelings of insecurity about potential economic crises as well as risks of war.[34] Crisis management after 2008 opened a new cycle of growth of the world economy, for example, but deepened the cleavage between 'winners' and 'losers'. Trump used a populist appeal to this cleavage to open a new period of American-led trade wars, not only with China but also with allies within the American Empire, with Europe and even Canada. The warning signs of a new worldwide recession had already been present before the global pandemic put a brake on the entire world market. A second global crisis in just over a decade has reinforced a general atmosphere of uncertainty and fear which blames the EU, national governments, and parties in government for their incapacity to solve these contradictions in the interest of the 'common people'. Further, the wars of the 'American Empire' against 'global terrorism' since 2001 not only failed, but grossly multiplied the number of refugees suffering from the consequences of war and climate change, as well as from poverty and political repression in their home countries.

Second, the period of neoliberal globalization has been marked by growing inequality between states and regions, but also within societies of developed capitalist countries. Globalization has transferred industries to the periphery. The portion of the working class protected by strong unions and parties shrank and lost power. Traditional industrial regions often turned into zones of social emergency, needing regional support funds, with high rates of unemployment, poverty, crime, and urban decay. In contrast, in major metropolitan areas parts of the high-waged, middle class were further upgraded by higher education

---

34   *The Global Risks Report 2020*, published by the World Economic Forum for the 50th anniversary of the 'Davos Meeting' (of the richest and most powerful elites of the world), lists the following as leading interconnected global risks: extreme weather events and failure of climate change mitigation and adaptation; large-scale cyberattacks and breakdown of critical information infrastructure and networks; high structural unemployment or underemployment and adverse consequences of technological advances; major biodiversity loss and ecosystem collapse, and failure of climate change mitigation and adaptation (World Economic Forum, 2020: 86–87).

levels and well-paid jobs in services and the new digital economy. Alongside, the few benefiting from occupational upgrades, the incomes in traditional working-class jobs stagnated causing personal debt to grow to maintain consumption levels. The risk of social descent into unemployment or into the ranks of a growing 'precariat' (part-time jobs without protection by collective agreements or social policy) becomes part of everyday social experience.[35]

Third, the working class recognizes the risks of the privatization of the pension system and of the healthcare system. 'Poverty in old age' is a real threat, and it has become part of the uncertainty of future life prospects. This creates fear and anger against those who are getting richer and richer and against a political class which has implemented neoliberalism and globalization; and misdirected resentment against refugees and migrants who receive state subsidies and accept low wages. It is the propaganda of right-wing populism that attacks open borders and free markets, the EU and 'globalization', in the name of the 'national interest' and the culture of 'white Europe'. The alienation of the organized political left from working-class experience – partly a result of the rise of middle-class academics into the leadership of left parties and unions – opened the window for a stronger influence of nationalist and racist agitation upon working-class consciousness. The political culture of the new progressive and cosmopolitan middle classes – focusing upon issues of gender equality, sexual identity, and human rights – largely ignores class questions, including the fear of working-class fractions facing social relegation. Private mass media, such as TV and internet social media, are instrumental in repressing class consciousness and solidarity. Class solidarity has always been an important weapon of working-class power and self-consciousness, but it is now limited as a consequence of trade union weakness, fewer strikes, and a decline in mass demonstrations.

Fourth, neoliberal policies gradually destroyed the 'social cohesion' that was promoted by strong unions and Keynesian full employment policies, and it encouraged a distribution of wealth and income marked by growing inequality. The 'Anglo-Saxon countries', where Reagan and Thatcher opened the neoliberal assault on unions and the welfare state, "have much stronger overall income inequality than continental Europe and still higher than the Nordic countries."[36] Inequality does not only appear through the growing divide between the 'rich' and 'poor' poles of societal income and wealth distribution; it also permeates the distance between rich and poor states, and

---

35   Nachtwey (2016).
36   Atkinson (2015: 23).

between regions and communities within the country. This uneven development of capitalism is reinforced by the movement of workers within deregulated labor markets from places with high unemployment, low wages, and poverty to regions and urban areas with better job opportunities and higher wages. Neoliberal policies have eroded the physical and social infrastructure of marginalized regions. The 'mouvement des gilets jaunes' in France has articulated these contradictions: the 'yellow vests' furiously attacked places with high symbolic value for the upper classes, for instance the shops along Paris's Champs-Élysées.[37]

In East Germany after unification in 1991, the 'socialist economy' completely crashed. Fiscal transfers from West Germany contributed to the reconstruction of the infrastructure of the cities. But below the shining surface, the structural socio-economic deficits of Eastern Germany have not been overcome. The development of the economy and the labor market after unification was characterized by labor migration towards the West, and by sharp differences between a few centers of growth and prosperity and the many abandoned villages and regions. In this division, the influence of neo-Nazi groups, racists, and nationalists has grown in recent years. The Alternative für Deutschland (AfD) became the strongest party in many parts of East Germany (nearly 30 percent in Saxony). The leading personnel of the AfD comes from the West, but they articulate protest against the contradictions of Germany's uneven regional development: the humiliation suffered by many as a consequence of unification; contempt for the 'political class' responsible for globalization, immigration, and European integration. Islam may be the central focus in their construction of a cultural and political enemy, but they also attack progressive gender politics and blame ecological struggles for the destruction of the German automobile industries.

Finally, they present themselves as allies of Putin and promise to cleanse Germany of the evil traditions of '1968' and the new left. German history must be steered away from its preoccupation with fascism and the Holocaust. Chancellor Angela Merkel attracts particular vitriol from the radical right-wing of the AfD which blames her and her allies for the 'ethnic death' ('Volkstod') of the German people. Hitler, the SS, and the Nazi Regime – including its crimes – are glorified by these groups. And they form fraternal relations with other Nazi groups in the Baltic states and Ukraine, which seek to restore a nationalist and fascist heritage of 'heroic deeds' in fighting communism.

---

37   Wahl (2019).

6   EU as European Empire?

The political system of the EU is characterized by a complicated distribution of competences between national states and the union. Political scientists distinguish different policies within a multi-level structure of statehood. In some fields – trade and agrarian policy, for example – the EU exercises an exclusive competence. The most important field of transnational legal regulation consists in the organization of the huge common market based upon the 'Four Freedoms' (of movement of goods, capital, people, and establishment of services) and the idea of transnational competition. The corporate lobby concentrates on this level of European decision-making in Brussels. The European High Court is – together with the European Commission – the 'guardian' of the treaties, and these judgments enter into national law and politics. Until recently, the main agents of European politics were convinced that the successful implementation of transnational market integration would require further steps transferring national competence in the fields of economic, monetary, and social policies, but also of international and security policies, to the transnational level of European regulation. The European Commission already controls national fiscal policies, and the member states of the Eurozone have lost monetary sovereignty to the ECB. Important fields of politics, such as taxation, fiscal, and social policies, still constitute the core of national sovereignty in the hand of national parliaments. There is no possibility, however, to transform the EU into a community of redistribution between the rich and the poor regions by existing transnational politics. In reality, national member governments always defended their sovereign competences within the process of European policy-making and within the hegemonic structure of political power within the union, dominated as it is by the governments of Germany and France. Compromises between common and national interests were the result of long and complicated processes of negotiations.

The path to a transnational 'European Empire' as a 'global player' was not only blocked by the asymmetry of economic, political, and military power between the member states, but also by the dialectics of neoliberal restructuring of the EU after 1991. Crisis management in the Eurozone after 2010 deployed policies of austerity, deficit reduction, and 'Troika' control of granting loans to the debtors. All these measures raised strong nationalist aversions between national governments and large parts of their populations. In Germany, for example, Chancellor Merkel and the government became objects of nationalist propaganda denouncing them as 'foreign actors' accountable for the misery of 'the people'. Over his entire term in office, US President Donald Trump put this line of nationalist confrontation at the center of his project to 'make America great again,' raising corresponding reactions not only in China but also in Europe. Germany and France propose to push forward a common security policy in order to strengthen the EU in the struggle for a new world order. The newly elected president of the European Commission, the German Ursula von der Leyen, is not only a confidant of Angela Merkel, but also the former Minister of Defence in Germany. This project is confronted, however, with different national interests as well as with manifest differences in strategic orientation between those inclined towards strengthening the NATO-alliance with the US and those favoring new relationships with Russia for a European system of peace and security.[38]

In parallel to these developments, the national state has emerged as the pivotal crisis-manager after 2008 in the EU space, and as a protector of the weak countries against the hegemony of Germany and its allies. In Poland and Hungary, nationalistic parties and governments have been especially successful in refusing to follow European politics (notably migration politics). These right-nationalist forces strengthen the functions of the national state in foreign and security policy,[39] but also do so in the fields of economic and social policies. The national state claims the role of 'protector of the weak' against the stronger nations within the EU. In the post-communist countries, this function of the state refers to the formation of a national bourgeoisie which must be protected against the dominance of powerful corporations and banks from Germany and other Western European states. At the same time, the Polish rural population – which is the basis for the power of the Catholic church and the Law and Justice Party (PiS) – must be protected against the consequences of free markets and the agrarian policy of the EU which has favored big agro-capitalism and sacrificed independent small farmers over the past decades. In Poland, criticism of the EU and German dominance goes together with a paternalistic extension of social policies supporting families in the countryside.

Within the multi-level system of international politics, the member states of the EU are – at the highest scale of political action – bound to constraints exerted by the world market and the struggle for world order. At the national scale they are bound to the rules of the EU, but national parliaments also remain the centers of democracy, the executors of national sovereignty, and the terrain upon which the struggle between political and social forces is fought out.[40] The struggle against neoliberalism and austerity, for redistribution of national wealth, against right-wing populism and neo-fascism must

---

38   Münkler and Münkler (2019).
39   The government in Poland prefers military cooperation with the US.
40   Deppe (2015).

be organized and won at the national level. This fight is also an international one as the forces of democracy and socialism operate and cooperate all over the world.

The left must, therefore, reject a philosophy of 'global democracy' that simply denounces national politics as reactionary. The relation of class forces, which is decisive for national politics and thus also European politics, is still primarily a result of struggles and conflicts which happen within the boundaries of national states. The capitalist state has to assure and organize the stability and the 'wealth of those societies in which the capitalist mode of production prevails' (Marx). But how this occurs is the result of class struggles for democracy and social justice against the barriers of capitalist states as the institutional 'condensation of relations of class forces' (Poulantzas). As Panitch expressed it in his classic essay,

> Not only is the world still very much composed of states, but insofar there is any effective democracy at all in relation to the power of capitalists and bureaucrats, it is still embedded in political structures which are national or subnational. Those who advance the nebulous case of an 'international civil society' to match the 'nébuleuse' that is global capitalist governance usually fail to appreciate that capitalism has not escaped the state but rather that the state has, as always, been a fundamental constitutive element in the very process of extension of capitalism in our time.[41]

The anti-capitalist left must learn to arbitrate the linkages between the scales of politics within social and political movements from below as well as with working-class struggles within the spheres of production and reproduction. The various campaigns and programs for a Green New Deal, in the US, Europe, and around the globe, give us an encouraging example of how global, national, and local struggles might be combined successfully and forge a path toward a new socialist politics.

---

41   Panitch (1994: 87).

CHAPTER 8

The UK's Organic Crisis

Colin Leys

In March 2019, three years after a narrow majority had voted in a referendum to leave the EU, the deadline for an agreement on the terms of the UK's departure was approaching, but the government lacked an overall majority and parliament was paralyzed. Public opinion remained deeply divided. Xenophobia and violent language had displaced reasoned argument. In 2016 a pro-EU Labour MP had been murdered in the street by a pro-Brexit fanatic. The EU's chief negotiator, Michel Barnier, told his political colleagues: "There is a very serious crisis in the UK, which in my view isn't a crisis linked to the text of Brexit. ... It is a much deeper crisis, a kind of existential crisis."[1] He was right: the misconceptions and illusions of the British politicians charged with the negotiations, and the polarization of public opinion and feelings, reflected something deeper and older – a long-developing but now intensifying breakdown of the UK's liberal-democratic representative system.

Two months later, in May 2019, with the two main parties still unable to agree on the terms of departure, the voters abandoned both of them. In the elections for the European Parliament a mere 9% voted for the governing Conservative Party, which had called the 2016 referendum, and just 14% voted for the opposition Labour Party. Thirty percent voted for the Brexit Party, formed a mere six months earlier. A "general crisis of the state," as Gramsci termed it, had arisen, in which "social classes become detached from their traditional parties ... that particular organisational form, with the particular men who constitute, represent and lead them, are no longer recognised by their class (or fraction of a class) as its expression."[2] "When such crises occur," Gramsci added, "the immediate situation becomes delicate and dangerous, because the field is open for violent solutions, for the activities of unknown forces, represented by charismatic 'men of destiny'."[3] But were the mechanisms of the UK's existing system of representation, and the existing constitution, not capable of resolving the crisis and restoring stability? Was a restoration of the status quo ante not the most likely result?

---

1   Desmet (2019).
2   Gramsci (1971: 210).
3   Gramsci (1971: 210).

1   **Brexit versus Social Democracy**

The starting point in seeking an answer to this question is the financial crash of 2007–08 and the transfer of its costs to the working class in the years of austerity that followed. Two opposed political responses emerged. The first was the election in 2015 of a socialist, Jeremy Corbyn, as leader of the Labour Party, followed by an unprecedented swing to Labour in a general election two years later (in 2017): forty percent of voters backed its platform of radical social democratic reform. The Conservatives, led by Theresa May, were left in office, but lost their overall majority. The second response came between those two elections: the victory of the Leave campaign in the June 2016 referendum, exploiting the anti-EU feeling fanned over several decades by the right-wing press and the far-right populist UKIP (United Kingdom Independence Party) leader Nigel Farage. By early 2019 this second, right-wing response had eclipsed the first.

Negotiations with the EU on the key terms of withdrawal began in March 2017 and had to be agreed by the end of March 2019.[4] But the agreement negotiated by Theresa May with the EU in 2018 was heavily defeated in parliament. Anti-EU Conservative MPs rejected it because the agreement involved keeping the UK indefinitely in the EU customs union, in order to avoid the EU having to close the Irish border, which would risk re-igniting conflict in Northern Ireland;[5] while the Labour Party rejected it because it failed to protect jobs and workers' rights and environmental standards embodied in EU legislation. As the March 2019 deadline for finalizing the agreement approached, the risk that no agreement would be reached, leading to a massive disruption of trade and production, meant that almost every other

---

4   The three key elements in the agreement were settling the UK's outstanding EU bills, settling the rights of the 3.7 million EU citizens in the UK and the 1.3 million UK citizens in the EU, and agreeing on a means of keeping open the EU's border between the Irish Republic and Northern Ireland, to which the UK and the Irish Republic was committed by treaty (the Belfast Agreement of 1998). If the UK left without an agreement these issues would immediately become acute international problems. The UK would also immediately become a 'third country' in relation to the EU, subject to the EU's external tariffs and with no access to the Single Market, entailing a severe drop in UK GDP and an acute problem for government finances. For various estimates of the cost of Brexit under different assumptions see Menon and Bevington (2018). What all such estimates rarely discussed was what these aggregates would mean for different sectors and places and the people who work and live in them.

5   This was also the position of the eleven members of the Democratic Unionist Party (DUP) from Northern Ireland, on whose votes Theresa May's minority government depended in parliament.

dimension of politics disappeared from view, including Labour's social democratic response to the crisis, which less than two years earlier had attracted
40% of the national vote.

The frustration and anger on all sides seemed easily explained. 'Brexiteers'
were angry that what Farage called 'the elite' were blocking the implementation of their vote to leave the EU. 'Remainers' were angry about the way such a
fateful decision was being made on the basis of a 52:48% majority vote in the
referendum, which Brexiteers insistently called the 'will of the people' – especially when it became clear that very few people (including many pro-Brexit
MPs, and some ministers) had understood what leaving the EU would mean
in reality, and that the winning margin might even have been secured by illegal spending by the Vote Leave campaign.[6] Labour activists were frustrated by
their hopes of a revived social-democratic advance being buried in the polarization over Brexit.

But the anger and frustration also had older sources, which made them
more intense. Ever since Margaret Thatcher converted the Conservative
Party from pragmatism to 'conviction politics' in the 1980s the UK's archaic
political system had been living on borrowed time. Its electoral system, constitution, economy and state apparatus had evolved in the era of empire, presided over by a patrician elite. The loss of the empire, followed by exposure
of the UK economy to global market forces after 1980, and the accompanying conversion of the political elite into agents of these forces, had exposed
the inherited political structure to stresses it was increasingly unable to
withstand.

2   The Failure of Representation

By 2019 most voters no longer felt there was much meaningful connection
between their votes in general elections and what governments did. The 'first
past the post' (FPP) electoral system had been crudely effective in reflecting
public opinion so long as two main class-based parties contested for power,
but the loss of class-based party allegiance had led to governments for which
smaller and smaller minorities of the electorate had voted. Conservative voters in seats with seemingly permanent Labour majorities, and Labour voters

---

6   "Brexit: Leave 'very likely' won EU referendum due to illegal overspending, says Oxford pro-
     fessor's evidence to High Court ... Analysis finds adverts reached 'tens of millions of people' in
     crucial days after spending limit breached – enough to change the outcome" (Merrick 2018).

in similarly 'safe' Conservative seats, saw the votes they cast as wasted; but so did Labour voters in seats with big Labour majorities, not least from 1997 to 2010, when Labour was in power but took their votes for granted and ignored their interests. Because proportional representation would inevitably lead to new break-away parties it had always been rejected by both Labour and the Conservatives.[7] The fact that the Brexit referendum had, exceptionally, offered voters a chance to determine something really important had a lot to do with the violent feelings that were aroused, especially in the so-called Labour heart-lands, by parliament's subsequent failure to agree on how to implement the decision.[8]

Meantime the ongoing professionalization of political life, which resulted in MPs becoming less and less like most of their constituents, and the parliamentary expenses scandal of 2009, had reduced respect for MPs to a new low and put a question mark against representative democracy itself.[9] In early 2019 74% of people said they trusted the military to act in the public interest, compared with only 34% who trusted MPs. 54% even agreed that Britain needed "a strong ruler willing to break the rules," and only 23% disagreed.[10]

---

7   The Liberal Democrats had a possible opportunity after the 2010 election to make PR a condition of their support for either of the two main parties in the hung parliament, but they settled instead for a referendum on changing to the Alternative Vote. AV would not have yielded proportional representation but would, it was argued, make parties more inclined to seek votes from a wider segment of their local electorate. In any case both Labour and Conservatives opposed it and it was defeated by 68% to 32%.

8   The alienating effects of the electoral system were aggravated by the *Fixed Term Parliaments Act* of 2011. The official rationale for introducing fixed terms was to remove the electoral advantage governments enjoyed by being free to call an election whenever they judged it would be advantageous to them; the immediate reason was to reassure the Liberal Democrats, as the junior parties in the Coalition formed as a result of the 2010 election, that they could not be dumped when the Conservatives saw a chance of winning an absolute majority. But the Act did not rule out an early election if a majority in the House of Commons agreed to one, and the reality was that it would always be difficult for the opposition to decline to fight one (as Labour's immediate agreement to Theresa May's proposal to call a 'snap' election in 2017 indicated). But the result also was that if a minority government lacked sufficient parliamentary support to conduct its business, but had enough support to prevent opposition MPs using the provisions of the Act to trigger an early election, it could still hold onto power, which is what happened in 2018–19: May could not get her Withdrawal Agreement through the Commons but was able to stay in office.

9   Thatcher had opposed increasing MPs' pay and tacitly encouraged reliance on expenses claims instead, leading to extensive abuse.

10 Hansard Society (2019).

3   A Non-binding Constitution

The crisis revealed the UK's so-called unwritten constitution as fatally lacking in regulative force. It is actually not unwritten but consists of a myriad of rules embodied in laws, precedents and commentaries, accumulated around the central doctrine that parliament is sovereign. There is no official codification of the rules and none of them enjoys any special protection. What was unconstitutional yesterday can become constitutional tomorrow if a government with a parliamentary majority so decides: for example in November 2019, when Theresa May's successor, Boris Johnson, wanted an early election to break the Brexit impasse, and could not get the two-thirds majority to call one as required by the *Fixed Term Parliaments Act*, he introduced a two-clause bill providing for an immediate election which was passed by a simple majority, on the principle that parliament is always sovereign and so cannot bind itself. More typically, since a lot of what are said to be constitutional rules are hallowed only by convention, a constitutional principle can simply be abandoned by a government when it becomes inconvenient.

For example, it wasn't even clear that the terms on which the country would leave the EU needed parliamentary approval. The government proposed to regard withdrawal as a matter of negotiating a treaty, without involving parliament, using the Royal Prerogative – a power formerly retained by the monarch, including for the deployment of the armed forces and making treaties. It was only forced to give this up by a ruling of the Supreme Court in a case brought by a group of well-resourced private citizens. In arriving at this ruling, the judges had no unambiguous document to appeal to, but only what they called "the UK's constitutional arrangements;"[11] and for that matter there was no rule that said the question was something for the court to decide. The right-wing *Daily Express* called the Supreme Court judges "enemies of the people." The establishment affected to be shocked by this, but the paper had a point. The people had been asked to vote; they had voted, and the government had said it would do what they had voted for. What entitled the courts to interfere? The court was not 100% sure itself (three of the eleven judges dissented).

Even more shocking to the commentariat was the decision by Boris Johnson, soon after succeeding Theresa May as prime minister in 2019, to prorogue (shut down) parliament for five weeks, until shortly before the extended deadline for the UK's exit from the EU, to ensure that MPs couldn't stop the government

---

11   The decision was based on the principle of parliamentary sovereignty: leaving the EU would entail changing laws passed by Parliament and only Parliament could do that.

then taking the country out of the EU 'without a deal', as demanded by the far right. Summoning and proroguing parliament is another royal prerogative, but since the seventeenth century it had been exercised solely to ensure the smooth operation of the legislature. Once again it fell to a group of citizens to seek a judicial review by the Supreme Court, which ruled the prorogation illegal and null and void. Some commentators saw in these rulings an emerging role for the Supreme Court in making the constitution generally enforceable against the government of the day, but without a codified constitution endowing the judges with such powers it seemed highly unlikely that they would want or be able to play such a role.

It was, in fact, a measure of the insular nature of the UK political system that no English politician of any party seems to have thought it problematic to try to settle such a major and complex constitutional issue as leaving the EU by a simple majority vote in a referendum, without requiring a larger majority or other special thresholds such as are required for constitutional change in almost all countries with written constitutions.[12] Across the UK the Leave vote won by the narrowest of majorities, but the Scots voted 62%:38% to remain. After the European Parliament elections in May 2019 Scotland's first minister demanded a fresh referendum on Scottish independence following Brexit. The Conservative government in Westminster made it clear it would not allow one, opening up the possibility of a Catalan-style confrontation.[13]

4   A Dysfunctional State

As Perry Anderson pointed out, at an earlier stage in the evolution of the crisis, the UK state had never been conceived of as a 'regulative intelligence' for

---

12   The leader of the Scottish National Party at Westminster called for approval by the devolved administrations of Scotland, Wales, and Northern Ireland to be required, but was ignored. No MP called for a 'super-majority' to be achieved in order for a Leave vote to be implemented.

13   Jeremy Corbyn did not rule out such a referendum but said he would not agree to one in the first three years of a Labour government, while Sturgeon said the SNP's support for a minority Labour government would depend on Labour's agreement to hold one. Northern Ireland had also voted to Remain, by a smaller but clear 54:46 majority. The risk that Brexit would lead to a resumption of violence by republicans opposed to the peace process was reduced by Johnson's acceptance of the need to leave Northern Ireland within the EU customs union. This replaced the need for a 'hard border' with the republic with a de facto customs border between Northern Ireland and the rest of the UK, and it had been bitterly opposed by Theresa May's Northern Irish allies, the Democratic Unionist Party, and by Johnson himself.

shaping national development.[14] When the need for such shaping eventually became inescapable, the chosen agents of change were not the senior civil service but global market forces. Capital controls were removed, and the economy opened up to the fullest possible international competition. The state apparatus was left to adapt the country to this, but without much guidance as to what this should mean.

The consequences were spelled out in 2013 in an analysis by Anthony King and Ivor Crewe of a dozen major failures of government policy between 1980 and 2010, many of them involving huge losses of public money and sometimes catastrophic impacts on hundreds of thousands of families – and another dozen failures that were then already in the making under the Coalition government which had taken office in 2010.[15] One set of causes were classed as 'human error', including policy-makers' sometimes breath-taking ignorance of the living and working conditions of the citizens they were legislating for; ideological blinkers; and, especially, the failure to think through, or even to think about, implementation. A second set of causes were 'systemic', including the centralization of power in the prime minister's office, but without the means of making it effective across government departments; the extremely short tenure of ministers in any one department; the lack of any effective accountability for either ministers or civil servants; the lack of serious parliamentary scrutiny of legislation; and a lack of expertise in government departments for managing major projects.

At the heart of most of these deficiencies were two factors. One was the background and training of senior civil servants. Once the decision was made to let market forces shape national development it was assumed that private companies would take over much work hitherto done by the state and that the main need was to downsize it. Between 1979, when Thatcher took office, and 2015, the central civil service was cut by almost a half.[16] But the recruitment and training of what remained was not reorganized to prioritize the technical competences needed to regulate and support a market-driven development path. The recruitment of senior civil servants with mainly humanities backgrounds continued. In 2012 just two percent of senior civil service specialist posts were for scientists or engineers.[17] Confronted with the growing need to undertake complex infrastructure projects, the response was often to

14   Anderson (1987).
15   King and Crewe (2013).
16   Nardelli (2015).
17   Government Office for Science, Department for Business, Innovation and Skills (2013).

outsource planning as well as implementation to private companies, with periodic expensive failures.

The other obvious factor was the effect of the electoral system in producing single-party governments based precariously on narrow majorities in marginal constituencies. Ministers felt the stakes were too high to allow opposition MP s to play any role in law-making that could be used to score critical points, or slow down legislation. 'Public bill committees', which were supposed to give 'pre-legislative' scrutiny to government legislation, to expose problems before policy positions are hardened, appeared positively designed to be useless.[18] Select committees of MP s developed some expertise in the policy areas they oversaw but had no power to influence policy or even compel witnesses to appear.[19] Few institutional barriers and no real 'veto points' existed to weed out bad ideas.

Besides the limitations of the inherited state model there were distinctive new weaknesses. The market-oriented shift to policy 'delivery' as the paramount bureaucratic virtue meant a loss of objectivity. The job of civil servants was no longer to test ministers' plans against criteria of the public interest but just to give effect to them. Evidence-based objections were brushed aside; ministers increasingly declined to respond to criticisms and in public statements 'spin' became the norm. Numerous areas of public service provision became unaccountable, being outsourced to private companies whose activities were treated as confidential and not covered by the *Freedom of Information Act* or other safeguards. The boundary between public and private interests became blurred. Conflicts of interest became commonplace and treated as inevitable: instead of being eliminated they were supposed to be 'managed'.[20] 'Informal' government, which shades easily into corrupt government, became normalized.[21] Official documents lost the respect they once enjoyed, and disregarding and suppressing evidence became commonplace. In general, the authority of the state, and its capacity to play a creative part in resolving the crisis, had been severely reduced.

---

18   King and Crewe (2013: 369–70).

19   Like so many constitutional matters, even the formal power of select committees to compel witnesses is vague to the point of being non-existing, and in any case doesn't cover ministers or, in the view of some ministers, their civil servants (White 2016).

20   Leys (2012).

21   A major example was yet another reorganization of the National Health Service (NHS), which was set in hand in 2014: managers 'worked around' (i.e., ignored) key provisions of the law laid down in the previous reorganization of 2012, which the government was unwilling to admit was unworkable and to repeal. See Leys (2016).

5   An Unproductive Economy

Underlying everything, and limiting the prospects for dealing with other dimensions of the crisis, was the chronic weakness of the UK economy, which neoliberal medicine had not cured. Behind the insistence of the leading Brexiteers that the UK was 'the fifth biggest economy in the world' and could trade and prosper outside the EU 'on WTO terms' lay an uneasy awareness of another reality.

The UK had been living above its means for almost forty years, with an accelerating deterioration setting in from 1999 onwards. A yawning deficit in the UK balance of trade in goods, due to deindustrialization, followed by persistent low levels of investment and lagging productivity, was partially offset by two main factors: first, a trade surplus in services, thanks to the foreign earnings of the multinational banking enclave in the City of London; and second, inward capital investment, attracted by the UK's membership in the EU, which offered foreign companies entry to the EU Common Market, and exceptionally tight restrictions on trade unions. Brexit threatened this economic model. A 'hard' Brexit could force investment banks to relocate significant portions of their work to Paris, Dublin, or Frankfurt, and drastically harm the prospects for manufacturers. The declining UK car industry, especially, had been revived in the 1990s by foreign vehicle companies seeking access to the EU's single market, and had become so closely integrated with production in other EU countries that by mid-2019 the prospect of uncertainty about Brexit helped to bring production almost to a halt, with two plants closed and threatened cuts or closures at most others.[22] The country's aircraft industry was also at risk, along with hundreds of smaller companies that formed part of European supply chains in a wide variety of fields.[23]

The exceptional openness of the UK economy to foreign investors also meant that over half of all the companies listed on the London Stock Exchange, and almost all those in the top 100, had become foreign-owned, while many of those with valuable technological assets were sold and their senior staff shipped abroad along with the companies' patents.[24] Conservative

---

22   The companies concerned stressed that the shift to electric cars was necessitating worldwide reorganization of production but did not deny that further production in the UK depended on continued free access to the EU. See also Campbell (2020).

23   Airbus, the UK's largest aircraft manufacturer, threatened to move production to the EU in the event of a hard Brexit, while Bombardier put its Belfast plant, which makes wings for Airbus, up for sale in May 2019.

24   See Brummer (2012).

government initiatives for 'rebalancing' the economy, such as 'The Northern Powerhouse' and 'The March of the Makers', involving various inducements to private enterprise to invest in former industrial regions, had had little impact and regularly succumbed to postponement.[25] The truth was that there was no strategy capable of creating stable employment and a modicum of security for all, not to mention responding to the environmental crisis, that did not call for a leading role for the state. But successive governments had rejected this approach, and the state apparatus had become even less capable of playing such a role than it had been before the neoliberal turn.

On top of these weaknesses came the financial crisis, which 'light touch' regulation of the banking system in the UK had played a major part in precipitating.[26] The Labour Chancellor Gordon Brown led the international response of running up public debt to bail out the banks, while under his Conservative successor George Osborne the postwar welfare state was progressively dismantled in the name of 'austerity'. Between 2011 and 2018 government funding to local authorities, which provided most social services other than education and health care, was halved, and centrally-provided social security support for individuals and families was also cut.[27] In 2019 about a quarter of all children were living in poverty.[28] By 2018 five million people were in self-employment, much of it precarious, and averaging little more than half the income of full-time employees.[29] In 2018 Philip Alston, the UN Special Rapporteur on Extreme Poverty and Human Rights, recorded his shock at "the immense growth in food-banks in the UK, the queues waiting outside them, the people sleeping rough in the streets, the growth of homelessness;" and at the fact that "local authorities, especially in England, which perform vital roles in providing a real social safety net have been gutted by a series of government policies. Libraries have closed in record numbers, community and youth centers have been shrunk and underfunded, public spaces and buildings including parks and recreation centers have been sold off."[30] At the same time tax cuts, tax avoidance and quantitative easing had made a tiny class of people immensely rich.

---

25   The new High Speed Rail (HS2) was supposed to link Manchester and Leeds to each other and to London. Predictably, the London-Birmingham link was prioritized and in 2019 even that was in doubt. HM Government (2016); Elliott (2016).

26   Panitch, Konings, Gindin and Aquanno (2009) and Tooze (2018: 80–90).

27   Freezing the levels of social security payments to people in work was estimated to have cut the annual incomes of the poorest families by £900-£1,800 a year: see Butler (2018) and Work and Pensions Committee (2019).

28   O'Leary (2019).

29   Wain, Sidhu, Vassilev, Mubarak, Martin and Wignall (2018).

30   Alston (2018: 1).

6   The Parties in Face of the Crisis

The 'historic blocs' on which both traditional conservatism and Labour's 'parliamentary socialism' had relied were fractured. In once-productive towns, ports, and mining regions throughout the UK, with boarded-up high streets and epidemics of drug abuse, which had been Labour strongholds, there was a strong current of lost pride and anger at the political elite that had presided over this dereliction. The far right, led by Nigel Farage, successfully directed this against an elite who had 'surrendered' power to 'Brussels' and encouraged unlimited immigration from the EU, 'taking jobs away' from English workers, diluting 'our values' and fostering domestic terrorism (from immigrant Muslims). The Brexiteers also appealed to nostalgia for lost imperial greatness, and its associated racism, which resonated with relatively prosperous Conservative voters in smaller towns and villages as well as with workers in the 'left behind' ex-industrial regions.[31] UKIP, which had won almost four million votes in the general election of 2015, as well as winning the EU elections in 2019, was now a serious threat to the Conservatives. Boris Johnson, who had positioned himself as the leader of the party's far right and replaced Theresa May as leader in July 2019, now declared the party ready to leave the EU without a 'deal' of any kind – a commitment which Farage had succeeded in making the touchstone of credibility on the issue – and promised to abandon austerity and embark on a large spending program to 'level up' regional living standards. This looked like an attempted 'passive revolution', aimed at absorbing the disaffected and rebellious elements in society into the established ruling bloc and restoring the old political order. But Farage had no interest in a return to business as usual, but only in pushing the mainstream continuously further to the right. It was also clear that the main players in the new Conservative leadership had no thought of abandoning the tenets of neoliberalism. On the contrary their wish was to purge the country of its remaining residues of social democratic, welfarist regulation and protections. Their vision for the UK's economic future was to reduce regulatory standards across the board.[32]

Corbyn's leadership team, in contrast, had a state-led plan for social and economic reconstruction. Its 2019 manifesto was still more radical than that of

---

31   For analyses of the mix of feelings to which the Brexit campaign appealed see Barnett (2017) and O'Toole (2018).

32   See for example Hannan (2016: ch. 6), which spells out the imagined benefits of Brexit in 2025: "We have become Europe's foremost knowledge-based economy; we lead the world in biotech, law, education, the audio-visual sector, financial services and software; new industries – from 3D printing to driverless cars – have sprung up ...."

2017, proposing a large program of public investment and renewed public ownership, aiming to reshape the economy and tackle the accumulated problems of unemployment, inequality, poverty, and homelessness. This project faced intense opposition from capital, the mainstream media, the US and, significantly, Israel: Labour was distracted and wounded by a disinformation campaign attacking the party, and especially Corbyn, who supported Palestinian rights, as anti-Semitic.[33] Moreover during New Labour's years in office party managers had prevented socialists from standing for election as MPs, so that by 2015 only a handful of Labour MPs, as opposed to the party's membership, fully supported the Corbyn leadership's project, while a large minority of them actively opposed it, and plotted to remove Corbyn from the leadership in moves that also aggravated the party's deep split over Brexit. Nonetheless, in the autumn of 2019 the party still represented a radical alternative set of solutions to the country's deepening crisis. In a November 2019 speech Blair described both Johnson's and Corbyn's projects as "two sets of fantasies," and called for a return to "the sensible mainstream of British politics."[34] But the true fantasy was to suppose that the 'sensible mainstream' could be restored. The right-wing populist forces that had set the political agenda from the referendum onwards were not a temporary aberration, but a response to the failure of the 'sensible mainstream' to resolve the country's organic crisis. Recognizing this, Boris Johnson opted to embrace them, adopting the slogan of "getting Brexit done" at any cost and expelling from the party 21 MPs, including several of the party's most experienced and capable members, who were not willing to agree. At a stroke the electoral arithmetic changed: the risk that Farage would split the 'Leave' vote was averted, and the Labour Party alone could now be identified as still resisting 'the people's will'. Having overcome the obstacle presented by the *Fixed Term Parliaments Act* Johnson went on to secure a decisive Conservative majority in a general election in December 2019.

7   Unknown Forces, Represented by Charismatic 'Men of Destiny'

The new political forces that were precipitated by the crisis were not literally unknown, any more than the fascists in various countries to whom Gramsci was referring in his analysis of the general crisis of the state. What was unknown, or rather unrecognized, was their potential for radically reshaping politics. This

---

33   For an introduction to this sorry tale see Philo, Berry, Schlosberg, Lerman and Miller (2019).
34   Reuters Staff (2019).

was partly because the radical nature of the crisis was unrecognized. But it was also because observers failed to notice the political vacuum created by the loss of an intimate connection between the Conservative Party and large-scale capital. By 2019 few leading companies of any kind in the UK were British-owned. As David Edgerton pointed out:

> Today there is no such thing as British national capitalism. London is a place where world capitalism does business – no longer one where British capitalism does the world's business. Everywhere in the UK there are foreign-owned enterprises, many of them nationalised industries, building nuclear reactors and running train services from overseas. When the car industry speaks, it is not as British industry but as foreign enterprise in the UK. The same is true of many of the major manufacturing sectors – from civil aircraft to electrical engineering – and of infrastructure. Whatever the interests of foreign capital, they are not expressed through a national political party.[35]

This was no less true of financial capital. The widely remarked silence of the City of London over Brexit partly reflected the judgement of the major international banks that most financial transactions would continue to be done in London whatever happened.[36] But it also reflected the fact that the senior executives of so many major companies in the UK didn't specially care: the fate of the inhabitants of the UK was not high on their political agenda. As Goldman Sachs had already noted, before the referendum in 2016, "Only a tiny sliver [of all the equity listed on the London stock exchange] is owned by households or the government, the only two sectors that have a long-term vested interest in the fate of the UK as a place to live."[37] The field was thus open for a few very rich individuals to exercise a novel level of political influence by donating large sums of money to the far right project.[38] Several of them bet, between them, a total of £8bn against the pound, which they expected to fall as a result of Brexit, and accordingly financed the Leave campaign in the referendum, or

---

35   Edgerton (2019a); see also Edgerton (2019b).
36   The *Financial Times* may have stayed silent on Brexit, but its leading columns and editorials became increasingly social-democratic, perhaps reflecting the writers' personal investment in living with the consequences of an even more deregulated, unequal and conflictual society, calling for "capitalism to be nudged in some more inclusive, more sustainable direction," for a shift from private to public investment, and even for the renationalization of public utilities (Ford, 2019).
37   Edwards (2016).
38   Geoghegan (2019).

Johnson's leadership campaign, or both.[39] They were committed to an extreme version of neoliberal ideology, and wanted complete freedom from the regulatory regime of the EU, which a no-deal Brexit would ensure.[40]

The Conservative Party had meantime become more and more susceptible to their influence. The 56 Conservative MPs who belonged to the European Research Group, from which several members of Johnson's cabinet were drawn, held the same views as the outsider 'disruptors', while the 21 Conservative MPs who baulked at inflicting a no-deal Brexit on the country were peremptorily expelled. Most of the remainder were chiefly concerned to keep their seats, which meant listening to the views of their local party members who had the power to deselect them, and who overwhelmingly supported Johnson, while the newly elected Conservative MPs in former Labour seats owed everything to him. The overall result was "a parliamentary party as servile as the Supreme Soviet."[41] And while the party's 180,000 members were committed to English nationalism and social conservatism rather than to neoliberalism, by 2019 they had reached a masochistic obsession with departure from the EU.[42] To get it, well over half of them said they were willing to accept, if need be, the break-up of the Union through the secession of both Scotland and Northern Ireland, an economic slump, and even the destruction of the Conservative Party itself.[43] At the Conservative conference in October 2019 the populist rage promoted by Farage overwhelmed all other views.[44]

The result of the December 2019 election cemented the far right in power. A third of Johnson's new parliamentary majority of 80 MPs had been elected in Leave-voting constituencies hitherto held by Labour, most of which were unlikely to have been won if Farage had stood candidates in them, as he originally proposed. Johnson now needed both to make voters in these constituencies feel that their economic interests were being attended to, and to make the far right feel that their project was being adequately implemented. This meant taking on significant elements of Farage's project, in addition to leaving the EU. By 2019 Farage had abandoned UKIP and formed a new Brexit Party,

---

39   Wearden (2019).

40   On the accommodation to the prospect of Brexit of a growing number of City-based investment bankers see Crow (2019); on the neoliberal views of some leading members of the far right in Johnson's government see Beckett (2012).

41   Wheatcroft (2020).

42   On the social and political attitudes of Conservative members see Walker (2018).

43   Smith (2019). The one price they said they were not willing to pay was a Labour government led by Corbyn.

44   Chakraborty (2019).

which unlike UKIP, with its chronic tendency to splits and scandals, was a 'virtual' party, at his personal disposal. As leader he was free to choose all its candidates for elections and decide what policies to promote – his first aim being to ensure that Johnson did not retreat from his commitment to a hard Brexit and the anti-immigrant, anti-welfare, small state policies on which they were both broadly agreed.

And while Farage presented the Brexit Party as a component of the established parliamentary system, the anti-Islam, anti-immigrant and neo-fascist elements he had previously succeeded in aligning with UKIP still saw themselves as the back-up enforcers of national-conservative counter-revolution, capable of mobilizing thousands of mainly young men – 50,000 on one occasion in 2017 – to intimidating rallies in London.[45] Political uniforms had been outlawed in the UK since 1936, or hundreds of Brexit-supporting activists would undoubtedly have been marching in them in 2019. Farage, "one of the most effective and dangerous demagogues Britain has ever seen,"[46] was well aware of their potential to threaten violence whenever the Conservatives needed a fresh push to the right – a latent threat which some Conservatives liked to use as a reason for their support for a no-deal Brexit. If there had been a second referendum (for which there was growing support in parliament in mid-2019), one 'government insider' said, "MPs wouldn't be able to leave a secure zone in SW1 [Westminster], they would be lynched."[47]

As a result, by December 2019 far right racist prejudices (against people of color, and especially Muslims), and a distinct anti-democratic current, had been mainstreamed; and to a far greater degree than was apparent in the mainstream media, since 49% of people now got much of their news – and four out of five people aged 16 to 24 got most of it – from social media:[48] "microclimates … in which simmering resentments are amplified and authoritarians can offer

---

45 For an overview of the far right in the UK see three papers published in 2019 by the Commission for Countering Extremism on the Commission's website: Lee (2019), Mulhall (2019) and Allen (2019).

46 Seymour (2019). To arrive at this position of significant power Farage had overcome a series of contradictions that were inherent in his project, not least the contradiction between his basic free-trade, de-regulatory aims, and his nationalist and protectionist appeal. The reality was that "If he had his way, many of his supporters would be working harder, longer, for less money, with less protection" – the opposite of what he let his working-class base imagine. "His offer to them is that, in a society of dog-eat-dog competition, they will not have to compete with foreign workers" (Seymour, 2015).

47 Parker (2019).

48 By 2019 social media were being used as a source of news by 19% of all adults and had become the main source of news for 83% of people aged 16 to 24. See Ofcom (2019).

a fantasy of liberation from them without biased brokers getting in the way."[49] If the 2017 election was the first in which social media significantly displaced the influence of the tabloid press, the 2019 election may have been the first in which a central role was played by targeted messages delivered to voters identified by online data profiling. Insulated from public criticism, these messages relied primarily on reinforcing existing prejudices and feelings, and traded freely in false information, personal smears and lies.[50]

The Conservatives' negative campaigning and dirty tricks in the 2019 election, and their overt contempt for established rules, tended to legitimate the 'post-truth' culture. Charged with undemocratic behavior for renaming the Conservative Party's website as 'FactcheckUK' during Labour's manifesto launch, in order to mislead voters into thinking its attacks on the launch were the judgements of an objective source, the Foreign Secretary Dominic Raab called it a legitimate response to "Labour's lies;" and, he added, "nobody gives a toss." His cabinet colleague Nicky Morgan concurred, saying "only the Westminster bubble" cared about it. When Channel 4 Television refused to accept a minister as a substitute for Johnson in a party leaders' election campaign debate a government spokesperson threatened that its legal remit would be "reviewed." And in reply to the Supreme Court's role in declaring the prorogation of parliament illegal, the Conservative manifesto promised a commission to ensure that judicial review "is not abused to conduct politics by another means or to create needless delays."[51] In February 2020 Johnson appointed as Attorney General a lawyer who was committed to removing any significant judicial limits on executive power.[52]

---

49   Shenker (2019: 233).

50   In his brilliant book *Nervous States* (2018), Will Davies asks how far progressive politics based on evidence and reason can survive in the age of digital media. "The question is how much, if any, of a pre-internet culture of public critique can survive in an age where every intellectual exchange can swiftly be derailed by a joke, a personal attack, a cry of victimhood or a strategic misunderstanding of the other's argument. What if none of it can?" (Davies, 2019). Like Shenker (2019) in *Now We Have Your Attention*, Davies concludes that the chances are poor. A glance through the racist, sexist, and evidence-free Twitter feed of one engaged right-wing voter during the 2019 election was a sobering experience for someone (myself) who hoped that rational progressive politics might yet have some traction.

51   Right wing Conservatives' dislike of the judicial review of government actions was long-standing. See Bowcott (2020).

52   "People we elect must take back control from people we don't. Who include the judges" (Braverman, 2020). But by "people we elect" Braverman clearly meant only the government: the examples she cited of illegitimate court action were those in which the courts had acted to restore to parliament powers which the government had usurped.

Behind all these plans lay the unprecedentedly powerful role of Johnson's chief adviser, Dominic Cummings. Cummings was a professional political strategist credited with a major role in winning both the Brexit referendum and the 2019 general election. He had well-publicized iconoclastic views on the inefficiency of the civil service and the organization of central government, and on the low caliber of most politicians.[53] In September 2019 he was given authority to dismiss the special advisers of any government minister – something he had already done, apparently without needing such authority, to an adviser of the Chancellor of the Exchequer in August. And in February 2020, when the same Chancellor refused to dismiss his remaining advisers and accept instead a team chosen by Cummings, it was the Chancellor who had to resign. By early 2019 there were over 100 special advisers across all ministries, meeting weekly under Cummings' chairmanship.[54]

Cummings had in effect become the country's project manager. The 'mother of parliaments' was thus being overtly displaced by a prime minister with a large, subservient parliamentary majority, acting within policy parameters set by one unelected political figure, Farage, and implemented by another, Cummings, neither of whom had any time for the checks and balances of liberal democracy. Politicians who shared this attitude prospered. When the Permanent Secretary (the senior civil servant) at the Home Office pointed out the problems and risks posed by the government's plans for limiting immigration, the minister demanded and eventually secured his removal; a government source said that the top civil servants at both the Foreign Office and the Treasury were also in line to be got rid of. Meanwhile the prime minister's office began trying to limit critical media coverage, banning ministers from appearing on the BBC's main radio news program and seeking to exclude journalists from news briefings if they or their paper or radio or TV channel were deemed hostile.[55]

The inclination of the mainstream media was to see all these steps as undesirable but marginal, likely to provoke resistance and eventually be reversed. But in the context of the crisis it seemed rather more likely that they would come to be taken as given, paving the way for further authoritarian measures when the new government began to face difficulties, as it undoubtedly would. Maintaining economic growth, and avoiding widespread economic disruption, would present big problems, especially if there was no trade agreement with the EU. Spending money in the disadvantaged North and Midlands would

---

53   See Collini (2020).
54   See Rutter (2020).
55   Di Stefano (2020).

not be popular with the Conservatives' electoral base in the South, or with the free-market ideologues in the cabinet; and spending on the scale needed to significantly 'level up' the country, as Johnson had promised, would require either unpopular tax increases, or risking the party's reputation for fiscal prudence.

As in other countries confronted with the rise of anti-democratic populism, those who thought that Johnson's embrace of it was unlikely to endure trusted in the countervailing power of the 'institutions'. But in reality, the institutions promised no serious resistance. The judiciary had little appetite for acting to restrict executive power. The Supreme Court's role in opposing the abuse of power over Brexit and prorogation was unsought-for, and it rested on the principle of supporting parliamentary supremacy when no party had a parliamentary majority: it was very unlikely to rule against a government which enjoyed a parliamentary majority. A more characteristic case was the judiciary's role in denying the Wikileaks founder, Julian Assange, an adequate opportunity to prepare his case against extradition to the US, and in declining to intervene to stop his grossly abusive treatment, as a remand prisoner, by the Prisons Service.[56] Like Captain Dreyfus a century earlier, the UK's most famous political prisoner did not find the institutions checking this abuse of power.[57] The Johnson government's stated intention of curbing the independence of the courts could not be explained by any obstacle they really offered to its policies.

The same was true of the supposedly impartial and objective BBC. When Corbyn was elected leader of the Labour Party in 2015, commentators expected the BBC to have to reposition itself, away from the middle of the relatively narrow gap between the politics of David Cameron's Conservatives and Ed Miliband's Labour Party, to the middle of the much wider gap between Theresa May and Jeremy Corbyn. But that did not happen: Corbyn and his team were treated as illegitimate. It was a reminder that the BBC was, in the words of one of its leading academic analysts, "ultimately ... an organisation accountable not to the public, nor even to parliament, but to the heart of government."[58] But the BBC's adherence to what had been the elite political consensus was no

---

56 Most accounts of the Assange case, including Wikipedia's, contain many inaccuracies. The statement by Nils Melzer, the UN Special Rapporteur on Torture and other Cruel, Inhuman or Degrading Treatment or Punishment, serves as a useful introduction to the issues: Melzer (2019). On the conduct of Assange's extradition hearings see the reports of the former UK ambassador to Uzbekistan, Craig Murray, available at https://www.craig-murray.org.uk/.

57 A fairer test of the judiciary's willingness to resist arbitrary power would, admittedly, arise if the case reached the appeal courts.

58 Mills (2019). See also Mills (2016; 2017).

longer enough for Johnson and his team. Ministers made clear their intention to cut it down to size.[59]

And while Johnson and senior ministers denounced 'the establishment' as enemies of the people, in reality it was no longer a significant or coherent force: as Aeron Davis has pointed out, neoliberalism had undermined it as much as the rest of the postwar social and political superstructure.[60] Cummings' determination to frighten the senior civil service into abandoning any claim to a policy-making role was really overkill: most senior civil servants had become as short-termist as hedge fund managers. And the current generation of corporate chief executives had become even more self-promoting and less concerned with any conception of the public interest than the previous one. As for the established church, it no longer had a significant presence in the lives of the population, or authority in public life, while the monarchy, having sought to extend its legitimacy in the shape of the 'royal family', had become a form of reality TV. Arbitrary power would not be seriously constrained by resistance from any of these quarters.

8   Coda: The Pandemic and Beyond

The new coronavirus arrived in the UK on 31 January 2020. Throughout February, despite increasingly urgent warnings from public health experts, nothing was done to prevent it spreading and by early March it was out of control. On March 23rd the government reluctantly decreed a nationwide lockdown. By the end of April, the economy was in freefall. By mid-July, the UK had the distinction of having the highest rate of Covid-19 deaths per 100,000 people in the world.[61]

The scale of the disaster, and the solidaristic response to it of most people, led commentators of all political persuasions to imagine that the pandemic must lead to a new era of consensus. The divisions and rancor of the last decade would be buried in a collective effort to rebuild the economy on a new, more egalitarian, and environmentally sustainable basis. This vision ignored the reality of the new Johnson-Cummings government, which consisted of ministers whose prime, if not sole, qualification for office was an unswerving commitment to leaving the EU, strategically led by an 'adviser' with a well-publicized contempt for constitutional conventions and a strong belief in his

---

59   Morgan (2020).
60   Davis (2018).
61   Johns Hopkins' Corona Virus Resource Center (2020).

own exceptional genius for getting things done. The response to the pandemic was a comprehensive failure, but it also showed how this government was likely to approach the problems presented by the long-term crisis of the state.

Its inaction in February was above all due to its obsession with Brexit. Ministers wanted to celebrate having left the EU on 31 January, not to concern themselves with an obscure new illness.[62] The weak initial response to the pandemic was also partly due to Cummings' disruption of established policy-making procedures for responding to a pandemic – procedures already gravely weakened by the Conservatives' earlier remodeling of the English National Health Service on market lines. But inaction was followed by a series of major policy failures: a critical delay in implementing lockdown, disastrous mishandling of safety in care homes, confused public messaging, and an extraordinary failure to establish a testing, case-finding, and contact-tracing system capable of preventing further surges of infection.

Ministerial incompetence, which was often painfully on view at public briefings, played a part in these failures, but also involved were two default policy positions: an overriding hostility to the public sector, and a faith in central management based on information technology.[63] To take one significant example: instead of building on the existing bases of local expertise in infection control and using NHS labs and other public laboratories, which had substantial capacity, the work was conceived as a nation-wide IT-based operation and contracted out to a consultancy firm with no relevant expertise in health, with the testing farmed out to private labs. By July only just over half of the contacts of infected people were being reached, and asked to isolate, and local public health officers were still not being given the information held at the center in time to close down new outbreaks, which were becoming more and more common as the national lockdown ended. A similar outsourcing approach was adopted for procuring protective equipment, with similar results.

---

62   Johnson did not even attend five successive meetings of the cabinet's 'Cobra' committee to discuss the pandemic in January and February, and obsessive hostility to the EU continued to mark the government's handling of the response. Even when the scale of the threat had been recognized, the government declined to join an EU-wide program to procure personal protective equipment for healthcare staff, and did the same in July in relation to the future procurement of vaccines.

63   The preference for the private sector also involved a great deal of conflict of interest. The contracts awarded to a range of companies in response to the pandemic, totaling some £2.5bn, were not subjected to public tender. Several of them involved an AI firm used by Dominic Cummings in the Leave campaign and the 2019 election, and one was for monitoring public reactions to a range of government policies after the pandemic response. Davies (2020).

The scale of the failure in dealing with the pandemic did not at first attract the level of public resentment that might have been expected. The injection of almost £200bn into sustaining the economy during the pandemic, including putting nine million workers on several months' paid 'furlough', produced an atmosphere of general relief; the appeal to national unity in face of the pandemic limited what critics, including the new Labour leader, elected in April, felt it appropriate to say; and the mainstream media continued to underplay the severity of the government's policy failures. But by the end of the year the recession was destined to leave several million of these workers and their families dependent on minimal long-term state support, on top of the penury in which 14 million others were already living. By July optimism had given way to anxiety, and Johnson's personal ratings fell. But the government's politics, and what they portended for the impending crash, were not widely commented on.

What was most immediately obvious was the continued pursuit of the concentration of power at the expense of institutions and conventions that limited it. Senior civil servants who resisted politicization were purged: the permanent secretary of the Home Office having been forced into resignation, the head of the civil service and the permanent secretary of the Foreign and Commonwealth Office were induced to take early retirement, having been relentlessly 'briefed against' by government insiders. All government communications, hitherto based in individual ministries and carried out by civil servants, to keep official communications free from party political bias, were centralized in the prime minister's office, and the civil service as a whole was warned that it was seen as an obstacle to efficiency and could expect what Cummings called "hard rain." In July Johnson set up a task force to plan the restoration of direct government control over the health service, whose legal independence, established by a previous Conservative government, this one had found irritating. The demand for absolute compliance also extended not just to ministers and their advisers. A Conservative backbencher who had the temerity to get himself elected to chair an independent security and intelligence committee in place of the prime minister's choice was summarily expelled from the parliamentary party.

Cummings' hand in all this was perfectly apparent, and his power was demonstrated in a very public way when he broke the government's lockdown rules by driving more than 300 miles out of London, and compounded the offence by making a further side trip on a pretext so ridiculous as to amount to a declaration of impunity. Anger was universal, but Johnson declined to reproach him, let alone dismiss him, reinforcing the widespread impression that the government was in effect being run by Cummings.

Liberal commentators thought Johnson's defense of Cummings undermined the government's claim to represent the people against the elite. But this was to misunderstand the nature of the new Conservative project. While of necessity enforcing the lockdown, Johnson and Cummings were also tacitly aligning themselves with that section of 'the people' who felt hostile to the establishment, especially Leave voters who had voted for them in December. Among these was a significant body of 'lockdown sceptics' who doubted if the measures were necessary, who had previously been encouraged by the leading Brexiteers to reject 'experts' (i.e., economists who said Brexit would be economically damaging), and who felt no affinity with the medical scientists on whose advice Johnson now said he was acting.

A similar political calculation explained Johnson's refusal to seek any extension of the transition period, ending on December 31, 2020, during which a trade agreement with the EU had to be concluded. Given the wide differences between the UK and EU negotiators' positions, the prospect of leaving without any agreement became increasingly likely, threatening to deepen the recession by severely damaging trade with the UK's largest export market. The effects would be most serious in the Midlands and northern towns that had voted Leave, where much of the UK's remaining manufacturing was located, but Johnson's pledge to Leave voters in these areas demanded it. And in the absence of a strong counter-narrative, whatever happened would be framed – and would be accepted by those who had voted Conservative in December 2019 – as better than having remained in the EU, or having elected a Labour government. Economists, whom Brexiters had previously blamed for overstating the future costs of leaving the EU, would be blamed again when the costs had to be paid.

And no strong counter-narrative was forthcoming. Keir Starmer, who had replaced Corbyn as Labour leader, was a former government lawyer who showed no inclination to challenge the government's drive to concentrate power in the hands of an unaccountable 'aide', or to articulate even a modestly social-democratic alternative vision of the future. And should the government's narrative be seriously challenged from any quarter, the far-right and neo-fascist forces nurtured by Farage as adjuncts could be quickly mobilized in its support, as the response to the Black Lives Matter protests following the killing of George Floyd in Minneapolis demonstrated. BLM activists in the UK, some of whom threw the statue of a notorious slave-trader into the harbor in Bristol, were denounced as unpatriotic far left metropolitans bent on destroying Britain's (white, Christian) heritage. The Football Lads Alliance and other right-wing organizations mobilized thousands of mainly young men to descend on London to 'defend' other statues that BLM activists saw as emblems of racism, and they forced the cancellation of a major BLM rally. Johnson signaled his sympathy for the defenders, declaring that while he opposed racism and deplored violence, removing statues was to "lie about our history."[64]

In itself the Johnson-Cummings diarchy was actually quite fragile. As the scale of the government's failures in handling the pandemic gradually became clear Johnson's personal ratings fell, and there was even speculation that he could be replaced. But the combination of far-right politics and the accumulation of unchecked power corresponded to the nature and requirements of the new social bloc which the crisis of the state had allowed Johnson and Cummings to construct, and would outlast them.

Author's Note

This chapter does not begin with an encomium to the work of the person in whose honor it was written, because it seemed superfluous. I knew Leo as a close friend for over forty years, and collaborated with him in various ways for many of them. He had the most powerful mind of any political economist I have known, and I was happy to play Dr Watson to his Sherlock Holmes and to relish the intellectual stimulation and warmth that this collaboration always involved. This chapter was meant as a warm tribute – however much (I added affectionately, writing in mid-2020) it might call for his corrective pencil. In the context of the wider losses inflicted by Leo's death, the loss to his close collaborators of his penetrating but always supportive commentary may seem minor, but it is none the less bitterly painful.

---

64 He also announced the creation of yet another commission to enquire into race inequalities (four inquiries had been held in the previous three years, hardly any of whose recommendations had been implemented). Its members were to be appointed by a close associate who was widely distrusted by racial minorities.

CHAPTER 9

The Coronacrisis

A Body Blow to the Rotting American State

Doug Henwood

The Covid-19 pandemic threw the US into a recession unlike any other.[1] Back in the old days, meaning three or four decades after the end of World War II, there was a textbook pattern to the business cycle. After a few years, an expansion would mature, the stock market would get exuberant and frothy, labor markets would tighten (meaning wages would start to rise more rapidly than the owning class liked, because tight labor markets increase workers' power), inflation would pick up, and the Federal Reserve would raise interest rates to provoke a recession. Stocks would decline, the overall pace of business would slow, unemployment would rise, and wage and price pressures would ebb. The owning class would then feel better about the balance of forces, the Federal Reserve would lower interest rates, and recession would turn into recovery and expansion.

All that began to change with the onset of the neoliberal era forty years ago. The deep recession of the early 1980s wasn't the muted affair of earlier decades. It was designed to crush labor and succeeded via a massive onslaught on unions and cuts in social spending. The cue to crush labor came from Ronald Reagan who responded to a strike by the air traffic controllers' union in 1981 by firing them all and replacing them. Private employers took up the practice, which for the early postwar decades was considered bad form. No longer.[2]

For all the talk of neoliberalism as a rolling back of the state, that class war from above was led by the Reagan administration and Paul Volcker's Federal Reserve. But the private sector contributed plenty. Wall Street went wild with takeovers and restructurings that led to job cuts, wage cuts, and speedup. The

---

1 This chapter is a revised and extended version of Henwood (2020).
2 There's no space here to discuss the international dimensions of these policies, notably the transformation of the heavily indebted Latin American economies through restructurings. New finance was made conditional on deregulation of domestic economies and opening to foreign trade and capital flows – a process led by the US Treasury and the IMF (once described by the economist Rudiger Dornbusch as "a toy of the United States to pursue its economic policy offshore.") Quoted in: [Editorial] (1999).

capitalist class, firmly in the driver's seat, demanded higher profits and higher stock prices above all other priorities. It mostly got what it wanted.

The last several decades have undoubtedly been a great time to be rich. But things haven't been so great for everyone else. And the whole system got more unstable. Instead of the neat boom and bust cycle I described earlier, we had insane bubbles, reckless speculative manias that would end in crashes. The first was as the leveraging mania 1980s turned into the 1990s; the second, as the dot.com mania of the 1990s turned into the 2000s, and the third as the housing mania of the early 2000s ended in the 2008 crash. Each recovery from those crashes got weaker and weirder, with the very upper brackets making out like bandits and much of the rest of the population feeling like the previous recession had never ended.

The point of this very compressed history is that the US economy was getting sicker for a long time, largely because of the regimen used to treat its previous ailments – the inflation and sagging productivity of the 1970s. Neoliberalism, by which I mean the belief that markets should be firmly insulated from any political influence and capitalists should be free to do as they please with little restriction, had seriously undermined the system's integrity. (When I say insulation from political influence I mean of the humane sort. Intervention to make the rich richer, or bail them out when they hit a wall, was perfectly ok – encouraged in fact.) The competence of the state, military and police functions aside, were consciously eroded. Public investment was squeezed, and our physical and social infrastructure left to rot. Class and racial disparities in health widened along with income inequality and economic precarity. Debt levels kept rising, and the cult of maximizing stock prices meant corporations didn't invest or hire. Many borrowed money just to buy their own stock to raise its price, leaving them in weak financial shape when this crisis hit.

1   **Systemic Decay**

This economic crisis is different from both sorts I've been describing. It's not the garden-variety recession of the post-World War II decades, nor is it like the financial crises of the neoliberal era. It's the result of mass illness disrupting normal economic life, making it impossible for people to work (though of course many were forced to at great peril) or shop or do all the things that keep the wheels of consumption and production spinning.

But this crisis hit a system that had been structurally weakened because of the systemic rot – the erosion of state capacity, declining health among a lot of the population, increasing financial fragility, inequality, precarity, and the rest. Fragility and precarity have been widespread even in what are nominally "good" times.

According to an annual survey of economic well-being by the Federal Reserve[3] – an institution that ironically shows more interest in the topic than most others in US society – done in October 2019, when the unemployment rate was under 4%:

- 16% of adults were unable to pay their monthly bills in full, and another 12% said they couldn't pay if they were hit with an unexpected $400 expense.
- Over a third couldn't meet an unexpected $400 expense either out of savings or using a credit card they'd pay off at the end of the month. The rest would either carry a credit card balance or throw up their hands in despair.
- One in four skipped medical or dental care because they couldn't pay.
- Almost one in five had unpaid medical debt.

These are averages. It's not surprising to learn that white people did better than average, and black and Latino people did worse. For example, almost four in five white people were doing ok or living comfortably, compared with about two in three black and Latino people. You could turn that around, though: even in a relatively good year, one in five white people were barely getting by. Almost four in five straight people were doing at least ok, compared with two in three identifying as lesbian, gay, or bisexual (yes, the Fed asked this question).

2   Dimensions of Crisis

So that was the situation going into the hellscape of 2020. In August, the official unemployment rate was 8.4%, more than twice what it was when the Fed took that survey in 2019. Unemployment had come down from a peak of almost 15% in April, as people were recalled to work, but the August reading was at the 92nd percentile of all months since the modern series began in 1948. The employment/population ratio, the share of the adult population working for pay, was 56.5% in August 2020, up from April's low of 51.3%, but lower than any time since 1965 (bracketing the early moments of the coronacrisis) – before the mass entry of women into the workforce. All these numbers

---

3   Board of Governors of the Federal Reserve (2020). While many on the left used to lament the Fed's insulation from the control of elected officials, that independence has paradoxically insulated it from the broad erosion of state capacity and even the cruelty that has come to dominate US politics.

are considerably worse than the 2008–2009 downturn, once dubbed the Great Recession, a name that now might be considered obsolete. While those numbers may improve as 2020 progresses, they're likely to remain deeply depressed for a long time. The Fed clearly expects the recovery to take years; in projections released in September 2020, it forecast unemployment to remain high through 2021, and expressed intentions to keep interest rates close to zero through 2023.[4]

Things would have gotten a lot worse, and the recovery, such as it was, much weaker, had it not been for the Coronavirus Aid, Relief, and Economic Security Act (aka the CARES Act), passed in late March 2020. It included way too much blank-check aid to big capital, and a badly designed and administered scheme to aid small business, known as the Paycheck Protection Act (PPP). The PPP, structured as loans that would be forgiven if borrowers retained their employees, was administered through banks, who decided on eligibility; there were many reports of arbitrary decisions, based on applicants' relationship with those banks.

There look to have been dodgy loans. ProPublica reported that temp firms got PPP money to "retain" employees that they were renting out to their clients, meaning they got paid twice for the same work.[5] An examination of loans by the House Select Subcommittee on the Coronavirus Crisis found "high risk for fraud, waste, and abuse," including multiple loans to individual companies, loans extended to companies excluded from doing business with the government because of bad behavior in the past, and applications approved despite missing key identifying information.[6] Several studies found that larger firms were aided at the expense of smaller, and hard-hit regions received less aid than less affected ones.[7] The program did preserve employment to some degree but it could have been designed much better; it did nowhere near as well at preserving employment as Germany's *Kurzarbeit* (short work) program, under which the government subsidized wages.[8]

But the CARES Act also did some very effective and humane things, notably one-time payments of $1,200 to most adults, and a dramatic expansion of the US's normally chintzy unemployment insurance (UI) program. UI is a joint federal-state project under which states set conditions of eligibility and levels

---

4   Federal Open Market Committee (2020).
5   DePillis (2020).
6   House of Representatives, Select Subcommittee on the Coronavirus Crisis (2020).
7   Liu and Volker (2020); Neilson, Humphries and Ulyssea (2020); Bartik, Cullen, Glaeser, Luca, Stanton and Sunderam (2020); Granja, Yannelis, Makridis and Zwick (2020).
8   Meyer (2020); IMF (2020).

of benefits. Those benefits vary widely, from a low of $181 a week in Louisiana to a high of $450 in Hawaii, with a national average of $306.[9] (The South generally has the lowest benefits of any region, averaging $261.) The CARES Act tacked on an additional $600 a week to those risibly small sums – a significant chunk of money that allowed, much to employer and Republican distress, more than two-thirds of jobless workers to make more than they did when employed.[10] Alas, those supplemental benefits ended in July 2020 and were not renewed, thanks mainly to Republican objections. Treasury Secretary Steve Mnuchin explained his reasons: "We're not going to pay people more money to stay at home than work."[11]

Additionally, the Act also provided benefits to workers, like freelancers, who were previously ineligible for unemployment insurance. As of the end of August 2020, 13.5 million workers were on traditional benefits, and another 14.5 million were on the special pandemic program – nearly 28 million in all, down from over 30 million in June but still a huge number.

The unemployment insurance provisions of the CARES Act were one of the most generous welfare state measures in the ungenerous history of the US. Job losses from late March onward resulted in steep declines in wage and salary income – almost twice as bad as the declines after the 2008 financial crisis and exceeded only by the onset of the Great Depression in the early 1930s. But those declines were more than offset by the huge increases in unemployment insurance (UI) benefits, along with the $1,200 checks. These payments were so large that overall personal income, as measured by the national income accounts, actually rose in the second quarter of 2020 despite the giant hit to wage and salary income.

Personal consumption spending collapsed in late March and early April but stabilized almost the very day the CARES Act passed and began rising when the payments started flowing. According to near-real-time daily tracking of debit and credit card spending compiled by the Opportunity Insights project, led by the economist Raj Chetty, spending had recovered to 95% of pre-crisis levels by mid-June.[12] With the expiration of the supplemental

---

9   Figures are for July 2020, retrieved from United States Department of Labor Employment & Training Administration (no date).

10   Ganong, Noel and Vavra (2020).

11   CNBC (2020). That attitude isn't stopping Mnuchin from looking to forgive loans extended to businesses under the PPP. Businesses who took the loans were supposed to keep employees on payroll; if they did, the loans would be forgiven. It's not clear how many did keep employees on the payroll, or how many gamed the system by laying off and then recalling workers before the deadline, but Mnuchin wants to forgive the loans without knowing what happened, (Tracy, 2020).

12   Opportunity Insights (2020).

benefits, however, spending slid through the summer, and at the end of August was probably about 10% below where it "should" be, based on historical trends.[13]

These numbers are, of course, aggregates. Lots of people almost certainly haven't been so lucky. Many reported huge difficulties in filing for unemployment insurance because our systems are so antiquated. According to Bloomberg – the news service, not the billionaire ex-mayor – a quarter of benefits went unpaid because of bottlenecks in the application process or delays in overwhelmed and antique state systems.[14] Despite the expansion of UI eligibility, just 63% of workers in households below the poverty line are eligible for benefits, compared with 87% overall. The one-time payments missed millions of low-income households who don't file income taxes because they're too poor to owe anything.

Supports are also meaner than they could be because over the last few decades, US social policy has emphasized work incentives more than other countries. Rather than providing robust income support for the temporarily or chronically unemployed, our programs have tried to get people working (through things like work requirements in some states for Medicaid and Supplemental Nutrition Assistance Program benefits) and topped up low earnings (via the Earned Income Tax Credit). These approaches are not equipped to handle a labor market crisis such as the one we've seen.[15]

Despite the payments, food banks have been doing record business, with one measure of demand up 70%. In one survey, a quarter of families reported running out of food.[16] According to an experimental weekly survey from the Census Bureau, as of the end of August 2020, 60% of the US population was getting enough of the food they wanted, down from 68% before the crisis. That's a significant increase, but it's striking that even in good times, the share making significant compromises or going hungry was so high.[17]

13 The logic is this: as of August 31, spending was 7% below pre-crisis levels. Given "normal" retail sales growth of around 4% a year, spending should be up 3% three-quarters of the way into the year, not down 7%. Add 3% and 7% and you get 10%.

14 Saraiva, Donnan and Pickert (2020).

15 Bitler, Hoynes and Whitmore Schanzenbach (2020).

16 Bitler, Hoynes and Whitmore Schanzenbach (2020).

17 United States Census Bureau (no date).

3   **Structural Damage**

Recovery from this recession is likely to be a long slog. As this is written, the virus is far from under control in the US. Since this is not a conventional old textbook recession, a story of what the mainstream calls overheating followed by an imposed cooling followed by a normal recovery, nor is it a financial crisis recession, where recovery is inhibited by a huge debt overhang and a freeze in the credit system. It's one caused by damage to the real sector – supply chains broken, workers kept off the job by sickness and death (and the fear of sickness and death), customers kept away by those same fears, firms bankrupted by months of closure who may never reopen and rehire. The Fed can pump money into the markets and the federal government can deficit spend on a previously unimaginable scale, but these problems will take time to heal.

The crisis brought forth a number of prescriptions that boil down to printing money, from the CARES Act itself to energized supporters of Modern Monetary Theory. While these maneuvers can take the edge off a crisis, money is valuable only for what it can buy, and if the productive sector is broken, running the presses (or tapping out the keystrokes) has limited curative potential.

We hadn't really recovered from the 2008 crisis before 2020 hit. Had the economy continued to grow in line with its 1970–2007 trend, GDP would be about 20% higher than it is now. The 2009–2019 expansion never narrowed the gap with that trendline that opened up in the recession – in fact, it widened as growth lagged the previous trend – and the lingering damage of 2020 will put an even greater distance between actual and trend. And while GDP is a very imperfect proxy for human welfare, it is one of capitalism's principal measures of itself, and it's a measure of the resources available in society to afford things.

Through the gloom, the stock market has powered higher, despite being very highly valued by historical standards on the cusp of the crisis. Why?

Stock investors are compulsive optimists most of the time, and so the markets have been convinced the virus is going to go away and everything will be better very soon. And the Federal Reserve has been pumping trillions into the markets for months; that's potent fuel for a speculative fire. From the end of February to the middle of June 2020, the Fed expanded its balance sheet by over $3 trillion, though it stayed flat in subsequent months. But it's not just money – it was the Fed's promises of indulgence as well. Especially powerful were promises of trillions in support, little of which has actually been extended; those sweet words set off strong market rallies in the minutes after their release.[18]

Most of the market's gains are concentrated in five big tech stocks, Facebook, Amazon, Apple, Microsoft, and Google. They're up 35% since the beginning of 2020; the rest of the market, as measured by the S&P 500 index, is down 5%.[19] A 5% decline is not big, given the damage to the real economy, but it tells a much different story from the tech biggies.

4 Rotting State

One of the most remarkable things the crisis has spotlighted is the profound erosion of US state capacity. And with this I depart from the well-known position held by Leo Panitch, in a publication designed to honor him, by sub-scribing to a narrative of American decline. By now that decline seems a well-established fact.

To take one prominent and important example, the Centers for Disease Control (CDC), previously one of the most respected such bodies in the world, has performed badly throughout the crisis. At the onset of the pandemic, the CDC's coronavirus test kits were unusable because of manufacturing prob-lems.[20] And as the crisis progressed, the Trump administration's direct over-ruling of the agency's scientific staff – rewriting press releases and health guidelines, intimidating staff, seeking editorial control over its flagship publi-cation – got ever-more egregious and openly reported.[21]

But as the test kit debacle suggests, the CDC's problems were long in the mak-ing, and predated Trump. Funding was squeezed coming out of the 2008–2009 recession, and young scientists became less enthusiastic about working there, a reversal of earlier practice. That same funding squeeze hammered state and local public health authorities, who were unprepared for the Covid-19 crisis.[22] We saw similar failures with the states' inability to handle the onrush of appli-cations for unemployment insurance, their systems running on 1960s-vintage COBOL software. Washington found it a challenge to send out the relief checks to everyone who qualified, and reliance on banks to handle the PPP because

---

18   Cox, Greenwald and Ludvigson (2020).
19   Foroohar (2020).
20   Willman (2020).
21   Diamond (2020). The flagship publication is the *Morbidity and Mortality Weekly Report.*
22   Interview with Himmelstein and Woolhandler (2020).

the federal government lacked the capability led to vast inefficiencies in the distribution of aid.

Much of this can be attributed to the relentless disparagement and underfunding of the public sector since the 1980s, to the point where the erosion of state capacity is undermining the system's capacity to sustain and reproduce itself. The pandemic is one dramatic instance of this, but so too is the climate crisis. Not even the simultaneous disasters of fires up and down the west coast and the destruction wrought by Hurricane Sally along the Gulf Coast, one of a new breed of wetter tropical storms spawned by climate change (because warmer air can hold more water), made much of an impression on a ruling class apparently committed to resolute inaction.[23]

This is where I could launch into a rendition of my current obsession: the rot of the American ruling class, driven by extracting the maximum profit in the shortest period of time, hang the consequences, unable to plan for the long term.[24] The contrast with the mid-20th century ruling class, which planned the postwar American imperial order with foresight and skill, is stark. But rather than do that, I want to focus on one particular aspect, the erosion of the two leading political parties' capability of organizing that ruling class.

Something important I learned from Leo Panitch (which in turn he picked up from Ralph Miliband) is that classes don't know their interests spontaneously, nor do they organize without parties, other organizations, and even states to lead the way. This is true even of ruling classes, despite their enormous advantage in resources over the ruled. The devolution of the Republican Party, from its role as the natural expression of the bourgeoisie, both high and petty, into first a hard-right party and then a Trump cult, is an important part of the story of elite rot.

There are many ways of making this point, but one would be to compare the Republican platforms of 1972, when Richard Nixon ran against George McGovern, with the 2020 platform, with Trump running against Joe Biden. The 1972 platform ran close to 25,000 words. In many ways it's a conservative document, emphasizing the role of the private sector in economic development, ginning up the War on Crime (and its close relative, the War on Drugs), and promoting the displacement of governmental responsibility down from the federal to the state and local level. But it had many passages illustrating why Garry Wills called Nixon "the last liberal." Strikingly, the platform devotes over 900 words to the environment, and another 600 to the closely related

---

23   Fountain and Schwartz (2020).

24   See Henwood (2018).

topic of energy and natural resources, and the positions advanced are a shock to anyone familiar with the philistine destructiveness that characterizes the current Republican Party (Trump's and otherwise). It promotes big spending and tighter regulations to improve air and water quality and land use, reduce ocean dumping and noise pollution, protect endangered species, and expand the federal parks system. It brags about Nixon's efforts to expand "leadership in international environmental activity." It promises to develop energy sources "without doing violence to our environment."[25]

The 2020 Republican platform is another beast entirely. It's not even a platform, really, but a "resolution regarding the Republican Party platform." Including that title, it runs 329 words, just over 1% of its 1972 ancestor's length, and after explaining how Covid-19 made the process of convening a platform committee impossible (something the Democrats had little difficulty overcoming, and funny coming from a party that has denied or minimized the pandemic since its outbreak), came to the core of the statement: "the RNC [Republican National Committee], had the Platform Committee been able to convene in 2020, would have undoubtedly unanimously agreed to reassert the Party's strong support for President Donald Trump and his Administration." The document then moves on to complain about unfair media coverage, denounce the "Obama-Biden administration," reiterates its enthusiastic support of "the President's America-first agenda," complains some more about the media, and – the third time the charm? – once again announces "the strong support of the RNC for President Trump and his Administration."[26] What was once the leading party of US capital – the Democrats were always mostly a party of capital that had to pretend otherwise for electoral reasons, making their loyalties more divided – has completed its transformation into a personality cult.

It's remarkable how little support from the upper bourgeoisie Trump has. Though there were exceptions, much of big capital lined up behind Hillary Clinton in 2016. Trump bought off a skeptical CEO class with tax cuts and deregulation, but as he faced re-election, the ranks of his corporate supporters thinned. Despite several decades in New York City real estate, most industry bigwigs are supporting Biden, both locally and nationwide. "A competent, rational and scientific-based response to Covid is essential for the real estate industry," said developer Douglas Durst. (In September 2020, Durst was tapped to become the next chair of the Real Estate Board of New York, the industry's

25   Republican Party Platforms (1972).
26   Republican National Committee (2020).

trade association. Trump never belonged.) An exception is Blackstone CEO Stephen Schwarzman, a strong Trump supporter and economic advisor, but donations to Biden coming out of his firm "far outnumbered" those to Trump.[27] As a friend who's a real estate banker in Florida, who got into the business through union pension funds and remains a Marxist, put it: "Trump has always been viewed as a blowhard lightweight by the real New York real estate crowd."

While the Republican Party has traditionally been seen as the pure party of capital, the Democrats often serve as understudies (though given that the working class is an important part of their electoral base, that can be an awkwardly contradictory role). But they've also devolved over the decades. In the 1990s, the business-friendly politics of Bill Clinton and his associates consolidated the gains of the Reagan years, further discrediting the welfare state, elevating the role of the financial markets in economic governance, intensifying the carceral state, and lowering working-class expectations. Dedication to austerity as the norm for public social spending was extended and deepened, as Clinton, declaring that "the era of big government is over," reversed Reagan's deficit spending and left office in 2001 with the federal budget in surplus for the first time since 1969.[28] Though it's certainly not to my liking, Clinton & Co.'s transformation of the Democratic Party was a gain for capital. Productivity, profits, and the stock market boomed; union representation fell from 16% of the workforce to 13%; after falling 81% in the 1980s, the number of strikes fell another 67% in the 1990s, for a cumulative fall of 97% between 1979 and 1999.[29]

Since then, the Democratic Party has little to offer capital except the promise of a "return to normalcy," Warren G. Harding's campaign slogan in the 1920 presidential election. Hillary Clinton's campaign was notoriously issue-free; there were position papers galore but no serious program. Biden doesn't even have much in the way of position papers. Across the spectrum, the political class in the US looks bereft of ideas.

5   WITBD?

It's not that the landscape isn't full of suggestions about what should be done.

---

27   Kromrei (2020).

28   While Clinton didn't exactly reverse "big government," it did shrink under his watch. When Reagan left office in 1987, federal spending, according to the national income accounts, was 22% of GDP; when Clinton left, it was 19%.

29   US Bureau of Labor Statistics (no date).

Most urgently, despite the partial economic recovery, millions of people need serious income support, at least $2,000 a month for at least six months. We need eviction and foreclosure moratoriums to prevent what looks like an inevitable wave of mass homelessness as people find it impossible to pay their rent and mortgages. State and local governments and school systems need big support; if they don't get it there will be massive job and service cuts that will generate misery and deeper depression. Schools can't reopen safely without a major infusion of resources.

Longer term, never has the Green New Deal seemed so practical, Nancy Pelosi's dismissive "green dream or whatever" comment to the contrary. It has everything we need: the massive public investment program to repair our rotting infrastructure, and the kinds of social spending we need to make the poor not poor and the working and middle classes comfortable and secure.

For decades, civilian public investment net of depreciation has hovered just above 0, meaning that we're doing little better to replacing things as they decay. (See Figure 9.1.) This economic statistic can easily be confirmed just by walking around anywhere in the US outside our richest neighborhoods. We need massive investment in public infrastructure on the model of the New Deal, both to fight the slump and to make this country habitable for the bottom 80–90% of the population. That infrastructure investment must not simply be more of the same – not airports and highways, but clean energy and high-speed rail. The investment program needs to be part of a conversion of an economy based on exploitation of workers and nature into something humane and sustainable. The New Deal also subsidized artists and writers, and the projects it created were often beautiful – not driven by the mean, philistine view of life that we usually associate with the public sector.

As an example of the new kind of investment we need, we could put now-unemployed auto workers back to work building vehicles that don't threaten life on earth. A model to think about was the (sadly unsuccessful) proposal to transform a plant in Ontario, Canada GM closed into something earth- and worker-friendly. That proposal would have nationalized the plant, put it under worker and community control, and converted it to producing electric vehicles for the public sector.[30] That could be a model for the transformation of the entire motor vehicle sector.

We also need to think about industries we don't want to see recover. The airline industry is in dire shape. It's also ecologically destructive and we need to imagine a world in which we all continue to fly much less. The cruise industry

---

30   Milton (2020).

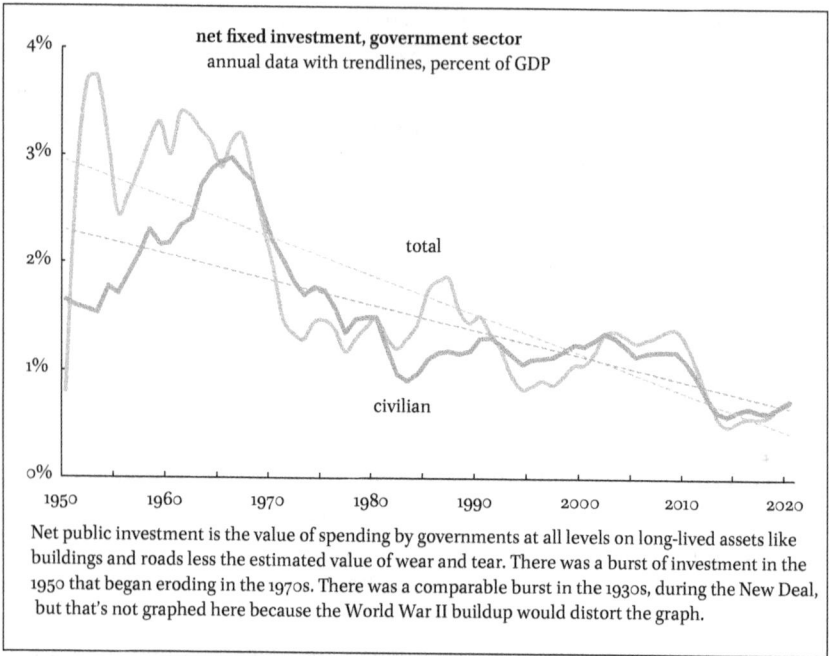

Net public investment is the value of spending by governments at all levels on long-lived assets like buildings and roads less the estimated value of wear and tear. There was a burst of investment in the 1950 that began eroding in the 1970s. There was a comparable burst in the 1930s, during the New Deal, but that's not graphed here because the World War II buildup would distort the graph.

FIGURE 9.1   Net fixed investment, government sector
SOURCE: BUREAU OF ECONOMIC ANALYSIS (2020)

is filthy and wrecks the towns where those giant ships dock, and it should be euthanized. This would be a propitious time to nationalize the oil and gas sector, undertaken with the idea of putting them out of business. We must move as quickly as possible to stop the use of fossil fuels, and as long as these entities exist, the political and economic obstacles to that necessity are nearly impossible to overcome. Political difficulties aside, the price tag would not be overwhelming. Because the price of oil has fallen so dramatically, the value of the major carbon producers has cratered. The five biggest US-based oil companies (Exxon Mobil, Chevron, ConocoPhillips, Phillips 66, and Valero) have a combined market capitalization of about $400 billion, which is equal to about an eighth of JPMorgan Chase's total assets and less than 2% of GDP. Shareholders will whine, but as the financial world wakes up to the inevitability of carbon's obsolescence, the value of their investments will tend towards o anyway. In all cases, workers should be protected, not displaced, but the underlying businesses should be wound down or severely shrunk.

The banking system is in decent shape now, surprisingly perhaps, but should serious recovery remain elusive, this will change as more people and businesses find themselves unable to service their debts. Nationalize several of the largest banks – and unlike the nationalizations in Sweden in the 1990s and the UK a decade ago, they should not be undertaken with the idea of returning them to private ownership as quickly as possible, after the government eats the losses. They should be run on entirely different principles – something like a financial utility, that provides basic services like checking and savings accounts, but not incomprehensible financial products.

There's no reason the nationalized banks couldn't be run to finance the Green New Deal. Some of the GND will have to be financed with traditional tax- and bond-financed public spending, but there's no reason these socialized banks couldn't participate.

Along with the nationalized banks, we should create something on the model of the Reconstruction Finance Corporation, to finance the GND. It would be a publicly capitalized bank that would evaluate and fund projects like clean energy generation and new models of food production.

At the same time, we should severely rein in, with an eye to abolishing, the shadow banking sector of private equity (PE) and hedge funds. PE has saddled companies with crippling levels of debt, which enrich their investors but put them at great risk of failure even in relatively good times. (A subset of PE, venture capital, can play a more constructive economic role, but it's quite small: there was less than $10 billion in early-stage financing from the sector last year.) Hedge funds do little but destabilize markets and serve no useful purpose.

And never has the need for Medicare for All been so clear. And the reason for that isn't only the need of freeing people from the anxiety of not being able to pay for essential care, but also because there is little in the way of planning for the distribution of health care resources beyond what The Market demands. A major part of the reason the US is so unprepared to handle the coronavirus crisis is that hospitals are built and outfitted according to where the money is, not where the needs are. Hospitals in both cities and rural areas are broke and closing in the middle of a health emergency. They need to be built where they can serve people who need them.

A lot of this may seem pie in the sky, but who ever thought there'd be a socialist caucus in the New York State legislature, as there will be in the next year's legislative session? The right still has political power, but it's widely discredited, and mainstream Democrats are out of ideas. We're deep in a massive economic and social crisis and we've got the energy and ideas and they don't. Now is not the time to be shy.

What makes this agenda less pie-in-the-sky than usual, aside from its screaming urgency, is that there are actually signs of revival on the left, with a growing number of self-identified socialists in city councils, state legislatures, and even a handful in the House of Representatives, with the count almost certain to rise significantly after the November 2020 elections. The Black Lives Matter protests of mid-2020 were probably the largest popular mobilization in US history – according to Gallup, 11% of US adults, and over a quarter of people in their 20s, participated in the protests, a phenomenal number.[31] Alas, there's not much in the way of organization or agenda behind the protests, but they are a sign of receptivity to radical ideas.

For organization and agenda, we do have the Democratic Socialists of America (DSA), which had over 70,000 members as of August 2020.[32] At least for now, the internal culture of the organization is nothing like the moribund one of the British Labour Party that Leo Panitch had been lamenting for years.[33] It's deeply collegial, rich with internal education, and active on many fronts, electoral and otherwise, and has certain parallels to the efforts of Momentum to work inside and outside the Labour Party to rebuild a new socialist movement in Britain. Of course, 70,000 in a country of 325 million is tiny, but it's grown through the pandemic, despite all the obstacles to meeting and recruitment. As Marx said in 1850, an observation that would apply to the US 170 years later, "les capacites de la bourgeoisie s'en vont" [the capacities of the bourgeoisie disappear] – but such a vacuum can be an opportunity for its antagonists.[34]

---

31   Long and McCarthy (2020).
32   Democratic Socialists of America (2020: 16).
33   Most recently in Panitch, Gindin and Maher (2020).
34   Marx (1850).

CHAPTER 10

The State, Trade Union Freedoms and the Impasse of Working-Class Power in Canada

Charles Smith

In 1984,[1] Leo Panitch and Donald Swartz published an essay in the pages of *Labour/Le Travail* examining the coercive powers that Canadian governments were using to restrict workers' ability to strike.[2] Panitch and Swartz's intervention came in the aftermath of the one-day national general strike against the state's imposition of wage and price controls in 1976's *Anti-Inflation Act*, the 1979 jailing of the Canadian Union of Postal Workers (CUPW) President Jean Claude Parrot after he refused to call off an illegal strike, and the cap on collective bargaining settlements in 1982's '6 and 5' program.[3] In reviewing the political-economic crisis plaguing North American capitalism at the time, Panitch and Swartz highlighted the inconsistencies in the capitalist state's stated commitment to 'free collective bargaining' in an era when the state and capital were actively working to restrict those rights by criminalizing the ability of workers to freely withdraw their labor. What was unique about this analysis was the historical observation that the erosion of free collective bargaining was itself contradictory as the state already restrained workers' collective freedoms through a "generalized rule-of-law form of coercion" embedded in the postwar form of 'industrial legality' across the capitalist world. Yet, what was unfolding in the crisis of the 1980s was an even greater restriction of those freedoms in which the Canadian state exercised "a form of selective, ad hoc, discretionary state coercion (whereby the state removes for a specific purpose and period the rights contained in labour legislation)."[4]

In the subsequent book-length expansion of the essay, Panitch and Swartz tracked the contradictory manner by which both federal and provincial governments repeatedly used temporary measures to restrict workers' capacities

---

1 A shorter version of this essay appeared in a roundtable discussion. See Smith (2021).
2 Panitch and Swartz (1984).
3 For a history of the federal government's intervention in collective bargaining and the clampdown on union freedoms in this period, see Aivalis (2018: ch. 7). On Parrot's incarceration, see Parrot (2005).
4 Panitch and Swartz (1984).

to freely bargain and strike whenever such actions became economically or politically problematic for the state and the corporate classes.[5] The authors were equally confounded by the fact that the newly minted Charter of Rights and Freedom's protection of freedom of association was interpreted by conservative judges to exclude both the right of workers to bargain or the right to strike.[6] By 2003, these 'ad hoc' restrictive measures and the capitalist state's disdain for workers' collective rights and freedoms were so frequent that it was safe to say that Panitch and Swartz's innovative concept of 'permanent exceptionalism' had become the new norm for all workers whose strike action threatened the power of capital or the state in any given conflict. Using this concept, Panitch and Swartz were able to identify the contradictory manner by which the use of back-to-work legislation by Canadian governments was "continually portrayed as exceptional, temporary, or emergency-related, regardless of how frequently they occurred or the number of workers who fell within their scope or were threatened by their example."[7] It is therefore not surprising, that what began to be deployed by the Canadian state in the 1950s, and used with increasing frequency since the end of the 1970s, the so-called 'temporary' and 'exceptional' nature of back-to-work legislation had become something much more than an 'ad hoc' policy instrument. Indeed, by 2021, legislated returns to work had over 144 separate occurrences.[8] For Panitch and Swartz, recognizing the coercive nature of back-to-work legislation in the era of so-called 'free collective bargaining' was important because it recognized the shifting power imbalance in Canadian labor relations was vital to understanding how class power was being restructured by state-led neoliberalism. This is why their book remains a foundational text in Canadian labor history, political economy, and labor studies.[9]

What Panitch and Swartz were able to recognize is that the right to strike in Canada was constantly being set against a looming political or economic emergency – real or imagined – that might disrupt capitalist accumulation.

---

5   Panitch and Swartz (1988).
6   Panitch and Swartz (2003). For more detailed discussion on the court's antagonism to workers' collective rights in this period, see: Fudge (1988). Larry Savage and I expand on this analysis in Savage and Smith (2017).
7   Panitch and Swartz (2003: 30–31).
8   Calculated from Panitch and Swartz (2003: Appendix 11); Canadian Foundation for Labour Rights (2020).
9   While publishing metrics are a deeply flawed way to measure influence, it is worth recognizing that a simple search of Google Scholar counts over 300 citations of *The Assault on Trade Union Freedoms* book and article. Within the pages of *Labour Le/Travail*, the book is cited routinely, with over 50 separate citations in a random search.

It was thus not surprising for the authors that when the capitalist offensive turned against the postwar Keynesian consensus in the 1970s, back-to-work legislation became the state's blunt instrument to discipline Canadian workers and weaken resistance to the otherwise violent process of neoliberalization.[10] The legal restraints on collective action reinforced the neoliberal policy changes designed to squeeze workers' capacities to fight for higher wages, as occurred during the earlier anti-inflation fights over wage controls; and they were equally effective in weakening the ability of teachers and nurses to challenge government-imposed austerity within the public sector throughout the 1990s and 2000s. Indeed, the complete norming of the permanent exceptionalism thesis in the Canadian state was demonstrated clearly – and unwittingly – by Conservative Prime Minister Stephen Harper when, in defending his decision to legislate Air Canada workers back-to-work in 2012, asserted that his government would,

> ... be darned if we will now sit by and let the airline shut itself down. Under these circumstances at the present time, this is not what the economy needs and it is certainly not what the travelling public needs at this time of year. As much as there's a side of me that doesn't like to do this, I think these actions are essential to keep the airline flying and to make sure the two parties find some way through mediation arbitration of resolving these disputes without having impacts on the Canadian public.[11]

Harper's position repeated the now consistent pattern of governments recognizing the legitimacy of industrial legality yet acting in a direct way to undermine any pretext of support for union associational rights when they challenge the policies of accumulation championed by governments and capitalists.

While Harper's government did not shy away from championing an anti-union animus, the present-day concoction of reactionary Conservatives

---

10   *Neoliberalization* is defined by Jamie Peck and Adam Tickell as a *process* that is shaped by the relative balance of class forces at any given moment within different capitalist formations. While parts of the neoliberal revolution became relatively hegemonic on a global level, Peck and Tickell warn us not to assume that neoliberalization will result in a "simple convergence of outcomes" across different states precisely because the balance of class power will differ between capitalist states. See Peck and Tickell (2002: 383). While the process of disciplining labor was universal across the capitalist world, it took on the form of intensified back-to-work legislation in Canada because it was meant to destroy the "social solidarity that put restraints on capital accumulation." See Harvey (2005: 75).

11   Bouzane (2012).

represents a crude form of a now decades-old pattern of the capitalist state undermining core labor freedoms. Notwithstanding this history, stubborn questions remain. Why do Canadian governments continue to use back-to-work measures, even though workers are utilizing the strike weapon (whether legally or illegally) far less than at any time since the 1940s? And how has the state's repeated use of back-to-work legislation contributed to a weakened movement now more reluctant to utilize the strike weapon? The answer to such questions lies in the Canadian state's long history of regulating workers' collective action through both the coercive and legitimacy functions of law; the legal system in capitalist societies has always been predicated on limiting and undermining working-class militancy. Canada's regulation of labor relations is unique in that both the ability of workers to bargain and to strike are specifically and narrowly defined by the capitalist state. In examining this history, this chapter will look at the first use of back-to-work legislation in 1950, in order to demonstrate that the basic elements of Panitch and Swartz's "permanent exceptionalism" concept – deference to public emergencies and temporary restrictions on legal rights to strike – were built into the foundation of Canada's current system of industrial legality. The way in which the Supreme Court of Canada has interpreted freedom of association in the Charter of Rights and Freedoms, which as of 2015 now includes a right for workers to collectively bargain and strike, will then be examined. It will be argued that back-to-work legislation continues to be the sharp edge of the ongoing state assault on post World War II union freedoms, disciplining labor to a point that strikes rarely disrupt the political and economic agendas of the country's ruling classes. Moreover, labor's response to these attacks, which has largely been through legal engagement with the courts, ends up reinforcing a legal regime that is structurally designed to weaken workers' collective ability to strike.

1   On Restrictions of Strikes in Canadian Labor History

In his 1977 essay on the Canadian state, Leo Panitch recognized that the early commitments by English settler politicians to embrace colonial Toryism witnessed an embryonic economic class (primarily tied to natural resource extraction, finance, and early manufacturing capital) utilizing the state to foster capital accumulation.[12] In Canada, this process first took the form of a violent dispossession of Indigenous territories, which Panitch later observed in

---

12   Panitch (1977b). On Toryism in this period see: Whitaker (1977).

his important essay on dependency and class, occurred with "exchange value predominat[ing] social relationships," which "had much to do with the fact that Canada was composed of 'white settler' colonies."[13] Built on the racist assumptions of white supremacy and colonialism, ruling classes in Canada used the state in violent and genocidal ways to appropriate Indigenous lands and territories and to utilize Indigenous labor in early capitalist industries throughout the country.[14] Later, the state became active in the recruitment of a landless working class first from Britain and later from Southern and Eastern Europe and Asia to labor and often die working on large public work projects and fledgling factories in the 19th and early 20th centuries.[15]

What Panitch further demonstrated was that because the process by which accumulation, coercion, and legitimation in this period was done to further capitalist expansion, it was both contradictory and uneven.[16] In that process, wealthy classes in the emerging cities were not able "extract a surplus through the direct imposition by force of greater absolute exploitation (as was the case with plantation agriculture)" and thus had to build an alliance of the largely male craft-work force with the Conservatives' ambitious national policy.[17] Somewhat ironically for economic nationalists, that alliance resulted not in an expanded domestic manufacturing class, but a relatively high-wage white male proletariat that weakened domestic capital's ability to squeeze labor through lower wages or a longer working day, thus contributing to the growing dependence on American branch plant capital to build and expand the Canadian manufacturing sector in Southern Ontario and Quebec. Yet, there was never any doubt that colonial elites were doing everything in their power to insulate and protect the domestic ruling classes from external pressure from American expansionism. The ties that the ruling Tories maintained with British financiers constructing the trans-continental railroad are just a small component of that history.[18] What is important for our purposes is that the uneven and

---

13   Panitch (1981: 14).

14   For an overview of this history see: Starblanket (2018). On Indigenous work and labor in the creation of Canadian capitalism see Parnaby (2006).

15   Bleasdale (2018). Bleasdale masterfully demonstrates the complex system in which the state directed the construction of the massive public works projects that built the foundation for Canada's future capitalist economy. In 19th century Canada, the construction of the so-called 'free' market was, in her estimate, tied to a massive public undertaking that was dependent upon a transient labor force that had to be imported (largely from the ranks of the British and Irish working classes), who upon arrival in Canada were both exploited and criminalized as they attempted to earn a living and create community in the colony.

16   Panitch (1981).

17   Panitch (1981: 14–15).

18   Naylor (1975).

contradictory manner by which the capitalist state acts to maintain the conditions for accumulation while simultaneously maintaining the tools to both coerce the working classes into submission through force or, as has been the case in the era of so-called free collective bargaining, through a form of political, legal, and economic legitimation.

Using Panitch's theorization of the capitalist state as our lens, it should come as no surprise to students of labor history that Canadian workers have never been entirely free to challenge the power of employers through the collective withdrawal of labor. Throughout the nineteenth century, the law constructed numerous criminal boundaries around workers' strike action.[19] Although many of these criminal restrictions were formally removed after 1872 in the alliance between the Tories and segments of the primarily white male working class, police and employer violence on picket lines were routinely utilized to break workers' strikes in the expanding areas of so-called non-skilled workers, especially when those actions proved threatening to the political and economic order.[20] While the process of violent coercion was certainly demonstrated, most famously during the 1919 Winnipeg general strike, that struggle was only the most sensational in a long history of state repression and violence that characterized strike activity in Canada prior to 1944.[21] To be sure, not all strikes in the pre-1944 period challenged the pillars of the capitalist economy or threatened to undermine the power of the state. While some erupted into violence, many others did not. Yet, whenever workers demanded recognition in industries where capitalists steadfastly refused to deal with the union, state or employer violence always loomed heavily in the background of any dispute.[22]

After unprecedented strike activity during World War II pushed the state to recognize in law basic freedoms of workers, state restrictions on collective activity took new but equally restrictive forms.[23] At the center of this new

---

19   Tucker (1991).
20   For an overview of these strikes see Palmer (1987); Cruikshank and Kealey (1987). On some of the tensions and contradictions in these regulations see Smith (2017).
21   On the employer and state collusion during the Winnipeg general strike see Kramer and Mitchell (2010).
22   The history of employer and state violence on picket lines is vast. For an overview, there is no better source than Palmer (1992). Other broad overviews include Morton (2007) and Heron and Smith (2020); Fudge and Tucker (2001) also examine numerous and violent strikes. For some specific case studies see Abella (1974).
23   McInnis (2002: 145–81). See also F. David Millar's (1980) exceptional history of the administrative structures constructed by the federal and provincial states to regulate the new collective bargaining legislation. For a more whiggish and sympathetic, if naïve, history of the state and the Liberal Party's construction of Canada's model of industrial legality during World War II see Hollander (2018).

regime of industrial legality was a turn away from open state and employer coercion in their relationship with unions, to be replaced with a mediated and structured legal process that put legal rights to collective bargaining at its center. Yet, acceptance of state-formulated collective bargaining came with equally competing demands for unions and workers to act 'responsibly' and thereby respect the ability of capital to accumulate. That implied that workers had to accept restrictions on the right to withdraw their labor, which included a ban on political, recognition, or mid-contract strikes.[24] Recognizing this contradiction, Panitch and Swartz cleverly observed that at the heart of this new system of legality were elements of coercion and legitimation that worked to reshape the class struggle from "what before had taken the appearance of the charge of the Mounties now increasingly took the form of the rule of law by which unions policed themselves in most instances."[25] This *quid pro quo*, as Judy Fudge and Eric Tucker remind us, was built on a foundation of where workers and their unions conceded their unrestricted ability to withdraw their labor "in the form of immunities for workers or unions, or in the form of duties imposed on employers that facilitate the freedom to associate and bargain collectively."[26]

Throughout the postwar period, while strikes occurred with some consistency, how and why they occurred became more predictable and more narrowly focused on concluding union collective agreements. Additional legal boundaries included mandated strike votes, and even then, strike action was further delayed until after both sides declared a legal impasse during collective bargaining. Once those steps were taken, workers were then required to participate in compulsory conciliation, and in most jurisdictions, governments implemented mandatory cooling-off periods before picket lines could be established.[27] Yet, for the system to have legitimacy amongst certain cross-sections of the working class, governments had to appear – on the surface at least – as neutral arbitrators in the class struggle. The dual elements of coercion and legitimation Panitch and Swartz identified at the center of industrial legality required workers and unions to maintain a degree of consent for the rules of the system to work effectively.

Under these new rules a different type of union and a different type of union leader was required. In the postwar period, a worker became a union leader by

---

24   Fudge and Tucker (2001: 273–74).
25   Panitch and Swartz (2003: 15).
26   Fudge and Tucker (2009–10: 355).
27   Fudge and Glasbeek (1994–1995); Fudge and Tucker (2000; 2001: 297–315; 2009–2010: 348–352); Drache and Glasbeek (1992: 8–31); Savage and Smith (2017:30–40).

developing an expertise in the new legal system of grievances, arbitration, and winning material gains during regular rounds of collective bargaining. Under this system, the skills of organizing and building a broader working-class consciousness through worker empowerment became of secondary importance. Moreover, while the strike remained an important tool within this new model of industrial relations, strikes themselves were highly regulated by the law and the courts and leaders were keen to make sure that the boundaries of class struggle adhered to the established legal order. Union leaders were thus responsible to "channel union activities away from spontaneous rank-and-file action" for fear of state reprisal in the form of injunctions, fines, or even imprisonment.[28] And in the context of the Cold War chill falling over labor movements in the 1950s, clamping down on worker militancy also meant purging the unions of communist and other far-left activists.[29]

Following the rules, however, does not guarantee that workers and their unions are free from abusive employer and coercive state intervention during labor disputes. Throughout the postwar period, courts continued to police the boundaries between the powers that flow from property ownership and workers' ability to challenge that dominance through the collective withdrawal of labor.[30] Perhaps the most glaring example of class biases of the laws surrounding strikes came in the form of judicial intervention in labor disputes through employer-obtained injunctions. These injunctions – grounded in the common law's defense of property and contract – were defended by business and the state on the grounds that collective picketing action tortuously interfered with employers' ability to run their business.[31] As unions themselves identified in the first postwar strike wave in the 1960s, once picketers' activities were diluted by the law, violence routinely escalated as picketers watched employers utilize the reserve army of the unemployed – 'scab labor' in worker vernacular – shuffle into their former jobs.[32] The state's promotion of picket line violence through easily obtained injunctions played a significant role in the labor radicalism of the 1960s, where worker challenges to employer, union, and even gendered and racialized power imbalances were often confronted by spontaneous strike action by a new generation of younger and militant workers.[33]

---

28 Jackson and Thomas (2017: 200). For a concrete case study examining the taming of worker collective action in the period see: Wells (1995).
29 On this question, see the classic study by Abella (1973).
30 Tucker and Fudge (1996).
31 On injunctions and torts see: Smith (2012). See also Tucker (2010) and Sangster (2004).
32 Canadian Labour Congress (1966: 32).
33 Palmer (2009: 212–41); McInnis (2012); Sangster (2004).

Although numerous government studies at both federal and provincial levels in this period recognized that injunctions were heightening tensions on picket lines, very few governments placed restrictions on employer abilities to obtain court orders restricting workers' collective actions.[34]

2   Enter Back-to-Work Legislation

Notwithstanding the numerous legal obstacles that unions must go through before they can engage in legal strike activity and the ease by which employers can obtain injunctions, governments continue to intervene in labor disputes. In fact, Canada remains one of the few countries in the world that routinely utilize the legislative weapon to formally intervene in legal strike activity to weaken the collective freedoms of workers to strike.[35] What accounts for this frequency? In many ways, the state's openness to utilize the instrument of back-to-work legislation is correlated with the construction of the regime of industrial legality itself.

Ironically, when the Liberal government led by corporate lawyer turned politician Louis St. Laurent became the first to use back-to-work legislation on August 30, 1950, it was based on a *quid pro quo* to the unions involved. In this dispute, seventeen separate railway and telegraph unions representing 125,000 workers walked off the job after failing to successfully bargain for improved wages and expanding union membership in non-union railway shops, including hotel and water employees.[36] Perhaps more important to the membership, however, was the insistence that the union not concede on the 40-hour work week, which the company had been stubbornly refusing to recognize at the bargaining table. In fact, the union had substantial support from the membership demonstrated by large mass meetings of 10,000 Canadian National Railway (CNR) and Canadian Pacific Railway (CPR) workers on the day the strike was announced – to push for a shorter work week given that excessive fatigue was an ongoing factor in health and safety issues on the railways.[37] Although the public company had conceded modest wage increases, it was only willing to shorten the normal work week to 44 hours (from 48) and offer

---

34   See Arthurs (1966); Carothers (1966); Task Force on Labour Relations (1968: 185–86).
35   International Labour Organization (1996–2017). Between 1970 and 2015, there were twenty-five complaints to the International Labour Organization's Freedom of Association Committee dealing with back-to-work legislation, all of which originated in Canada.
36   *Toronto Star* (1950a).
37   List (1950).

vague commitments to bring in the 40-hour week at some point in the future if the union agreed to lower its wage demands.

Representing the largest strike in Canadian history to that point, the railway dispute placed pressure on all sectors of the economy, especially as the state mobilized for participation in the Korean War. In fact, the day the strike was called newspapers were filled with fear-mongering stories of communities in northern regions "starving" within days,[38] warnings of massive layoffs across the country,[39] and the typical bemoaning of unions abusing the strike weapon to punish the general "public."[40] A.R. Mosher, President of the Brotherhood of Railway Employees and Frank Hall, Chairman of the negotiating commit-tee responded to these claims by apologizing to the Canadian public, placing the blame solely on the rail companies and their disregard for the health and safety of the workers on the line. Mosher went so far to hint at the internal anti-communist fights within his Canadian Congress of Labour (CCL), even suggesting that the rail company's inaction and disregard for the health and safety of the workers was providing added "comfort" to "subversive elements by this strike." He went on to emphasize that "these elements will be glad to see a slowing down of a war effort directed against the Communists of North Korea."[41] Criticizing CNR president Donald Gordon and the alleged commu-nists in his own union, Mosher aligned his public relations strategy with what Irving Abella describes as the "frenzy of anti-communism which swept the continent in the wake of the onset of the Korean war"[42] to point out the greed of the railway capitalists while also playing on nationalist sentiments to win public support at the beginning of the Cold War's first armed conflict.[43]

The unions were also quick to point out that the Liberal government's indif-ference to the working conditions of railway workers. Having been deeply involved in the negotiations through the conciliation process, and after the appointment of a special mediator in an attempt to avoid backlash from the numerous companies dependent on the rail system, the Liberals wasted little time in attempting to end the strike. The government's urgency was reflected in the fact that the day the strike began, the Liberals mobilized the Royal

---

38   *Globe & Mail* (1950a); *Toronto Star* (1950b).

39   *Globe & Mail* (1950b; 1950c; 1950d); *Toronto Star* (1950c).

40   [Editorial] (1950).

41   *Globe & Mail* (1950e).

42   Abella (1973: 159).

43   On Mosher's anti-communism against unions operating on the railway, see the discus-sion to expel the United Electrical Workers from the CCL in 1949 and 1950 in Abella (1973: 150–63).

Canadian Air Force to fly MPs back to Ottawa to hold a special "strike session" of Parliament in order to end the strike through binding arbitration.[44] Although Prime Minister St. Laurent himself endeavored to broker a deal through negotiations during the first days of the strike, the Cabinet also leaked information stating that the eventual legislation would come with a threat of following the back-to-work order or risk losing their pension and seniority rights.[45] As Parliament debated the issue, the threat of state-imposed arbitration brought calls of solidarity from unions across the country, with the United Electrical Workers (UE) and large locals within the United Auto Workers calling for a mass strike in support of the railway workers.[46] In the words of the *Globe and Mail* labor reporter Wilfrid List, the government's actions further "tightened the growing alliance" between the CCL and the Trades and Labour Congress (TLC) in their common anti-communist and pro-nationalist political orientations, but also in their shared belief in the sanctity of the new labor regime of industrial legality.

When Parliament debated the issue, St. Laurent outlined his government's reasoning for intervention – how and why the state had to end even legal strikes. Despite claiming allegiance to "the principle of collective bargaining" and the legal "institutions which have proved their value to the national economy of Canada," the government had no choice but to "deal with what amounts to a national emergency."[47] St. Laurent insisted that his government was not intending to intervene in the process of collective bargaining between "equal powers" and recognized that the "strike had not been in violation of any law," but that in situations of national emergency even the most sacred of "normally private rights may at times amount to what becomes public wrongs."[48] In such an instance, St. Laurent elaborated, the ability for workers to bargain and strike freely may inflict an "injury that the insistence on private rights may do to the public weal is sometimes so great that it has to be given serious consideration because the existence and security of the state is the first and prior consideration for each and every one of us."[49] Although Co-operative Commonwealth Federation (CCF) members opposed the legislation, the eventual back-to-work bill was supported by the union leadership because the government conceded to wage increases and to the 40-hour work week (later in 1951) that could not

---

44   *Toronto Star* (1950d; 1950e).
45   *Globe & Mail* (1950f).
46   *UE News* (1950).
47   Canada (1950–51: 11).
48   Canada (1950–51: 11–13).
49   Canada (1950–51: 12).

be eroded by arbitration. In other words, the back-to-work bill imposed binding arbitration – something the unions universally opposed – but the government restricted the arbitrator's ability to impose a contract lower than the wage, workweek, and bargaining extension demands acceptable to the union leadership.

While smiling pictures of Mosher and Hall appeared the next morning in the *Toronto Star* alongside a booming headline declaring, "Unions Commend St. Laurent," the unions faced criticism for accepting the back-to-work order. The United Electrical Workers, recently ousted from the CCL for its alleged communist sympathies by Mosher himself, denounced the government's actions and was critical of the union leadership for not challenging the back-to-work order.[50] Meanwhile social democratic CCF Premier of Saskatchewan, Tommy Douglas argued that,

> ... the introduction of the principle of compulsory arbitration shows how far we have drifted from democratic procedures in Canada. Collective bargaining is now to be replaced by binding 150,000 workers to the decision of one individual from whose ruling there is no appeal. This may make the Employers' Association and the Manufactures' Association happy but it will cause great concern to those who believe in the democratic right of workers to bargain collectively.[51]

Responding to this criticism, the Canadian Brotherhood of Railway Employees celebrated the fact that "the principle of the forty-hour, five-day work week" was now acknowledged by government statute, notwithstanding the fact that it was buried in the back-to-work order. Mosher predicted that the government's recognition of the 40-hour work week in the back-to-work bill would "be used by thousands of other workers throughout Canada to gain similar improvements in their conditions of employment."[52] Mosher further elaborated in his annual presidential address to the union that the "strike was one hundred per cent effective." To be sure, Mosher acknowledged that the "calling off of the strike in compliance with the law" was "subject to derogatory remarks by some." Yet, he remained convinced that the gains made through the back-to-work order were an important material benefit for his members and not accepting the back-to-work order "would probably have resulted in

---

50   *UE News* (1950).
51   Douglas (1950).
52   *The Canadian Railway Employees' Monthly* (1950a: 284).

far more drastic and repressive legislation."[53] In arriving at this conclusion, the union leadership believed that the material gains provided by the back-to-work order necessitated following the law and conceding their right to freely bargain and to strike.

3   The State and the Never-Ending Use of Back-to-Work Legislation

St. Laurent's foray into legislating the railway workers back-to-work set the pattern for how governments would apply this legal tool in the future: workers deemed essential or important enough to threaten national or provincial interests, or those that maintained the potential to disrupt important sectors of the economy would be legislated back-to-work, usually with the promise of some form of third-party arbitration. Once public sector workers won similar legal freedoms in 1966 and 1967 at the federal level (and somewhat later in the provinces),[54] the public nature of strikes placed government in the dual and contradictory role of employer and legislator. That dual role and the government's broad interpretation of what constitute a crisis – so aptly demonstrated in the 1950 rail dispute – suggested that public sector conflicts allowed governments to bypass workers' strikes through legislative intervention. And while legislative intervention allows for the use of third-party arbitration, that process takes the issue out of the hands of workers and hands it to high-priced lawyers and professional arbitrators.[55] Yet, there is some evidence to indicate that even the usage of third-party arbitrators to settle disputes allows governments to avoid a political or economic crisis but does little to actually address the workplace grievances that led to strike action.[56] The point for the government, however, is that workers continue to work and while the state can claim its allegiance to the regime of industrial legality, those rights are always subject to limitations when it is economically or politically necessary for capital and the state.

---

53   *The Canadian Railway Employees' Monthly* (1950b: 286).
54   Saskatchewan was the only province to allow its public sector workers to bargain and strike before 1968. In 1944, the CCF government of Tommy Douglas included public workers in its *Trade Union Act*.
55   On the role of interest arbitration during a strike, see Doorey (2017: 156–57).
56   In 2018 the Canadian Union of Postal Workers (CUPW) walked off the job after repeated attempts to have the employer address excessive hours of work and serious health and safety issues for rural mail carriers. The Trudeau Liberals nevertheless intervened and legislated CUPW back-to-work because the government was worried about the strike's implications for the Christmas retail season. Over two years later, CUPW reported that the health and safety issues remained unresolved. (*CBC News*, 2020).

Panitch and Swartz were among the first scholars to recognize that the formula utilized by the St. Laurent Liberals had become a blunt instrument in the hands of the capitalist state as the ruling classes embraced neoliberalization, roughly in the period from 1975 to 2002 in order to end 115 separate strikes. To be sure, public sector struggles have remained ground zero of government intervention in both legal and illegal strike activity. In private sector disputes since the 1980s, there is often no such urgency as governments are more than willing to let private workers linger on picket lines if private employers can withstand prolonged strike action using legal injunctions and scab labor. This is especially true outside of British Columbia and Quebec where no government of any political stripe has actively considered let alone implemented anti-scab legislation, which would restrict employer abilities to break legal strikes through the use of scab labor. These issues were clearly highlighted in 2020, when the conservative Saskatchewan Party government refused to intervene in an ongoing private sector dispute in the Co-Op Oil Refinery, notwithstanding the fact that the government-appointed mediator recommended a settlement that was accepted by the union.[57] In this dispute, Unifor workers were repeatedly unable to stop the flow of scab labor into the plant because a court-imposed injunction prevented the union from "impeding, obstructing, or interfering with the ingress or egress to or from the applicant's property," and was only able to delay those attempting to cross the line "as long as necessary to provide information, to a maximum of 10 minutes, or until the recipient of the information indicates a desire to proceed, whichever comes first."[58] Put more concretely, those wishing to cross the line merely had to indicate their desire to receive no information and drive through the picket line. Such wording made Unifor's picket line weaker and allowed the company to drag the union back to court when any worker action was deemed to impede access to the company's property. And notwithstanding these egregious examples of government support for employer's breaking of union picket lines, even private sector strikers are not immune from reactionary government intervention when those strikes appear to threaten the perceived stability of a local economy. In 1983, Grant Devine's Conservative government ended a dairy strike in Saskatchewan while Harper quickly legislated Air Canada and CP Railway workers back to work in 2011 and 2012 because of arbitrary threats to the "economy." These actions demonstrated that governments were more

---

57   Eneas (2020).
58   *Consumer's Co-operative Refineries Ltd., v. Unifor Canada, Local 594*, Queen Bench for Saskatchewan, QBG 3302, 2019.

than willing to push aside the regime of industrial legality when it suited their interests.[59]

To be sure, governments are utilizing back-to-work legislation less frequently than in the turbulent period of neoliberalization in the 1970s and 1980s. Yet there still have been over 29 instances since 2002 where governments have ended legal strikes. In 2018, the Liberal government of Justin Trudeau once again reached back into the now decades-old government playbook to legislate legally striking CUPW workers back-to-work because of the perceived national threat to the Christmas retail season. Lobbied by business organizations to legislate CUPW workers back-to-work to "save the holidays for Canadian consumers,"[60] the Trudeau Liberals acted to end the strike. In so doing, both Prime Minister Trudeau and Labour Minister Patty Hajdu claimed that while "legislating an end to a labour dispute is never the best option," the Liberals had to take this action because the "ongoing work stoppage has had significant negative impacts on Canadians, businesses, international commerce, Canada Post, its workers and their families, and with "Canadians and Canadian businesses feeling serious impacts, our government is prepared to legislate a path forward to keep goods moving."[61] The blunt actions of the capitalist state in legislating these legally striking workers back-to-work would not have been surprising for Louis St. Laurent (nor for that matter Panitch and Swartz), as this blunt instrument has now become the standard policy tool for governments to address worker strikes that challenge the profitability of private corporations or, for that matter, public strikes that may only be a matter of significant political or public inconvenience, as well as those that threaten to disrupt the political or economic status quo. These actions by the state have direct implications for the ability of workers to freely strike. Since the 1970s, workers in all sectors are utilizing the legal (and illegal) strike weapon with far less frequency than at any moment since the end of World War II (Figure 10.1).

Clearly the decline in worker strike activity has weakened the ability of workers to challenge unilateral decisions made by government and capital, especially when those decision result in plant closures, technological change, government privatization, or outsourcing. In short, the ongoing assault on workers' associational freedoms highlighted by Panitch and Swartz has not simply weakened the movement, it has also undermined workers' capacity to think beyond the existing regime of industrial legality to expand and deepen their collective freedoms.

---

59   Warren and Carlisle (2005: 241).
60   McCarthy (2018).
61   Pedwell (2018).

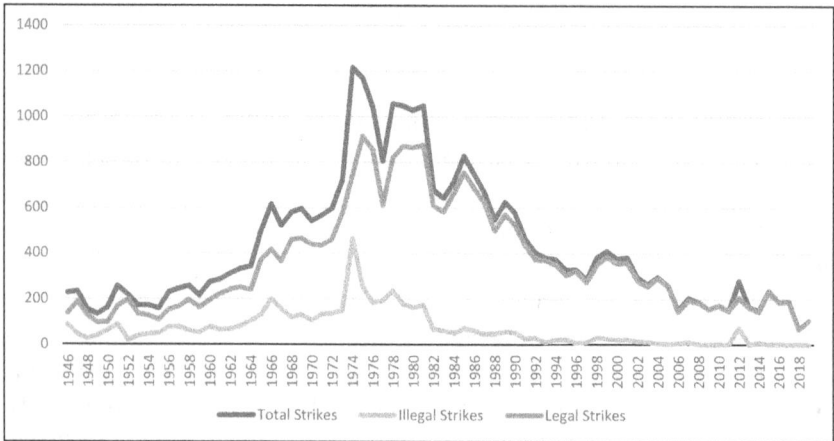

FIGURE 10.1 Total strikes in Canada, legal and illegal, 1946–2019
SOURCE: STATISTICS CANADA (2020); ILLEGAL STRIKES CALCULATED FROM
EMPLOYMENT AND SOCIAL DEVELOPMENT CANADA, WORK STOPPAGE
DIRECTORY, 1946–2019.[62]

4 Workers' Freedom of Association and the Charter of Rights and Freedoms

Although Panitch and Swartz recognized that Canadian governments' usage of back-to-work legislation undermined the free associational rights of workers, their analysis did not end with the actions of government alone. They were equally critical of the judicial branch of the capitalist state and these actors' collective hostility to interpreting the Charter of Rights and Freedoms in a manner that protected workers and their unions. In fact, when labor unions first brought three freedom of association challenges before the Supreme Court in the late 1980s, one of the central questions in what became known as the *labor trilogy* was the extent to which freedom of association protected a collective freedom to strike.[63] As Panitch and Swartz demonstrate, the rulings in the labor trilogy cases reflected long-held judicial biases towards workers' collective freedoms, and equally problematic was that these hostilities provided "juridical and ideological space for a broader assault in the private and public sectors on collective bargaining by virtue of the breadth of its ruling

---

62 I have discussed strikes and this data in more detail in Smith (2020).
63 These decisions were released simultaneously and included: *Reference re Public Service Employee Relations Act (Alta.)*, [1987] 1 S.C.R. 313 [*Alberta Reference*]; *PSAC v. Canada*, [1987] 1 S.C.R. 424; and *RWDSU v. Saskatchewan*, [1987] 1 S.C.R. 460.

that freedom of association did not constitutionally protect workers' rights to bargain collectively and strike at all."[64] This observation was made clear in the *Alberta Reference* case, where unions attempted to argue that the provincial government's unilateral withdrawal of public sector workers' legal ability to strike (replaced with binding arbitration) violated their associational freedom in the newly established Charter of Rights.[65] Unions argued that for Charter-protected freedom of association to have real meaning, workers had to be free to form a group that is then capable of acting collectively. For unions, of course, those collective actions included collective bargaining and, if that broke down, striking. In short, unions interpreted freedom of association as any worker would: individuals had to be free to organize into a union of their choice and that union then had to be free to challenge employer power through the collective withdrawal of labor.

Centuries of individual rights of contract and deference to the rights of property, however, pushed the Supreme Court in a much different ideological direction. In a 4–2 decision, the Supreme Court ruled that freedom of association did not include the ability to strike. In arriving at that decision, three of the four majority judges adopted a stunningly short four-paragraph "plain meaning" interpretation of freedom of association that union activities such as collective bargaining or engaging in strike action are "modern rights" created by legislation and therefore "not fundamental rights or freedoms."[66] In his concurring decision, Justice McIntyre adopted a longer if equally contradictory definition of freedom of association, recognizing that it "advances many group interests, and of course, cannot be exercised alone" but that "it is nonetheless a freedom belonging to the individual and not to the group formed through its exercise."[67] For the court, then, it was therefore impossible for individuals to "create an entity which has greater constitutional rights and freedoms than they, as individuals, possess."[68] Having arrived at this conclusion, McIntyre then observed that the only plausible definition of freedom of association was one that allowed groups to perform activities that are lawful for individuals to perform alone. Based on that rationale, and conscious that they did not want to upset the so-called balance between business and labor, the Supreme Court of Canada's pronouncement was that freedom of association was simply an individual right.[69] In dissent, Chief Justice Dickson (along with Justice Wilson)

64   Panitch and Swartz (2003: 74).
65   Panitch and Swartz (2003: 51–83).
66   *Alberta Reference* at para 144.
67   *Alberta Reference* at para 155.
68   *Alberta Reference* at para 155.
69   *Alberta Reference* at para 182.

adopted the position of the unions, acknowledging that if associational freedom "only protects the joining together of persons for common purposes, but
not the pursuit of the very activities for which the association was formed,
then the freedom is legalistic, ungenerous, indeed vapid."[70] While the Chief
Justice's ardent critique of the majority's reasoning remains rare in Supreme
Court jurisprudence, the dissent carried little immediate weight. In cases
throughout the remainder of the 1980s and 1990s, the court continued to deny
that freedom of association (and freedom of expression) included a primary[71]
or secondary[72] ability to picket or the ability to bargain.[73] The Supreme Court
also ruled that there was no constitutional protection for unions from criminal contempt charges while on legal strike,[74] and in a sympathetic nod to the
permanent exceptionalism philosophy being promoted by Canadian governments, that the "public interest" had to take precedent over workers' freedom
to collectively bargain or strike.[75]

Notwithstanding the Supreme Court's hostility to workers' collective legal
freedoms throughout the 1980s and 1990s, unions continued to engage the
courts in order to expand constitutional labor rights. There is broad debate
within the union and labor law scholarship as to why unions continued to see
the courts as an important terrain of struggle, notwithstanding the fact that
courts had rarely been sympathetic to workers' collective freedoms. In our
book, Larry Savage and I argue that the trend of unions engaging the Charter
and courts accelerated for two contradictory reasons. First, governments
pushed the boundaries of what constituted an emergency and used their
power to side-step even a semblance of respect for labor freedoms long-established within the existing system of industrial legality. Second, and perhaps
more importantly, because workers were repeatedly losing ground against capital and because governments were increasingly undermining their capacities
to strike, unions were constantly on the defensive. In this view, hiring lawyers
and engaging judges in the legal minutia of labor law became an easier strategy for labor leaders to challenge government than organizing and expanding working-class power against ongoing neoliberalization in both the private
and public sectors.[76] Equally important, as unions became weaker and less

70   *Alberta Reference* at para 81.
71   *BCGEU v. British Columbia (A.G.)*, [1988] 2. S.C.R. 214.
72   *RWDSU v. Dolphin Delivery*, [1986] 2 S.C.R. 573.
73   *Professional Institute of the Public Service of Canada v. Northwest Territories* (Commissioner), [1990] 2 S.C.R. 367.
74   *United Nurses of Alberta v. Alberta (Attorney General)*, [1992] 1 S.C.R. 901.
75   *Canadian Union of Public Employees, Local 301 v. Montreal (City)*, [1997] 1 S.C.R 793.
76   Savage and Smith (2017: 207–20).

threatening to the political and economic status quo, evolving judicial support for the rights of minorities in other areas began influencing judicial reasoning on the rights of workers. Influenced by the arguments of Panitch and Swartz, we concluded that unions went to court not as an offensive strategy but rather to defend long-established legal gains, notwithstanding the existing contradictions within that system of legality. Quite simply, unions were channeling resistance towards legal, rights-based claims rather than the traditional collective strategy that had led to the creation of industrial legality in the first place: membership mobilization, civil disobedience, and collective workplace militancy.

Perhaps surprisingly given historical precedent, union leaders were partially rewarded in these legal strategies in 2007 when the Supreme Court ruled in *Health Services and Support – Facilities Subsector Bargaining Assn. v. British Columbia*, (BC *Health Services*) that freedom of association included a constitutional right for workers to collectively bargain, which also included a corresponding duty on employers to bargain in good faith.[77] Responding to the malicious and unilateral actions of the British Columbia Liberal government of Gordon Campbell, the Supreme Court embraced Justice Dickson's "purposive" definition of freedom of association in the 1980s, ruling that the Charter now protected "the capacity of members of labour unions to engage, in association, in collective bargaining on fundamental workplace issues."[78] While the court framed its ruling as only narrowly applying to a "process of collective action to achieve workplace goals," and not constitutional protection for "the fruits of the bargaining process," the decision nevertheless expanded significantly on the ability of unions to challenge governments intent on weakening public sector unions from bargaining.

The Supreme Court's newfound willingness to read collective dimensions into the Charter's freedom of association provisions and the continued offensive by right-wing governments all but guaranteed that the questions of labor freedoms would continue to be fought out in court. In 2007, the right-wing Saskatchewan Party formed government after sixteen years of ostensibly pro-labor New Democratic Party (NDP) governments. The new government took direct aim at weakening the collective freedoms of labor unions in both the public and private sectors. The Saskatchewan Party's labor law changes consisted of Bill 5, the *Public Service Essential Services Act* (PSESA), and Bill 6, the *Trade Union Amendment Act* (TUAA). The PSESA unilaterally took away the

---

77   *Health Services and Support – Facilities Subsector Bargaining Assn. v. British Columbia*, [2007] 2 SCR 391 [BC *Health Services*] at para 97.

78   BC *Health Services* at para 19.

right of almost every public sector worker in the province to strike, with the
government arguing that essential services had to be maintained in order to
protect the general public against strike interruption. The TUAA represented
the usual changes to labor legislation made by right-wing governments, including: expanded employer speech provisions; ending card check certification
procedures, replacing them with a mandatory vote procedure; and raising the
numerical threshold for union certification. While the government defended
its labor law changes as preserving "balance" and "democracy"[79] in the workplace, scholars have repeatedly shown that such changes hand employers significant legal tools to defeat unionization drives and thus drive down union
density.[80]

In 2015, the Supreme Court sided with the unions and ruled for the first time
that the Charter included a *collective* freedom to strike. Writing for the majority, Justice Abella determined that judicial interpretation of collective associational freedoms indicated that the constitutional "arc bends increasingly
towards workplace justice."[81] In making that declaration, Abella determined
that the freedom to strike is a central component of a "meaningful collective
bargaining process in our system of labour relations," which is supported by
Canadian labor history, by court jurisprudence, and by international commitments.[82] As the court had determined in *BC Health Services* that "meaningful
collective bargaining" was a constitutionally protected freedom, Abella now
recognized that engaging in that process was impossible without a credible
threat for workers to withdraw their labor. In her mind, the freedom to "collectively withdraw services for the purpose of negotiating the terms and conditions of employment – in other words, to strike – is an essential component
of the process through which workers pursue collective workplace goals."[83] As
the ability to strike furthered the process of collective bargaining, it now fell
to reason that the same values were magnified by the collective withdrawal of
labor. In Abella's mind, the strike allowed workers to "come together to participate directly in the process of determining their wages, working conditions
and the rules that will govern their working lives."[84] Under such circumstances,
workers are able to act collectively to resist "imposed terms and conditions"

79   Government of Saskatchewan (2007: 5).
80   Riddell (2004); Slinn (2004).
81   *Saskatchewan Federation of Labour v Saskatchewan,* [2015] 1 SCR 245 [*SFL v. Saskatchewan*]
      at para 1.
82   *SFL v. Saskatchewan* at para 3.
83   *SFL v. Saskatchewan* at para 46.
84   *SFL v. Saskatchewan* at para 54.

of employment and thus further their human dignity by levelling the power imbalance between themselves and employers. It was particularly important, the court reasoned, to recall that the simple engagement in strike action does "not guarantee that a labour dispute will be resolved in any particular manner, or that it will be resolved at all."[85] Rather, pressure is placed on both workers and employers to peacefully solve the dispute through "good faith negotiations." The court determined that it is the process of good-faith negotiation through the collective bargaining process and (if necessary) through strike action that furthered collaborative decision-making. Having determined that the ability to withdraw one's labor furthered the individual and collective dimensions enshrined in the Charter's values, Abella concluded that the time had come to give the freedom to strike "constitutional benediction."[86]

The 2015 decision culminated almost three decades of constitutional wrangling by unions, lawyers, and judges to inject associational freedoms for workers into the constitution. To be sure, these victories in court now give the labor movement unparalleled legitimacy to defend existing legal gains. Yet, to date, their application has been uneven. These constitutional rights have done little to stop governments legislating strike workers back to work, nor has it encouraged new labor freedoms such as sectoral bargaining or extending legal protections to non-standard employees in new sectors of the capitalist economy. In this sense, while the court has addressed Panitch and Swartz's critique of lending 'ideological weight' to the ongoing assault on trade union freedoms, the newfound constitutional rights have yet to address the ongoing assault on the core freedoms of working people and their unions.

5   The Ongoing Assault on Trade Union Freedoms

Notwithstanding the narrow legal victories achieved in court, the now four-decade assault on the Canadian labor movement is clearly taking its toll on labor militancy and labor organizations more generally. Part of this change is driven by capitalist restructuring within states. Unions once dominant in manufacturing and natural resources are dwindling at the same time that we are witnessing a now two-decade 'proletarianization' of new workers in services and even professional job categories, leading to what Panitch recognized in 2001 as "the spread of more unstable, casual and contingent employment"

---

85   *SFL v. Saskatchewan* para 57.
86   *SFL v. Saskatchewan* para 3.

across the capitalist world.[87] The inability of unions to break into these sectors has clearly weakened the movement, as once mighty unions are either merging with larger entities to survive, engaging in solidarity-killing raiding, or making concessions at the bargaining table, none of which is stemming the outward flow of capital across the country.[88]

These economic, political, and legal pressures represent the ongoing process of neoliberalization in Canada, where governments and capital are now *dependent* on weakening the bargaining power of workers in order to maintain competitiveness. That dependence raises serious concerns for all working people, as the restriction of the associational freedoms of workers is not simply an attack on the legal institutions that recognize union freedoms, but one that gives voice and power to all workers. Without such freedoms, democracy itself becomes negotiable for capital and its state allies. It is therefore essential, as Panitch and Swartz suggest in their conclusion of *The Assault on Trade Union Freedoms* that,

> ... freedom of association for workers is an essential condition of democracy. Achieved through long, arduous, even bloody, struggle, it was only accepted by the state at real cost to the further mobilizing capacities of unions. Moreover, it was always, in a capitalist society, open to challenge. Reforms, even reforms basic to liberal democracy, are always subject to limits and never guaranteed forever. They must be defended, extended, and transformed to further strengthen workers' capacity to conduct class struggle – or else they are always in danger of atrophying, or worse, being reneged on.[89]

Put simply, Panitch and Swartz's analysis recognizes that the long assaults on workers' associational freedoms to bargain and strike first highlighted by the St. Laurent Liberals and later practiced with some regularity by federal and provincial governments is not simply a question over legal institutions or the legal freedom to bargain but rather over "the substantive meaning of democracy in Canadian society."[90]

---

87   Panitch (2000: 367).
88   On some of these issues, see Heron and Smith (2020: ch. 7). On labor's inability to stop the outward flow of capital, see the particularly devastating story of Caterpillar in London, Ontario chronicled by Ross and Russell (2018).
89   Panitch and Swartz (2003: 240).
90   Panitch and Swartz (2003: 240).

The linkages between the political, economic, and indeed, legal freedoms of association for working people and democracy are rarely mentioned in contemporary theories of democracy, law, or the state. In *The Assault on Trade Union Freedoms*, Panitch and Swartz expand and deepen theories of the state by recognizing that the historical struggle of working people to resist capitalist exploitation – often legally protected and enforced by the state – is at the center of the democratization forces within liberal capitalist societies. It almost goes without saying that the underlying principle that workers and their unions have always used to challenge that power is one of solidarity.[91] As the open assault on trade union freedoms by the Canadian state continues, one of the ongoing challenges for workers, as Panitch reminds us, is the broad and daunting task to "learn how to 'reinvent solidarity'," against these authoritarian crackdowns on worker freedoms.[92] Although labor's victories in the courts have opened a small door to expanding workers' constitutional freedom of association, government has not shied away from side-stepping even these constitutional freedoms in the face of economic or political 'emergencies'. For socialists and worker advocates, then, the continued erosion of associational freedoms for workers suggests that the law – while an important defensive tool for workers – cannot replace the longstanding principles of solidarity nor can it alone offset the power that capitalist classes maintain in its relationship to the capitalist state.

91   On this concept in relationship to labor politics, see Swartz and Warskett (2012).
92   Panitch (2000: 389).

PART 4

Transforming Class Politics and the State

∴

CHAPTER 11

Transformative Agency from a Time of Revolt to a Time of Pandemic

Hilary Wainwright

The tyranny of the immediate is a powerful force. Sometimes it is a force to be resisted, when the pressures of office entangle would-be radical activists in short-term institutional battles diverting them from strategic efforts to transform those self-same institutions. At other times, 'the immediate' involves a dramatic break with normality that reveals the structural realities that these institutions maintained. Just as an earthquake reveals the pattern of deep structural tensions in the earth's geological substructure, leading to radical decisions such as relocating cities or closing mines, so in such moments in social or economic life, the demands of the immediate deserve our concentrated attention. Far from being resisted, they must be turned instead into an impetus for focused study to guide transformative action – the kind of action that would have been impossible in 'normal' times. Far from crushing us into the confines of existing institutions, such moments – with all their risks, dangers, and tragedies – can open up and indeed require a radical change in our perspectives in order to fully understand the deep shifts in material reality and social consciousness, and the new opportunities they open up.

1   Old Problems Radically Reconfigured

I write now in the summer of 2020, in the midst of the social upheaval produced by the Covid pandemic, the social, human, and personal consequences of which have made it difficult to concentrate on much else.[1] The problems on which I worked with Leo Panitch are dramatically reconfigured by the revelations and lasting repercussions of the pandemic.[2] The humane and potentially

---

1   Being in isolation, though able to participate in numerous virtual conversations, my experiences and perceptions of the crisis are inevitably personal and limited – reacting like many others to the disturbing background of the action and inaction of the government of Boris Johnson – a government of extreme social irresponsibility, inhumanity, and lack of integrity.

2   Concerning transforming the state, overcoming the limits of sectoral trade unionism, and whether or not the Labour Party can be transformed into an instrument of radical change.

transformative responses to a deadly virus, whose origins lie in the human exploitation of nature[3] and whose social impact has been decisively influenced by structures of inequality and power and by collective and individual human agency, remain quite uncertain. I will be arguing that Leo's recent writing, with Sam Gindin, on the development of popular capacity to organize and to build democratic power needs now to be the center of an agenda of study and practice on the radical left. The implication of the arguments explored here is that this capacity-building work is now closely associated with a process well underway and in need of being taken seriously, of rethinking political organization of the left in the context of what we know to be the structural limits of representative democracy even with a party or (in the case of the Labour Party) a leadership, from the radical left – limits that have proved more profound and more pervasive than we had anticipated.

Recently, after analyzing the failure of the radical party of the Greek left, Syriza, to realize its radically transformative promise when elected to government in January 2015, Panitch and Gindin concluded that, "If a socialist government is not to be stymied by the inherited state apparatuses, decisive focus on developing the agency and capacity for state transformation will be required."[4] As a result of the explorations of this chapter, I would add that this capacity-building of which they write will need to include the capacity – autonomous of the cycles of representative politics – to build popular control over production – production of the essentials of daily life (including health care in all its variety, food, housing, recreation, and the environment) and over manufacturing and the means of communication (hence over the design, development, and installation of the new information and communication technologies). This, especially concerning the production of the essentials of daily life, was a lesson of the crisis of Syriza,[5] and concerning both aspects of production; it is also, I will suggest, an implication to be drawn from the collective social responses to the pandemic and the imperatives of a transition to a low-carbon economy under the threat of climate change.

In this chapter, I want to begin an investigation (which cannot possibly be completed in the span of a short chapter) into the possibility and character of transformative agency in an era of defeat and now of pandemic. My thinking in describing this as a potentially transformative moment has been inspired by three kinds of citizen responses to the pandemic. Their significance requires further investigation, especially of whether underlying social and economic

---

3   Davis (2020).
4   Panitch and Gindin (2018a: ch. 6).
5   See Karitzis (2017).

tendencies favor or limit their sustainability; so, my references to them are intended as suggestive rather than definitive.

2   **Three Potentially Transformative Responses to the Pandemic by Organized Citizens**

All three are the product of the immediate (and short-lived) moment when the priority of public health – of overcoming the pandemic or at least minimizing the numbers of those who died – dominated society, driving political decisions, overriding the imperatives of profit and capital accumulation. Government decisions – inconsistent and unstable as they have been – set a frequently unconvincing framework, but an autonomous, sometimes critical collective social creativity emerged to meet urgent social needs. My first example is the role of workplace trade union organization in converting airplane manufacture into urgently needed ventilators[6] – however it is but one example of trade unions reaching beyond the routine priorities of wage bargaining and defense of working conditions, recognizing and deploying the use value of their skills, and extending the scope of their organization and their demands to address the urgent public health issues affecting not only their own members but society as a whole, especially the most vulnerable social groups. I'm thinking here notably of the principled and strategic campaign of the teachers' union (National Education Union, NEU) protecting communities as well as teachers against the government's rushed, unprepared, and dangerous attempt to open schools with scant regard for public health.

My second example is the way in which, for many people, including in my own neighborhood of Hackney Wick, far from meaning social isolation, 'lockdown' became turning the home, the neighborhood, and the personal mobile phone into the bases and the tools of active social networks of material aid and solidarity – though carried out with cautious attention paid to maintaining physical distance and wearing protective masks. (Indeed, the production of masks and other personal protective equipment has often been part of the processes of mutual self-help.) Through these purposefully social networks, local acquaintances became friends with needs or with capacities and new sustaining relationships flourished, spreading across a neighborhood and beyond, sometimes initiated and helped by a pre-existing infrastructure – a local Labour Party with members active in local tenants and community groups, a

---

6   See Wainwright (2020a).

self-organized community group with a long history of street-by-street mobilization like the Marsh Farm Outreach Group in the Marsh Farm Estate of
Luton.[7] Sometimes a responsive and flexible but massively under-resourced
local council has provided what help they can. These networks often spawned
or were associated with new forms of food distribution, care provision – for the
young, the old, the homeless. In some cases, the experience – at three months,
sufficiently long to form a habit – has inspired lasting new thinking and practice, including new, deeper forms of political organization rooted in the problems of everyday life that will undoubtedly intensify. But these improvised
organizations cannot survive without sustained material support.

Finally, I witnessed the rapid growth of an unprecedented level of knowledge and curiosity amongst the public, nourished and strengthened by critical
scientists who, infuriated by the government's suppression of open debate on
scientific advice, established independent sources of scientific advice from
those of the government. The most notable was created by Sir David King,
a previous Chief Scientific Advisor who could not stand back in the face of
the government's incompetence and irresponsibility, and created instead
what became an influential source of alternative expertise and popular self-
education in science – Independent Sage – challenging the government's crass
claim 'to follow the science' as if there was no debate, no plurality of views.
This debate and independent advice became a resource for people making
their own calculated risks rather than relying entirely on government instruc-
tions. And indeed, King saw the role of Independent Sage as being to advise the
public as much as the government.[8]

The Independent Sage provides a highly informative weekly briefing at
which members of the public, along with journalists and members of parliament, ask questions and contribute suggestions. The result has influenced self-
confidence as regards public policy beneath the party-political, Westminster
radar, and potentially strengthened popular capacity and self-confidence to
act autonomously from government in the public sphere. It has also acted as
a watchdog on the government's use of the private sector, and its ignoring of
the local and regional network of public health officers that could have helped
to ensure an effective network of testing, tracing, and isolating.[9] It no doubt
feeds into a consciousness of the need to rebuild an infrastructure of public
health as we work towards zero Covid-19, but also plan how to live with it in the
long term. I will argue that scientific knowledge of public health has become a

---

7   See Wainwright (2007) for the background to this organization.
8   See Wainwright (2020b).
9   What Neil Ascherson (2018), in another context, presciently referred to as 'the Serco State'.

condition of effective solidarity organizing and therefore an essential capacity to be developed.

At first sight, these three developments seem expressions 'only' of an emerging common sense, based in different ways on citizens organizing practical and productive solidarity with fellow citizens to meet social needs. And this is indeed part of what these examples amount to. Many a Zoom discussion now refers, optimistically, to such developments as harbingers of 'a new normal'. In their different ways though, they also involve a very precarious material practice that breaks from the normalities of an economy driven by private accumulation.

I intend to explore the extent to which the experience of the pandemic has quickened changes slowly accumulating under the rotten but resilient institutional framework of an exhausted old order persisting beyond its time. It is an order originating in the changes similarly quickened by the Second World War – the last crisis of such a global and profound consequence. This influences how far there is a potential basis for strategies to turn this crisis, with all its many personal tragedies, into an opportunity to create a humane society whose institutional priorities are those of social need and human wellbeing. Just as the changes brought about in 1945 cannot be understood without some reference to tendencies and antagonisms at work in the decades before the war, both in terms of economic and political institutions and in terms of popular consciousness, so today we cannot develop strategies for the future without identifying pre-Covid dynamics that the pandemic and response to it, in some sense, quicken or bring to the fore. It is the nature of these pre-Covid dynamics, in all their complexity, which will shape the nature of the 'normal' that could follow what responses the pandemic produced.

3   The Long View: Underlying Tendencies and Forces for Change

To investigate the character of these underlying tendencies involves different levels of reality, and I will draw on the insights of writers, including Leo Panitch and Sam Gindin, whose work takes the long view.

Panitch and Gindin are concerned, most notably in *The Making of Global Capitalism* but also in their other writings, with the balance of class power. They investigate the consequences of capitalist competition on the organizations and power of both ruling and working classes. They start from the tendency of capitalist competition to produce increasing concentration and centralization, and hence the increasingly dominant position of large oligopolistic companies. They go on to argue that far from this leading to a decline of

competition and the emergence of a homogeneous and unified corporate capitalist class, in close alliance with the state, there is an intensification of competition.[10] A crucial feature of the new institutional environment produced by
corporate competition is the way that the growth of the multinational corporation leads to a competitive drive, a relentless search for new sources of profit
and accumulation of capital. These dynamics lead to the dissolution of industrial sectors. The increased mobility of capital leads to acquisitions and investments across sectors so that a single corporation has many diverse industrial
interests. With this goes the weakening and break-up of the craft, sectoral basis
of organized labor and a consequent shift in the balance of power towards
capital, aided by legislation destroying labor rights.

Panitch and Gindin's explanation of the way in which the ground on which
the organizations of the industrial working class stood has been swept away
through the rise of the multinational corporation (MNC) is very convincing.[11]
However, to grasp the new challenges facing workers today in the context of
the pandemic and also the underlying changes that preceded and help to
shape this context, we need to combine their institutional analysis with a
deeper focus on the issues concerning technological change.

4   Technological Change and Questions for Systemic Change

Panitch and Gindin list technological innovation as one of the factors, alongside price, marketing, and cutting labor costs, deployed by corporations as they
intensify competition. Marx understood technological change as central to the
dynamism of capitalism, on the basis of its importance as a means to competitive advantage. He comments on this throughout his work, including in the
Communist Manifesto, and analyzes this in the most depth in his *Grundrisse*.
In a notably clear and accessible exegesis of this text, David Harvey points to
the two distinctive features of Marx's analysis of the character of technological

---

10   Panitch (2001).
11   The way they develop their analysis of the recent role of the MNC into an analysis of
      global geopolitics is also very important, but it does not directly concern our argument in
      this chapter. They argue that the expansion of the role of MNCs, and the way that through
      them foreign capital became a force in different national economies, undermines the
      applicability of nation-state based inter-imperialist rivalry through the international-
      ization of the American state. (The present crisis of the US state, both from domestic
      instabilities and in relation to China, an international rival competing on terms not
      understood by US realpolitik, must be understood as an active part of the context of pos-
      sible systemic change following the pandemic.)

change under capitalism.[12] First is the significance of technological innovation itself becoming a business; second is the tendency for the knowledge and skill of the workers to be incorporated into the machine – as what Marx termed 'dead labor' – and the consequent increase in productivity leading to the "general reduction of the necessary labour," or amount of labor needed to meet the needs of society. This development poses the possibility of free disposable time for all – "a condition for the emancipation of labour."

With the development of microelectronics, software, and computer-related industries plus the worldwide web, social media, and modern telecommunications, we are in the midst of what in Marx's terms is a new phase in the appropriation of surplus value – this time in the form of 'surplus time' influencing the whole of society and connected to the production of new scientific and technical knowledge, and what others, most notably Carlota Perez, describe as a new 'techno-economic paradigm.[13]

The spread of such a change in technological systems does not determine other institutional and political levels of society, though certain managerial and institutional forms will favor the realization of the new potential productivity, while others associated with vested interests in the old technologies will block it. Of themselves, these forms do not have their own political logic. For example, the combination of central coordination and horizontal self-control that favors, and is facilitated by, the new information and communication technologies can be found in the multinational corporations of Silicon Valley as well as the peer-to-peer open software initiatives of Barcelona and other centers of the social movement left.

But two issues of political significance are raised by the new productive potential of technological change. One is the question of the purpose to which the new productive potential might be put; a question raised by the very fact of system-wide change and a question posed more starkly in the context of

---

12   Harvey (2020).
13   Carlota Perez (2002) is another writer whose work is grounded in studies of capitalism over *the longue durée*. Her work is not directly in the Marxist tradition, but it has been influenced by the Marxist economist of science, Chris Freeman, and his work on long waves. Perez focuses on the relationship between financial cycles and changes in what she calls techno-economic paradigms, saying: "understanding the nature of the paradigm can provide the most appropriate tools for becoming a fully conscious and effective actor in the process of institutional modernization" (Perez, 2004: 238). In her analysis, as the change in techno-economic paradigm – the new source of wealth-creating potential – unfolds in the economy, its logic propagates throughout all of society modifying the taken-for-granted criteria that guide all sorts of organizations and eventually resulting in maximum social synergy.

a system-wide threat – whether the societal health threat of a pandemic or the planetary threat of climate change, or another threat also effectively concerning the whole of society – that of mass unemployment. This leads to the second question of political importance, which is the particular significance of the latest technological changes for labor.

Marx discusses in the *Grundrisse* how the increased productivity resulting from technological change and what he describes as "the transformation of the production process from the simple labour process into a scientific process" leads to the creation of surplus labour time, which under capitalism is appropriated as surplus value. In that sense, argues Marx, capital "quite unintentionally – reduces human labour, expenditure of energy to a minimum. This will redound to the benefit of emancipated labour and is the condition of its emancipation."

The Covid pandemic and the lockdowns/confinements have brought this issue of working hours dramatically to the fore as working hours and locations are thrown into fluidity and uncertainty; and at a time when in many industries management has plans to automate or is already well-advanced in the process. As governments end furlough payments and companies announce mass redundancies, the demand for shorter working hours, and to redistribute the available work, is unusually high on trade union agendas – more out of desperation as they see their membership figures plummet than out of considered strategic thinking. But, under pressure from the members who remain, it is likely to stay high on trade union agendas, even though at present employers, especially big corporations, are resistant.

There are also parts of industry where the process described by Marx as a corollary of technology becoming an economy-wide business – the application of technology and science in the production process – has favored the emergence of a strategically significant group of workers who, over the past four decades or so, have become a relatively well-organized part of the trade union movement, certainly in the UK and many other developed capitalist countries. I'm thinking here of the design and research staff whose skills and knowledge, including tacit knowledge that is not easily automated or replicated, is essential to the competitive advantage that comes from a company's capacity to innovate. These workers, whether members of ASTMS (the Association of Scientific, Technical and Managerial Staff) or AUEW-TASS (the Technical, Administrative and Supervisory Section of the Engineering Workers Union) in the past, or now as members of UNITE, have been amongst the most militant and strategic activists in the engineering industry. In the 1970s, along with skilled shop floor engineers, some of them led a number of struggles around 'alternative plans for socially useful production' – refusing management's declaration that they were 'redundant' by insisting that, on the contrary, they were surrounded by unmet needs for whose solution their skills were essential.

The most well-known of these workers organizations, the Lucas Aerospace Shop Stewards Combine Committee, also developed the concept of 'human-centered technology'. Mike Cooley, a leading member of the Combine Committee, worked on this concept and the struggle for it to be realized in the context of the transition in advanced industrial design – very much underway at Lucas Aerospace – from traditional drafting at a drawing board to computer-aided design. He used the term, in context of the new computer-aided technology, to stress the aim of preserving or enhancing human skills, in both manual and office work, in environments in which technology is introduced to undermine workers' skills.[14] It became an idea central to the struggle over the direction, design, and application of the new information and communication technology. This tradition of socially conscious designers and research staff – confident of the social usefulness of their skills, organized in the union and actively working with the shop floor union reps without any deference to, and minimum respect for, overpaid senior management – lives on in the drawing offices and research laboratories of the major engineering corporations. Moreover, with their national union officers preoccupied with collapsing industries everywhere they look, and with it a collapsing membership, these strategically placed activists are open to collaboration with local activists and intellectuals working on strategies for a Just Transition to a low-carbon economy, often organized around the idea of a Green New Deal. In several areas in the UK, this kind of collaboration is taking trade unionism beyond its traditional, defensive preoccupation to lay the basis for alternative strategies for production, pragmatically gaining support from sympathetic Labour MPs and parts of the Labour Party.[15]

What, though, of the workers' organizations emerging in those sectors of the economy based on the new technologies which have been massively strengthened by the pandemic – accelerating as it has preexisting trends towards online sales and just-in-time supply chains where speed of turn-over

---

14   In the cases I have observed, Rolls Royce for example, this management obstinacy in the face of company-wide demands for shorter hours and a sharing out of work stems partly from the fact that they were implementing long-term restructuring (that included redundancies and closures), which they had planned before the pandemic, when the issue of shorter working hours was not high on trade union agendas. In certain individual plants, especially those where the workforce was mainly involved in research and design, they were more flexible, and negotiated deals involving a redistribution of work.

15   Such a group exists in Coventry of trade union leaders from Solihull, Ainsty (mainly research and design staff), and Coventry Green New Deal.

is central to maximizing profit? Giant, windowless warehouses, surrounded by container yards and lorry parks, have become the new post-industrial factories. And potentially the precarious workers in these 'factories' have a new strategic bargaining power, if they become organized. This is the one sector of the economy that is recruiting in large numbers. The work is intense and the mainly agency workers are subjected to much abuse and sexist and racist bullying. But the kinds of workers being recruited show signs of rebellion. Callum Cant, a writer on the frontline of organizing precarious workers, and longtime Corbyn supporter, comments: "As the crisis continues, young workers expelled from city centre retail and service jobs are likely to end up sucked into the logistical vortex. This demographic already radicalised around issues of work, including working hours might well act as the spark that sets off a logistics worker movement of our own."[16] This points to a basis, in the UK at least, for Panitch and Gindin's call "to start anew at creating the kinds of working-class political institutions which can rekindle the socialist imagination."[17]

A further network of people exploiting what Marx described as the liberating potential of moving from a simple labor process to a scientific labor process are those who since the late 1980s have been developing open source software, and with it a collaborative ethos in the process of technological innovation based on freely shared source code.[18] Alongside and often overlapping with them are the diverse creators of a peer-to-peer economy based, as the term implies, on co-operation between equals. Whereas the open software movement has its origins in the counterculture of the late 1960s, and deepened through the radicalism and internationalism of the alter-globalization movement at the turn of the century, the peer-to-peer movement began through mutual self-help amongst medical patients in the 1970s and has now become a practical movement for an economy based on mutuality and production for social need.[19] The invention of the 3D printer has significantly boosted the

---

16 Cant (2020). Organizations such as Autonomy and also the New Economics Foundation have made issues of working hours and self-management central practical issues for a new generation. Many are working in or for new trade unions – Independent Workers Union of Great Britain (IWGB) and United Voices of the World (UVW) – who in turn work closely with a number of established unions, such as the Bakers Union and parts of UNITE. These and other developments point towards a radicalization of a significant minority of these workers around questions of work.

17 Panitch and Gindin (2014). Ursula Huws (2020) provides an excellent analytic framework for understanding the new forms of organization developed by successive groups of workers, whose work is shaped by new technologies and who also have access to the new tools made possible through this technology.

18 See Weber (2004).

19 The P2P Foundation provides the most comprehensive guide to the peer-to-peer movement.

capacity of this movement to create common goods. The work of the peer-to-peer movement escalated, informally more than formally, during the pandemic, with collaborative community and peer-to-peer making of the medical equipment that governments failed to provide. Community Centre and family sitting rooms were turned into mini-factories, making masks, visors, and even ventilators.[20]

The work of Open Software networks has been taken up successfully by private companies working in the market, but has faced more obstacles in the public sector – in spite of its advantages "in reducing costs, and increasing independence and transparency in the management of critical resources, services and infrastructure."[21] There is, however, a reversal of the trend, as Free and Open Source Software (FOSS) is becoming the new standard and hundreds of public organizations are currently engaged in a process of learning by doing in FOSS development.

This discussion of the values, purposes, and choices involved in the realization or appropriation of the potential of the new electronic information and communication technology indicates that technology is designed, developed, and installed in contexts where powerful historical, cultural, and political influences are at work. Any analysis then of the underlying forces which shape the responses to the crisis into which the Corona pandemic in bringing the exhausted institutions and technologies of the old order needs to trace underlying shifts in social values.

5   Underlying Shifts in Social Values: A Fifty-Year Process

Again, this cannot be done in one chapter, with the complexity that is necessary. So, I will focus on tendencies of particular relevance to identifying the character of transformative agency. Here I find myself tracing, often unwillingly (for fear of nostalgia), the repercussions of the rebellions of 1968. This moment of an international convergence of rebellions – Vietnam, Paris, Mexico, California, and across the US, ricocheting to Berlin, London, and Belfast and, with its far-reaching challenge to authority in the home, the school, universities, factories, and government, in the Soviet bloc as well as in the US-dominated West, certainly shook the institutions of the old order, and had in that sense the makings of a paradigm-shifting moment. But the movement was institutionally

---

20   See Lisdorf (2020).
21   Quoting from an excellent and comprehensive report. Berlinguer (2020).

and organizationally weak, and it was defeated by the free-market right that had for some time been preparing to benefit from the exhaustion of the post-war settlement. Culturally, however, and in terms of the values and capacities of working people, the experience instilled a belief in comprehensive human rights and a persistent questioning of all forms of authority that survived into the second decade of the twenty-first century, and refused to allow the market to override 'the right to breath' (as Cameroon philosopher, Achille Mbembe eloquently put it) when Corona struck.[22] Anthony Barnett perceptively traces the consequences of 1968 for the values that survived the following 50 years of market supremacy, and are now evident in the humane public pressures on free-market governments, most notably in the UK.[23]

While agreeing with much of Barnett's analysis, I will sketch a further dynamic, directly associated with the resources that the legacy of these years makes available for transformative agency today. It hinges on the search insti-gated by the events of 1968 for forms of democracy sufficiently strong to chal-lenge complacent and immoral elites, and sufficiently open to give form to the widespread feelings of helplessness, so that people see the political and economic sources of their private needs and organize to change society. It has been a search conducted through experiment and practice as much as through theory. This search is intensified in this time of pandemic, but its origins lie in 1968, and the generation formed by their role in ending the US war on Vietnam, their part in the civil rights movement, their founding of the women's libera-tion movement, their shaking of the paternalistic institutions of higher educa-tion, and their experiments with participatory democracy and struggles to con-trol production. It is perhaps of special significance in relation to the Labour Party, and in a sense runs through Panitch's important engagement with and reflections on the struggles of the UK left to overcome the parliamentarism which Ralph Miliband, our common mentor, comrade, and friend, analyzed with such precision and profundity in *Parliamentary Socialism*.[24]

The origins of the Labour Party, founded in 1900, lie in the formation of the Labour Representation Committee (the direct predecessor of the Labour Party), whose founding principle was that of *representing* labor, as an orga-nized but subordinate interest in British capitalism, to achieve legal rights and protections against the attacks of capital. Clause 4 – the commitment to bring the commanding heights into common ownership – was added to the party's constitution, while at the same time the party declared its loyalty to the British

22   Mbembe(2020).
23   See Barnett (2020).
24   Miliband (2009 [1961]).

state and all this implied in terms of MP s' deference to the monarch/state in parliament as distinct from accountability to the people. Certainly, Clause 4 did not imply that the unions, the industrially organized working class, would play any part in the process of bringing parts of industry into common owner-ship. On the contrary, anything so political was to be left to the Parliamentary Labour Party and the parliamentary process. The zenith of representation was presumed to be government, and the party's goal soon became to deploy the state to meet the needs of working people *within* the existing economy (redis-tributing wealth but leaving the production of wealth to the capitalist market).

It achieved this goal in 1945 and continued to pursue it throughout the 1950s and 1960s. By the late 1970s however – probably earlier – the growth of corporate power meant that the fiscal and monetary mechanisms for influ-encing the economy on the Keynesian economic model that had been so cen-tral to Labour's program for government were no longer effective. Keynesian economics had assumed that it was possible to influence the mechanisms of the capitalist market to create full employment, and to generate the wealth to redistribute through the welfare state. As the competitive logic of the cap-italist market generated an increasing tendency to oligopoly and monopoly on a global scale, the instruments of Keynesian demand management became blunt. This also opened up the need for new economic instruments to influ-ence employment levels more directly, through intervening in production itself. At first this was attempted through elected governments or ministers working with corporate management, using a mix of subsidies/incentives, but this had little impact, partly because of the defeat of Tony Benn and the stron-ger, more interventionist alternative economic strategy that he championed.

In particular, the collaborative relationships that Benn built with shop floor organizations, like the Lucas Aerospace shop stewards, amounted in effect to state-supported direct intervention in production –exactly what had been his-torically spurned by the Labour leadership – reducing the power of corporate management and increasing the possibility of meeting the interests of labor. Looking back, this represented the beginning of a significant move away from liberal representative democracy by a minority of the Labour Party and the unions, breaking two of liberal democracy's key distinguishing features: the separation of politics from production which Labour, following Keynes, left to the market. Under representative democracy, politics must adjust to the mar-ket – as do both Keynesian and Monetarist economics. A second feature of liberal democracy is that it treats citizens simply as individual voters, atom-ized from each other, connecting to the polity only through the vote and the election of a representative to whom the citizen abrogates all responsibility. Again, Benn broke this by building productive collaborations with citizens as organized workers, and worked with them on policy, implementation, and in effect, strategy. It's no wonder that the British establishment, strongly supported by the US government, turned on Tony Benn and ensured that his power to intervene in production on the side of labor was destroyed – along with efforts to destroy Benn himself as a political influence.

One of Panitch's greatest achievements in all his work as an engaged scholar was to document this decisive and revealing period in the history of the Labour Party.[25] Here is a telling vignette: "While U.S. Secretary of State William Rodgers harboured 'cosmic' fears in 1976 that Tony Benn might precipitate a policy decision to turn its back on the IMF, which might in turn lead to the whole liberal financial system falling apart, Rodgers quickly found he could count on the support of the rest of the Labour Party, let alone the Treasury and the Bank of England and MI5."[26]

It is significant that Tony Benn himself was influenced by the radical movements of 1968 and the early 1970s, and their move away from a narrowly representative and parliamentary politics. Indeed, his inspiration to democratize the party was less of an inner party affair and more about the need to reach out to these movements. Quoting Benn, Panitch describes how "Benn's vision to counter the basically undemocratic market alternative to social democracy 'now emerging everywhere on the right' " in the 1970s was by connecting "the Labour Party to the political energy fuelling the student uprisings, worker militancy and radical community politics." Benn's message above all involved "extending our representative function so as to bring ourselves into a more creative relationship with many organisations that stand outside our membership." "The promise of Benn's message" was thus that "a Labour government will never rule again but will try to create the conditions under which it is able to act as the natural partner of a people, who really mean something more than we thought they did, when they ask for self-government."[27]

Panitch also notes that it was these ideas of Benn's, ideas quite beyond the parliamentarist traditions of Labour,[28] that shaped Jeremy Corbyn's political formation in the 1970s. Benn's national project for democratizing the Labour Party, and his own bid for the party leadership, was defeated. But his ideas concerning industrial strategy, and direct intervention in production, lived on amongst local activists – most notably in London where community and

---

25   See especially Panitch and Leys(1997: ch. 6).
26   Panitch (2001: 161–62).
27   Panitch and Gindin (2018a) quoting Benn (1970 and 1971: 277–79).
28   Benn would think of himself as a parliamentarian but refused, unlike most Labour MPs, to be a parliamentarist – the object of Miliband's critique.

workplace movements, along with the women's movement and anti-racist initiatives, still had some strength and self-confidence, and were indeed radicalized by the reactionary character of the Thatcher government.

Consequently, the Greater London Council (GLC) under the radical leadership of Ken Livingstone[29] took these breaks with Labour's conservative and parliamentarist form of representative democracy further and was more explicit about them; the experience could be described as a microcosm of transformative economic change. Its London Industrial Strategy (LIS) was based on the idea that "the growth of unemployment and of unmet need, the decline of private and public industries – all indicate a deep failure of policies based on adjusting to the market. What is required is a change in direction in economic strategy, *towards direct intervention in production*."[30] The GLC was also explicit about the importance of a relationship between Londoners as organized citizens and their own autonomous organizations – trade unions, community organizations, Police Monitoring groups. Again, the LIS was explicit: any transformative intervention in industry could not be achieved by the state alone, 'intervening' from above with the expertise of the planner. In the past, it argued, "the resources and the powers to plan have remained at the centre within the state or shared with management. Worker or community involvement has taken on a secondary, consultative form, commenting on plans drawn up within the public authority." The GLC, by contrast, introduced the idea of 'popular planning' which stresses '*sharing power*' (my emphasis), empowering those without official power. The end result on many occasions, for instance the People's Plans in Docklands and in Coin Street, the campaigns against hospital closures, and the alternative plan at Ramparts Engineering (examples of citizen economic initiatives supported by the GLC and often emerging out of resistance to corporate decisions), is an alliance around policies worked out together. Such alliances, would "allow more power than either the GLC or the trade union and community groups would have on their own."[31]

---

29   The Greater London Council was the tier of government that covered the whole of London. In 1981 a radical Labour administration was elected on the basis of an ambitious program: building new homes; slashing the fares on public transport; creating fair employment conditions for women, gays and lesbians, and ethnic minorities; reshaping the public procurement function with social and employment purposes in mind; and opening up and democratizing the land use planning system. An ambitious London Industrial Strategy was to be implemented through the Greater London Enterprise Board, the Popular Planning Unit, the Greater London Training Board, and use of the Council's Procurement function and land use planning powers. See www.glcstory.co.uk and www.robinmurray.co.uk.

30   Greater London Council (1985: 17, my emphasis).

31   Greater London Council (1985: 53).

Whatever its wider alliances with organized citizens, as a municipal government the Livingstone GLC could not, of course, bring about system change. Moreover, any lessons that can be drawn for national politics must be qualified by the fact that its elected councilors were not constrained by oaths of loyalty to the monarch, and through the monarch to the state, the military and so on; consequently, they could carry through their engagement in social movements into the Council, and act more like delegates accountable to their communities rather than MPs beholden to the state. Put briefly, this municipal experience gave high-profile institutional form to the kinds of relationships between electoral sources of power and the direct, popular forms of power that would be necessary to bring about system change at a national and international level. In particular, its break from a predominantly representative form of social democratic politics involved an important shift away from policies as 'plans' – blueprints from above – towards the idea of a 'strategy' – a concept with military origins, implying, in the words of the London Industrial Strategy again: 'conflict, limited resources, and a ground-level perspective which was always having to guess what was over the horizon'. In the case of London,

> what it implied in practice was a view of the London economy as composed of innumerable battlegrounds, involving a struggle for jobs against the pressures of the market ... each case was fought over a particular terrain, with its specific balance of forces – of local communities, workforces, perhaps the support of a borough council in one case, of a local resource centre in another. Each case required its own strategy, geared at first to the immediate terrain.[32]

This approach focuses attention on strategies for organizing and capacity-building which *lay the conditions* (my emphasis) for radical policies by an elected government, as much as on the policies themselves. In *Renewing Socialism* (2001), Panitch quotes approvingly a remark to similar effect by Robert Cox: once "a historical movement gets underway, it is shaped by the material possibilities of the society in which it arises ... as much as by the ... goals of its supporters;" and Cox concludes that "in the minds of those who opt for change, the solution will most likely be seen as lying not in the enactment of a specific policy program as in the building of new means of collective action informed by a new understanding of society and polity."[33]

---

32   Greater London Council (1985: 2).
33   Robert Cox quoted in Panitch (2001: 160–61).

This was in effect the approach of the 1982–86 Labour GLC, which met with limited success, building as it was on movements that were struggling to survive in an otherwise hostile environment. Cox's emphasis on strategy and the balance of power provides a useful perspective not only for understanding the GLC, but also the conditions under which Jeremy Corbyn became leader of the Labour Party and then failed to become Prime Minister.[34] A full understanding of this requires a careful analysis of the uneven state of social movements, and most significantly the weakness of the labor movement, following the abolition of the GLC and the defeat of the miners. Uneven because while the traditional organizations of the labor movement – that is, the trade union movement in the mines, the docks, and manufacturing industry – were effectively destroyed by Thatcher and the processes of industrial restructuring that she reinforced. Some other movements made advances, most notably the peace movement of the early 1980s against cruise missiles, which was as massive in its mobilization as it was imaginative in its tactics.[35]

The movement in support of the 1984/85 miners' strike was another example of the growing tendency to choose practical direct action, building autonomous power based on solidarity. Support groups outside the mining communities twinned with pits and women's support groups in the pit villages, regularly delivering material aid and spending time in the communities, rather than limiting their focus to passing resolutions and lobbying MPs.[36] But against a right-wing establishment determined to destroy the National Union of Mineworkers (NUM), which it saw as the heart of the labor movement itself, this movement was doomed – whatever its impact in changing the lives of hundreds of women in the mining communities as well as their supporters in the cities. The following two decades of political activity from the left, especially of new generations of activists, emphasized direct action, or 'DIY politics' as some of those active described it. From the movements defending the 'Right to Rave' – by organizing raves against hostile Tory legislation – through to the alter-globalization movement, which moved rapidly from stalking and disrupting the summits of the global elites to continental and global gatherings that both insisted and demonstrated that Another World Is Possible, left politics (with a small, non-party 'l') was about building what was termed

---

34 This approach also inspired Panitch's thinking in Albo, Langille and Panitch (1993).

35 Most notably the Greenham Common Women's Peace Camp, originally a direct attempt to disrupt the US Cruise Missile Base, and the people-to-people diplomacy of the European Nuclear Disarmament Campaign that linked peace movement activists in the West with dissident activists working for peace and democracy in Eastern Europe.

36 See Massey and Wainwright (1986).

'people power' and only pragmatically engaging with electoral politics. It was less 'in and against the state' and more 'outside of' and 'in spite of' the state.

Meanwhile, the left inside the political institutions, most notably the Labour Party, had reached a dead end – insofar as they confined themselves to parliament. So much so that Labour leader Tony Blair boasted that he could leave the small band of Socialist Campaign Group MPs as 'a sealed tomb' rather than go through the bother expelling them.[37] No wonder he and his allies were in shock when one of these supposedly ghostly figures, Jeremy Corbyn, won the leadership of the Party!

The shock was greatest amongst those, commentators and politicians alike, for whom parliament is the axis around which all politics moves, and who therefore had no understanding whatsoever of the underlying forces for change. Yet the people who joined the queues or climbed through windows to hear Jeremy Corbyn in 2016 were mainly those who had lost all hope in parliamentary paths and had in small ways begun to make their own way through fighting exploitative landlords, organizing workers, often like themselves, on zero-hour contracts, organizing direct support for refugees in the UK and internationally. And Jeremy Corbyn had supported them; though an MP of many years, he was not a parliamentarian, and spent a good deal of his time engaged with movements outside parliament. Movement activists without a party card supported him. This was especially significant after an ambiguous attempt, during the leadership of Ed Miliband, to reform the union 'block vote' opened up the possibility of activists from outside the party having a say in the Party leadership, which after decades of Tory government, seemed worth a try.[38]

Now is not the moment for a full analysis of the Corbyn years, with all their contradictions, complexities, successes, and failures. What is relevant for our argument here about the persistent trend towards creating sources of political, social, cultural, and economic power, including political voice, autonomous from parliamentary politics, is that as Corbyn advanced and the attacks on him from the right intensified, the overwhelming strength of embedded and enduring parliamentarist political institutions became apparent at every level of the Labour Party, from local branches to the national and regional apparatus with its close relation to the Parliamentary Party, reinforced by the pressures of the UK electoral system and the lack of diversity in the mainstream British media plus personal vested interest and the power of habitual routines. This power of the inherited power structures proved too great for the informal, enthusiasm-driven

---

37   Simpson (2014).
38   This glorious story is told vividly in Nunn (2018).

ed to the primacy of electoral routines and the pressures of the internal power struggle typical of the Labour Party's culture. In that sense, using Cox's insight, the material possibilities at the time of 'the Corbyn moment' in terms of the strength of "a new movement with a new understanding of society and politics" did not match the ambition of Corbyn's policies, and the movement supporting Corbyn did not have the autonomous capacity to consolidate and organize the activism that it inspired throughout society. Its energies got sucked into the hostile vortex of the parliamentary politics that it had historically spurned.

Two consequences can be noted for our purposes here. First, the end result was that the new extra-parliamentary, non-electoral organizational energies that Corbyn's leadership attracted to the Labour Party – into its ambit, even if not into its formal membership[39] – ended up renewing Labour's electoral campaigning, from more extensive canvassing returns to an approach to canvassing that developed relationships on which local parties could build, rather than simply conducting a transaction to win a vote. This worked well in several cities where the local Labour Party and Momentum had been active campaigning organizations, and the local Labour Council had not taken working-class Labour voters for granted – often because of electoral competition and a mobile population. But a more friendly 'relationship-building' canvassing method was not enough in the so-called 'Red Wall' constituencies to make up for a deep mistrust of Labour after decades of being taken for granted by nepotistic Labour Council, compounded by concerted media and political attacks on Corbyn.[40] This points to the need for an entirely different modality, whereby the party could directly meet people's needs in a way that enables them to understand the social sources of their private problems, and gain the collective strength to bring about change. Secondly representative institutions were in a sense hostile terrain, epitomized by the way that the mainstream media defined politics almost entirely through Westminster. Perhaps the Corbyn leadership did not establish sufficient autonomy from the pull of these powerful institutions. After the unexpectedly high vote Corbyn won in 2017, Labour began to define itself as the government-in-waiting, which meant

---

39 Many young Corbyn supporters whose main energies are in non-Labour Party campaigns now report how 'I never joined the Labour Party, but I did go door stepping with them'.
40 Whose message about changing local councils to be responsive to local people could never be heard above the cacophony of vicious attacks.

that in practice, it made the parliamentary stage the main stage – even though amongst some there was an awareness that without an organized movement in workplaces and communities, they could not succeed.[41] These voices of disquiet, however, were overwhelmed by the tyranny of immediate electoral pressures alongside the constant attacks on Corbyn from within the Parliamentary Labour Party and the party apparatus.

The devastation of the 2019 defeat – in a sense all the more devastating because Corbynistas had invested so much in the election campaign and the possibility of their leader becoming Prime Minister – led to lessons being ruthlessly and self-critically learned. The result most relevant to my argument has been a transformation of Momentum under an entirely new leadership.

Built out of the campaign for Jeremy Corbyn to be leader, Momentum originally had two purposes: to strengthen support for Corbyn inside the party, and movement-building in communities and workplaces. Leading members talked about forming renters unions and organizing precarious workers. However, as Mish Rahman, one of the members of the new committee, commented: "In reality building grass roots power did not get the support it needed."[42] Momentum, however, was not simply its national directorate; branches were more or less autonomous, and some took the movement-building purpose seriously. Moreover, The World Transformed (TWT) established itself as an autonomous organization, though closely associated with Momentum and with the Labour Party. Its annual festival has been held in parallel and in interaction with the main Labour Party conference and took place in 2020 online. TWT has now turned itself into a year-round, locally as well as nationally based organization, and resource for popular political education. Many of those who joined the party from grassroots movements, attracted by Corbyn's leadership, believed they had a license as it were from the new leadership to continue with their involvement with the local tenants' organization or other extra-parliamentary

---

41   John McDonnell in particular made a point, in all his speeches around the country, to call for organized action around alternative policies *before* Labour was in government. It's interesting that the two insiders working on policy in the Leaders Office who have written publicly about the lessons to be learned from the Corbyn years stress the importance now of concentrating on the movement-building that was lacking when Corbyn was leader, because of the constant attack he was under from the PLP and the lack of co-operation at crucial moments from important parts of the party apparatus. See the assessment by Andrew Fisher, one of Corbyn's policy advisors, in Fisher (2020). See also Robertson (2020).

42   At a panel organized by Momentum on local campaigning at the 2020 The World Transformed Festival.

organizing, but, under Corbyn, with the possible added benefit of Labour Party support.

This meant that a good proportion of Momentum members maintained their movement-building commitment throughout the period of Corbyn's leadership and had no intention of giving it up after the election defeat of 2019 with the election of Keir Starmer as Labour Leader (who has no sense whatsoever of the importance of sharing power, or even of what it means as part of a strategy of social transformation), whether or not they remained members of Labour (and for many that was no longer a big issue, now putting their energies into non-electoral organizing, myself included). These people supported a change of leadership for Momentum, and earlier in 2020, a new leadership was elected on the basis that it would reorient the organization towards building grassroots power.

Several months later, this new leadership presented a panel at the 2020 virtual TWT festival on 'Building Local Power'. Cardiff Momentum talked about how it works with the local branch of Acorn, the grassroots housing organization, in campaigns to reduce rents, stop evictions, and build council houses. The Momentum organizer stressed how they see their role as being to 'support these campaigns not to lead them, and to train their members into becoming organisers'. Liverpool Momentum has responded to the huge homeless problem in the city with an imaginative plan for ecological housing. Tower Hamlets worked with and supported the local union branch in fighting a mayor intent on service cuts. They focused especially on organizing service users to complement the unions' workplace organizing, and to ensure that the unions built the needs of users into their strategy. North Tyneside Momentum described an election campaign for a radical socialist mayor whose campaign was based on meeting local everyday needs, and who had committed to sharing power and supporting local movements and campaigns in the process. Their pro-Corbyn candidate won with a large majority.

Corbyn supporters are also involved in key struggles over what is emerging as the post-pandemic capitalism. We have referred earlier to the boom in logistics that makes it the one sector of the economy that is recruiting in large numbers. Corbyn supporters are active in the unionization and organization of these and other groups of precarious workers – for example in restaurant and delivery services, another post-pandemic growth area.

They are building a new kind of organization, rather than just a more radical innovative form of representative politics. The organizing and methodology is impressive, especially in the shift that all these diverse experiences indicate, away from a preoccupation with inner Labour Party battles.

Instead of an organization whose prime function is securing majority Labour representation, the new leadership of Momentum is creating an organization whose function is empowerment, to share its resources inside or outside the state to build strategic popular power. Some Corbyn-supporting Labour MPs and ex-MPs are thinking in a similar direction.

Laura Pidcock, for example, the eloquent and locally rooted MP who lost her seat in North West Durham, argues that now is the time to establish meaningful relationships with local people and their communities, to "organize ... in the true sense" rather than "to get better at door knocking, which is essentially data collection."[43] She talks instead of opening Labour offices and clubs to provide food and other personal support for people under pressure – and that pressure is growing – as well as space and resources for young people to organize music, art, dancing, and other activities for which there is no space in their homes. The idea would be both provision of a service to meet pressing needs and also a practical educational experience in democratic self-government.

What if this was part of a social and economic strategy? Could this approach of directly supporting self-organizing also lead to a shift towards social controls over production? This would be to follow Marx in his emphasis on socialism as a matter of the transformation of production rather than exclusively distribution; an emphasis that is all the more necessary in the face of the contemporary challenges of climate change and re-equipping under-resourced health systems to meet the needs of the continuing pandemic. A purely distributional socialism does little to address the need for a transition to a low-carbon economy, or the related need to expand the capacity of the health service. But to follow the logic of a strategic, movement-building approach as distinct from an electoral and policy emphasis implies an expansion of labor movement capacity-building around production. This has two sides to it: first, identifying the role of a political organization in changing the balance of power *now*. The second is asking deeper and broader questions about what capacity-building in production would in fact involve for the trade unions and other campaigning, activist organizations.[44]

---

43   Pidcock (2020).

44   A word of clarification concerning 'capacity-building' would be helpful here. The term 'capacity-building' has been somewhat devalued and depoliticized in the wave of a disingenuous enthusiasm for an apolitical community organizing that swept the UK with the attempts at a feel-good rhetoric of Tony Blair (New Deal for Communities) and David Cameron (Big Society). I mean it to refer to education, preferably rooted in and reflecting on experience, in organization building and consciousness-raising in the context of a movement working for radical social transformation.

6   Organization-Building and Consciousness-Raising Around Production

We can return to Airbus Unite branch's response to the call for the conversion of plants to produce ventilators to inspire answers to these questions. A spread of such conversion initiatives to health equipment more generally (not just ventilators, whose benefits are under review) would require some coordination with campaigns in and around the health service, based on a health workers' audit of equipment needs for expanded procurement and therefore manufacture of what was needed in the context of a decline in traditional, high-carbon manufacturing markets (like Aerospace). We would need an organization that could play the kind of combined coordination and consciousness-raising role that the Lucas Aerospace Shop Stewards Combine Committee played when it led workers to "think as if they were planners," as Mick Cooney, one of the shop stewards, put it,[45] and to encourage both industrial workers (on the manufacturing, supply side) and health workers (on the need, demand side) to imagine how their skills could be used for socially useful purposes. The idea would be to develop new strategic thinking about changes that could be campaigned for here and now, exploiting the sense of emergency that is awakening people's humane and social sensitivities, shaking them to reach beyond their traditional roles and gain confidence and power in the possibilities of productive change.

This experience around ventilators during the height of the pandemic is already influencing the consciousness of workers in industrial companies like Airbus and Rolls Royce to see conversion to low-carbon products as nothing exceptional, but as socially desirable and something of which they are fully capable. And here again, on the issue of a transition to low-carbon forms of production, a political organization could play a vital role in bringing together industrial trade unionists and environmental activists and researchers, building support for conversion plans as part of a strategy against the dramatic and disastrous growth of redundancies.

For this emphasis on building power over production now as a condition for political change in the future, trade union organizations will need to develop a consciousness of their constructive capacity to produce solutions to the challenges posed by the pandemic and by climate change. The absence of a radical leadership of the Labour Party is of course a setback here, but on the other hand the Conservative government's mixture of incompetence and contempt for working people is leading responsible and socially minded trade unionists,

---

45   Interview with author in Wainwright (1982).

especially at a factory level, to feel that insofar as they can see an alternative direction, it is they who need to act – no one else will.

For a period, this strategic organizing both in manufacturing and also in the more widespread production of the essentials of everyday life, will be localized and dispersed. Is this not where some kind of political organization comes in? But not one that is organized around representation and policy alone. Strategy, as distinct from policy, implies a view of society and the economy composed of innumerable battlegrounds, involving a struggle for jobs against the pressures of the market; each case was fought over a particular terrain, with its specific balance of forces – of unions, local communities, democratic media, perhaps the support of a borough council in one case, or of the government in another. Each case requires its own strategy, geared at first to the immediate terrain. Thus, the model of a party whose predominant function is representation, on the basis of a set of policies to be implemented from above by the state is no longer appropriate. A strategic approach, rather, implies extra-parliamentary action at different levels, by unions and social movements, working in collaboration with supportive elected representatives who are willing to share the resources and platform to which they have access.

If, building on Panitch and Gindin, "in a very real sense, we are starting over ... free ... from the moorings of either 1917 or 1945 that have so badly tethered previous attempts at party-building or renewal,"[46] then developing the capacities for a political organization able to encourage and support the development of strategic movements in production and in the wider society is the priority. Without these new organizing capacities, including knowledge of issues of production, science, and technology, we will just fall back into the default routines of organizations that have failed.

7   **Labor Schools of Strategic Organizing**

This implies that a massive learning exercise is needed – preferably through experience, by doing, whereby activists, whether inside or outside the party, learn the basics of organizing in workplaces that have yet to be unionized, whether they be in entertainment, retail, or logistics, and equip themselves with the know-how to build society-wide support for these initiatives. They also need to learn the basics of building a tenants or residents organization and develop alliances able to stand up to the council over its eviction policy,

---

46   Panitch and Gindin (2015: 20).

its approach to immigrants, and its development plans and, ideally, to have the know-how to put forward alternative plans. Such a learning process would need, above all, to involve the unions in developing a political trade union-ism that goes beyond the immediate issues of the workplace and takes action over the purpose and consequences of their work – whether in manufactur-ing, around high-carbon emissions, or public services, where responsiveness to users, especially in the age of Covid-19, is central. The list could go on.

My argument here is close to that of Panitch and Gindin when they urged a return to the model of the early-twentieth century days of the labor move-ment, when political activists put their energies into building basic organiza-tional foundations. Here I would reinforce but also develop their concluding remark in *The Socialist Challenge Today*: "If a socialist project today is not to be stymied by the inherited state apparatuses [and, I would add, by the electoral-ism of left political parties] decisive focus on developing the agency and capac-ity for state [and, I would add, economic] transformation will be required."[47]

I have a whimsical proposal on which to end, which sums up the key change that I have suggested has been taking place for the past fifty years, the decades that both Leo Panitch and I lived through, and on which we reflected and wrote as we engaged and organized; a change now deepened by the impact and civic response to the Covid pandemic. The thought is that whereas socialist activists in 1900 were busy creating the Labour *Representation* Committee (the organi-zation that led to the foundation of the Labour Party), we need to busy our-selves creating *Labour Schools of Strategic Organizing* by whatever names and forms are appropriate, recognizing the need to build on what already exists. In a sense such schools are already emerging in the more creative and inter-active of the Zoom meetings that have now become a daily occurrence. Much must be done: to improve their educational, as distinct from expressive, value; to extend their reach beyond the already committed; and, as soon as possi-ble, to be engaged in actually organizing together face-to-face and beyond our normal comfort zones. Such physical, sociable experiences are a vital part of true consciousness-raising. They are but one example of the new develop-ments which have been quickened by the pandemic, on which strategies for a humane society can creatively and modestly build in what is in many ways a bleak political environment.

47   Panitch and Gindin (2018a: 89).

CHAPTER 12

Class Politics and Strategies for Party-Building

Michalis Spourdalakis

The class–party relationship has historically been one of the most complex and thus controversial issues for the left. That is because, class and class stratification compose the ground for any left political strategy, while at the same time, the effectiveness of strategic choices are determined by the party's organizational and political efficiency. Thus, the relation between class and party has been one of the most debated questions, both theoretically and practically, among left activists. Especially after the 1960s, these debates became more intense. It was then that the relatively stable social division of labor and the overall social cleavages that defined parties' development limited the organizational choices of all parties, regardless of their tradition and orientation to a mass party structure. The social, cultural, ideological, and political developments that emerged in the late 1960s challenged party organizational certainties. This is something that the crisis of the 1970s and the neoliberal hegemony challenged further, undermining parties' organizational and representational capacities. Consequently, it is not a surprise that the latter has forced the left to consider the party–class relation again.

More concretely, the collapse of so-called actually existing socialism caused a major setback, even to that part of the left and the Marxists who were critical of 'historical socialism'. In addition, capitalist integration on a world scale, what we came to call 'globalization', along with the rise and fall of the anti-globalization movement, and finally the huge cluster of technological innovations, have radically changed the terrain of the current political scene. Under these conditions, the crisis of representation, propelled by the fiscal crisis, made the question of party-building vital, not simply for the advancement of the left, but for its mere survival. The enormous challenges facing the left, above all the versatile and seemingly almighty hegemony of neoliberalism, have led to a widespread pessimism and even despair among leftists. This can only be curbed by collective action, namely, through the organization and practice of left parties. The democratic capacity of political parties and their key role in socialist transformation never escaped the analytical and political concerns of Leo Panitch in his path-breaking work.[1] This is something which,

---

1   Indeed, Panitch's contribution was far reaching on the social and political functions of the party, and it presented a view that is neither formalistic nor instrumentalist as in the Leninist tradition. See for example: Panitch (2001: esp. ch. 7); Albo, Panitch and Zuege (2018: esp. 275ff).

as so many other contributions to this volume underline, stemmed from his commitment to social transformation and to the continuous struggle for the democratization of political power.

This chapter will begin with a brief critical presentation of the various approaches to the relation between the political party and society as it is understood by the mainstream. Then it will turn to the Marxist understanding of the class–party relationship with regard to recent socio-political dynamics. I will conclude by sharing some ideas on the political and social challenges of building a radical left party in the current conjuncture.

1   The Mainstream Contribution

If one wishes to do away with the shortcomings of reductionism, then you cannot but approach the question of party development as a result of the parameters deriving from: social conflict and antagonism; the formal, informal, and customary rules and conditions; and as the positive regulatory and customary conditions of the political struggle in a given social formation. Political conflict and antagonisms that develop during electoral competition are key to understanding parties, but these dynamics are not sufficient for understanding the relationships between political and social forces. On the contrary, party antagonisms are the result of long-term and multidimensional socio-political processes, which must be examined in detail if we want to fully grasp party dynamics. In other words, as Gramsci emphasized, it is inconceivable to consider "the counting of votes as the actual societal condition or as the only reflection of the party–society relationship."[2]

Mainstream theorists, who at best see social antagonisms as secondary in advanced liberal democracies, consider the party–society relationship to be of a brokerage type. That is because they emphasize the parties' functions of interest aggregation and interest articulation as the main processes for the accommodation of social interests.[3] Apart from stating the obvious, i.e., pointing out that parties respond in one way or another to social demands, this approach seems to be based on false assumptions as it implies that parties can accommodate all interests. It is not a given that parties are compelled to respond to demands (aggregation) and then to accommodate them by converting them into responsive policies (articulation). The problem of this approach is not so much that it ignores the obvious differentiation of the strength of social

---

2   Gramsci (1971: 192ff).
3   For example, see: Janda (1970).

interests but rather that it seems particularly deterministic, when in reality, consideration of interests (aggregation-articulation) does not necessarily result in responsive policies. Love and marriage do not necessarily go together.

Along these lines, although coming closer to addressing the issues of political conflict and competition, is the Downsian approach.[4] Downs raises the issue of political conflict as a central factor in his analysis. To him, parties should not be examined outside the framework of the conflict expressed in the electoral market. Downs has clearly been inspired by the principles guiding individual behavior in the classic micro-economic model. Thus, he argues that parties are nothing but groups of rational individuals who come together under pressure of their self-interests in order to compete and win in the electoral market. The latter is somehow the guarantee that the winning interests will be fulfilled. Although this approach is more sophisticated than the simple 'brokerage model', because it places the party–society relationship closer to the heart of the political struggle, it suffers from the birth defects of its initial theoretical principles. Micro-economic theory assumes the rationality of 'homo economicus', which is expected to guide the actions not only of the individuals involved but also of their collective institutions and agencies (corporations, unions, and of course political parties). Downsian theory tends to see political parties in the same vein and thus collapses the relationship of parties to society into a relationship between individuals.

This rather simplistic approach to parties has very little methodological usefulness. Above all else, political parties are organizations. Of course, parties are made up of individuals and thus are to some degree subject to the control of their members. However, a party cannot be understood merely as the sum of the individuals that makes them up. Like all organized institutions, parties develop a logic, which, although not unrelated to the individual party members, has a dynamic of its own.[5] Otherwise, for example, how could we explain the rigidity displayed at times by parties vis-à-vis their supporters, even when it concerns immediate electoral gains?[6] Furthermore, how could we explain how subjective and individual interests are articulated and expressed in collective action?[7] Finally, how could we understand the constraints which have been imposed upon parties, by class, religious, linguistic, ethnic, or other cleavages,

---

4   See Downs (1957).

5   Panebianco in a way defines this 'logic' as the 'genetic model' of political parties, which defines their founding traits and thus are the least mutable (Panebianco, 1988: 50–53).

6   For example, the frequency of cases in which parties choose leaders who are not the most popular individuals is a case in point.

7   Balbus (1974: 281–83).

and upon which political parties base, although not exclusively, their existence and dynamic?

Other mainstream scholars view political parties merely as transmission belts between the state (and/or the governmental) apparatus and society. As such, parties undertake a number of ex officio functions, which are crucial to the smooth functioning of the entire system.[8] Again, the focus is on their functions: 'political socialization'; 'political recruitment'; 'providing leadership';[9] 'formulating public policy'; and 'structuring the vote'. These functions are seen as the basis upon which the relationship between the party and society is formed. There are however two major problems with this approach. First, these functions are difficult to identify, and in addition, they simply describe the parties' presence in the socio-political environment and not the actual party–society relationship. Secondly, this understanding does not apparently make any distinction between the 'functions' of the different parts of the political spectrum. It would be rather simplistic to accept the idea that a left-wing or working-class party performs the same kind of political functions as their counterparts at the other end of the political spectrum.[10]

The problem with all these approaches to the 'party–society/class' question does not lie in their dismissal of societal conflict, as one might have imagined, but rather in their fractionalized and individualistic perception of that conflict. These theoretical approaches did not manage to cut the umbilical cord from the individualism of the liberal tradition and surpass the liberal understanding of society as a multitude of independent individuals whose interests are articulated in an autonomous and subjective fashion. In fact, these interests are not seen as originating within the structure of the system, which, though in a contradictory fashion, collectivizes individuals. Although collective political expression is taken as given, the interests which support and influence it become understood subjectively and in a fragmented fashion. To be more specific, although the capitalist social formation is characterized by the concentration of social interests that are situated in structurally distinct locations, the liberal analysts insist on considering these interests as if they were the

---

8   See: Neumann (1956: 396–400); Merkl (1970: 272–84); Curtis (1968: 134–40); Almond and Powell (1966: 73–112); Macridis (1967: 17).

9   See for example Lipset (1963: 239). In fact, Gramsci in his "Modern Prince", talks about the "task" of political parties to perform this "mass function which selects leaders" (Gramsci, 1971: 191, 146). However, his statement should not be misunderstood and equated with similar arguments made by mainstream theorists. Gramsci, in his symbolic language, refers to the revolutionary party and not to parties in general.

10   This is certainly a methodological conclusion that is drawn even in some classic studies of the same tradition. For example, Epstein (1967: esp. 130–200).

outcome of personal choice. As a result, the social category (or class) to which a person belongs becomes an issue of personal preference and as such, these classes become, in the end, just another factor influencing the party–society/ class relationship.

Thus, on the one hand, most mainstream scholars, without dismissing class divisions, have for decades now reached the conclusion that given "the decomposition of capital and labour, it is highly doubtful whether the concept of class is still applicable to the conflict groups of post-capitalist societies."[11] In such approaches, there is a clear lack of cohesiveness between groups with common economic interests. Naturally, conclusions along these lines distance party theory from the issue of the party–class relationship, and turn it in the direction of a whole series of other cross-class conflicts (i.e., religious, geographic, etc.).[12] On the other hand, the 'orthodox' Marxists tend to focus exclusively on the class–party relationship in such a way as to reduce one to the other.[13]

A comprehensive and methodologically useful analysis of the party–society and class relationship would have to distance itself from both of these conceptions. To approach the party–class relationship, we should begin with an examination of the party–class relationship, focusing in particular on current class dynamics (alignments, de-(re-)alignments). Then account should be taken of those social differences, contradictions, and conflicts that have been called super-structural and that usually over-determine and/or disguise the class base of political parties. This examination is essential as these contradictions and conflicts frequently acquire an autonomous existence vis-à-vis the class dynamic and display an amazing inertia.

2   The Relative Autonomy of Party from Class

As one may have expected, the Marxist literature tends to place more emphasis on the party–class relationship. It does not, however, provide us with a systematic analysis of the question. Only in the context of other analyses can one find some theoretical insights and useful methodological conclusions, which may constitute the starting point of a more comprehensive approach. Before we attempt to draw out these insights, it must be stressed once again, that any

---

11   For example, Dahrendorf (1967: 57).
12   For a comprehensive presentation of the issue see: Alford (1963: 18–20ff).
13   See for example: Goertzel (1976: 136–37); and San Francisco Bay Area Kapitalistate Group (1977: 19).

examination of the relationship between party and class should be under-taken differently for parties from different ends of the political spectrum. Over and above some general principles that govern the party–class relationship, it is not possible for all types of parties – with such diverse and, by definition, adversarial political traditions – to have the same relationship with their social base. After all, parties and party families are inspired and guided by different and competing strategic goals and social visions. It is for this reason that in the following pages, after a brief general introduction to the issues, we will examine first the relationship of the 'bourgeois' parties with social classes, and then the relationship between the left-wing parties and their social base.

The real material existence of any social class is the result of its political organization. Classes or class factions acquire their distinctiveness and effectiveness as soon as they organize (through and) into political parties. Parties are creations of their classes through this process and as such are assigned certain tasks. On the one hand, they are to protect and advance the interests of class(es) or the social alliance that created them, and on the other, they are to suppress the interests of the other classes. The latter function indicates that political parties as the "nomenclature for classes" are not simply "a mechanical and passive expression of those classes but (that they) react energetically upon them in order to develop, solidify and universalize them."[14] In other words, "through their political and ideological activity" political parties are critical "organizers of the relations between classes."[15]

However, no matter how much one stresses the importance of political parties for social classes and strata, it would be erroneous to assume that there is a one-to-one relationship between them. Such an assumption would be a crude reduction, which for many reasons is inappropriate.

First, it is clear, even if we accept the claim that capitalism by nature creates primarily two opposing classes (bourgeois and working class), that capitalist social formations – i.e., the totality of all the existing modes of production within the particular historical and territorial framework of a primarily capitalist society – contain a number of social groups/remnants from previous modes of production.[16] Thus, it is no surprise that these social strata, perhaps more so than other social groups, have a wide range of political choices and expressions, and are anything but stable. At times, some of these strata ally their interests with the aims of the bourgeoisie and the parties that best represent them; and some with the aspirations and the political goals of the working

14   Gramsci (1971: 152, 227); Poulantzas (1973: 78, 247).
15   Brodie and Jenson (1980: 9).
16   Brodie and Jenson (1980: 14).

class; or sometimes, more rarely, manage to create or control some other party formation.

Second, it is not only the inertia of the 'old' class(es) and social strata which prevents us from identifying party and class, but also the appearance of new social groups. The development of a social formation is not linear, nor can it be anticipated in a deterministic fashion. On the contrary, the dynamic of a social formation is the result of a myriad of internal contradictions and external factors, the outcome of which depends both on the result of and the conditions of the waging of the class struggle at all levels. It is exactly this process which determines the appearance or the disappearance of new social strata, who find themselves in a peculiar and often unique location vis-à-vis the primary classes produced by the antitheses between capital and labor.[17] These new classes and/or factions are faced with a dilemma similar to that of the 'old' (remnant) social groups – to join the bourgeois or the working-class political organizations or perhaps to form one of their own.

However, over and above this line of argument, which prevents the tautology of party and class, the historical conjuncture of recent years has led to social reorganizations that allow us to characterize our time as transitional. For over a decade now, since the outbreak of the most recent deep economic and political crisis, this is clearer than ever before. It appears to shed doubt upon and lead to a reconsideration of the existing manners of political arbitration. In fact, there have been two primary lines of analysis, which attempt to understand the developments of the societies of 'late capitalism'. The first approach, which is rather dated, was based on the expansion of the phenomena of social inequalities as a result of the economic crisis during the 1980s which led to the conclusion that the advanced capitalist societies tend to develop extensive phenomena of social exclusion and what was called the 'two-thirds society'.[18] In a second approach, others focus upon the tendencies and overall macro developments of the 'post-industrial' society[19] or to 'third wave' societies[20] leading not only to new social contradictions and alignments[21] but also necessarily to new types of

---

17   Brodie and Jenson (1980).
18   See for example: Glotz (1985; 1986: 36ff).
19   See chapter 2, section II and also: Touraine (1971); Bell (1976); Block (1990); Esping-Andersen (1993: esp. 7–31). A number of scholars have expressed reservations about the concept of the 'post-industrial', in particular the implicit notion that industrial capitalism has been superseded. On this, see: Cohen and Zysman (1987).
20   Toffler (1981: esp. 137ff).
21   Gouldner (1979); Gorz (1982).

political expression and organization.[22] The boom in the field of cultural and post-colonial studies has clearly contributed to the problematique in the same direction. Despite the often-superficial conclusions, there is no doubt that this problematique of modern sociology is based on some genuinely radical developments within our advanced capitalist societies which constitute a further reason to reject the idea of a one-way relationship between party and class.

Third, we have already shown how parties are primarily (but not exclusively) the creation of class interests. As such, they not only promote the interests that by definition they represent, but they also seek to disorganize or rather to organize in a distorted fashion, the articulation of the interests of other classes. The latter takes place through not only omissions and the political inertia of the parties but also through the planning and carrying out of specific initiatives. In other words, as Gramsci put it, this characteristic of parties is nothing other than a "balancing and arbitrating function between the interests of their (class) and those of the other groups," which is necessary for the achievement of their primary goal – i.e., securing and developing the interests of the class(es) they primarily represent.[23] In advanced capitalist societies, this function of political parties seems particularly important and vital, because no class or stratum maintains the absolute majority and strength to enforce its political will and to establish hegemony on its own. As a result, identifying party with class would be an oversimplification since it would not allow an approach to and an analysis of this important "balancing and arbitrating function" of parties.

Fourth, as we mentioned above, by definition, parties live for and are subject to political competition and the struggle for political power. If that competition is at least a partial expression and result of the class struggle, then it is logical to argue that political parties find themselves at the center of class antagonism and of the class struggle. Thus, due to their position at the crossroads of political power on the one hand, and given their vital function in organizing, reorganizing, and disorganizing the class struggle, parties cannot but reflect the totality of the processes of class struggle. Taking this into consideration, it would be absurd to argue that any party is "the unilateral, unequivocal instrument of just one class or class fragment."[24] On the contrary, political parties internalize the entire complexity of class relations and consequently become

---

22   This is an argument, which has been made for some time now. See for example: Hindess (1971: esp. chs. 1, 2, 7, and 8); *Monthly Review*, special issue on "Technology, the Labor Process and the Working Class," July-August 1976, especially articles by Ehrenreich and Ehrenreich (1976: 10–18) and by Braverman (1976: esp. 122–24).

23   Gramsci (1971: 148).

24   Bourque (1979: 131).

the arena for part of the class struggle. It follows that "it is inside the party (in addition to a number of other locations) that the hegemony of one class or fragment is imposed upon other classes or fragments."[25] This insight provides a starting point for the examination of both the organizational structure and the mechanism of decision-making for parties' strategies and policies.

Finally, the actual articulation and pursuit of alternative political strategies within a given social formation further prevents us from unilaterally identifying party and class. The possibility of the choice of tactics and/or policies cannot but affect the political expression of the social classes. It appears that a recognition of this phenomenon led Poulantzas to make the distinction between the "political scene,"[26] which is defined as "the field of political parties' action," and the "political interests and practices" of social classes. In fact he makes the useful observation that the "political scene ... is often dislocated in relation to the political practices and to the terrain of political interests of the classes, represented by the parties in the political scene."[27] This dislocation suggests not only that the reduction of a party to a class is unthinkable, but also that it would be legitimate, if not necessary, to claim that there is a relative autonomy of the political party vis-à-vis the interests of the social class(es) it primarily represents. This relative autonomy is a particularly useful notion in analyzing and understanding the conflicts that are often apparent between the class(es) and factions of the power bloc and parts of the bourgeois class, or even the phenomenon of working-class or populist parties expressing and supporting the interests of the bourgeoisie.

Taking a detour for a moment, we must point out that these conclusions are particularly useful in the analysis of the development of bourgeois parties in the two main phases of their history that coincides with the stages of capitalist development – competitive and monopoly/advanced. In the first phase, political parties were 'used' as unifying tools for the diverse and often conflicting interests of the individual members of the bourgeoisie. The political effectiveness of the bourgeoisie was vital at the time, as it had to establish its political hegemony over the declining feudal order. In this effort, the bourgeois

---

25   Bourque (1979).

26   Poulantzas argues that "in capitalist formations the political scene is a privileged place in which the open action of social forces can take place by means of their representation by parties ... The metaphors of presence in the political scene, of the place of a class in this scene (whether in the forefront or not), etc. *are constantly related to the modalities of class representation by parties and to the relations between the political parties*" (Poulantzas, 1973: 247).

27   Poulantzas (1973: 251).

parties had to accommodate to some degree, for tactical reasons, the political interests of the working class and other popular strata within their struggle. When the capitalist class(es) established themselves in full command of the social, political, and ideological order of the system, the aims of the parties changed. Thus, today, the bourgeois parties no longer need to organize and unite the interests of all parts of the bourgeois class in the same way. Given its hegemonic role, the bourgeois class does not necessarily need to have its own party, because it is able to "utilize the existing parties turn by turn."[28] To some extent, these remarks are at the base of recent analyses of the crisis of party democracy. From the left, Peter Mair has declared that "the age of party democracy has passed," and Wolfgang Streeck has contended that the liberalization of markets has ended the uneasy relation between capitalism and democracy and thus undermined representative institutions. And from a more conservative perspective, Bernard Manin has gone so far as to attribute the decline of parties to the elitist nature of elections and to the fact that parties cannot keep their programmatic promises, while Frances McCall Rosenbluth and Ian Shapiro claim that the party crisis is the paradoxical result of parties' efforts to decentralize power and engage the electorate.[29] Gramsci's observation on the contingent relationship between bourgeois rule and political parties has achieved wide resonance.

After accepting the thesis of parties' relative autonomy from their founding social class(es), as well as the argument that the bourgeois class does not necessarily need a party of its own, we are led to the question of the definition of 'bourgeois' parties. To put it differently, if direct class (bourgeois) participation in a party is not proof of its orientation, then the question naturally arises: what are the criteria for distinguishing a bourgeois party?

Therborn has approached this question with the insightful observation that the bourgeoisie, with or without its own party or parties, has demonstrated the ability to exploit the peculiarities of class differentiation. As this is the result of the social and technical division of labor, the bourgeoisie has the capacity to organize the "population around the capitalist enterprise and the capitalist state on the basis of various ideologies."[30] In other words, the ability of a political party to effectively organize social classes and strata in such a way demonstrates its 'bourgeois' nature. However, in spite of the fact that this analysis avoids the shortcomings of instrumentalism, it contains a number of other problems which curtail its analytical usefulness.

---

28   Gramsci (1971: 155).
29   See: Mair (2013); Streeck (2017: esp. 93–112); Manin (1997); Rosenbluth and Shapiro (2018).
30   Therborn (1978: 194).

284

SPOURDALAKIS

The critical remarks of the previous paragraphs do not allow us to conclude that class participation in any party constitutes, or could constitute, the
determining factor in the characterization of a party. However, this does not
mean that class is a peripheral consideration either. Even when it is generally
accepted that a working-class party acts in the interests of capital while the
bourgeoisie is organized in other party(ies), this does not mean that there is
no difference between competing parties and party families. Class participation in a party may not be the determinant but it frames the outside limits of
party action and can never turn completely against the interests of the founding class(es) of the party in question. On the other hand, a party's effectiveness or ineffectiveness in organizing the social interests of the society more
generally "around the capitalist enterprise and the capitalist state" alone does
not constitute the sole criterion for the definition of a bourgeois party. Such a
deduction would lead to problematic political conclusions, such that the party
itself could be characterized as 'bourgeois' or 'working class' depending on the
particular conjuncture.

The criterion of 'organizational effectiveness' remains useful for classifying
political parties despite its analytical limitations. In order to be fully appreci-
ated, however, it needs to be combined with criteria of 'class participation' and
'political discourse'.[31] Therefore, in addition to 'organizational effectiveness'
(i.e., positive to capitalist interests), a party must also meet the requirements
of the appropriate (bourgeois) 'class participation' and the proper 'political
discourse'[32] (i.e., "definition of the issues as in but not of, the existing society")[33] in order to gain the 'honor' of being called 'bourgeois'.

The relationship of the so-called bourgeois parties to society conceals yet
another dimension that is not covered methodologically in the preceding analysis. This is the problem of the formation of political leadership in the bourgeois class. More specifically, the question arises of how the bourgeoisie – by
definition heterogeneous – manages through the vehicle of a political party
to establish "a governing authority ... which exercises control in effect and
practice."[34] This important question cannot be answered with generalizations

---

31   Bourque (1979: 134ff).
32   We define political discourse as the totality of tacit, explicit, and symbolic practices
    (speeches and actions) which are the outcome of antagonisms and compromises among
    different interests and strategies, and which determine and set the boundaries of every
    human activity. For a historical presentation of discourse theory see Macdonell (1986).
33   Therborn (1978: 195).
34   Pareto (1966: 268–69). Pareto's remark is well taken although the notion of class for him is
    different if not opposite to the Marxist problematic presented here.

based solely on theoretical abstractions. Of course, various approaches have attempted to make theoretical contributions on the issue, but, given the tremendous diversity of the historical and regional experiences they cover, these contributions typically fall far short of the mark. A notable exception of course is the monumental work of Ralph Miliband, as Panitch recently reminded us.[35] Indeed Miliband, in *The State in Capitalist Society*, based primarily on the British and French experiences, reaches interesting conclusions concerning the relationship between the bourgeois classes, governmental leadership in general, and party leadership in particular.[36] Therborn, at a higher level of abstraction, observes that the "reconciliatory function" of the leadership of these parties (a vital function of the dominant class), which becomes particularly obvious during election periods, makes them "less accessible to ... the ruling class." In fact, the latter consequence is considered "the price (which) has to be paid by the bourgeoisie for the advancement of its party."[37]

This observation is particularly useful in understanding the conjunctural contradictions that occur from time to time between the leadership of bourgeois parties and the different parts of the bourgeois class, or even of the power bloc. A further question must still be posed concerning the particular process through which the political leadership of the bourgeois class is brought forward and formed. The answer to such a question can only be given after an examination of the historical conditions that form the particular political party within the framework of a given political formation. We do not of course propose a simple empirical approach to the issue. However, since political and party competition, despite appearances, tends to have a more converging than diverging dynamic, the examination of the actual articulation between political leadership, political parties, and dominant class(es) cannot be a strictly abstract exercise. To put it differently, a concrete and detailed analysis of the relationship between party leadership and social base is vital in outlining party politics and dynamics.

The relationship between left-wing, socialist, and generally working-class parties with their social base, as we have already indicated, differs from the so-called bourgeois parties. Let us briefly examine the specific trends of these parties that do not permit a complete application of the above-mentioned methodological principles. As our discussion on party–class relations focuses on party-building for the radical left, it is important to turn to these differences.

---

35   Panitch (2019).
36   Miliband (1969: ch. 7).
37   Therborn (1978: 193).

All Marxists traditions have stressed the need for and the importance of the party in the development and the stabilization of the political unity of the working class. The 'party' had been entrusted with the transformation of the fragmented and individual economic interests of the working class into a united revolutionary political practice capable of materializing the socialist vision. In contrast to other social classes which historically make up the political forces aimed at the taking of or the control of power, the working class has one further aim in sight, which at least initially appears contradictory. In so far as the proletariat revolution is the beginning of the classless society, the proletariat is the first social class in history that aims to gain power not to ensure its ongoing political and social domination, but in order for it to wither away.[38] In fact, it is within this contradiction that the (historically) tragic nature of the working class is to be found. It is the proletariat's own party, its political organizer and expression, which objectively leads it on its tragic course. This last hypothetical scenario leads to the plausible theoretical claim that even in the case of the parties of socialism which were historically working-class parties, a paradoxical distance – a 'relative autonomy' – develops between them and the working class(es) they are supposed to express and organize.

3   The Party-Building Challenge

In addition to the theoretical remarks of the previous section, there are important social and political developments that reinforce the paradox of the relative autonomy of radical left parties (socialist and/or communist) from the working class itself. The technological and other structural needs of accumulation have led in recent decades to important social developments. New social strata have appeared which, regardless of how one defines them (new middle class, new working class, and so forth), have characteristics which do not correspond either to the historical characteristics of the working class or to the characteristics of the traditional middle class. Even if we agree with the view concerning "the contradictory class location"[39] of these strata, there is no doubt that, at least occasionally, broad sections of these new strata embrace visions

---

38   Magri (1970).
39   The notion was developed by E. O. Wright, in the context of the debates on class stratification in advanced capitalism during the late 1970s. For a comprehensive and more refined analysis of the notion, see Wright (1985: 19–64). For a critique that challenges the usefulness of the notion in order to "understand ... the complexities" of advanced capitalist societies, see Meiksins (1989: 173–83).

of reforming and/or transforming capitalist society. Large factions participate in left-wing parties and as a result influence them. This cannot but force 'the parties of the working class' to partially distance themselves from their own founding social agent, especially if one considers that structural changes of the accumulation regime have led to a numerical reduction of the traditional working class. At the same time, this autonomy provides the potential of responding to the demands of the emerging new social strata, which appear to constitute new subjects of social transformation.

This should not lead to the conclusion that recent social developments will necessarily result in some form of *catchall-ism* for the parties of socialism. What it means is that new strata have to be added to those who have always been considered the social agents of the socialist transformation. This is because the contradictions of capitalist development bring new social forces into the traditionally socialist, working-class parties. However, these strata have distinct origins, historical experiences and behavioral habits, as well as demands that are different from those attributed to the working class. At the same time, their political tendencies are more diverse than convergent. The political behavior and political choices of a part of these strata, for example those from the agricultural population, will differ from the behavior and the choices of other parts – from the marginalization of the traditional middle class or from those social strata who are proponents of 'post-materialist' demands. It is precisely for this reason that a wide range of strategic choices have opened up for political parties of socialism. This in its turn strengthens the tendency towards the relative autonomy of these parties from the choices of their social base.

Based on this line of analysis, we clearly cannot view parties inspired by the 'vision' of socialist transformation as fully committed agents devoted to the implementation of the working class 'project'. This is more than obvious if one considers that the rationalized anarchy of capitalism gives birth to and sharpens everyday problems and contradictions, which cannot be reduced directly to the process of capitalist accumulation. These multifold contradictions, by their nature, bring together a cluster of classes and social strata from various multilateral movements and political initiatives. Organizations concerned with the environment, urban issues, civil rights, welfare state cuts, and issues of world peace are some of the now common examples of these radical cross-class movements. The developed capitalist societies have not only brought problems and conflicts to the surface, which do not have an obvious relationship to the capital-labor contradiction, but have also given rise to a series of so-called 'post-material interests' which, until the 1960s, essentially had not entered the left's agenda. The conflicts around gender and sexual orientation, climate change and the environment, as well as the dramatic increase of refugee flows and the demands that emerge from these have recently found their place on the agenda of the traditional or otherwise radical left parties. Although this development, in one way or another, is something that has been with us at least since the middle of the past century, in the past couple of decades it has drastically changed the social base of these parties. Despite the fact that these issues definitely have a class dimension, the programmatic reference to them forced radical left parties to distance themselves even further from the working class and to build their base on a more cross-class alliance.

Regardless of whether one views these new fields of socio-political issues as 'post-materialist' or not, there is little doubt that social participation in left parties is changing. This in turn has had an impact on the strategy of these parties, as was observed long ago when this phenomenon first appeared. As Claus Offe insightfully noted at the time, "in a period of economic strain, not only the clash of material interests, but, in addition, a broad spectrum of post-material interests and causes ... will together make up the scenario of political conflict."[40] Furthermore, this plurality of radical demands, especially in the past two decades after the political experience of the anti-globalization movements, has led a number of radical left parties of our time (e.g., the Communist Party of Portugal, Bloco, Syriza, etc.) to distance themselves not just from the working class, but even from those social strata that composed their generic model.

The idea of the relative autonomy of the political party from its social base (generic or otherwise) is very useful for opening up discussion of the challenge of party-building for the radical left. The ideas and proposals that derive from this notion do not provide a ready-made organizational manifesto for the future direction of the radical left, but rather, offer a starting point for open and critical discussion about strategic planning. In this spirit, one should treat the following pages as an effort to set the stage for overcoming the widespread pessimism of the left. Since the discussion and practical application of ideas always have to do with the evaluation of specific historical circumstances, they should be confronted with audacity and sobriety. Otherwise, it will be very difficult to strike the necessary balance between voluntarism and effectiveness. A few points require initial attention and discussion.

Political parties are the products of socio-historical cleavages. Although economic cleavages and inequalities are important, they are by no means always determinant. This non-reductionist understanding of cleavages means that the conditions and the timing that activate these cleavages are equally

---

40   Offe (1980: 12).

important because these will determine the political party's *genetic model* and in turn the conditions of its dynamic.[41] This dynamic has to do primarily with the social alliance that constitutes the social base of the party organization, which is committed to socialist transformation. In other words, it is important to consider and analyze the specific circumstances of its creation and development and to understand the modalities of its establishment and its impact. The latter largely defines the organizational and the programmatic capacities of the parties.

Recent developments on the left have naturally raised the question of which 'left' are we referring to. Any effort to establish a radical left party should encompass the entire tradition of the left, radical, and labor movements. This conclusion flows from a consideration of key political developments of the past few decades. Indeed, after the collapse of so-called 'actually existing socialism' and the disarray of the Western Marxists critical of it after 1989, the dissipation of anti-globalization protest through the early 2000s, the 'Pasokification' of social democracy in the last decade, the limited impact of the anti-austerity movements that sprung up after the 2007 economic crisis, and finally the stalemate of the extra-parliamentary left initiatives and organizations, no one can think of the future of the radical left without aspirations of unifying the entire left tradition. This should be the primary goal. It should be a unity that capitalizes on all the advances of the left and at the same time overcomes the shortcomings of these traditions.

There are at least two assumptions that must be made before one begins thinking strategically about the future of the radical left. These are that: (a) parties before anything else are organizations and party organization is the determining factor for programmatic and political party capacity; and (b) given that left political agencies (parties, movements, initiatives) have at best had limited effectiveness, the future of the radical left must be based on the historically accumulated organizational, programmatic, and ideological practice.

More concretely, the political organization of the radical left should in all its initiatives and functions demonstrate that it is learning the 'lingua franca' that is constantly being produced by ever-changing new social dynamics. The radical left should drop its dogmatic hang-ups and learn and understand the language not just of the working class but also of the unemployed, the poor, the refugees and the immigrants, and especially of the youth that has no experience with the lingua and practice of the old left. In addition, the radical left

---

41   Panebianco (1988).

must leave behind its reservations concerning the new means of communication and social media, in its search for new and effective organizational practices.

Finally, the radical left of our times should not look backwards. Of course, we must retain an historical awareness of our history, but we must do away with the frictions and the demarcations among the various left traditions that hinder the unity of the entire left. This unity can only be built by capitalizing upon the positive residues of all traditions and locales of the entire left. This can only be a successful process if the party somehow adopts an 'against and beyond' logic vis-à-vis these traditions.

For the traditional communist left, this means going 'against and beyond': economism; social reductionism; the instrumentalist and essentially liberal conception and use of the state; the opportunistic understanding of formal democratic institutions and of civil rights; the anthropomorphic perception of imperialism; and finally, the monotonous rhetoric of internationalism that often hides a deep-seated nationalism. The effect of these dogmas, which Avishai Ehrlich has ingeniously called 'polyleninism',[42] has been to divide and fragment the left for many decades. Nevertheless, from the communist left tradition, we should still preserve and appreciate the existential commitment to the cause of social transformation as well as the capacity to organize and mobilize subordinate classes, especially the traditional working class.

For the so-called reformist left (the various forms of social democracy), going 'against and beyond' means overcoming parliamentarism, governmentalism, uncritical adoption of the market, an understanding of subordinate class demands as undemocratic populism, and the bureaucratization of the state. On the other hand, one should appreciate their commitment to assume the responsibilities of governing and their optimism to reform and to alleviate the hardships arising from ever-increasing inequalities, although the latter may nowadays seem like an impossible task.

For the extra-parliamentary left, 'against and beyond' should mean doing away with sectarianism and the agoraphobia of political power that eschews governmental responsibilities in a spirit of moral self-righteousness. At the same time, we can learn from this tradition how to remain steadfast in the face of setbacks and to find the courage to overcome them when left organizations find themselves on the margins of politics.

And finally, for the social movements, the task of 'against and beyond' is to transcend the repertoire that they have inherited, since the post-materialist

---

42   See Panitch (2013: 113–24).

tendency to focus on single issues often hinders efforts to build connections with wider issues and with socialist transformation. On the other hand, the social movements can enrich the agenda of the mainstream socialists as well as their means of organizing and mobilizing. This is something that cannot be overlooked in the project of building a radical left party.

Leo Panitch's writing made important contributions to the contemporary problematique for the left of class- and party-building. In tracing out political developments in the British Labour Party over the past decades, in a long struggle to remake it as a socialist party from Tony Benn to Jeremy Corbyn or to re-position it as a conventional governing party from Tony Blair to Keir Starmer, Panitch put forward a set of 'guidelines' for a crucial future project for the left. Setting off from his widely-noted article (authored with Sam Gindin) on 'transcending pessimism'[43] as a debilitating process that can only lead to political conformism, Panitch argued that the strategy of left party-building must be a balanced blend of the two Gramscian strategies of 'war of position' and 'war of movement', of gaining institutional position and of a series of class struggles that open fissures in the existing balance of forces and power. This requires a struggle over the state, inside the state itself and outside the state, as well as insisting on the extension of popular power and capacities for self-governance. In doing so, Panitch stressed the importance of democratizing the state, especially after the negative impact of neoliberal 'new public management' that has transformed the capacities of the public service into so many vehicles for privatization and marketization. This is, he contended, central to developing 'new forms of accountability' that could control the de-radicalization of left parties in their engagements with the state, by transforming parties into vehicles of political mobilization that extend beyond elections to social struggles to meet the day-to-day needs of members and communities.[44]

The party-building process for socialists is neither, and never has been, a one-off affair, nor a one-hundred-meter dash to the finish line. It is a marathon, full of defeats, retreats, and setbacks. A race that we must navigate while rebuilding our ships along the way.

---

43   Panitch and Gindin (2000).
44   Panitch and Leys (2020). For discussion of 'parties of a new kind' that are needed for socialist politics to regain a mass presence today, see: Panitch, Gindin and Maher (2020) and the essays on socialist strategy in Panitch and Albo (2016).

Decades ago, Joan Baez said it well :

> You left us marching on the road
> and said how heavy was the load.
> The years are young,
> the struggle barely had its start...
> And we are still marching
> in the streets with little victories
> and big defeats

Bobby, JOAN BAEZ, 1972

CHAPTER 13

Notes toward a Plausible Socialism

Sam Gindin

Marxists have, with some notable exceptions, tended to pay only rhetorical or cursory attention to what the world at the end of the socialist rainbow might actually look like.[1] More immediate issues awaited, and socialism's details could, it seemed, be postponed until 'later'. The present moment seems to validate that traditional perspective. Even though socialism is once again part of political speak there is no significant call, from friend or foe, to elaborate socialism's future contours.

Yet it would be hasty, and a misread of the apparent evidence, to put aside explorations of how socialism might solve its riddles. As welcome as the rhetorical popularization of 'socialism' may be, it comes with an erosion of its content; for a good many, 'socialism' references not a new world but rather a significantly more progressive *capitalism*, something that does indeed demand far less of an imaginary. More important, while it's true that even those who pose socialism in its radical historical sense seem to face few demands to explain its detailed workings, this can be expected to change as socialism becomes a more imminent possibility. Can we really expect to win large numbers of people to a protracted struggle for profoundly new ways of producing, relating, and being, *without* addressing whether what we're fighting for is really workable?

For those already committed to living their lives *as if* socialism is possible, the uncertain realization of socialism may not be a barrier.[2] But for those not yet there – the vast majority – the 'as if' won't be good enough. Socialists will have to offer more if they "expect people to take the risks necessary to change things."[3] How much more, of course 'depends', but it is crucial that this not be understood as a matter of *proving* that socialism is possible (the future can't be verified) nor of laying out an exhaustive blueprint (as with projecting capitalism before its arrival, such details can't be known). Rather, the challenge lies in making the case for socialism's *plausibility.*

---

1 This chapter is a revised and extended version of Gindin (2018).

2 This sentiment comes from Bensaid (2005).

3 Hahnel (2012: 7).

1   Problematizing Socialism

1.1   *When Hope Rings Oddly in Our Ears*

The *Communist Manifesto*'s famous rebuke of the utopians for building 'castles
in the air' went beyond the tension between dreaming and doing, though it
of course spoke to that as well. Without an historical lens, Marx and Engels
argued, the utopians simultaneously lagged and yet prematurely raced ahead
of history. Lagged in missing the significance of a newly emerging revolutionary actor, the proletariat; rashly raced ahead in absorbing themselves with
detailing a distant world that could then just be envisaged in the most general
and abstract terms. Only in the process of fighting to transform capitalism,
they insisted, could the collective capacities for building socialism emerge,
and only in the process of confronting the new dilemmas thrown up, might
institutional solutions surface.

The consequent Marxist emphasis on analyzing the political economy of
capitalism, grasping its dynamics and contradictions, and facilitating the formation of the dispossessed into a coherent class with the potential to remake
the world, is clearly basic to the socialist project. Yet it doesn't justify, especially
in the current conjuncture, the common Marxist disdain for utopian contem-
plations. In the wake of the epochal defeat of the socialist left and the consequent widespread fatalism over transformative alternatives, it's not enough to
focus on getting there. It is now at least as important to convince prospective
socialists that there really is a 'there' to get to.

And yet it can't be denied that, looking back to when Marx and Engels were
writing, there is a convincing edge to their warnings against a fixation on an
unknowable future. At that early stage of capitalism, the car – never mind the
airplane, electronic computer, and internet – had not yet been invented. Trade
unions were just appearing, universal suffrage was still an epoch away, the
modern state wasn't yet recognizable, and above all the Russian revolution and
the new questions it posed had not yet burst onto the political stage. To have
debated then what socialism might later look like certainly does, in retrospect,
confirm how presumptuous it would have then been to devote much attention
to the workings of a socialist society.

Moreover, capitalism's relative infancy at the time left that period compar-
atively more open to envisioning its rejection. The barriers of traditional cultural, religious, and family ties blocked capitalism's full sway and the absorption of the working class into the new social system remained incomplete.
By 1873, when Marx coined the derisive catchphrase "writing recipes for the
cook shops of the future," socialism was in the air in a way that it no longer is

today.[4] It was widely discussed among workers, and in London it was "fashionable for even West-end dinner-parties to affect an interest in and knowledge of it."[5] Mass socialist parties were emerging across Europe, and this was widely followed, whether anxiously or hopefully. In the US, though a mass socialist party never took hold, the second half of the nineteenth century ushered in a "long era of anti-capitalism" that included an 'urge to overthrow the new order of things."[6]

This openness to socialism persisted after World War I. The preface to a newly translated work of Karl Polanyi notes that in the early 1920s, he was "just one of many social scientists who found accounting, prices and socialism to be the most exciting topic of the day."[7] At the end of the 1920s the president of the prestigious and far from radical American Economic Association opened his keynote by declaring that "Like most teachers of economic theory, I have found it quite worthwhile to spend some time studying any particular problem at hand from the standpoint of a socialist state."[8] Later, Murray Rothbard, a lifetime disciple of the arch-conservative Ludwig von Mises, lamented that when he entered grad school after World War II "the economics establishment had all decided, left, right, and center, that ... economically, socialism could work just as well as capitalism."[9] With socialism having such a degree of economic credence, the further elaboration of its functioning was decidedly less pressing than developing the politics of getting to it.

That era is, however, over; those earlier openings to a different world, however qualified, have today strikingly narrowed.[10] The oft-noted paradox of our

4   Many of the early founders of neoclassical economics considered themselves socialists though they feared the revolutionary movements of the 1870s. On the fascinating history of the development of neoclassical economics and its relationship to theoretical models of socialism, see Bockman (2011: ch. 1).
5   Morris (1889).
6   Fraser (2016: 152, 178).
7   Bockman (2016).
8   In going on to address how a society without private property in the means of production might determine prices and allocate resources, he confidently asserted that its authorities "would have no difficulty finding out whether the standard valuation of any particular factor was too high or too low," concluding that "this much having been learned, the rest would be easy" (Taylor, 1929).
9   Rothbard (1991).
10   Erik Olin Wright begins his monumental treatise on 'real utopias' by wistfully recalling that "There was a time, not too long ago, when both critics and defenders of capitalism believed that 'another world was possible'. It was generally called 'socialism'." Wright continues on to lament that "Most people in the world today, especially in its economically developed regions, no longer believe in this possibility" (Wright, 2010: 1). Wright himself

times is that even as popular frustrations with capitalism intensify, belief in transformative alternatives continue to languish. There is clearly an appetite for change, and an 'anti-capitalist' discourse pervades protests, but the elevated language of hope in a *systemic* alternative "rings oddly in our ears."[11] The persistence – and even strengthening – of capitalism through great crises seems to further verify its permanence. The *Manifesto*'s faith in capitalism's 'grave diggers' comes up against the atomization of workers, the depth of their defeats, their multi-dimensional integration into capitalism, and their painful inability to defend past gains, never mind advance radical agendas. The overwhelming prospect of taking on a global capitalism that seems beyond the purview of any particular state, seemingly leaving us with no tangible target, reinforces a pervasive cross-generational sense that 'there is no alternative'. The liberatory confidence that the *Manifesto* radiated has been replaced with a ubiquitous skepticism and worse, 'radical change' is often a calling card of the right.

In these dispiriting times the need for structures to more effectively organize and mobilize struggles is clear enough but transcending pessimism and reviving revolutionary hope needs an animating vision as well, a utopia that is both dream and possible reality.[12] However valid Marx and Engel's historical criticism of the utopians may have been for their era, there is a compelling case – equally historically-driven – to take a different turn in *our* times. A good number of Marxists have indeed increasingly argued that far from seeing the preoccupation with alternatives as a diversion, it is the very absence of alternatives that contributes to the left's marginalization.[13] Some of their work is relatively abstract and this is understandable as part of developing new ideas. Some is more concrete and popular. But in both cases, this subculture of socialist thought remains on the margins. Developing a more systematic consideration of socialism's possible functioning, even if what we offer remains relatively general, incomplete, and even speculative, has today become a requirement for reviving a receptivity to achievable utopias and the willful action to achieve them.

---

reflects a lowering of left expectations in that he retreats from the classical starting point of the full socialization of the means of production.

11   Fraser (2016: 162).

12   See Panitch and Gindin (2000).

13   Michael Albert and Robin Hahnel have been evangelizing on the need for alternatives since the early 1990s. See Albert and Hahnel (1990). More recently, Peter Hudis observed that the "past does hang like a dead weight upon the living – especially when alternative visions of a postcapitalist society that can animate the imagination of humanity are hard to come by" (Hudis, 2013: 213). See also Radice (2013).

An institutionally elaborated alternative is now elemental to encouraging social movements to press beyond protest, to sustaining socialists who are wavering, and to recruiting the newly discontented. Such an alternative has, in Ernst Bloch's poetic capture of both despair and hope, become an indispensable spur "to make the defeated man try the world again."[14]

1.2   *Capitalism as Socialism's Dialectical Enabler*
There is a seductive tradition in certain strains of Marxism, rooted in both their theory and political strategy, that looks to assure the unconvinced that the difficulties involved in the construction of a socialist society have been vastly exaggerated. Capitalism, it's argued, is itself inadvertently laying the base for socialism and as such is socialism's 'dialectical enabler'. Yet most working people well understand from their experience of capitalism that building a new society will be far from simple. To engage those that we expect to lead in the making of socialism by *mis*leading them about the difficulties involved is not just patronizing, but ultimately self-defeating. What is needed is not comfort food but an honest presentation of the risks, costs, complexities, and quandaries building a socialist society will face, together with credible examples and promising indications of how the problems might be creatively addressed.

The historical development of capitalism removed certain barriers to a future socialist society and introduced a working class with the potential to act as the agent that might play a leading role in social transformation. But the dilemmas facing the socialist project cannot be conjured away by overstating the usefulness to socialism of much of what will be inherited from capitalism. Capitalism has, for example, eased but not ended scarcity and the tensions that go with it. Though it has vastly advanced the productive forces, especially in the West and in Asia, scarcity – the need to make choices between alternative uses of labor time and resources – is unlikely to end outside of utopian fantasies. Popular demands, even when transformed into collective/socialist demands, are remarkably elastic: they can continue to grow. Think especially of better health care, more and richer education, greater care for the aged, the expansion of art and of cultural spaces – all of which require labor time and generally also complementary material goods, and thus impose choices.

Furthermore, the calculation of scarcity can in particular not ignore the extent to which leisure – the 'realm of freedom' – is universally available. Even if we produced enough of what we wanted and liked our work, as long as some of that labor isn't completely voluntary, of the right kind, and workers

---

14   Bloch (1996: 198).

periodically prefer to not show up or leave early, then effective scarcity of either labor time or the good/service persists. And once scarcity is acknowledged as an inherent and permanent reality, the question of socially structured incentives can't be ignored. This is not just a matter of motivating adequate hours of work, but of affecting its intensity and quality, as well as influencing where that work is best applied (i.e., society's overall division of labor and the allocation of the social surplus).

Similarly, the notion that the planning undertaken by globe-spanning corporations 'proves' the institutional practicality of socialist planning does nothing of the sort. It is not only that the scale of organizing a total society in a non-market way is of a different order of magnitude and substance than addressing a single, even vast, corporation, nor that internal corporate calculations under capitalism have an advantage that centralized socialist planning would not have – i.e., they can make comparisons with markets and market-driven standards standing on their very doorstep. More fundamentally, corporate planning is based on structures that give management the flexibility and authority to allocate labor power. To plan in a way that denies commodified labor and includes autonomous worker decisions involves the invention of a *completely new productive force* – the collective capacity to democratically administer and coordinate workplaces.

Might the breath-taking explosion of computer power and big data, along with the hopes for artificial intelligence, represent such a new productive force? Daniel Saros has forcefully argued that socialists could not in earlier periods answer how a democratic socialism might work because at that point it *couldn't* in fact function effectively. It is only today, with the advances in computer power, Saros argues, that socialism has become possible. He offers an elegant, computerized model to demonstrate this. In essence, consumers with computerized access to catalogues of all possible goods and services (think a far more elaborate Amazon), and to every production unit capable of providing those goods and services, would set down their finely detailed choices at the beginning of the planning period and the production units could use this for their own plans, with the center making adjustments in prices as needed.[15]

There is clearly great potential in these new technological capacities to address specific planning problems like inventory control, the logistics of just-in-time delivery, and using algorithms to predict individual consumer preferences.[16] Far more significant are the exciting possibilities of reconfiguring computer power so it provides decentralized information and 'feedback

15   Saros (2014). See also Morozov (2019).
16   Leigh Phillips and Michal Rozworski, though writing in the tradition of expecting capitalism to unintentionally advance the capacities for socialism, make very thoughtful

structures' to facilitate the decisions of worker collectives and link them to other workplaces.[17] And a version of Saros' model may be helpful here. But inflating the ability of machines to solve the overall problems of socialist planning repeats the technicist illusion.

The problem here goes beyond contestation over whether future breakthroughs in computer power will be able to cope with the voluminous data involved in the simultaneous interactions and continual vicissitudes of a living society. As the Soviet example illustrated, the *systematic withholding* of accurate information by managers and workers is a sobering warning that the output computers give us depends entirely on the quality and completeness of the information going in (garbage in, garbage out).[18] And even where the information provided is not manipulated, the necessary information from both consumers and producers may – as Friedrich Hayek, the conservative Austrian economist famously emphasized – be 'tacit' and often only discovered in the process of carrying out actual decisions. Consumers may indeed sit down at their computer desks and set down their meticulous wish-lists, but they are also profoundly influenced by the physical process of browsing in grocery stores, restaurants, hardware stores, furniture and appliance stores, clothing stores, and so on. And the particular methods for producing the requested goods and services as well as the inputs required might be comprehensively catalogued at a point in time, but they are also not fixed. Rather, they are *constantly* modified, often dramatically, in the very process of producing them. More powerful computers are undoubtedly a very promising tool, but not a resolution to socialism's centralization-decentralization dilemmas.[19]

A common response to such cautions is to emphasize the radical changes in consciousness and culture brought about through the 'revolutionary praxis' of ending capitalism. The edifying impact of participating in capitalism's defeat is unquestionably central to the construction of the new society. The escape

---

contributions on, among other things, the development of new corporate technologies and administrative capacities. See Phillips and Rozworski (2019).

17 A fascinating early experiment in applying the democratic potentials of computerization to a socialist society emerged in Chile but ended with Pinochet's counter-revolution. This experiment wasn't just about universalizing access to computers but their facilitating active planning from below. See Medina (2011).

18 See Lebowitz (2012: ch. 1).

19 It is telling that just as the Polish political economist Oskar Lange was emphasizing the potentials of computers in the 1960s – markets, Lange had suggested, "may be considered a computing device of the pre-electronic age" – what was getting the practical ear of central planners was the call by liberal reformers for the *increased* role of markets. See Lange (1973 [1967]: 401).

from the debilitating resignation wrought by capitalism and the exhilarating discovery of previously unknown individual and collective capacities and ways of relating, working, and living are clearly indispensable to advancing the building of socialism. Yet extrapolating a functioning socialism from the heady period leading to the revolution won't do.

To start, there is the generational problem. As time goes on, fewer people will have experienced the revolution's rousing élan. There is as well the reality that the skills and orientations developed in the course of political mobilization against capitalism don't necessarily match the democratic sentiments and governance skills required for constructing a new world. And even among the revolution's original participants, the heightened consciousness of that moment can't simply be projected into the ensuing, more mundane world of meeting daily needs. As some of the most committed and able workers come to hold privileged positions as society's new administrators, it can't be assumed they will be immune to bureaucratization and self-interest.[20]

Crucially, even with a leap to the heroic assumption that universal socialist consciousness has been achieved, the question remains of how individuals or workplace collectives, limited by their own fragmented locations, figure out what the right overall thing to do *is*. The highest levels of socialist consciousness cannot, in themselves, answer this. It is one thing to assert that workers will make the decisions in their workplace, but how, for example, would workers in an appliance plant weigh whether to increase their use of aluminum, as opposed to leaving it for more valuable social purposes elsewhere? Or, in deciding how to allocate their year-end 'surplus', how much should be reinvested in their own operations versus other workplaces? Or if a group of workers wanted to exchange some income for shorter hours, how could they measure and compare the benefits to themselves versus the loss of products or

---

20   Christian Rakovsky, a participant in the Russian revolution and later a dissident internally exiled under Stalin, keenly noted this corrosion of the revolutionary spirit. "The psychology of those who are charged with the diverse tasks of direction in the administration and the economy of the state, has changed to such a point that not only objectively but subjectively, not only materially but also morally, they have ceased to be a part of this very same working class." This, he argued, was true in spite of a factory director being 'a communist, in spite of his proletarian origin, in spite of the fact that he was a factory worker a few years ago'. He concluded, with some despondency, that "I do not exaggerate when I say that the militant of 1917 would have difficulty in recognizing himself in the militant of 1928," Rakovsky (1928). While this reflects the special circumstances of the Russian experience, it would be a mistake to ignore the vulnerability of all revolutions to such regressions.

services to society? How, in other words, are the interests of particular workers and society as a whole reconciled?

For some socialists, the combination of all these hopeful elements – the definitive defeat of capitalism, the end of scarcity, the power of computer technology, higher social consciousness – culminates in the 'withering away of the state', and with that the oppressions that emanate from states. Of course, if states are reduced to only being oppressive institutions, then the democratization of the state *by definition* brings the end of the state (a 'fully democratic state' becomes an oxymoron).[21] But this tends to pass over a whole range of critical issues: the effectiveness of needed centralized institutions; balancing state power with greater participation from below; how to initiate and institutionalize experiences and learning that would not rest so heavily on the moment of revolutionary praxis, but constitute a *constant* praxis that fosters socialist education, consciousness, and culture.[22]

If the state is instead seen as a set of specialized institutions that not only mediate social differences and oversee judicial discipline, but also superintend the replacement of the hegemony of class and competitive markets with the planning of the economy, this lends itself to a different take.[23] If a state in some form is expected to persist, then a prime strategic concern is the *transformation* of the inherited capitalist state into a specifically socialist, democratic state that is central to the creative rethinking of all institutions.[24]

It is, in short, one thing to build on the productive forces inherited from capitalism and the consciousness developed in the transition towards socialism, but quite another to place inflated socialist hopes on capitalism doing the heavy lifting for us. The extent to which capitalism's productive and administrative achievements can be popularly reproduced, adapted, and applied in a democratic and socialized form is a question to be problematized, not something to be presumed.[25]

---

21   This is the grounds on which Ernest Mandel asserts that the "proletarian state … is the first state that begins to wither away at the very moment of its appearance," Mandel (1971). Lebowitz has rightly countered that "it does not matter if they prefer to call these articulated councils a non-state or the 'Unstate', as long as all agree that socialism as an organic system requires these institutions and practices in order to be real" (Lebowitz, 2016: fn 30).

22   Paul Auerbach (2016) places the question of education and constant human development at the center of his socialist alternative.

23   See Panitch (1986c: 232–35).

24   See Albo, Langille and Panitch (1993).

25   Lenin too, it seemed, was at first sanguine about the complexities of constructing a socialist economy. On the eve of the Russian Revolution, he looked ahead to a socialist stage in which "[T]he whole of society will have become a single office and a single factory' and

2   Framing Socialism

2.1   *Worker Control versus Planning*

The fundamental precondition for a socialist society is 'social ownership' of the means of production, distribution, and communication. The twin foundations for this are worker control of workplaces and democratic planning. How to actually manifest social ownership – how to relate these two foundational elements – is the central quandary of constructing a socialist society.

Aside from self-employment and small co-ops, socialist ownership resides in municipal, regional, or national state bodies. But it is the workers in each workplace who collectively run these operations. Central planners oversee these workplaces and address the concerns of society as a whole: the trade-off between leisure and output, and between present consumption and investment in the future; ensuring a degree of equality across firms, sectors, and regions; international economic and political relations; and ever-more crucial, seeing to it that the environment is incorporated into *all* social decisions. The tension between worker control and democratic planning lies in their operating in distinct but interrelated spheres that must be mediated. To the extent that workers make decisions in the narrower interests of their own workplaces, this undermines claims to those decisions being 'democratic'. Moreover, as noted earlier, these fragmented workers have limited ways of knowing what constitutes the general interest. The plan on the other hand must be prevented from running roughshod, in the name of the general interest, over workplace autonomy.

The two poles are not equal in power. Planners have special access to system-wide information and have their heavy hand on the 'vast and complex administrative system of allocation'. This carries the danger, as illustrated in the former USSR, of a crystallization among those occupying the commanding heights of the economy – central planners, ministry heads, workplace managers, municipal administrators – into what the Soviet central planner Yakov

---

declared that the 'accounting and control necessary for [workplace and state administration] have been *simplified* by capitalism to the utmost and reduced to the extraordinarily simple operations – which any literate person can perform – of supervising and recording, knowledge of the four rules of arithmetic, and issuing appropriate receipts." Whether or not this was only a reflection of the hyperbole that comes with looking to inspire revolutionary confidence, its speciousness was soon devastatingly revealed. Kautsky, later likewise asking "what forms will the socialist economy assume?", began his answer with "It will certainly not form a single factory, as Lenin once thought." As it turned out, Lenin rather quickly and soberly changed his position. See Lenin (1970: 361) and Kautsky (1925).

Kronrod called a self-reproducing 'social oligarchy'.[26] As that oligarchy pushes for compliance to its rigid plans, it also brings forth increased authoritarianism and bureaucratization (Kronrod was not alone in this argument but was especially insistent on it). Though workers have some countervailing power based on their specific knowledge and their capacity to frustrate plans from above, worker disruption of production is a negative power; fragmented workplaces cannot substitute for, and are unlikely to maintain sustained challenges to, central planners.

Alongside the risk of the planners undermining democratic decision-making stands unease about the effectiveness of comprehensive planning. As Kronrod noted in the 1970s, economic and social life are simply too diverse, too dynamic, and too unpredictable to be completely planned from the top. No amount of central planning capacity can fully anticipate the continuous changes encouraged by socialism among semi-autonomous local groups, nor – given that many of those changes occur simultaneously, each change has extensive repercussions across workplaces and communities, and involve time-consuming negotiations across multiple actors – can central plans respond without pronounced and disruptive lags. Putting too great a weight on 'the plan' can therefore be counterproductive; plans work best if they concentrate on a limited number of key variables and don't overload themselves with too much detail.

Overburdened central planning and tensions between workplace control and the general interest have led to consideration of various mechanisms to mediate and overcome these dilemmas. The extension of liberal freedoms – contested elections, transparency of information and decisions, an independent press, public forums to discuss priorities – are one aspect of limiting the arbitrary power of the center. But such freedoms, as demonstrated by capitalism itself, are too thin to adequately check the concentrated power of central bodies. Michael Albert and Robin Hahnel have suggested that the only way of overcoming this contradiction between the workplace at the base and planning from above is to introduce 'planning from below'.[27] Their creative proposal of a series of iterative plans and negotiations between workers, suppliers, and consumers can play a significant role here, perhaps more in some sectors than in others. And that role may very well grow in significance over time through institutional learning and the application of computer technology. Yet

---

26   Kronrod's 'drawer book', so named because he expected the censors to prevent it ever
      leaving his drawer, didn't reach public eyes until after the fall of the Soviet Union. This
      pathbreaking work is admirably excavated in David Mandel (2017).
27   Albert and Hahnel (1990).

it is unconvincing as a comprehensive solution to the complexities raised earlier in coordinating a dynamic society.

What of the role of markets? Marx rightly argued that praising the voluntary and efficient nature of markets apart from the underlying social relations
in which they're embedded fetishizes markets. But markets are also fetishized
when they are rejected in principle, and treated as having a life of their own,
independent of the underlying relations. Markets that simply accommodate
choices, rather than express uneven power and competitive relations, should
be welcome to the socialist project. Who, for example, can imagine a socialism without a marketplace of coffee shops and bakeries, small restaurants and
varieties of pubs, clothing stores, craft shops, and music stores?

But the very nature of labor, land, and capital markets undermines basic
socialist principles and therefore must be unequivocally rejected. The argument runs as follows. Planning – the ability to conceive what is about to be
constructed – is a universal characteristic of human labor: "What distinguishes
the worst architect from the best of bees is that the architect raises his structure in imagination before he erects it in reality."[28] A core critique of capitalism is that the commodification of labor power robs workers of that human
capacity to plan. Individual capitalists plan, capitalist states plan, and workers
as consumers also plan. Yet in selling their labor power to get the means to live,
workers as *producers* surrender their planning capacities and human potential to create. This original sin of capitalism is the foundation for the broader
social and political degradations of the working class under capitalism. With
socialism, the reduction of labor power to a commodity controlled by others
must be eradicated.

Land (nature) is the common inheritance of not only the living but also
future generations, and as the climate/environmental crisis in particular makes
frightfully clear, commodifying nature to serve private profits portends ecological catastrophe (private control of land is likewise destructive of our 'built'
environment).[29] So too must capital markets be eliminated because choices
over where investment goes structure every facet of our lives and shape future
goals and options. Economic indices can be brought into making such decisions, but the main benefit of such indices – their ability to compare alternatives based on a narrow range of monetary economic measures – is offset by
the unquantifiable complexities of assessing what is to be valued. And though
credit will exist under socialism to support consumers as well as small co-op

28   Marx (1976: 284).
29   Bellamy Foster (2018).

start-ups or workplace collectives dealing with the gaps between buying and selling, in general the same is not the case for financial markets based on the creation of financial commodities.

Yet even with such a radically constrained system of markets, the use of prices and profitability to assess how valuable an input might be if used elsewhere, and how valuable others consider the final product or service, risks moving beyond prices as mere 'parameters' and 'indicators' to also reintroduce some of the anti-social consequences of price mechanisms. Though ending private ownership of the means of production addresses the critique of the inter-class relations underlying markets (no more bosses), *intra*-class conflict between workplace collectives linked through competitive markets remains. At the extreme, the competitiveness fostered becomes a back door to labor-market-like pressures on workers to conform to competitive standards.[30] The *external* pressures to maximize the earned surplus brings pressure to replicate the 'more efficient' *internal* divisions of labor of old and the deference to expertise and toleration of workplace hierarchies, undermining the substantive meaning of worker control.[31] And with such competition and its narrow criteria also comes a downgrading of other workplace priorities: a tolerable work pace, health and safety, solidaristic co-operation, democratic participation.

If markets are reluctantly accepted as a *practical* necessity for mediating the local with the general interests of society, can the inherent tendencies of markets to competition and anti-egalitarian consequences be effectively contained even if markets are restricted to the relationships between workplaces and consumers and to commercial transactions among workplaces themselves (e.g., between final assemblers and suppliers)? Only, we argue below, if they are also checked by other institutions.

2.2   Layers of Planning

Socialism demands a state of a new kind, one with not just a commitment towards the deepest internal democratization, but also constantly developing structures and capacities to bring about greater democratization at all levels of society. Indispensable here – and to economic effectiveness as well – is the sectoral and territorial devolution of key state planning functions to civil society. This leads beyond the paradigm that identifies 'planning' with the central state to a society structured around semi-autonomous *layers of planning:* planning within workplaces and planning across particular sectors, central planning

---

30   For powerful critiques of market socialism, see Mandel (1988) and McNally (1993).

31   Standards and parameters set by the state can have a similar negative impact on worker autonomy and workplace relations.

and regional planning. The transformations of the state, of civil society, and of the relationship between them have the potential to make the polity run more democratically and the economy run more effectively.

For example, state ministries that were so powerful under Soviet-style planning (e.g., automotive and steel, mining, transportation, education, health) would, with existing as well as new capacities, be reconstituted as 'sectoral councils' composed of elected delegates from the workplaces in each sector. These councils would bring a material check on the center far beyond what fragmented workplaces might do. They would as well have the authority and capacities to shape the relationship among the workplaces they oversee, and to curb, or at least significantly moderate, the negative implications of the markets the workplaces deal in.

Workplaces develop unevenly. Some, for reasons related to both natural advantages and internal organization, will be more effective than others. Where surpluses generated are the property of the respective workplaces, this allows for higher levels of investment for some workplaces that can reproduce their advantages. The responsibility of the sectoral councils, in fundamental contrast to the logic of competitiveness, would not be to support the 'most competitive' but to proactively equalize conditions across firms. One mechanism for doing this would be the centralization of the larger part of research and development, and the sharing of such knowledge across the sector. Others would involve regular sectoral conferences to share techniques and innovations; cross-workplace exchanges through which workers can learn best practices; teams of 'fixers', including both engineers and workers, to trouble-shoot problems and address bottlenecks in workplaces that are falling behind.

A portion of the surpluses earned in each workplace collective would be used for communal or individual consumption, serving as an incentive for increasing the workplace's surplus. But a significant portion would be taxed – by both the sector and the central planning administration – to prevent reinvestment being a function of the size of the surplus. The sectoral council would then, based on the taxes it collects and investment funds allocated to the sector from the central authority, reallocate investment funds to firms according to social priorities (e.g., bringing up the effectiveness of lagging firms, expansions to hire emerging local pools of young workers, larger investments in certain parts of the country to equalize regional growth).

That partiality to equalizing conditions across the sector would likely lead to resistance from some workplaces, and this practical reality could affect the balance between material incentives and egalitarianism. Though this would partially be offset by workplaces opposed to intensive competition, the more general acceptance of the bias towards equality would depend on the extent

to which socialist ideals have permeated the workplace collectives and sectoral councils, an ideological orientation that should strengthen over time. The
emphasis on equality on the part of the sectoral councils would also be backed
up and reinforced by the central plan and the conditions that come with its
investment allocations to the sectors.

In this context, and with the absence of income from capital and the social
wage carrying great weight relative to individual consumption, the effective
variation in the conditions of workers will lie in a relatively narrow, egalitarian range.[32] This should minimize socialist angst over workers having some
individual earnings with which to choose which particular goods or services
they prefer (other than that prices include social costs such as environmental
impacts).[33] Nor is there much reason to worry about the existence of credit.
With basic necessities essentially free, housing subsidized, and adequate pensions in retirement, pressures to save or borrow would largely be limited to
different time preferences over the life cycle (e.g., saving for a trip at retirement
or wanting an appliance now). So, workplace or community credit unions, or
for that matter a national savings bank may, under nationally supervised conditions and interest rates, mediate credit flows between lenders and borrowers
with no threat to socialist ideals.

Of the greatest importance – and in powerful contrast to capitalist workplaces – within this socialist framework, workers would not live under the constant discipline to compete. It's only in such a context, with the containment
of pressures to conform to standards of surplus maximization, that worker
autonomy and control can have substantive rather than only formal meaning.
Only in such circumstances might the space be opened for workers to make
choices that can demonstrate what everyday worker control and decommod-
ification might genuinely mean.[34] Inside the reincarnated workplace, basic
rights do not vanish when the border into the workplace is crossed. The rigid
division of labor (including the rigidities built by workers in self-defense) is
transformed into a world of experimentation and cooperation. Hierarchies
can be flattened – not by dismissing the importance of those with special

---

32   On reasonable assumptions, the value of the social wage – free health care, education,
      transit, child care, and subsidized housing and culture – would be at least three times that
      of individual consumption.

33   Income isn't based on receiving 'the fruits of your own (personal) labor' since work is
      a collective, not private activity. with the after-tax surplus shared equally among them
      (modified by hours worked, the intensity or unpleasantness of the work, and – gradually –
      more and more on the basis of need).

34   For a stimulating take on possibilities re the division of labor, see Albert and Hahnel
      (1990: 15–26).

skills, but by integrating them as mentors ('red experts') committed to democratizing knowledge and making complex issues understandable. With workers given the time, information, and skills to regularly participate during worktime in planning production and resolving problems, it becomes possible to finally imagine a decisive blurring of the historic separation between intellectual and manual labor.

The culture of rights and responsibilities that might emerge in this context, especially the new self-confidence of people seeing themselves as more than 'just workers', could not be confined to the workplace. It would flow into the local community and beyond, raising democratic expectations of all institutions, especially the socialist state. This new social authority of the working class, materially reinforced by the weight of the worker-led sectoral councils in influencing and implementing the national plan, corrects a previously missing check on the central planners and establishes the footing for assertive initiatives from below. In this world without capital or labor markets, with tight institutional constraints and countermeasures against subsuming labor power to the discipline of competition, it could be credibly argued that the commodification of labor has been effectively done away with.[35]

Alongside the devolution of ministry power to the worker-controlled sectors would come territorial devolution. As with the sectoral councils, this serves to diffuse power in society and allow the otherwise overloaded center to concentrate on its own most important tasks. Regional and sub-regional devolution bring planning closer to those most affected by and most familiar with local conditions, and would greatly multiply the numbers participating in planning processes. The municipalization of certain workplaces – through regional/sub-regional ownership of hospitals, utilities, energy distribution, transportation, housing, communications, schools (and even some local manufacturing) – would facilitate bridging the production and consumption dimensions of people's lives through local community councils. Though the social may take somewhat of a backseat relative to coping with economic dilemmas in socialism's early years, as socialism matures and productivity is increasingly expressed in reductions of working hours and increased leisure, the role of the local community councils – with their emphasis on rethinking cities, expanding the provision of daily services, developing sociality, encouraging art and cultural expansiveness – could be expected to gain in comparative significance.

---

35 International relations raise a host of issues not addressed here, ranging from the complex relations with capitalist countries to relations of solidarity with the global south (passing on technology and skills and paying 'fair prices', negotiating planned relations with other socialist countries).

All of this does not necessarily mean a weakening of the state's effectiveness; it is in fact likely these steps will strengthen that effectiveness. This is so not only because planning mechanisms that are responsible for fewer variables can concentrate on the most important ones and so become both less intrusive and more effective; it is also that having stronger sectoral and regional institutions can allow for leveraging these institutions to better carry out democratically determined plans. Moreover, the very dispersal of power makes the importance of a coordinating body, even if less directly hands on, ever more important, and may lead to the central planning board having to take on new functions such as monitoring and regulating markets, introducing new mechanisms for revenue generation in the unfamiliar world of extended markets, and radically revising education curriculums so as to develop the popular capacities essential for the explosion of active democratic participation in planning.

2.3   *In Praise of Messiness*
Socialism doesn't dismiss efficient economic organization and dynamic economic development. Addressing society's needs with a minimum of pressure on resources and the environment, while trying to maximize leisure time ('free time'), is fundamental to developing the productive potentials of all, including the capacity for enjoyment of society's cultural riches. Yet in contrast to the paper elegance of equilibrating markets and the predetermined coherence of plans, the economic framework discussed here confronts a significant measure of 'messiness'.

This messiness is more than a corollary of introducing a radically new mode of production and living, with all the unknowns and the consequent reliance on experimentation and learning through doing. Nor is it a matter of the persistence of numerous differences in preferences and regional legacies. Rather, the framework raised here incorporates a good many *systemic* tensions and even contradictions. These emerge out of "the socialization of the means of production [being] a process and not a once-for-all act" that may not tend "automatically in a particular direction ... [and] may even be regressive."[36] In our case, the messiness is reinforced by the multiple layers of planning and economic mechanisms involved: the central planning board, workplaces with a substantive degree of autonomy, powerful industrial and territorial sectors, iterative negotiations, markets with sometimes blurred borders, new state forms. Fundamental too is in this regard is the weight of checks and balances in decision-making and the turbulence of truly mass participation.

---

36   Brus (1973, 89–91).

Hayek takes these complexities of socialism a step further. Capitalism too is messy, but the messiness, he claims, tends towards resolution, order, and dynamic advance. Only a system based on private property and its incentives could elicit the needed information, especially the 'tacit' information and knowledge not expressly articulated or even consciously grasped by those directly involved and only revealed/discovered through social interactions in markets. Shadow markets and indicative prices are not enough. Socialism's exclusion of private property, incentives, and market-based discovery, Hayek asserts, condemns it to static ineffectiveness and longer-term stagnation.[37]

Von Mises, after an earlier embarrassing failure to theoretically prove socialism's impossibility, shifted his emphasis in a more credible direction and added another dimension to the critique.[38] The special strength of capitalism, he argued, was to deal with the uncertainties surrounding knowledge through profit-seeking entrepreneurs and the related trading in risk. This brought about the unexpected breakthroughs that no other institutional combinations, especially those based on central planning, could accomplish.

The declarations of both Hayek and von Mises can however be readily turned on their heads. It is in fact the very institutions of private property and the competitive drive for profits that make a *hoarding* of information functional under capitalism. This is the case not only among capitalist firms but also for their workers, who often hold back some of their knowledge ('soldiering') because the benefits go primarily to the employer, and the information/knowledge passed on may lead to tougher production standards for the workers. Hayek paid little attention to workers – the information he was primarily interested in was that of employers and consumers – and this also led him to ignore the development of the future capacities of workers and their potential contribution of untapped information and knowledge.

Hilary Wainwright has notably added that the methodological individualism at the root of Hayekian thinking (the basic units generating knowledge being individual actors) leaves no room for the valuable information that

---

37   Hayek (1945).

38   Oskar Lange, a socialist trained in classical economics, countered von Mises by showing that even on the terrain of classical economics, an economy without private property in the means of production could function rationally. This theoretical coup was however limited by the shallowness of the socialism introduced at this level of abstraction. Lange's analytical model paid scant attention to institutional mechanisms, substantive worker control, and the potential contradictions in market incentives mediating localized interests and the general interests.

emerges out of formal and informal *collective* discussions.[39] This observation overlaps with economists conceding that certain 'externalities' affecting society as a whole creep into market functioning. These exceptions range from the neglect of environmental costs to gross inequalities in income and power that waste the potentials of 'the many' and undermine substantive democracy – hardly life's marginalia but rather the very *stuff* of life, and increasingly so.[40]

As for von Mises' emphasis on the capitalist entrepreneur, the history of technological breakthroughs was always about more than a series of isolated thinkers suddenly seeing lightbulbs flash above their heads. Mariana Mazzucato has shown, in her detailed study of some of the most important American innovations, that it was the state which was in fact "willing to take the risks that businesses won't" and "has proved transformative, creating entirely new markets and sectors, including the Internet, nanotechnology, biotechnology, and clean energy."[41] The distinguishing aspect of the capitalist entrepreneur was not his/her ability to innovate, but to *commercialize* innovations that were largely achieved by others. Greed, it turns out, need not be the only driver of innovation. Dynamic efficiency can also come from socially concerned scientists and engineers given the resources and opportunity to address society's needs, as well as from the mutual cooperation within worker collectives, and the interactions of workplace committees with their suppliers and clients. The socialist challenge in this regard is to encourage a far broader *social 'entrepreneurship'* focused on innovations in how we live and govern ourselves at every level of society.

There is of course nothing wrong with *striving* for a comprehensively tidy model as long as 'perfection' does not become a false standard. Capitalism, too, has its own innumerable and profound imperfections, yet this famously didn't prevent Marx and Engels from singing its praises: "The bourgeoisie ... has been the first to show what man's activity can bring about. It has accomplished wonders far surpassing Egyptian pyramids, Roman aqueducts, and Gothic cathedrals; it has conducted expeditions that put in the shade all former Exoduses of nations and crusades."[42] But – and this is crucial – underlying their celebration

---

39 Wainwright (1994). The Hayekian individualist bias extends as well to the nature of the goods considered important. Apart from services difficult to privatize like the military, Hayek's outlook was largely restricted to the individually purchased goods that went along with individual compensation, with little appreciation of the range of public goods so vital in any assessment of social life.

40 See in this regard the speech by Joseph Stiglitz in receiving the shared Nobel Prize for economics for work on how asymmetrical information undermines much of classical economic theory (Stiglitz, 2001).

41 Mazzucato (2013: 3).

42 Marx and Engels (1998 [1848]: 5).

of the specific achievements of capitalism lay the role of capitalism in opening our eyes to the far greater social potentials that *humanity* "can bring about."

Inspired by Norman Bethune's acknowledgement of the "ugly and uncomfortable mess" that characterized the Soviet Union in the mid-1930s, and Bethune's defense of that mess with an analogy to the pain and agony that women experience alongside the glorious beauty of giving birth, Panitch makes the more general argument that "the act of creation is not to be shunned because it is a messy business."[43] If we see socialism not as a static end point, but a complex and uncertain act of experimentation, discovery, learning, and invention, then disorderliness may indeed be hard-wired into socialism's DNA. But it is a *constructive* disorderliness, pitting the 'creative messiness' of socialism against the 'creative destruction' of a capitalism increasingly characterized, in terms of the social and the environmental, by the destructive. Socialism's messiness is, in this light, not a shortcoming but a sign of life, growth, openness, and richness.

2.4   *Conclusion: From There to Here*
Addressing the plausibility of a future socialist society can't help but raise the implications of that discussion for strategic orientations in the here and now. Yet though ends and means overlap, there is no direct line from the nature of socialism to the means for getting there. Each of the two involves distinct undertakings, in distinct circumstances, with distinct strategies and structures. Better then to avoid strained linkages and turn to underlying commonalities. In this regard, the special Marxist focus on working-class capacities brings together vision, critique, and strategy.

The socialist vision references a society structured to meet and develop the full and mutual capacities of all. The critique of capitalism that follows is based on how the social relationships of capitalism undermine that individual and collective potential. Capitalists, through their ownership of the means of production, buy and control the labor power of workers and organize it into a more powerful collective productive force, pocketing the difference. In having to sell their labor power to reproduce themselves, workers thereby alienate a vital aspect of their humanity – their creative capacity to *do*. The political challenge lies in how those who are so dependent on capital to make a living, who only participate in social labor through the mediation of their employers, whose capacities are so deformed and narrowed by their place within capitalism and whose immediate anxieties distance them from possible futures – how can this disempowered class morph into a social force capable of leading the fight

---

43   Panitch (1986c: 242–43).

to defeat capitalism and then move on to construct and administer an alternative world? More: how can they even *contemplate* such a role?

Three particular orientations follow for the struggle to get from here to there. First, ending capitalism does not revolve around a cumulative addition of policies, but of *capacities*. That is, in struggling for progressive policies, special weight needs be placed on how particular reforms and struggles build workers' confidence, unity, organizational skills, and vision of an alternative future.[44] Second, though worker control is a socialist goal, the road to socialism does not run through sitting on corporate boards, gaining more corporate shares, or increasing the number of prefigurative islands of worker-controlled workplaces. This is so because the *context* of worker control is so decisive. The pervasive pressure to compete or die not only reproduces permanent worker uncertainty, but also brings pressures to compromise on whatever inner democratic workings could be developed within firms, perverting the substance of 'worker control'. Additionally, the class impact of competitiveness is asymmetric. While competition does destroy particular capitalists, the survival of the fittest generally bolsters capitalists as a *class*; for workers, competition undermines their primary source of strength – solidarity – and so weakens them as a contending class.

Limiting competitiveness is consequently fundamental to building working-class power within capitalism and to creating the domestic space for moving on to build socialism. This points to replacing market discipline with a degree (at first rudimentary) of democratic economic planning. On the one hand, this necessitates limiting the undemocratic 'freedom' of both global and domestic private capital flows. On the other, it demands the expansion of productive spaces that have a degree of autonomy from markets. The opportunities here lie in: (a) expanding social services; (b) placing utilities under state and community control (while broadening the definition of 'utilities'); and (c) concretizing the New Green Deal through the planned conversion of productive facilities to address the environmental crisis (easiest with facilities scheduled for closure, but not stopping there).[45] Within these spaces liberated from the authoritarian discipline of markets, it becomes possible to experiment with substantive worker control, and balancing the concerns of workers, communities, and the larger social interest.

This gets us to the fundamental question of transforming the capitalist state. Though this may start within capitalism, it is only with capitalism's

---

44   See Gorz (1968).
45   See Maher, Gindin and Panitch (2019: 24–26).

overthrow and the radical reinvention of the nature of the state that the revolutionary rebuilding of society truly begins. To speak of the state as a *capitalist* state reflects that more than the personnel of the state – not unimportant of course – is involved. The targets of change are the extensive structures and capacities within the overall state that evolved, over a long period of time, to address the particular needs and problems of a capitalist economy. Organizing inside, against, and outside the state is essential to the state's transformation, yet this itself does not adequately specify what needs to be done. Protest movements outside the state, for example, tend to be sporadic and overwhelmed by both the inertial powers of the existing state and the sustained pressures of supporting the still-capitalist economy. This is made all the more difficult because though the state directly impacts people's lives, its main institutions are concentrated in nation's capital city, and that physical distance from daily life leaves the notion of 'transforming the state' even more abstract.

It is such limits that led Leo Panitch to argue that demands for a different kind of state must be approached more organically: "We should not initially approach this in terms of getting it on the state's policy agenda ... the *first step in a new strategy* is to get labour movements to think again in terms that are not so cramped and defensive, to think ambitiously again and then, once mobilized in such frame of mind, to make radical demands on the state of this kind."[46]

In considering unemployment as an example, Panitch suggested that rather than demanding answers from the state when we don't have the power and ability to implement such demands, the focus might be on the apparently more modest establishment of elected 'Job Development Boards' in each community. The mandate of these new institutions would be to guarantee all who want a job either employment or training towards a prospective job (much like the education system guarantees everyone at least a basic education). This common-sense proposal has the advantage, against prematurely and naively trying to 'transform the state', of engaging people in concrete struggles in their communities – while gradually adding complementary structures to undertake popular education around these projects and provide training, engineering, and research capacities. This decentralizes the space of the state and broadens its role, and it also quickly raises further demands – like the need for funds to be redirected in this direction, the protection of local markets from imports, the role of planned government procurement – that can escalate the development of new and different kinds of state interventions and state capacities.

---

46   Panitch (2000: 381).

What envisaging a plausible socialism brings to the project of challenging capitalism is the inspiration of, and confidence in, a larger credible vision. Laying out the specifics of the alternative society, even in fairly general terms, may suggest particular steps on the road to defeating capitalism that will also make it easier to bring about socialism, e.g., a degree of cohesion and trust within the class along with new cultural sensibilities; new analytic, administrative, and organizational capacities; the expansion of economic spaces free from global discipline. Yet these are only suggestive; revolutionary strategies can't be directly derived from a model of socialism. As for the emphasis in this essay on the complexities and contradictions involved in manifesting a socialist society (socialism's 'messiness'), this same sober sensibility is well worth, we'd argue, bringing into strategic considerations for the defeat of capitalism.

CHAPTER 14

Between the State and the Streets

A Study in Socialist Sobriety

Bryan D. Palmer

Canada does not lack for significant homegrown socialist intellectuals.[1] But few have had the impact, here and abroad, of Leo Panitch. His reach across the academic disciplines of history, sociology, political science, and political economy has registered in writing, teaching, editing, and campaigning over the course of five decades. No Canadian socialist of his generation rivaled Panitch in terms of his contribution, influence, and reputation among radicals.

At the level of scholarly production alone, the contribution has been immense: at least 10 authored or co-authored books; 33 edited or co-edited collections; 100s of journal articles and chapters; some 90 PhD dissertations, MA theses, and Masters Research Essays supervised; guest lectures throughout Canada, the United States, and around the world. Panitch played pivotal roles in two important journals, co-founding *Studies in Political Economy* in the 1970s and co-editing the *Socialist Register* from the mid-1980s until 2020. A public intellectual featured in most magazines of the left, from *Canadian Dimension, Monthly Review,* and *New Left Review* to *Red Pepper* and *Actuel Marx,* Panitch was also a regular contributor to mainstream publications like the *Globe and Mail* and *The Guardian.*

The entirety of this research and writing was animated by a direct concern with building the possibilities of socialism in our time. This project, born in the Jewish socialist milieu of Leo's upbringing in Winnipeg, took a precocious Panitch through classes with *Canadian Dimension* editor Cy Gonick to the London School of Economics, where he worked with the Marxist critic of parliamentary socialism, Ralph Miliband.[2] He returned to Canada, hired as a professor in the Politics Departments of Carleton University and then York University.

Never far from the political struggles of his time, Leo certainly harbored radical nationalist sympathies in the late 1960s and early 1970s. He undoubtedly had loose connections with the Waffle eruption in the New Democratic Party

---

1 This chapter draws heavily on Palmer (2017).
2 Ralph Miliband's major writings include *Parliamentary Socialism: A Study in the Politics of Labour* and *The State in Capitalist Society.*

(NDP). But accidents of intellectual choices taken, with respect to the location of his dissertation work, intervened. It was as a graduate student in England that Panitch first cut his teeth politically in the 1970s. Tony Benn's attempt to radicalize the Labour Party proved a formative moment that solidified a life-long interest in the excruciatingly drawn-out crisis of social democracy.[3]

Back in Canada in the 1975–1984 years, Panitch figured centrally in the Ottawa Committee for Labour Action (OCLA), a pioneering effort to revive popular socialist and labor mobilization during a time of much reconsideration on the left. The Waffle had largely disintegrated. New communist movements that emerged out of the 1960s and flourished in the early-to-mid 1970s were in the throes of dissolution. And Pierre Elliott Trudeau's youthful politics, which paid lip service to participatory democracy and basked in the limelight of Just Society possibilities and economic nationalism, succumbed to austerity's alignments: wage control initiatives; attacks on public sector unions, most evident in the jailing of J.C. Parrot, leader of the militant Canadian Union of Postal Workers; and the 1982 '6 and 5' restraint program.[4]

This set the stage for what is one of the most important accounts of the end of the era of free collective bargaining in Canada. Panitch and his OCLA co-worker, Donald Swartz, chronicled the first chapter in what would be a long austerity book of neoliberal restraint. The state declared virtually all public sector employment as a kind of "permanent exceptionalism" to the entitlements of the industrial pluralist regime that institutionalized trade union rights of association and negotiated contracts in the aftermath of World War II. The Panitch-Swartz volume provided an impressive analysis of how class war, in the changed context of the mid-1970s and beyond, was now being waged from above. *From Consent to Coercion: The Assault on Trade Union Freedoms* (2003), originating as an essay in the journal *Labour/Le Travail,* first appeared in 1985 and hinted at the relations developing among radical political economists and social historians of the working class.[5]

With his move to Toronto's York University, Panitch continued to meld socialist scholarship and politics. At moments of seeming breakthrough – the election of the NDP government in Ontario in 1990; the thaw attendant on the collapse of Stalinized socialism in the USSR in the 1990s; or the rise of the Party of the Radical Left in Greece with the fracturing of the European Union in more recent times, Panitch was ever present, lending his perspective.

---

3   See, for instance, Panitch (1986a; 1986b); and Panitch and Leys (1997).
4   Some of this history has recently been addressed in Graham with McKay (2019).
5   See Panitch and Swartz (1984; 2003).

Such high points obscure the day-to-day work he has done, often amid difficult challenges and the ubiquitous fractiousness of the left. Panitch was dogged in his advocacy and dissemination of the socialist idea. He did this through various cultural activities and causes, not the least of which has been the promotion, time and time again, of alternatives to the mainstream media, and support for beleaguered dissidents.

Over the course of the 1970s until his death in 2020, Leo emerged as Canada's most widely recognized and internationally acclaimed public intellectual of the revolutionary left. There is no other Canadian socialist as likely to be read, heralded, even on occasion repudiated, in Athens and Sao Paulo, in Alexandria and Sydney, in Johannesburg and Oslo, as Leo Panitch. Few can match his range, often breathtaking in its sweep, encompassing a wide appreciation of classic writings by Marx, Luxemburg, and Lenin. A profound interdisciplinary grasp of contemporary scholarship is complemented by a resolute and sober (I will return to this word) insistence on the primacy of the politics of class struggle, in all of their richness, that nonetheless refuses to back away from difficulties and limitations.

No brief comment can fully address the complexity and breadth of Panitch's contribution. It evolved over time. Originating in a concern with the state and how class formation and class struggle established particular ends, Panitch's *oeuvre* extended to the global consolidation of the American Empire and its utilization of mechanisms of financialization in the current conjuncture.[6] Never absent from any of this work was the dynamism of class struggle, an undercurrent of the inevitable conflictual nature of class relations that structures developments of all kinds.

The book entitled *The Making of Global Capitalism: The Political Economy of American Empire* (2012) – the result of Panitch's collaboration with long-time friend and former Research Director of the Canadian Automobile Workers, Sam Gindin – is perhaps the pinnacle of this research agenda. Awarded a number of prizes in the United Kingdom and Canada, the book is a rich study underscoring how globalization has not dismantled nation-states and powerful centers of capital accumulation, but rather concentrated the iniquitous distribution of wealth and shored up the institutions of capitalist hegemony. Much could be said about this impressive text, but what I want to stress here is how it relates to Panitch's commitment to socialism, and the ways in which he and Gindin situated their analytic orientation to the specificities of political intervention.

---

6 Among many early studies in the first phase of Panitch's analytic project, consider Panitch (1976; 1977; 1986a). The capstone of his later work on American Empire is of course Panitch and Gindin (2012).

To illuminate all of this, I commence with Gramsci, someone whom Panitch draws on lightly in his writing. Gramsci nonetheless provides a useful scaffold on which to order consideration, not only of Panitch's voluminous writings, but his activities as a socialist intellectual and architect of socialist practice. Gramsci, as Perry Anderson once commented, and as Peter Thomas has more recently elaborated, developed three seemingly separate understandings of the state in relation to society. He posited at one time or another an understanding of the necessity to differentiate civil society from and surrounding the state; the state separated from and surrounding civil society; and political society and civil society fused in a general notion of the state.[7] These positionings, of course, constituted three contradictory sensibilities about the relation of state and civil society, of governance and class formation/struggle. Out of this mélange, Gramsci suggested that the making of socialism in the West would require a war of position, the struggle of the working class to achieve hegemony within the state, effecting its transformation.

Leaving aside many complexities, including the different conjuncture of class forces in the East of Revolutionary Russia in 1917 and in the West of a more-sturdy civil society which enveloped the state in democratic foliage, Gramsci posed the difficulty, in many ways, that Panitch's engagements with state and class formations ultimately struggled to address. How can the bourgeoisie and the proletariat alternate, in Anderson's words, "simultaneously as the hypothetical subjects of the same passage," as the class forces that determine the state and its objectives, as, in effect, "historically equivalent."[8] Hegemony in this sense is reduced to a matter of transforming the state by merely *reversing* the class forces orchestrating the apparatus of governance. It is as if a kind of class substitutionism will automatically resolve the mysteries of state and power in class society. Replacing the bourgeoisie by the proletariat within the state will necessarily result in the transformation of the state, leading the way toward the remaking of civil society, ushering in socialism.

Simplistic commentary often attributes the failure of the Soviet Revolution of 1917 to just this kind of substitutionism. Lenin is held up as the culprit responsible, in Luxemburg's 1918 words, for the revolutionary proletarian state being overtaken by a "clique."[9] In Poulantzas's later claim, Leninism was responsible for the mistaken assumption that the state could merely be replaced by an "apparatus of Workers Soviets, or councils."[10]

---

7   See, for instance, Anderson (1976); and Thomas (2009: 50–51).
8   Anderson (1976: 20).
9   Luxemburg (1940 [1918]: ch. 6).
10 Poulantzas (1978c: 257–61).

Panitch struggled, successfully but with difficulty, to avoid these kinds of all-too-simplistic reductions. He was cognizant of the complexities involved in the transformation of the state, not just at the moment of revolutionary reconstruction, but also in the midst of shifts within the mercurial and often volatile politics of long bourgeois dominance, framed as this recurring hegemony is by the regularity of crises.[11] It was Panitch's sober judgment that, in the absence of a truly revolutionary opposition, the crises of capital in the post-1975 period did not lead to crises for capitalism. Instead, states orchestrated by their fixation on power engaged in wars of maneuver within a global order, leaving the working class often reeling in the wake of subsequent tumult. Such insight does lead to sober reflection regarding all of those who would cry revolution when, in Panitch's view, no such revolution is actually on the agenda of possibility.

In the absence of such a transformative reality, the centrality of the state looms large. If it cannot, as a pivotal force sustaining class rule, be brought down, what, indeed, is to be done? Can it be entered and realigned in ways congruent with socialist possibility in the future? Can the forces of the left engaging in this politics within the state actually survive the inevitable pressures of accommodation, which are many, and range from the obviously blunt to the more nuanced and subtle sophistications of enticement, culminating in the kinds of concessions that can perhaps collapse into capitulation? Alternatively, how can the politics of the left challenge and transform the state if they remain sufficiently distanced from it to avoid being drawn into its sphere of pragmatic influence?

Such interrogations necessarily confront the quagmire posed by Gramsci's explications of the relationship of state and civil society. They also run headlong into debates on the left about what kind of organization might be envisioned that will best secure the optimum outcome from wrestling with the bourgeois state, struggling to turn it into a vehicle of utility in the creation of a new kind of civil society. These questions are at the heart of how revolutionaries approach the issue of the state and societal transformation in times that are decidedly non-revolutionary. Countering Panitch are those articulating the need to speak in a different idiom, although it is of course the case that the range of perspectives articulated has been great, running the gamut from unthinking ultimatism to more reasoned, transitional arguments.

I am sure Leo sometimes saw me as an oppositional, even ultimatist, voice. On some levels I am content to plead guilty as charged. We argued, over

---

11   See, for instance, Panitch and Gindin (2016); and Albo, Gindin and Panitch (2010).

decades, about socialism, class struggle, and the alternative politics of anti-capitalism. As socialists of slightly different temperament and orientation, our arguments, and I will not rehearse them here, have been serious and undeniable, and they all relate to the issues and relations of protest and politics that I will return to at the close of this tribute.[12] I raise this point to accent that socialism will not be made without the airing of different perspectives, which will often be posed as serious political divergence, even giving rise to battles over fundamental questions of tactics and strategy. All of this will, inevitably, produce awkward tensions on the left, but in the ensuing clarification of thought and practice, advances will be made.

Our times are non-revolutionary. This demands a certain humility among all of us who are on the revolutionary left, but who hold to different sensibilities. Leo's sober reflections will no doubt be needed in any reconfigured socialist movement. That said, it is also the case that no revolutionary movement has ever been made by the entirely sober minded.

Leo's sobriety, I would suggest, was in some senses overdetermined by his focus on the state. This led him from a concern with state structures in Canada as constitutive of political-economic development in particular directions (a dominant concern of the early 1970s) to the possibility of a Bennite transformation of social democracy in the United Kingdom. But the defeat of this radicalizing initiative within the Labour Party culminated in the sad demise of parliamentary socialism. The Blairite Third Way did much to eviscerate the tarnished hope that social democracy could be revived within the Labour Party. This process of defeat was paralleled by the rise of the neoliberal state in Canada, and its declaration of war on the working class. Global capitalism's late-twentieth century ascendance only deepened and extended this increasingly unbalanced hegemony, securing capital a firm grasp on the social relations of both production and governance that had eluded it for decades. From the Canadian concerns of Panitch's and Swartz's *Assault on Trade Union Freedoms* to Panitch's and Gindin's understandable and empirically demonstrated refusal to see American Empire as having been displaced, this trajectory of research trends resolutely in the tracks of capitalist power's materialist manifestations.

---

12   Among areas where Leo and I disagreed: trade union and left-wing opposition to an early neoliberal initiative under the Social Credit government of British Columbia in 1983 and how and what it was possible for the mobilization of resistance, Solidarity, to achieve; the approach to the election of social democrats to power (Bob Rae's 1990 electoral victory in Ontario); and, less articulated, the difficult dilemma posed for European dissidents, such as Greece's Syriza, amid the crisis of the European Union.

Exploring this march of capitalist fortification, Panitch was moved to sobriety. Chronicling and analyzing the rise of the capitalist state constitutes, among other things, a history of power's victories. And the accent on the state lends this power and its relentless advances and accumulations a certain inevitability, an inviolate articulation of a reality not to be denied. Panitch was, of course, centrally concerned with class struggle, but his writings were structured within a state-bounded appreciation of determination, a perspective of much value but one that colors political interpretation in ways that inevitably leave possibility shrouded in the distorting shadows of power. Workers and their struggles, viewed through the prism of the state and its capacity to structure labor, necessarily tend to be refracted in specific, sobering ways. The state's containments appear in bold relief, while the challenges, so often deflected, deformed, and defeated by state power, tend to wither under the heated glare of concentrated authority. In Marx's formulation, "Men make their own history, but they do not make it just as they please;" Panitch's orientation invariably leaned to the latter half of this brief sentence's packed analytics, a realist's abstemious tilt.[13]

Precisely because of this alignment, and where it led Panitch, he and Gindin placed great accent on the need for the left to focus on the state, perhaps even to enter into it, as part of the process of building socialist possibility. They called this move, in a recent article in the *Socialist Register*, a shift from "protest to politics," which I read as something of a Gramscian tilt toward the merger of state and civil society. The necessity for socialists, they argued, was to recognize the impossibility of insurrectionism and the debilitations of social democratization. Looking to Syriza's experience in Greece, the two Sanders electoral campaigns for the Presidency in the United States, and the kneecapping of Corbynism in the British Labour Party, Panitch and Gindin present analysis of the need for new kinds of working-class political organization – party formations – and new thinking on what entering the state means.[14]

I am not a sober person, but I can appreciate the stand Panitch and Gindin take and which Panitch had long presented, in various ways. But I will leave this recognition with a thought: if a touchstone of socialism is indeed the recognition that it is fundamentally important in the building of any socially transformative possibility to address the state, is sobriety alone the guide to how this is done? Can we so easily talk of shifting from protest to politics, with the suggestion that this path is one structured through engagement with the state – an engagement that will always raise to the forefront ambiguities about

---

13   Marx (1968: 97).
14   Panitch and Gindin (2018a).

an interventionist/accommodation coupling? I know Panitch did not, in any simplistic way, embrace the view that socialists can simply, through a takeover of parties like Labour in the United Kingdom, the New Democrats in Canada, or, certainly, the Democrats in the United States, bring into being the new Jerusalem. But in the formulation of transcending protest through an elevation of the socialists' game plan to the higher plane of politics, there is a danger of slipping into this mindset. It is with my unsober inclinations that I react to this kind of slippage, albeit in recognition of the importance of Panitch's eminently sensible socialist sobriety.

I am still drawn, as an advocate of class struggle and the socialist promise, to Marx's recognition, spelled out in *The German Ideology*, that "the revolution is necessary, therefore, not only because the ruling class cannot be overthrown in any other way, but also because the class overthrowing it can only in a revolution succeed in ridding itself of all the muck of ages and become fitted to found society anew."[15] This cleansing, I would suggest, is not likely to come through an orientation that draws lines of hard separation between politics *and* protest. I find the phrasing of Panitch and Gindin unfortunate, if only because it will be interpreted quite undialectically: politics lies beyond and transcends protest. My own view is that politics, in the age of late capitalism, *is* protest, or it will not amount to much. Even acknowledging the points Panitch and Gindin are making, it is perhaps crucial to discuss the tactics and strategies of left oppositions in our time as embracing linked activities that are undertaken simultaneously and connect spheres of political reconstruction. It is not so much that we should be positing a hierarchy of politics above protest, or a shift from the performance of resistance to the practical engagement with power, but that what the revolutionary left needs is an orientation that builds its presence both outside of politics as currently constituted *at the same time* as it exercises pressure that is felt inside the structures of governance where change of an immediate and needed kind can take place. In many ways this is similar to arguments that have stalked left-wing thought for more than a century and a half, in which the relationship of reform and revolution have been endlessly debated.

A dialectical approach suggests that these are not oppositional ends, but related ones, in which the crucial issue is perhaps how a strategic appreciation of transitions from immediate and realizable policy change can be implemented in ways that further galvanize understandings of the need for socio-economic transformation. Staking the fortunes of the left on a

---

15   Marx and Engels (1976: 53).

singular placement of energies and activities premised on an oppositional understanding of what can be done in the metaphorical streets versus the seemingly more decisive corridors of power is surely a dead end, as the sorry denouement of the Sanders and Corbyn experiments inside the Democratic and Labour Parties reveal. As robust as were these mobilizations for change, they existed within acute limitations, as Panitch and Gindin long acknowledged, even stressed. Their curtailment and ultimately defeat *within* their respective parties of longstanding accommodation to capitalist imperatives could only have been staved off or extended into other organizational advances for the left with the development of more, not less, protest. But this was not the path either Sanders or Corbyn chose to follow. Without an understanding of just how hostile to the left and how fundamentally compromised in their relation to capitalism – to adopt about as benign a designation as it is possible to imagine – these conventional party formations are should be crystal clear after the events of 2019–2020. And in a sense, although this was never Panitch's and Gindin's meaning, this is what the phrasing of "from protest to politics" will obscure to many people. If it is important to contend for authority and policy direction in ways that register *within* the state, it is crucially important to recognize that being *there,* in the ways that Sanders and Corbyn either aspired to or were in part successful in achieving, will never be enough.

Left politics, as arm-twisting with state power, will inevitably succumb to a wide variety of forces undermining its revolutionary substance if the rallying cry is only *inside* the established institutions of governance. It must have, as a parallel politics of resistance, *outside* agencies of protest, and it may well be that these need to be built as entirely new structures of alternative, the beginnings of which might well seem somewhat distanced from any possible immediately concrete transformative outcomes. What Mike Davis insisted was fundamental to a reconstitution of the United States revolutionary left in the 1980s still resonates with the realities of our current conjuncture, however much the velocity of change seems to have been accelerating of late. "The long-term future of the US left," Davis wrote in 1986, "will depend on its ability to become both more representative and self-organized among its own 'natural' constituencies, and more integrally a wing of a new internationalism." Judged against this standard, the Sanders campaigns of 2016 and 2020 surely measure up ambiguously at best. And Davis continues, in what is a perhaps less than sober vein: "It is necessary to begin to imagine more audacious projects of coordinated action and political cooperation among the popular lefts in all countries of the Americas."[16] This, in the Age of Trump, Make America Great Again, and Covid-19, not to mention Bidenesque compromise and conciliation, also seems salient. Separating protest and politics, let alone imposing on their differentiation a hierarchical ordering, may well be unnecessary, if not counterproductive. New parties of socialist commitment will likely begin as *protest* before they have any realistic hope of moving into spheres where they will have any chance of affecting *politics* as governance.

This is not unrelated to what we can appreciate about the tension between the sober and the *not so* sober. Marx recognized the necessity, at times, of throwing sobriety's cautions to the winds of revolutionary possibility. *The Eighteenth Brumaire of Louis Bonaparte* (1852), as a case in point, can hardly be considered a one-sidedly sober text, with Marx declaring:

> Proletarian revolutions, like those of the nineteenth century, criticize themselves constantly, interrupt themselves continually in their own course, come back to the apparently accomplished in order to begin it afresh, deride with unmerciful thoroughness the inadequacies, weaknesses, and paltriness of their first attempts, seem to throw down their adversary in order that he may draw new strength from the earth and rise again, more gigantic, before them, recoil ever and anon from the indefinite prodigiousness of their own aims, until a situation has been created which makes all turning back impossible, and the conditions cry out: *Hic Rhodus, hic salta* [*Here is Rhodes, leap here.*]

We live in times reminiscent of the Eighteenth Brumaire, with the "bourgeoisie [having] no choice but to elect" a "patriarchal benefactor of all classes" who aims to turn all the property and labor of the nation into "a personal obligation to himself."

The state, in this rule of "the king of buffoons," is apt to become "parts of the institution of purchase." The personnel of governance and authority are less likely to take on the appearance of the flight of an "eagle ... more like a *raven*." Marx's description of the rush to office of Bonaparte's regime brings to mind the making of the Trump or Boris Johnson administrations: "A bunch of blokes push their way forward to the court, into the ministries, to the head of the administration and the army, a crowd of the best of whom it must be said that no one knows whence he comes, a noisy, disreputable, rapacious bohème that crawls into gallooned coats with grotesque dignity." Such situations produce deformation, and throw:

---

16   Davis (1986: 314).

the entire bourgeois economy into confusion, violates everything that seems inviolable ... makes some tolerant of revolution, others desirous of revolution, and produces actual anarchy in the name of order, while at the same time stripping its halo from the entire state machine, profanes it and makes it at once loathsome and ridiculous.

Times of crisis such as our own, then, often call out for a dialectical response, one crucial component of which will undoubtedly be sober reflection. But the audacity to leap, even occasionally, into political spaces where outcomes cannot be known with absolute certainty, might also be necessary. The trick – and it is neither an insurmountable one nor an easy strategic balance to strike – is to prepare the decision to be daring with a judgment of what is possible that does not always foreclose the necessity and validity of bold acts.[17]

Faced with the dire consequences of a continuity in the deformed politics of bourgeois denouement that constitute the disorder of our times, Panitch understandably turned to the necessity of socialists taking politics from the streets of protest to a politics of transformative possibility. This, of course, is what all socialists want. As with all strategic moves, however, it is in the transition to transformation that the questions perplexing us will be worked out and answers provided in practical outcomes. I do not believe that Leo believed in some hard and fast distinction between protest and politics, whatever his analytic push in his later writings. Too much of Panitch's political organizing involved developing cultural alternatives, along with creating opportunities for resistance within civil society, for any such simplistic scapegoating. He always understood his contribution, moreover, to be taking place alongside the reciprocal activities and analytic interventions of others, many of whom he saw addressing the struggles of workers and the possibilities of socialist practice that take place beyond the state, in arenas of extra-parliamentary endeavor. In Panitch's case, his research and writing concentrated on what the state does, how it structures possibilities, and why it must be transformed. It is perhaps inevitable that particular dimensions of the socialist project appear in bolder relief, and that those are bounded by determinations that condition an understandable moderation of the politics of possibility.

Panitch's sober sensibilities have a great deal to tell us about both the necessity of socialist revolution and how it will be made. The state, about which he informed us so richly in many brilliant studies, is central to this process, made more problematic in the aftermath of Marx's failed nineteenth-century

---

17   The quotes from Marx in the above paragraphs are from Marx (1968: 100, 179–180).

revolutions and those successful, and then compromised, revolutions of the twentieth century. Things will invariably look different in the socialist advances of our twenty-first century, and our research and writing, as well as our political interventions, must appreciate the complexities attendant on the significance of the state.

Just as Marx and Engels were forced to reconsider their politics of revolution in the aftermath of the Paris Commune, so must we, more than a century later, confront how states script socialist possibility. As global capital marches forward in its proverbial seven league boots, it does so in the aftermath of the implosion of the Soviet Union, the negotiations of 'actually existing socialist' states with a resurgence of acquisitive individualism within their political economies, the ongoing crises of capitalism and the impending break-up of the European Union, the rise of populist adventurism on a world stage, and the ways in which nature is wreaking its revenge on decades of capitalist despoliation and destruction, the demise of biodiversity manifesting itself in the 2020 Covid-19 pandemic.

Panitch's sobriety will be needed in the necessary reassessments contingent on these developments. If complemented by audacity, this body of considered reflection will contribute mightily to socialists making history, albeit not quite as any one of us might choose. This, ultimately, will prove Leo's legacy, a lasting engagement with the kind of revolutionary transformation all socialists seek.

Postscript

Greg Albo, Stephen Maher and Alan Zuege

The history of political theory has seen more than a few efforts to elaborate a science of politics which could serve as a manual of power for ruling classes to maintain their rule. There have been far fewer contributions to the making of a 'critical political science' for a radical transformation intent on overturning class power. Karl Marx, of course, marked a pivotal turning point. His 'ruthless criticism' exposed the class limits of liberal freedoms in the emerging democratic states set against the unfreedoms of workers in capitalist forms of exploitation and conditions of factory despotism. But it was Antonio Gramsci who first and foremost took up the challenge of a critical – indeed revolutionary – political science appropriate to the forms of government and class power in modern capitalism. In his *Prison Notebooks*, Gramsci observed that with the "decline in the concept of political science ... 'Politics' became synonymous with parliamentary politics or the politics of personal cliques." But an "impoverishment of the concept of the State ... ensued from such views. If political science means science of the State, and the State is the entire complex of the practical and theoretical activities with which the ruling class not only justifies and maintains its dominance but manages to win the active consent of those over whom it rules, then it is obvious that all the essential questions of sociology are nothing other than the questions of political science."[1]

Gramsci's formulation for the study of politics was, to say the least, enormously ambitious – an analytical dissection of the mechanisms of state power capable of generating critical knowledge integral to the making of emancipatory political projects. It was in the midst of the political turmoil that spanned the 1960s and 1970s that Nicos Poulantzas and Ralph Miliband followed Gramsci's lead, and took up an explicit political science of capitalist states in their respective, now classic, texts *Political Power and Social Classes* (1968) and *The State in Capitalist Society* (1969). As Miliband put it in his intervention, with the exception of Gramsci, "Marxists have made little notable attempt to confront the question of the state in the light of the concrete socio-economic and political and cultural reality of actual capitalist societies. Where the attempt has been made, it has suffered from an over-simple explanation of the inter-relationship between civil society and the state." A 'return to the state'

---

1 Gramsci (1971: 243–44).

could not be limited to a merely sociological refutation of the vapid democratic claims of pluralist political science. As it was for Gramsci, it had to also
be an affirmation of a necessary transformation of the existing political order
and state system. Again Miliband: "... despite all the immense obstacles on the
way, the working class and its allies in other classes will acquire that faculty [of
ruling the nation]. When they do, the socialist society they will create will not
require the establishment of an all-powerful state on the ruins of the old. On
the contrary, their 'faculty of ruling the nation' will, for the first time in history,
enable them to bring into being an authentically democratic social order, a
truly free society of self-governing men and women."[2]

    This was a position as common to Poulantzas as to Miliband, and an insis-
tent theme across the New Left. Both a more critical political science and a
more potent collective political practice demanded shifting the strategic
focus beyond simple recipes for 'taking state power' in itself. Instead, a radical democratization had to be front and center, conceived as a process of
capacity-building, social mobilization, and ultimately political rupture of the
representative and administrative apparatuses of the state, allowing the direct
intervention and participation of 'the people' into the state while facilitating
the materialization of new forms of direct democracy.

    It was in the theoretical and political cauldron of these two decades that
Leo Panitch was formed as a socialist intellectual and practicing critical political scientist. After studying political science and economics at the University
of Manitoba, he took his doctorate at the London School of Economics (1974)
under the guidance of Miliband himself. Leo's thesis, an investigation of postwar trade union politics in relation to the British state, was directly engaged
with the turmoil of the time and would later come out as a book under the
title, *Social Democracy and Industrial Militancy: The Labour Party, the Trade
Unions and Incomes Policy, 1945–1974* (1976).[3] Indeed, the time, place, and scope
of research provided the perfect opportunity to practice a critical political science of the state in the vein of Gramsci, Poulantzas, and Miliband. For at the
core of state management of the economic crisis was incomes policies to control inflation and contain working-class struggles that were shifting income
shares in their favor. But despite national variation in corporatist institutions
across capitalist states, they had in common the drive to control wage-setting
and limit union organizing in workplaces. In this, the structural contradictions
common to all capitalist states, Leo argued, were also revealed: on the one

---

2 Miliband (1969: 8, 247).
3 Panitch (1976).

hand, the class bias materialized in the very institutions of the liberal state; and, on the other, the limits of social democracy's strategy of 'socialism in one class' that accepted the political parameters of existing state practices to sustain accumulation. This was a highly original formulation, operationalized here to penetrate the concrete logic of incomes policies in the midst of a major capitalist crisis, capturing what a critical science of politics could offer to socialist theory and practice. And in certain crucial ways this formative project laid the theoretical and political groundwork for Leo's future research: attention to the specific ways class and social inequalities are inscribed directly into the apparatuses of the state and its modes of operation; the impasse of social democracy; the necessity of remaking parties and unions as vehicles of struggle and education; the inescapable need to bring class struggle inside and yet against the existing state; and the call for an historically and institutionally sensitive Marxist political science.

It was this critical political science of the state, combining an academic field of study and the political practice of a public intellectual committed to socialist politics, that Leo brought back to Canada in 1972 when he took up a post in the Department of Political Science at Carleton University in Ottawa. Upon his return he immediately gathered a like-minded group of politically committed scholars to collaborate on a project that became *The Canadian State: Political Economy and Political Power* (1977), a central reference in any account of critical political science and Marxism in Canada. This was followed up by a signal text (written with Donald Swartz), *From Consent to Coercion: The Assault on Trade Union Freedoms* (1986), that detailed the coercive turn by the Canadian state using back-to-work legislation to undermine workers' associational and collective bargaining rights and thereby to sustain the political conditions for capital accumulation.

These studies constituted a first phase of Leo's research on trade unions and the state in the midst of capitalist crisis. A second, if overlapping, phase covers his exploration of the limits and possibilities of democratic forms of rule in capitalist societies – classic questions of political science and socialist strategy alike. The postwar settlement reflected a relative shift in the balance of class forces, strengthening labor unions in the workplace and working-class parties in elections. But these modes of representation were breaking down in the economic and political instabilities of the 1970s. The ensuing crisis of representation, Leo argued, took multiple forms: the decline of corporatism as a central institution regulating the capital-labor relation in the wake of capital's new offensive against trade union power; the impasse of social democracy as Keynesianism was displaced by neoliberal policy agendas; and the growing struggle of unions to organize workers in new sectors. In a word, the old

socio-economic order was transforming, and the form of the state was changing along with it, as policy regimes and modes of administration were restructured in the neoliberal drive to 'free markets' and 'remake bureaucracy'.

These were essential themes of Leo's writings gathered in *Working Class
Politics in Crisis* (1986), and in the essays written for the annual *Socialist
Register*, which Leo joined as co-editor in 1985. The analysis of the crisis of
working-class representation also set the frame of reference for Leo's influential study of the British Labour Party, *The End of Parliamentary Socialism*
(1997), co-authored with Colin Leys. This text was a careful investigation of the
making of the British 'Third Way' under Tony Blair, but also of the inability of
the Bennite left to block this shift, never mind to accomplish their own socialist re-make of the party – a story hardly unique to Britain. These volumes provided a clear and provocative series of contentions on the class contradictions
of liberal democracy and the emerging threat to democracy and working-class
politics posed by the consolidating neoliberal state.

This set an agenda for what might be considered a third phase of Leo's
research – taking stock of an increasingly integrated global capitalism, under
the hegemony of US 'empire', and its implications for the institutional materiality of capitalist states. In writing about 'globalization and the state', beginning with his formative essay in the 1994 *Socialist Register*, Leo advanced two
central claims.[4] First, even with global value chains and integrated systems of
production, exchange, and finance, the responsibilities of national states were
hardly declining – on the contrary, states were forming crucial policy capacities to actively support the global expansion of capital and to manage the
contradictions and crises associated with international accumulation. Second,
the US state had a pivotal role to play – and actively undertook it – in 'superintending global capital' through its 'informal empire' within the international
state system. The US Treasury and Federal Reserve in particular became indispensable state agencies in support of global capitalism, offering unparalleled
coordinating capacities and economic instruments for the management of the
world economy. These themes of Leo's writing in the 1990s and 2000s formed
the foundation of what is now a standard reference on the capitalist state and
world market in the period of globalization, *The Making of Global Capitalism*
(2012), co-authored with Sam Gindin. But there was also the contentious conclusions – set against the common sense of so much of the contemporary left –
that notions of American economic decline and inter-imperial rivalry between
the core capitalist states involved a fundamental misreading of the nature of

---

4 Panitch (1994).

capitalist competition and the state system in the period of neoliberalism. Rather, the most pressing political questions, Leo argued, were about how to construct alternative political organizations and strategies for democratizing the state that might address the crisis of working-class representation, the gross social inequalities within and between nations, and the anti-democratic – even authoritarian – tendencies developing within capitalist states.

If these three phases to Leo's research and writing can be presented in a sequential narrative, they are also somewhat arbitrary if held to rigidly. For the themes from all these phases continued to traverse Leo's most recent writing, in the *Socialist Register* and in recent books, on the crises of 'post-democracy', the shifting terrain of the geo-political order and state system, and the continuing struggles of socialist movements to find pathways toward new political organization and democratic transformations beyond the capitalist state.

The various themes and trajectories of Leo's research, emerging from a life-long commitment to the practice of a critical political science, informed his teaching as well – most recently at York University's Department of Political Science where he taught for more than thirty years. Upon his retirement a two-day conference, 'Transcending Pessimism, Reimagining Democracy', was held in his honor at York in October 2017. This followed on similar sessions run during the joint meetings of the Canadian Political Science Association and Society for Socialist Studies, also to discuss Leo's contributions to political science and socialist thought in Canada. For more than four decades, Leo had steadfastly worked at building an intellectual and activist community on the left through his extensive publications, his teaching of hundreds of graduate students at Carleton and York, and his editorship of the *Socialist Register* since 1985. The conference brought together economic researchers, colleagues, current and former students, and political comrades from across Canada and, indeed, around the world. In this, the discussions reflected a common engagement with Leo's writing, but also a shared commitment to the practice of a critical political science in Gramsci's sense formed within, or influenced by, the Marxist tradition. That is, a collective vision of a radical transformation "converting the state," as Marx expressed it, "from an organ standing above society into one completely subordinated to it."[5] To this end, Leo once advised that we brace for this daunting challenge of 'state transformation' with what he called 'revolutionary optimism': "Optimism of the intellect in fact involves being sensitive to contingency in human history, with contradiction and crises not the only variables determining the scope and possibilities of such contingency, but

---

5   Marx (1966[1875]: 17).

also the capacities of collective human agency as especially crucial variable factors in developing transformative institutional forms. ... What is needed is a careful, sympathetic probing of the barriers which attempts at transformative change are running up against, and the limits and problems being confronted or evaded, the better to learn from them when we come back and have to face the contingencies of trying to develop the capacities to effect political change in our own countries."[6]

Leo's sudden passing at the end of 2020 was an incalculable loss for the global left. But for the editors and contributors to this volume, and indeed for socialists around the world touched by Leo, the commitment to the project of critical political science, the spirit of 'revolutionary optimism', and the pursuit of an alternative democratic future beyond capitalism must continue.

6 Panitch (2016: 360, 361).

References

[Editorial] (1950) "The power of life and death." *Globe & Mail*, 24 August.

[Editorial] (1999) "World central bank." *Journal of Commerce*, 7 January.

Abella, I. (1973) *Nationalism, Communism, and Canadian Labour*. Toronto: University of Toronto Press.

Abella, I. (ed.) (1974) *On Strike: Six Key Labour Struggles in Canada*. Toronto: James Lewis & Samuel.

Abrams, P. (1988) "Notes on the difficulty of studying the state." *Journal of Historical Sociology* 1(1): 58–89.

Aglietta, M. (1979) *A Theory of Capitalist Regulation: The US Experience*. London: Verso Books.

Aivalis, C. (2018) *The Constant Liberal: Pierre Trudeau, Organized Labour, and the Canadian Social Democratic Left*. Vancouver: UBC Press.

Albert, M. and Hahnel, R. (1990) *Looking Forward: Participatory Economics for the Twenty First Century*. Boston: South End Press.

Albo, G. (1997) "A world market of opportunities? Capitalist obstacles and left economic policy." In Panitch, L. (ed.) *Socialist Register 1997: Ruthless Criticism of all that Exists*. New York: Monthly Review Press.

Albo, G. (2002) "Neoliberalism, the state and the left: A Canadian perspective." *Monthly Review,* 54(1): 46–55.

Albo, G. (2003) "Cracks in the facade: The US and the world economy." Paper presented at the University of Innsbruck.

Albo, G., Gindin, S. and Panitch, L. (2010) *In and Out of Crisis: The Global Financial Meltdown and Left Alternatives*. Oakland, California: Spectre PM Press.

Albo, G., Langille, D. and Panitch, L. (eds.) (1993) *A Different Kind of State?: Popular Power and Democratic Administration*. Toronto: Oxford University Press.

Albo, G., Panitch, L. and Zuege, A. (eds.) (2018) *Class, Party, Revolution*. Chicago: Haymarket Books.

Alford, R. (1963) *Party and Society*. Chicago: Rand McNally.

Alford, R. and Friedland, R. (1985) *Powers of Theory: Capitalism, the State, and Democracy* Cambridge: Cambridge University Press, 1985.

Allen, C. (2019) "National action: Links between the far right, extremism and terrorism." Commission for Countering Extremism. Available at: https://www.gov.uk/government/publications/national-action-links-between-the-far-right-extremism-and-terrorism.

Almond, G. and Powell, G.B. (1966) *Comparative Politics: A Developmental Approach*. Boston: Little Brown & Co.

Alston, P. (2018) "Statement on visit to the United Kingdom by Professor Philip Alston, United Nations Special Rapporteur on extreme poverty and human rights.".

Althusser, L. (1971) "Ideology and ideological state apparatuses: Notes towards an investigation." In *Lenin and Philosophy and Other Essays*. New York Monthly Review Press.

Andersen, J.G. (1984) "Decline of class voting or change in class voting? Social classes and party choice in Denmark in the 1970s." *European Journal of Political Research* 12: 243–259.

Anderson, P. (1976) "The antinomies of Antonio Gramsci." *New Left Review* 100: 5–78.

Anderson, P. (1987) "The figures of descent." *New Left Review* 161: 20–77.

Arrighi, G. (2005) "Hegemony unraveling." *New Left Review* 32: 23–80.

Arrighi, G. (2007) *Adam Smith in Beijing: Lineages of the Twenty-first Century.* New York: Verso Books.

Arrighi, G. (2008) *Adam Smith em Pequim: origens e fundamentos do século XXI.* São Paulo: Boitempo.

Arrighi, G., Mamashita, T. and Selden, M. (eds.) (2003) *The Resurgence of East Asia.* London: Routledge Press.

Arthurs, H. (1966) *Confidential Memorandum on Injunctions.* Ontario Department of Labour, Archives of Ontario, RG 3-26 Box 189, Premier J.P. Robarts General Correspondence Strikes-Exparte Injunction January 1966-June 1966.

Ascherson, N. (2018) "Ancient Britons and the republican dream." *openDemocracy.* Available at: https://www.opendemocracy.net/en/opendemocracyuk/ancient-britons-and-republican-dream/.

Aschoff, N.M. (2017) "The glory days are over: Trump's victory signals a deep crisis of neoliberalism." *Jacobin*, 20 March. Available at: https://jacobinmag.com/2017/03/the-glory-days-are-over-2.

Atkinson, A.B. (2019) *Inequality. What Can Be Done?* Cambridge, Mass.: Harvard University Press.

Auerbach, P. (2016) *Socialist Optimism: An Alternative Political Economy for the Twenty-First Century.* New York: Palgrave Press.

Avery, J.M., Peffley, M. (2005) "Voter registration requirements, voter turnout, and welfare eligibility policy: Class bias matters." *State Politics & Policy Quarterly* 5(1): 47–67.

Balbus, I. (1974) "The Concept of Interest in Pluralist and Marxian Analysis." In Katznelson, I. (ed.) *The Politics and Society Reader.* New York: David McKay Co.

Ban, C. (2013) "Brazil's liberal neo-developmentalism: New paradigm or edited orthodoxy?" *Review of International Political Economy* 20(2): 298–331. Available at: https://doi.org/10.1080/09692290.2012.660183.

Barnett, A. (2017) *The Lure of Greatness: England's Brexit and America's Trump.* London: Unbound.

Barnett, A. (2020) "Out of the belly of hell: COVID-19 and the humanization of globalization." *openDemocracy*, 21 May. Available at: https://www.opendemocracy.net/en/opendemocracyuk/out-belly-hell-shutdown-and-humanisation-globalisation/.

Barrow, C.W. (1993) *Critical Theories of the State: Marxist, Neo-Marxist, Post-Marxist*. Madison: University of Wisconsin Press.

Barrow, C.W. (2001) "Corporate power and political science: A review essay." *New Political Science* 23(1): 147–55.

Barrow, C.W. (2002) "The Miliband-Poulantzas Debate: An intellectual history." In Aronowitz, S. and Bratsis, P. (eds.) *Paradigm Lost: Revising State Theory*. Minneapolis: University of Minnesota Press.

Barrow, C.W. (2008) "Ralph Miliband and the instrumentalist theory of the state." In Wetherly, P. Barrow, C.W. and Burnham, P. (eds.) *Class, Power and the State in Capitalist Society: Essays on Ralph Miliband*. New York: Palgrave Press.

Barrow, C.W. (2016) *Toward a Critical Theory of States: The Poulantzas-Miliband Debate After Globalization*. Albany: State University Press of New York.

Barrow, C.W. (2017) "The political and intellectual origins of New Political Science." *New Political Science* 39(4): 437–72.

Barrow, C.W., Didou-Aupetit, S. and Mallea, J. (2003) *Globalisation, Trade Liberalism, and Higher Education in North America*. Dordrecht: Kluwer Academic Publishers.

Barrow, C.W., Wetherly, P. and Burnham, P. (2008) "Introduction." In Wetherly, P., Barrow, C.W. and Burnham, P. (eds.) *Class, Power and the State in Capitalist Society: Essays on Ralph Miliband*. Houndsmill: Palgrave Macmillan.

Barrow, C.W. and Keck, M. (2017) "Symposium/State – Globalization theory and state theory: The false antinomy." *Studies in Political Economy* 98(2): 1–20.

Barrow, C.W. (2019) "Marxist political theory, diversity of tactics, and the doctrine of the long civil war." *New Political Science* 41(4): 622–53.

Bartik, A., Cullen, Z., Glaeser, E., Luca M., Stanton, C. and Sundream, A. (2020) The targeting and impact of Paycheck Protection Program Loans to small businesses." NBER Working Paper 27623. Available at: http://www.nber.org/papers/w27623.

BCGEU v. British Columbia (A.G.), [1988] 2. S.C.R. 214.

Beck, U. (1997) *Was ist Globalisierung? Irrtümer des Globalismus – Antworten auf Globulisierung*. Frankfurt/Main: Suhrkamp Verlag.

Beck, U. and Grande, E. (2007) *Cosmopolitan Europe*. Cambridge: Polity Press.

Becker, G.S. (1993) *Human Capital: A Theoretical and Empirical Analysis with Special Reference to Education*, 3rd Edition. Chicago: University of Chicago Press.

Beckett, A. (2012) "Britannia unchained: The rise of the new Tory right." *The Guardian*, 22 August.

Beckett, A. (2019) "A Labour defeat, yes, but this was not nearly as bad as 1983." *The Guardian*, 19 December. Available at: https://www.theguardian.com/commentis-free/2019/dec/19/left-labour-michael-foot-tony-blair.

Bell, D. (1960) *The End of Ideology*. New York: Basic Books.

Bell, D. (1976) *The Coming of Post-Industrial Society*. New York: Basic Books.

Bellamy Foster, J. (2018) "Marx, value and nature." *Monthly Review* 70(3). Available at: https://monthlyreview.org/2018/07/01/marx-value-and-nature/.

Benn, T. (1970) "A new politics: A socialist renaissance." Fabian Tract 402, September.

Benn, T. (1971) "Democratic politics: Fabian Autumn Lecture 3." In *Speeches by Tony Benn*. Spokesman Press.

Bensaid, D. (2005) "On a recent book by John Holloway." *Historical Materialism* 13(4): 169–192.

Bensel, R. (1990) *Yankee Leviathan: The Origins of Central State Authority in America, 1859–1877*. Cambridge: Cambridge University Press.

Berlin, I. (1969) "Two concepts of liberty." In *Four Essays On Liberty*. Oxford: Oxford University Press.

Berlinguer, M. (2020) *Commons, Markets and Public Policy*. Transform! ePaper, January. Available at: https://www.transform-network.net/fileadmin/user_upload/2020-01-commons_3.pdf.

Best, M.H. and Connolly, W. (1976) *The Politicized Economy*. Lexington, Mass.: D.C. Heath.

Bieling, H. and Deppe, F. (2003) "Die neue europäische Ökonomie und die Transformation von Staatlichkeit." In Jachtenfuchs, M. and Kohler-Koch, B. (eds.) *Europäische Integration*, 2nd. Ed. Opladen: Leske+Budrich.

Bieling, H. (2010) *Die Globalisierungs- und Weltordnungspolitik der Europäischen Union*. Wiesbaden: vs Verlag.

Bitler, M., Hoynes, H., and Whitmore Schanzenbach, D. (2020) "The social safety net in the wake of COVID-19." NBER Working Paper 27796. Available at: http://www.nber.org/papers/w27796.

Bleasdale, R. (2018) *Rough Work: Labourers on the Public Works of British North America and Canada, 1841–1882*. Toronto: University of Toronto Press.

Bloch, E. (1996) *The Principle of Hope*, Volume 1. Cambridge, MA: MIT Press.

Block, F. (1977) "The ruling class does not rule: Notes on the Marxist theory of the state." *Socialist Revolution* 7: 6–28.

Block, F. (1980) "Beyond relative autonomy: State managers as historical subjects." In Miliband, R. and Saville, J. (eds) *The Socialist Register 1980*. New York: Monthly Review Press.

Block, F. (1990) *Postindustrial Possibilities*. Berkeley: University of California Press.

Board of Governors of the Federal Reserve (2020) "Report on the economic well-being of U.S. households in 2019–May 2020." Available at: https://www.federalreserve.gov/publications/2020-economic-well-being-of-us-households-in-2019-preface.htm.

Bockman, J. (2011) *Markets in the Name of Socialism: The Left-Wing Origins of Neoliberalism*. Stanford: Stanford University Press.

Bockman, J. (2016) "Socialism and the embedded economy." *Theory and Society* 45(5): 385–427.

Boggs, C. (1986) *Social Movements and Political Power: Emerging Forms of Radicalism in the West*. Philadelphia: Temple University Press.

Bohoslavsky, E. and Morresi, S. (2016) "El Partido PRO y el triunfo de la nueva derecha en Argentina." *Amérique Latine Histoire et Mémoire. Les Cahiers ALHIM* 32. Available at: http://journals.openedition.org/alhim/5619.

Bond, P. and Garcia, A. (2018) "Amplifying the contradictions: the centrifugal BRICS." In Panitch, L. and Albo, G. (eds.) *Socialist Register 2019: A World Turned Upside Down?* London: Merlin Press.

Bonefeld, W. (1992) "Social constitution and the form of the capitalist state". In Bonefeld, W. Gunn, R. and Psychopedis, K. (eds.) *Open Marxism*, Vol I. London: Pluto.

Bonefeld, W. (1993) *The Recomposition of the British State During the 1980s*. Aldershot: Dartmouth.

Boschi, R. and Gaitán, F. (2009) "Politics and development: Lessons from Latin America." *Brazilian Political Science Review* 4. Available at: http://socialsciences.scielo.org/pdf/s_bpsr/v4nse/a06.pdf.

Bothwick, G, Ellingworth, D., Bell, C. and Mackenzie, D. (1991) "Research note: The social background of British MPs." *Sociology* 25 (4): 713–17.

Boudieu, P. (1994) *Language and Symbolic Power*. Cambridge: Harvard University Press.

Bourque, G. (1979) "Class, nation and the Parti Quebecois." *Studies in Political Economy* 2: 129–158.

Bouzane, B. (2012) "PM defends action on Air Canada." *Montreal Gazette*, 10 March.

Bowcott, O. (2020) "What is judicial review and why doesn't the government like it?" *The Guardian*, 11 February. Available at: https://www.theguardian.com/law/2020/feb/11/what-is-judicial-review-and-why-doesnt-the-government-like-it.

Bowles, S. and Gintis, H. (1982) "The crisis of liberal democratic capitalism: The case of the United States." *Politics and Society* 11(1): 51–93.

Bowles, S. and Gintis, H. (1987) *Democracy and Capitalism: Property, Community, and the Contradictions of Modern Social Thought*. New York: Basic Books.

Bowles, S., Gordon, D.M. and Weisskopf, T.E. (1984) *Beyond the Wasteland: A Democratic Alternative to Economic Decline*. Garden City, N.Y.: Anchor Books.

Bratsis, P. (2002) "Unthinking the state: Reification, ideology, and the state as a social fact." In Aronowitz, S. and Bratsis, P. (eds.) *Paradigm Lost: State Theory Reconsidered*. Minneapolis: University of Minnesota Press.

Braverman, H. (1976) "Two comments." *Monthly Review* 28(3): 119–124.

Braverman, S. (2020) "People we elect must take back control from people we don't. Who include the judges." *Conservative Home*, 27 January. Available at: https://www.conservativehome.com/platform/2020/01/suella-braverman-people-we-elect-must-take-back-control-from-people-we-dont-who-include-the-judges.html.

Bresser Pereira, L.C. (2007) "Estado y mercado en el nuevo desarrollismo." *Nueva Sociedad* 125: 110–25.

Bresser Pereira, L.C. (2020) "Argentina, developmentalism and populism." *Bresser Pereira*. 15 January. Available at: http://www.bresserpereira.org.br/Articles/2013/64.Argentina-desenvolvimentismo-populismo-i.pdf.

Brewer, A. (1990) *Marxist Theories of Imperialism: A Critical Survey*. London: Routledge Press.

Bridges, A.B. (1974) "Nicos Poulantzas and the Marxist theory of the state." *Politics and Society* 4(2): 161–90.

Brodie, J. and Jenson, J. (1980) *Crisis Challenge and Change: Party and Class in Canada*. Toronto: Methuen Publications.

Brown, W. (2015) *Undoing the Demos: Neoliberalism's Stealth Revolution*. New York: Zone.

Bruff, I. and Ebenau, M. (2014) "Critical political economy and the critique of comparative capitalisms scholarship on capitalist diversity." *Capital & Class* 38(1): 3–15.

Brummer, A. (2012) *Britain for Sale*. London: Random House.

Brus, W. (1973) *The Economics and Politics of Socialism*. London: Routledge Press.

Bryan, D. (1992) "International accumulation and the contradictions of national monetary policy." *Science & Society* 56(3): 324–352.

Bryan, D. (1995) *The Chase Across the Globe: International Accumulation and the Contradictions for Nation States*. Boulder, Colorado: Westview Press.

Bugiato, C. (2014) "A política de financiamento do BNDES e a burguesia brasileira." *Cadernos do Desenvolvimento* 9(14): 83–103.

Bugiato, C. (2017) "A importância do BNDES na política externa do governo Lula." *Cadernos do Desenvolvimento* 12(21): 43–69.

Bukharin, N. (1973 [1915]) *Imperialism and World Economy*, New York: Monthly Review Press.

Bullock, I. (2017) *Under Siege: The Independent Labour Party in Interwar Britain*. Edmonton: AU Press.

Burbach, R. and Robinson W.I. (1999) "The fin de siecle debate: Globalization as epochal shift." *Science & Society* 63(1): 10–39.

Bureau of Economic Analysis (2020) "Table 5.2.5." Available at: https://apps.bea.gov/iTable/index_nipa.cfm.

Burgmann, V. (2005) "From syndicalism to Seattle: Class and the politics of identity." *International Labor and Working-Class History* 67: 1–21.

Burnham, P. (2008) "Parliamentary socialism, labourism and beyond." In Wetherly, P. Barrow, C.W. and Burnham, P. (eds.) *Class, Power and the State in Capitalist Society: Essays on Ralph Miliband*. New York: Palgrave Press.

Butler, P. (2018) "Welfare spending for UK's poorest shrinks by £37bn." *The Guardian*, 23 September. Available at: https://www.theguardian.com/politics/2018/sep/23/welfare-spending-uk-poorest-austerity-frank-field.

Callinicos, A. (2007) "Does capitalism need the state system?" *Cambridge Review of International Affairs* 20(4): 533–549.

Callinicos, A. (2009) *Imperialism and Global Political Economy*. Cambridge, England: Polity Press.

Cammack P. (1989) "Review article: Bringing the state back in?" *British Journal of Political Science* 19(2): 261–290.

Campbell, P. (2020) "Can Britain's car plants stay open after Brexit?" Financial Times, 10 February. Available at: https://www.ft.com/content/97fef2b8-4915-11ea -aeb3-955839e06441.

Campbell, P. (2020) "Can Britain's car plants stay open after Brexit?" *Financial Times*, 10 February. Available at: https://www.ft.com/content/97fef2b8-4915-11ea-aeb3 -955839e06441.

Campos, L., González, M. and Sacavini, M. (2010) "El mercado de trabajo en los distintos patrones de crecimiento." *Realidad Económica* 253: 48–81.

Canada (1950–51) *Official Report of Debates House of Commons, Third Session-Twenty-First Parliament, 14–15 George VI*.

Canadian Foundation for Labour Rights (2020) *Restrictive Labour Laws Directory*. Available at: https://labourrights.ca/restrictive-labour-laws.

Canadian Labour Congress (1966) "Campaign Against Strike Injunctions." *Canadian Labour* 11(11): 32.

Canadian Union of Public Employees, Local 301 v. Montreal (City), [1997] 1 S.C.R 793.

Cant, C. (2020) "In Britain's low-pay economy, warehouse workers could start calling the shots." *The Guardian*, 3 September. Available at: https://www.theguardian.com/commentisfree/2020/sep/03/britain-low-pay-economy-warehouse -workers-online-retail.

Carnes, N. (2012) "Does the numerical underrepresentation of the working class in Congress matter?" *Legislative Studies Quarterly* 37(1): 5–34.

Carnes, N. (2013) *White Collar Government: The Hidden Role of Class in Economic Policy Making*. Chicago and London: University of Chicago Press.

Carnes, N. (2016) "Dialogue: Working class – why are there so few working class people in political office? Evidence from state legislatures." *Politics, Groups and Identities* 4(1): 84–109.

Carnoy, M. and Shearer, D. (1980) *Economic Democracy: The Challenge of the 1980s*. Armonk, N.Y.: M. E. Sharpe.

Carnoy, M. (1984) *The State and Political Theory*. Princeton: Princeton University Press.

Carothers, A.W.R. (1966) *Report of a Study on the Labour Injunction in Ontario*. Toronto: Ontario Department of Labour.

Castells, M. (1997) *The Information Age: Economy, Society, and Culture*, 2 Vols. Oxford: Blackwell Publishers, Inc.

Castells, M. (2000) *The Rise of the Network Society*, 2nd Edition. Malden, MA: Blackwell Publishers.

Caves, R. (1982) *Multinational Enterprise and Economic Analysis*. Cambridge: Cambridge University Press.

CBC News (2020) "Canada Post employees protest in Montreal after 2 years without collective agreement," 31 January. Available at: https://www.cbc.ca/news/canada/montreal/canada-post-montreal-protest-1.5447160.

Chakraborty, A. (2019) "The Tories' 'angry white men' act is desperate and dangerous." *The Guardian*, 2 October. Available at: https://www.theguardian.com/commentisfree/2019/oct/02/tories-angry-white-men-david-cameron-conservatives-republicans.

Chang, H. (2003) *Globalisation, Economic Development, and the Role of the State.* London: Zed Books, Ltd.

Clark, T.N. (2003) "The breakdown of class politics." *The American Sociologist* 34(1–2): 17–32.

Clark, T.N., Lipset, S.M. and Rempel, M. (1993) "The declining political significance of social class." *International Sociology* 8(3): 293–316.

Clarke, S. (1988) *Keynesianism, Monetarism and the Crisis of the State.* Aldershot: Edward Elgar.

Clarke, S. (1991) "Introduction." In Clarke, S. (ed.) *The State Debate.* New York: Macmillan.

Clarke, S. (ed.) (1991) *The State Debate.* New York: St. Martin's Press.

CNBC (2020) "CNBC exclusive: CNBC transcript: Treasury Secretary Steven Mnuchin speaks with CNBC's 'Squawk Box' today." *CNBC*, 23 July. Available at: https://www.cnbc.com/2020/07/23/cnbc-exclusive-cnbc-transcript-treasury-secretary-steven-mnuchin-speaks-with-cnbcs-squawk-box-today.html.

Coates, D. (1989) *The Crisis of Labour: Industrial Relations and the State in Contemporary Britain.* Oxford: Phillip Allan.

Cohen, S. and Zysman, J. (1987) *Manufacturing Matters: The Myth of the Post-Industrial Economy.* New York: Basic Books.

Collini, S. (2020) "Inside the mind of Dominic Cummings." *The Guardian*, 6 February. Available at: https://www.theguardian.com/politics/2020/feb/06/inside-the-mind-of-dominic-cummings-brexit-boris-johnson-conservatives.

Consumer's Co-operative Refineries Ltd., v. Unifor Canada, Local 594, Queen Bench for Saskatchewan, QBG 3302, 2019.

Cosentino, A., Isasa, M. Carreras Mayer, P. de Achával, F., Coretti, M. and Dall'o, F. (2017) *Crisis y reestructuración de deuda soberana: una visión sistémica de la perspectiva de los mercados emergentes.* Buenos Aires: Eudeba.

Costa, A., Kicillof, A. and Nahón, C. (2004) "Las consecuencias económicas del Sr. Lavagna. Dilemas de un país devaluado." *Realidad Económica* 203: 70–100.

Cox, J., Greenwald D. and Ludvigson, S. (2020) "What explains the COVID-19 stock market." NBER Working Paper 27784. Available at: http://www.nber.org/papers/w27784.

Cox, R. (1987) *Production, Power, and World Order: Social Forces in the Making of History.* New York: Columbia University Press.

Cox, R. (1992) "Global Perestroika." In Miliband, R. and Panitch, L. (eds.) *Socialist Register 1992*. London: Merlin Press.

Crothers, L. (2010) *Globalization and American Popular Culture*, 2nd edition. Lanham, MD: Rowman and Littlefield Publishers, Inc.

Crouch, C. (2004) *Post-Democracy*. Cambridge: Polity Press.

Crow, D. (2019) "Top bankers shift tone over horror of no-deal Brexit." *Financial Times*, 9 August. Available at: https://www.ft.com/content/b2d275aa-ba73-11e9 -96bd-8e884d3ea203.

Crozier, M., Huntington, S.P. and Watanuki, J. (1975) *The Crisis of Democracy: On the Governability of Democracies*. New York: New York University Press.

Cruikshank, D. and Kealey, G. (1987) "Strikes in Canada, 1891–1950: Methods and sources and the data." *Labour/Le Travail* 20: 85–145.

Curtis, M. (1968) *Comparative Government and Politics*. New York: Harper & Row.

Dahrendorf, R. (1967) *Class and Class Conflict in Industrial Society*. Stanford: Stanford University Press.

Damill, M., Frenkel, R. and Rapetti, M. (2005) "The Argentinean debt: History, default and restructuring." *Economia-Revista Da ANPEC* 6(3): 29–90.

Davies, R. (2020) "Concern over 'opaque' Covid-related contracts awarded around world." *The Guardian*, 1 September. Available at: https://www.theguardian.com/world/2020/ sep/01/concern-over-opaque-covid-related-contracts-awarded-around-world.

Davies, W. (2018) *Nervous States*. London: Vintage.

Davies, W. (2019) "Let's eat badly." *London Review of Books* 41(23). Available at: https:// www.lrb.co.uk/the-paper/v41/n23/william-davies/let-s-eat-badly.

Davis, A. (2018) *Reckless opportunists: Elites at the end of the Establishment*. Manchester: Manchester University Press.

Davis, M. (1986) *Prisoners of the American Dream: Politics and Economy in the History of the US Working Class*. London: Verso Books.

Davis, M. (2020) *The Monster Enters: COVID-19, Avian Flu, and the Plagues of Capitalism*. New York: OR Books.

Dean, J. (2009) *Democracy and Other Neoliberal Fantasies. Communicative Capitalism and Left Politics*. Durham: Duke University Press.

Delacourt, S. (2013) *Shopping for Votes: How Politicians Choose Us and We Choose Them*. Medeira Park BC: Douglas and McIntyre.

Deleuze, G. and Guattari, F. (1987) *Thousand Plateaus: Capitalism and Schizophrenia* London: Athlone Press, 1987.

Democratic Socialists of America (2020) *Democrat Left* 48(2).

Dempsey, N. and Loft, P. (2019) "Turnout at elections." Briefing paper number CBP 8060, House of Commons Library, 5 July.

Department of Labor Employment & Training Administration (no date) *Monthly Program and Financial Data*. Available at: https://oui.doleta.gov/unemploy/claims-sum.asp.

DePillis, L. (2020) "The small biz double-dip: temp companies got cheap government money, got paid by clients for the same workers." *ProPublica*, 27 July 2020. Available at: https://www.propublica.org/article/the-small-biz-double-dip-temp-companies-got-cheap-government-money-got-paid-by-clients-for-the-same-workers.

Deppe, F. (1993) "Von der 'Europhorie' zur Erosion – Anmerkungen zur Post-Maastricht-Krise der EG." In Deppe, F. and Felder, M. (eds.) *Zur Post-Maastricht-Krise der Europäischen Gemeinschaft*. FEG-Arbeitspapier Nr. 10, Marburg, S.

Deppe, F. (2012) *Gewerkschaften in der Großen Transformation: Von den 1970er Jahren bis heute*. Köln: PapyRossa Verlag.

Deppe, F. (2013) *Autoritärer Kapitalismus*. Hamburg: Demokratie auf dem Prüfstand.

Deppe, F. (2015) *Der Staat*. Köln: PapyRossa Verlag.

Deppe, F. (2016) *Politisches Denken im 20. Jahrhundert. Band 2, Zwischen den Weltkriegen*. Hamburg: VSA-Verlag.

Deppe, F. (2017) "Die Krise der Europäischen Union – deutsche Hegemonie – europäische Linke." In Candeias, M. and Demirovic, A. (eds.) *Europe – What's Left? Die europäische Union zwischen Zerfall, Autoritarismus und demokratischer Erneuerung*. Münster: Westfälisches Dampfboot.

Deppe, F. (2020) "Brexit schlägt Sozialismus." *Z. Zeitschrift marxistische Erneuerung* 121: 18–26.

Deppe, F., Felder, M. and Tidow, S. (2003) "Structuring the state – The case of European employment policy." In Kohler-Koch, B. (ed.) *Linking EU and National Government*. Oxford: Oxford University Press.

Desmet, L. (director) (2019) *Brexit: Behind Closed Doors* [Motion picture]. London: Films of Record.

Diamond, D. (2020) "Trump officials interfered with CDC reports on Covid-19." *Politico*, 11 September. Available at: https://www.politico.com/news/2020/09/11/exclusive-trump-officials-interfered-with-cdc-reports-on-covid-19-412809.

Di Stefano, M. (2020) "No 10 accused of 'sinister' tactics in media dispute." *Financial Times*, 3 February. Available at: https://www.ft.com/content/b2ff3b3e-46ab-11ea-aeb3-955839e06441.

Doherty, A. (2019) "Momentum activists are trying to make Jeremy Corbyn prime minister: An interview with Emma Rees." *Jacobin*, 13 November. Available at: https://www.jacobinmag.com/2019/11/momentum-labour-party-emma-rees-election.

Domhoff, G.W. (1967) *Who Rules America?* Englewood Cliffs, N.J.: Prentice-Hall, Inc.

Domhoff, G.W. (1978) *The Powers That Be: Processes of Ruling Class Domination in America*. New York: Vintage Books.

Domhoff, G.W. (1990) *The Power Elite and the State: How Policy is Made in America*. New York: Aldine de Gruyter.

Domhoff, G.W. (1996) *State Autonomy or Class Dominance? Case Studies on Policy Making in America*. New York: Aldine de Gruyter.

Doorey, D. (2017) *The Law of Work: Industrial Relations and Collective Bargaining.* Toronto: Edmond.

Douglas, T.C. (1950) Statement for Leader-Post, Re: Back-to-Work Legislation (The Maintenance of Railway Operation Act (August 30, 1950), Saskatchewan Archives Board, TC Douglas Fonds, F117, R 33.1, File Number 810, (31), Press.

Downs, A. (1957) *An Economic Theory of Democracy.* New York: Harper & Row.

Drache, D. and Glasbeek, H. (1992) *The Changing Workplace: Reshaping Canada's Industrial Relations System.* Toronto: Lorimer.

Draper, H. (2018) "The principle of self-emancipation in Marx and Engels." In: Albo, G., Panitch, L. and Zuege, A. (eds.) *Class, Party and Revolution: A Socialist Register Reader.* Chicago: Haymarket Books.

Dunning, J. (1981) *International Production and the Multinational Enterprise.* London: George Allen & Unwin.

Eckstein, O. (1978) *Great Recession: With a Postscript on Stagflation.* New York: North-Holland Publishing Co.

Edgerton, D. (2019a) "Brexit is a necessary crisis – it reveals Britain's true place in the world." *The Guardian*, 9 October. Available at: https://www.theguardian.com/commentisfree/2019/oct/09/brexit-crisis-global-capitalism-britain-place-world.

Edgerton, D. (2019b) *The Rise and Fall of the British Nation: A twentieth century history.* London: Penguin Books.

Edsall, T.B. (1984) *The New Politics of Inequality.* New York: W.W. Norton and Co.

Edwards, J. (2016) "Half the FTSE 100 is owned by foreigners who might sell if there is a Brexit." *Business Insider*, 20 June. Available at: https://www.businessinsider.com/goldman-sachs-half-the-ftse-100-is-owned-by-foreigners-brexit-2016-6.

Edwards, S. (2019) "On Latin American populism, and its echoes around the world." *Journal of Economic Perspectives* 33(4): 76–99.

Ehrenreich, J.A. and Ehrenreich, B. (1976) "Work and Consciousness." *Monthly Review* 28(3): 10–18.

Eley, G. (2002) *Forging Democracy: The History of the Left in Europe 1850–2000.* Oxford: Oxford University Press.

Elliot, L. (2016) "March of the makers remains a figment of Osborne's imagination." *The Guardian*, 12 January. Available at: https://www.theguardian.com/business/2016/jan/12/march-of-the-makers-osbornes-economy-manufacturing-output.

Eneas, B. (2020) "Co-op refinery labour dispute: Unifor accepts special mediator recommendations, FCL does not accept in full." *CBC News*, 22 March. Available at: https://www.cbc.ca/news/canada/saskatchewan/special-mediator-recommendations-fcl-unifor-1.5506135.

Epstein, L.D. (1967) *Political Parties in Western Democracies.* New York: Frederick A. Praeger Publishers.

Ercan, F. and Oguz, S. (2007) "Rethinking anti-neoliberal strategies through the perspective of value theory: Insights from the Turkish case." *Science & Society* 71(2): 173–202.

Erdilek, A. (1992) "The role of foreign investment in the liberalization of the Turkish economy." In Nas, T.F. and Odekon, M. (eds.) *Economics and Politics of Turkish Liberalization*. Bethlehem: Lehigh University Press.

Eribon, D. (2016) *Rückkehr nach Reims*. Berlin: Suhrkamp.

Esping-Andersen, G. (ed.) (1993) *Changing Classes. Stratification and Mobility in Post-industrial Societies*. London: Sage Publications.

Essex, J. (2007) "Getting what you pay for: Authoritarian statism and the geographies of US trade liberalization strategies." *Studies in Political Economy* 80: 75–103.

Evans, G. (ed.) (1999) *The End of Class Politics? Class Voting in Comparative Perspective*. Oxford: Oxford University Press.

Evans, G. (2000) "The continued significance of class voting." *Annual Review of Political Science* 3: 401–17.

Evans, G, and Tilley, J. (2012) "The depoliticization of inequality and redistribution: Explaining the decline of class voting." *Journal of Politics* 74(4): 963–76.

Evans, P., Rueschemeyer, D. and Skocpol, T. (eds.) (1985) *Bringing the State Back In*. Cambridge: Cambridge University Press.

Evans, P. (1997) "The eclipse of the state? Reflections on stateness in an era of globalization." *World Politics* 50(1): 62–87.

Farber, S. (2018) "Donald Trump, lumpen capitalist." *Jacobin*, 19 October. Available at: https://www.jacobinmag.com/2018/10/donald-trump-lumpen-capitalist-class-elections.

Federal Open Market Committee (2020) "Table 1. Economic projections of Federal Reserve Board members and Federal Reserve Bank presidents, under their individual assumptions of projected appropriate monetary policy, September 2020." *Board of Governors of the Federal Reserve System*. Available at: https://www.federalreserve.gov/monetarypolicy/files/fomcprojtabl20200916.pdf.

Felder, R. (2013) "Neoliberal reforms, crisis and recovery in Argentina (1990s-2000s)." PhD thesis, York University.

Felder, R. and Patroni, V. (2018) "Precarious work in recession and growth: A new structural feature of labour markets in Argentina?" *Review of Radical Political Economics* 50(1): 44–65.

Fine, B. (2013) "Beyond the Developmental State: An Introduction." In *Beyond the Developmental State: Industrial Policy into the Twenty-First Century*. London: Pluto.

Fine, B. and Harris, L. (1979) *Rereading Capital*. New York: Columbia University Press.

Fisher, A. (2020) "I was at the heart of Corbynism. Here's why we lost." *openDemocracy*, 10 September. Available at: https://www.opendemocracy.net/en/opendemocracyuk/i-was-heart-corbynism-heres-why-we-lost.

Ford, J. (2019) "Labour is right: Britain's private utility model is broken. High returns from private monopolies cannot be justified." *Financial Times*, 19 May.

Foroohar,R.(2020)"BigTech,neoliberalismandwhatcomesnext."*FinancialTimes*,27July. Available at: https://www.ft.com/content/31bab53a-b27a-419f-a592-8eee6d5b860e.

Foucault, M. (1972) *The Archaeology of Knowledge & The Discourse on Language.* New York: Harper and Row Publishers.

Foucault, M. (1980) *The History of Sexuality, Vol. 1: An Introduction.* New York: Vintage Books.

Fountain, H. and Schwartz, J. (2020) "Hurricane Sally's fierce rain shows how climate change raises storm risks." *The New York Times*, 16 September. Available at: https://www.nytimes.com/2020/09/16/climate/hurricane-sally-climate-change.html.

Fraser, S. (2016) *The Age of Acquiescence: The Life and Death of American Resistance to Organized Wealth and Power.* New York: Little Brown and Company.

Friedman, M. (1962) *Capitalism and Freedom.* Chicago: University of Chicago Press.

Fudge, J. (1988) "Labour, the new constitution, and old style liberalism." Queen Law's Journal 13: 61–111.

Fudge, J. and Glasbeek, H. (1994–1995) "The legacy of PC 1003." *Canadian Labour and Employment Law Journal* 3: 357–399.

Fudge, J. and Tucker, E. (2000) "Pluralism or fragmentation?: The twentieth-century employment law regime in Canada." *Labour/Le Travail* 46: 251–306.

Fudge, J. and Tucker, E. (2001) *Labour Before the Law: The Regulation of Workers' Collective Action in Canada*, 1900–1948. Toronto: Oxford University Press.

Fudge, J. and Tucker, E. (2009–10) "The freedom to strike in Canada: A brief legal history." *Canadian Labour and Employment Law Journal* 15(2): 333–353.

Fukayama, F. (1992) *The End of History and the Last Man* . New York: The Free Press.

Gaggero, A. and Wainer, A. (2004) "Burguesía nacional. Crisis de la convertibilidad: el rol de la UIA y su estrategia para el (tipo de) cambio." *Realidad Económica* 204: 14–41.

Gaggero, J. and Rúa, M. (2013) "Fuga de capitales III. Argentina (2002–2012): magnitudes, evolución, políticas públicas y cuestiones fiscales relevantes." Centro de Economía y Finanzas para el Desarrollo.

Gallego, A. (2010) Understanding unequal turnout: Education and voting in comparative perspective. *Electoral Studies* 29: 239–248.

Ganong P., Noel, P. and Vavra, J. (2020) "US unemployment insurance replacement rates during the pandemic." Becker Friedman Institute for Economics at the University of Chicago Working Paper 2020–62. Available at: https://bfi.uchicago.edu/wp-content/uploads/BFI_WP_202062-1.pdf.

Garcia, A. (2017) "BRICS investment agreements in Africa: more of the same?" *Studies in Political Economy* 98(1): 24–47.

Garcia, A. and Bugiato, C. (2019) "Repensando o Estado e Imperialismo nas Relações Internacionais: as contribuições teóricas de Leo Panitch." *Revista de Estudos Internacionais* 10:2.

Garcia, A. and Kato, K. (2020) "A road to development? The Nacala Corridor at the intersection between Brazilian and global investments." In Satgar, V. (ed.) *BRICS and the new American Imperialism: Global rivalry and resistance.* Johannesburg: Wits University Press.

Gardner, B. (2019) How Jeremy Corbyn's predicted defeat would be the worst since 1935." *The Telegraph*, 12 December. Available at: https://www.telegraph.co.uk/politics/2019/12/12/jeremy-corbyns-predicted-defeat-would-worst-since-1935-election.

Geoghegan, P. (2019) "The Tory party is so dependent on big money it now represents only a tiny elite." *The Guardian*, 9 December. Available at: https://www.theguardian.com/commentisfree/2019/dec/09/money-matters-elections-tories-ultra-rich-brexit-donors.

GER-GEMSAL (2013) "Bienes comunes en la hegemonía extractivista. Disputas y resistencias." In Norma, G. and Teubal, M. (eds.) *Actividades extractivas en expansion ¿Reprimarización de la economía Argentina?* Buenos Aires: Antropofagia.

Gest, J. (2018) *The White Working Class: What Everyone Needs to Know.* New York: Oxford University Press.

Gibson, R. and Römmele, R. (2001) "Changing campaign communications: A party-centered theory of professionalized campaigning." *Harvard International Journal of Press/Politics* 6(4): 31–43.

Giddens, A. (1998) *The Third Way: The Renewal of Social Democracy.* Malden, MA: Polity Press.

Gilens, M. (2013) *Affluence and Influence: Economic Inequality and Political Power in America.* Princeton: Princeton University Press.

Gill, S. (2003) *Power and Resistance in the New World Order.* New York: Basingstoke.

Gindin, S. (2018) "Socialism for realists." *Catalyst* 2(3).

Gindin, S. and Panitch, L. (2002) "Schätze und Schund. Eine Rezension zu 'Empire' von Hardt und Negri." Offenbach: Ränkeschmiede. Texte zur internationalen ArbeiterInnenbewegung. Nr. 13/Oktober.

Globe & Mail (1950a) "Meat famine faces north," 22 August.

Globe & Mail (1950b) "300,000 workers idle; Toronto lucky so far," 24 August.

Globe & Mail (1950c) "1,000 layoffs daily in Ontario over strike; Meat prices take jump," 26 August.

Globe & Mail (1950d) "700,000 unemployed expected within week; Ontario suffers least," 25 August.

Globe & Mail (1950e) "Let's be in the poorhouse together, says Mosher," 24 August.

Globe & Mail (1950f) "Government plans ultimatum: Work or lose pension," 28 August.

Glotz, P. (1985) *Manifest Fur Eine Neue Europaische Linke.* Berlin: Wolf Jobst Siedler Verlag Gmbh.

Glotz, P. (1986) *Μανιφέστο για τη Νέα Ευρωπαϊκή Αριστερά, Αθήνα, Οδυσσέας.* Athens: Odysseas.

Glyn, A. and Sutcliffe, B. (1972) *Capitalism in Crisis.* New York: Pantheon Books.

Goertzel, T.G. (1976) *Political Society.* Chicago: Rand McNally.

Gold, D.A., Lo, C.Y.H. and Wright, E.O. (1975a) "Recent developments in Marxist theories of the capitalist state, part I." *Monthly Review* 27: 29–43.

Gold, D.A., Lo, C.Y.H. and Wright, E.O. (1975b) "Recent developments in Marxist theories of the capitalist state, part II." *Monthly Review* 27: 36–51.

Gorz, A. (1968) "Reform and revolution." In Miliband, R. and Saville, J. (eds.) *Socialist Register 1968.* London: Merlin Press.

Gorz. A. (1982) *Farewell to the Working Class.* London: Pluto Press.

Gough, I. 1979. *The Political Economy of the Welfare State.* London: Macmillan Press, Ltd.

Gouldner, A.W. (1979) *The Future of Intellectuals and the Rise of the New Class.* New York: Continuum.

Government Office for Science (2013) *Future of the civil service: Making the most of scientists and engineers: Executive Summary.* London: Department for Business, Innovation and Skills. Available at: https://assets.publishing.service.gov.uk/government/uploads/system/uploads/attachment_data/file/283203/bis-13-594es-review-science-engineering-in-civil-service-summary.pdf.

Government of Saskatchewan (2007) *Speech from the Throne 2007: Securing the Future.* Regina.

Graham Jr., O.L. (1976) *Toward a Planned Society: From Roosevelt to Nixon.* New York: Oxford University Press.

Graham, P. with McKay, I. (2019) *Radical Ambition: The New Left in Toronto.* Toronto: Between the Lines.

Gramsci, A. (1971) *Selections from the Prison Notebooks.* Translated and edited by Q. Hoare and G. Nowell Smith. New York: International Publishers.

Granja, J. Yannelis, C. Makridis, C. and Zwick, E. (2020) "Did the Paycheck Protection Program hit the target?" *SSRN.* Available at: https://papers.ssrn.com/sol3/papers.cfm?abstract_id=3585258.

Grayson J.P. (1979) "Review of *The Canadian State: Political and Political Power* by Leo Panitch." *American Political Science Review,* Vol. 73(2): 651–52.

Greater London Council (1985) *LIS: London Industrial Strategy.* London: Greater London Council.

Green, J. (2019) "AOC's organizing app is spreading to democratic socialist campaigns." *Bloomberg Businessweek,* 26 March. Available at: https://www.bloomberg.com/news/articles/2019-03-26/aoc-reach-app-helps-build-voter-support-for-democratic-socialists.

Green, M.E. and Ives, P. (2009) "Subalternity and language: Overcoming the fragmentation of common sense." *Historical Materialism* 17: 3–30.

Grugel, J. and Riggiriozzi, P. (2018) "Neoliberal disruption and neoliberalism's afterlife in Latin America: What is left of post-neoliberalism?" *Critical Social Policy* 38(3): 547–66.

Haas, E.B. (1958) *The Uniting of Europe: Political, Social and Economic Forces, 1950–1957.* Stanford: Stanford University Press.

Habermas, J. (1970) *Toward a Rational Society.* Boston: Beacon Press.

Habermas, J. (1998) "Die postnationale Konstellation und die Zukunft der Demokratie." In *Die postnationale Konstellation. Politische Essays.* Frankfurt/Main: Suhrkamp.

Habermas, J. (1999) "The European nation-state and the pressures of globalization." *New Left Review* 235: 46–59.

Habermas, J. (2001) *The Postnational Constellation: Political Essays.* Translated and edited by Max Pensky. Cambridge: Polity Press.

Hahnel, R. (2012) *Of the People, By the People.* Chico, CA: AK Press.

Hall, J.A. and Ikenberry, G.J. (1989) *The State.* Minneapolis: University of Minnesota Press.

Hanna, D. (2016) *What Next.* London: Head of Zeus.

Hansard Society (2019) *Audit of Political Engagement 16: The 2019 Report.* London: Hansard Society. Available at: https://www.hansardsociety.org.uk/publications/reports/audit-of-political-engagement-16.

Hardt, M. and Negri, A. (2000) *Empire.* Cambridge, Massachusetts: Harvard University Press.

Harris, A. (2020) "Bernie Sanders reached out to Black voters. Why didn't it work? *The Atlantic*, 10 March. Available at: https://www.theatlantic.com/politics/archive/2020/03/bernie-sanders-black-voters/607789/.

Harvey, D. (1999) *The Limits to Capital.* London: Verso Books.

Harvey, D. (2001) *Spaces of Capital: Towards a Critical Geography.* New York: Routledge Press.

Harvey, D. (2003) *The New Imperialism.* Oxford: Oxford University Press.

Harvey, D. (2005) *A Short History of Neoliberalism.* New York: Oxford University Press.

Harvey, D. (2007) "In what ways is 'The New Imperialism' really new?" *Historical Materialism* 15(3): 57–70.

Harvey, D. (2018a) *Marx, Capital and the Madness of Economic Reason.* Oxford: Oxford University Press.

Harvey, D. (2018b) "Realities on the ground: David Harvey replies to John Smith." *Review of African Political Economy.* Available at: http://roape.net/2018/02/05/realities-ground-david-harvey-replies-john-smith/.

Harvey, D. (2020) "David Harvey: We need a collective response to the collective dilemma of coronavirus." *Jacobin.* Available at: https://jacobinmag.com/2020/4/david-harvey-coronavirus-pandemic-capital-economy.

Hayek, F. (1945) "The use of knowledge in a society." *American Economic Review* 35(4): 519–530. Available at: https://www.econlib.org/library/Essays/hykKnw.html.

Health Services and Support – Facilities Subsector Bargaining Assn. v. British Columbia, [2007] 2 SCR 391.

Heider, D. (ed.) (2004) *Class and News.* Lanham: Rowman and Littlefield.

Heitmeyer, W. (2018) *Autoritäre Versuchungen.* Berlin: Suhrkamp.

Held, D. (1995) *Democracy and the Global Order: From the Modern State to Cosmopolitan Governance.* Stanford: Stanford University Press.

Held, D., McGrew, A., Goldblatt, D. and Perraton, J. (1999) *Global Transformations. Politics, Economics and Culture.* Stanford: Stanford University Press.

Held, D. and McGrew, A. (eds.) (2000) *The Global Transformations Reader: An Introduction to the Globalization Debate.* Cambridge: Polity Press.

Henri-Levy, B. (1977) *Barbarism with a Human Face.* New York: Harper and Row.

Henwood, D. (2018) "Trump and the new billionaire class." In Panitch, L. and Albo, G. (eds.) *Socialist Register 2019: A World Turned Upside Down?* London: Merlin Press.

Henwood, D. (2020) "We have no choice but to be radical." *Jacobin,* July 30, 2020. Available at: https://www.jacobinmag.com/2020/07/green-new-deal-unemployment -economic-crisis.

Heron, C. and Smith, C. (2020) *A Short History of the Canadian Labour Movement,* 4th Edition. Toronto: Lorimer.

Hibbs Jr., D.A. (1976) "Industrial conflict in advanced industrial societies." *The American Political Science Review* 70(4): 1033–1058.

Hill, K.Q. and Leighley, J.E. (1992) "The policy consequences of class bias in state electorates." *American Journal of Political Science* 36(2): 351–365.

Himmelstein, D. and Woolhandler, S. (2020) Personal Interview, April 20.

Hindess, B. (1971) *The Decline of Working-Class Politics.* London: MacGibbon & Kee Ltd.

Hirsch, H. (1995) *Der nationale Wettbewerbstaat. Staat, Demokratie und Politik im globalen Kapitalismus.* Berlin/Amsterdam: Edition ID-Archiv.

Hirst, P. and Thompson, G. (1996) *Globalization in Question: The International Economy and the Possibilities of Governance.* Cambridge, England: Polity Press.

HM Government (2016) *Northern Powerhouse strategy.* Available at: https://www.gov. uk/government/publications/northern-powerhouse-strategy.

Hobsbawm, E.J. (1968) "Karl Marx's contribution to historiography." *Diogenes* 16(64): 37–56.

Hobsbawm, E. (1996 [1990]) *Nationen und Nationalismus. Mythos und Realität seit 1780.* Frankfurt: Campus Verlag.

Hollander, T. (2018) *Power, Politics, and Principles: Mackenzie King and Labour, 1935–1948.* Toronto: University of Toronto Press.

Holloway, J. (1994) "Global capital and the national state." *Capital and Class* 18(1): 23–49.

Holloway, J. and S. Picciotto (eds.) (1978a) *State and capital. A Marxist Debate.* London: Edward Arnold.

Holloway, J. and S. Picciotto (1978b) "Introduction: Towards a materialist theory of the state." in Holloway, J. and Picciotto, S. (eds.) *State and capital. A Marxist debate.* London: Edward Arnold.

Holtzman, L. and Sharpe, L. (eds) (2015) *Media Messages.* New York: Routledge Press.

House of Representatives, Select Subcommittee on the Coronavirus Crisis (2020) "Preliminary analysis of paycheck protection program data." *Congress of the United States.* Available at: https://coronavirus.house.gov/sites/democrats.coronavirus.house.gov/files/2020-09-01.PPP%20Interim%20Report.pdf.

Hudis, P. (2013) *Marx's Concept of the Alternative to Capitalism.* Chicago: Haymarket Books.

Hunter, P. and Holden, D. (2015) *Who Governs Britain: A Profile of MPs in the 2015 Parliament.* London: The Smith Institute.

Huws, U. (2020) "Reaping the whirlwind: Digitalization, restructuring, and mobilization in the Covid crisis." In Panitch, L. and Albo, G. (eds.) *Socialist Register 2021: Beyond Digital Capitalism. New Ways of Living.* London: Merlin Press.

Hymer, S. (1979) *The Multinational Corporation: A Radical Approach.* Cambridge: Cambridge University Press.

IMF (2020) "Kurzarbeit: Germany's short-time work benefit." *IMF News,* 15 June. Available at: https://www.imf.org/en/News/Articles/2020/06/11/na061120-kurzarbeit -germanys-short-time-work-benefit.

International Labour Organization (1996–2017) *Freedom of association cases.* Available at: http://ilo.org/dyn/normlex/en/f?p=NORMLEXPUB:20060:0::NO:::.

Jackson, A. and Thomas, M.P. (2017) *Work and Labour in Canada: Critical Issues.* Toronto: Canadian Scholars Press.

Jacobs, E. (2012) *Understanding America's White Working Class: Their Politics, Voting Habits, and Policy Priorities.* Governance Studies at Brookings.

Janda, K. (1970) *A Conceptual Framework for Comparative Analyses of Political Parties.* Beverly Hills: Sage Publications.

Jenkins, R. (1987) *Transnational Corporations and Uneven Development: The Internationalization of Capital and the Third World.* London: Methuen.

Jessop, B. (1977) "Recent theories of the capitalist state." *Cambridge Journal of Economics* 1(4): 353–73.

Jessop, B. (1982) *The Capitalist State: Marxist Theories and Methods.* New York: New York University Press.

Jessop, B. (1990) *State Theory: Putting the Capitalist State in its Place.* Cambridge/ Oxford: Polity Press, 1990.

Jessop, B. (1991) "On the originality, legacy, and actuality of Nico Poulantzas." *Studies in Political Economy* 34(1): 75–107.

Jessop, B. (2002) *The Future of the Capitalist State.* Cambridge: Polity Press.

Jessop, B. (2011) "Poulantzas's State, Power, Socialism as a modern classic." In Gallas, A., Bretthauer, L., Kannankulam, J. and Stutzle, I. (eds.) *Reading Poulantzas.* London: Merlin Press.

Johns Hopkins' Corona Virus Resource Center (2020) *Mortality Analysis*. Available at: https://coronavirus.jhu.edu/data/mortality.

Kannankulam, J. (2003) "Authoritarian statism and right-wing populism." Paper submitted to the Workshop on State and Globalisation: Perspectives from Germany and Turkey. Frankfurt University.

Karitzis, A. (2017) *The European Left in Times of Crisis*. Amsterdam: Transnational Institut.

Katz, C. (2014) "¿Quées el neo-desarrollismo? I- Una visión crítica. Economía." *La página de Claudio Katz*. Available at: https://katz.lahaine.org/que-es-el-neo-desarrollismo-i-una-vision-critica-economia/.

Kautsky, K. (2011 [1925]) *The Labour Revolution*. Translated by H.J. Stenning. Abingdon and New York: Routledge Press.

Kennard, M. (2019) "How the UK military and intelligence establishment is working to stop Jeremy Corbyn becoming prime minister." *The Daily Maverick*, 4 December. Available at: https://www.dailymaverick.co.za/article/2019-12-04-how-the-uk-military-and-intelligence-establishment-is-working-to-stop-jeremy-corbyn-from-becoming-prime-minister.

Kennedy, G. (2009) "Republican discourses and imperial projects: Liberty and empire in American political discourse." *Spectrum: Journal of Global Politics* 1(1): 53–68.

Kesselman, M. (1982) "The state and class struggle trends in Marxist political science." In Ollman, B. and Vernoff, E. (eds.) *The Left Academy: Marxist Scholarship on American Campuses*. New York: McGraw Hill.

Keucheyan, R. (2013) *The Left Hemisphere: Mapping Critical Theory Today*. London: Verso Books.

King, A. and Crew, I. (2013) *The Blunders of Our Governments*. London: Oneworld.

Kirchner, N. (2003) "Discurso del Señor Presidente de la Nación Doctor Néstor Kirchner ante la Honorable Asamblea Legislativa." 25 May.

Kolko, G. (1963) *The Triumph of American Conservativism: A Reinterpretation of American History, 1900–1916*. New York: Free Press.

Konings, M. (2015) *The Emotional Logic of Capitalism*. Stanford: Stanford University Press.

Konings, M. (2018) *Capital and Time: For a New Critique of Neoliberal Reason*. Stanford: Stanford University Press.

Koop, R. (2012) "Marketing and efficacy: Does political marketing empower Canadians?" In Marland, A., Giasson, T. and Lees-Marshment, J. (eds.) *Political Marketing in Canada*. Vancouver: UBC Press.

Kozul-Wright, R. (1995) "Transnational corporations and the nation state." in Michie, J. and Smith, J.G. (eds.) *Managing the Global Economy*. Oxford: Oxford University Press.

Kozul-Wright, R. and Rowthorn, R. (1998) *Transnational Corporations and the Global Economy*. London: Macmillan.

Kramer, R. and Mitchell, T. (2010) *When The State Trembled: How A.J. Andrews and the Citizens' Committee Broke the Winnipeg General Strike*. Toronto: University of Toronto Press.

Kromrei, G. (2020) "Real estate donors backing Biden over Trump." *The Real Deal*, 10 September. Available at: https://therealdeal.com/2020/09/10/real-estate-donors-backing-biden-over-trump/.

Kulfas, M. (2016) *Los tres kirchnerismos: una historia de la economía argentina*. Buenos Aires: Siglo XXI Editores.

Laclau, E. (1975) "The specificity of the political: The Poulantzas-Miliband Debate." *Economy and Society* 5: 87–110.

Laclau, E. and Mouffe, C. (1985) *Hegemony and Socialist Strategy: Towards a Radical Democratic Politics*. London: Verso Books.

Lange, O. (1973 [1967]) "The computer and the market." In Nove, A. and Nuti, D.M. (eds.) *Socialist Economics*. Middlesex, U.K.: Penguin Books.

Larcinese, V. (2007) "Voting over redistribution and the size of the welfare state: The role of turnout." *Political Studies* 55(3): 568–85.

Lebowitz, M. (2012) *The Contradictions of Real Socialism*. New York: Monthly Review Press.

Lebowitz, M. (2016) "What is socialism for the twenty-first century?" *Monthly Review* 68(5). Available at: https://monthlyreview.org/2016/10/01/what-is-socialism-for-the-twenty-first-century/.

Lee, B. (2019) "Overview of the far right." Commission for Countering Extremism. Available at: https://www.gov.uk/government/publications/overview-of-the-far-right.

Lees-Marshment, J. (2001) "The marriage of politics and marketing." *Political Studies* 49(4): 692–713.

Lefort, C. (1988) *Democracy and Political Theory*. Cambridge: Polity Press.

Lefort, C. (2012) *Machiavelli in the Making*. Evanston: Northwestern University Press.

Le Goff, J. (1988) *Your Money or Your Life*. New York: Zone Books.

Lehmbruch, G. and Schmitter, P.C. (eds.) (1982) *Patterns of Corporatist Policy-Making*. Beverly Hills: Sage Publications.

Lehndorff, S., Dribbusch, H. and Schulten, T. (eds.) (2017) *Rough Waters: European Trade Unions in a Time of Crisis*. Brussels: European Trade Union Institute.

Lembcke, J. (1988) *Capitalist Development and Class Capacities: Marxist Theory and Union Organization*. Westport, Conn.: Greenwood Press.

Lenin, V.I. (1970 [1917]) "State and revolution." In *V.I. Lenin Collected Works*. Moscow: Progress Publishers.

Lenin, V.I. (1996 [1917]) *Imperialism: The Highest Stage of Capitalism*. London: Pluto Press.

Lenin, V.I. (1925) "State and revolution." In *Selected Works,* Volume 2. Moscow: Progress Publishers.

Leys, C. (2012) "The dissolution of the mandarins: The sell-off of the British state." *Open Democracy*, 15 June. Available at: https://www.opendemocracy.net/en/opendemoc-racyuk/dissolution-of-mandarins-sell-off-of-british-state.

Leys, C. (2016) "The English NHS: From market failure to trust, professionalism and democracy." *Soundings* 64: 11–40.

Lindblom, C.E. (1982) "The market as prison." *Journal of Politics* 44(2): 324–32.

Lipset, S.M. (1963) *Political Man*. New York: Anchor Books.

Lisdorf, A. (2020) "Open-source medical supplies battle COVID-19." *Shareable*, 14 April. Available at: https://www.shareable.net/open-source-medical-supplies-bat-tle-covid-19/.

List, W. (1950) "Unions work on new set of proposals." *Globe & Mail*, 22 August.

Lister, M. (2007) "Institutions, inequality and social norms: Explaining variations in participation." *British Journal of Politics and International Relations* 9: 20–35.

Liu, H. and Volker, D. (2020) "Where have the Paycheck Protection loans gone so far?" *Federal Reserve Bank of New York*, 6 May 2020. Available at: https://libertystreete-conomics.newyorkfed.org/2020/05/where-have-the-paycheck-protection-loans-gone-so-far.html.

Logiudice, A. (2011) "Pobreza y neoliberalismo: La asistencia social en la Argentina reciente." *Entramados y Perspectivas* 1(1): 61–90.

London-Edinburgh Weekend Return Group (1980) *In and Against the State*, 2nd edi-tion. London: Pluto Press.

Long, S. and McCarthy, J. (2020) "Two in three Americans support racial justice pro-test." *Gallup*, 28 July. Available at: https://news.gallup.com/poll/316106/two-three-americans-support-racial-justice-protests.aspx.

Luxemburg, R. (1940 [1918]) *The Russian Revolution*. New Yorker: Workers Age.

Lyotard, J.F. (1984) *The Post-Modern Condition: A Report on Knowledge*. Minneapolis: University of Minnesota Press.

Macdonnell, D. (1986) *Theories of Discourse: An Introduction*. Oxford: Basil Blackwell.

MacGilvray, E. (2011) *The Invention of Market Freedom*. Cambridge: Cambridge University Press.

MacLeod, A. (2019) "Study reveals How UK intelligence works with media to Smear Jeremy Corbyn." *MintPress News*, 6 December. Available at: https://www.mintpress-news.com/new-study-reveals-uk-intelligence-smear-campaign-against-jeremy-corbyn/263231/.

Macridis, R. (ed.) (1967) *Political Parties*. New York: Harper & Row.

Magri, L. (1970) "Problems of the Marxist theory of the revolutionary party." *New Left Review* 60: 97–128.

Maher, S., Gindin, S. and Panitch, L. (2019) "Class politics, socialist policies, capitalist constraints." In Panitch, L. and Albo, G. (eds.) *Socialist Register 2020: Beyond Market Dystopia, New Ways of Living*. London: Merlin Press.

Mahler, H., Fisahn, A., Wahl, P. and Eberhardt-Köster, T. (2018) *EU in der Krise: Hintergründe, Ursachen, Alternativen.* Hamburg: Vsa Verlag.

Mair, P. (2013) *Ruling the Void.* London: Verso Books.

Mandel, D. (2017) *Democracy, Plan and Market: Yakov Kronrod's Political Economy of Socialism.* Germany: ibidem Press.

Mandel, E. (1967) "International capitalism and 'supranationality'." In Miliband, R. and Saville, J. (eds.) *The Socialist Register 1967.* New York: Monthly Review Press.

Mandel, E. (1970) *Europe versus America? Contradictions of Imperialism.* London: New Left Books.

Mandel, E. (1971) *The Marxist Theory of the State.* London: Pathfinder Press.

Mandel, E. (1988) "The myth of market socialism." *New Left Review* 169: 108–120.

Manin, B. (1997) *The Principles of Representative Government.* Cambridge: Cambridge University Press.

Manzer, R. (1978) "Review of *The Canadian State: Political and Political Power* by Leo Panitch." *Canadian Public Policy* 4(3): 405–08.

March, J.G. and Olsen, J.P. (1984) "The New Institutionalism: Organizational factors in political life." *American Political Science Review* 78(3): 734–49.

Marchart, O. (2007) *Post-Foundational Political Thought: Political Difference in Nancy, Lefort, Badiou and Laclau.* Edinburgh: Edinburgh University Press.

Martinez, A.G. (2019) "How Alexandria Ocasio-Cortez shapes a new political reality." *Wired*, 9 January. Available at: https://www.wired.com/story/how-alexandria-ocasio-cortez-shapes-new-political-reality/.

Marx, K. (1850) "England's 17th Century Revolution." *Marxists Internet Archive*. Available at: https://www.marxists.org/archive/marx/works/1850/02/english-revolution.htm.

Marx, K. (1966 [1875]) *Critique of the Gotha Programme.* New York: International Publishers.

Marx, K. (1968) "The Eighteenth Brumaire of Louis Bonaparte." In Marx, K. and Engels, F. *Selected Works.* Moscow: Progress Publishers.

Marx, K. (1976) *Capital: A Critique of Political Economy*, Volume 1. London: Penguin Books.

Marx, K. (1979 [1852]) "The Eighteenth Brumaire of Louis Bonaparte" In *Marx-Engels Collected Works*, Vol. 11. London: Lawrence & Wishart.

Marx, K. (1993 [1939]) *Grundrisse.* London: Penguin Books.

Marx, K. (1996 [1885]) "Capital: A critique of political economy, Vol. 2: The process of circulation in capital." In *Marx-Engels Collected Works*, Vol. 36. London: Lawrence & Wishart.

Marx, K. (1998 [1894]) "Capital: A critique of political economy, Vol. 3: The process of capitalist production as a whole." In *Marx-Engels Collected Works*, Vol. 37. London: Lawrence & Wishart.

Marx, K. and Engels F. (1976a [1846]) "The German ideology." In *Marx Engels Collected Works*, Vol. 5. London: Lawrence & Wishart.

Marx, K. and Engels, F. (1976b [1848]) "The Communist Manifesto." In *Marx-Engels Collected Works*, Vol. 6 (Autumn 1845- March 1848). London: Lawrence & Wishart.

Marx, K. and Engels, F. (1998 [1848]) *The Communist Manifesto*. Rendelsham, U.K.: Merlin Press.

Marx, K. and Engels, F. (2012 [1848]) *The Communist Manifesto*. London: Verso Books.

Massetti, A. (2010) "Limitaciones de los movimientos sociales en la construcción de un estado progresista en Argentina." *Argumentos. Revista de crítica social* 12: 81–108.

Massey, D. and Wainwright, H. (1986) "Beyond the coalfields: The work of the miners' support groups." In Beynon, H. (ed.) *Digging Deeper*. London: Verso Books.

Mazzucato, M. (2013) *The Entrepreneurial State: Debunking Public vs. Private Myths*. London: Anthem.

Mbembe, A. (2020) "The universal right to breathe." Translated by C. Shred. *In the Moment*, 13 April. Available at: https://critinq.wordpress.com/2020/04/13/the-universal-right-to-breathe/.

McCarthy, S. (2018) "Retailers urge Ottawa to end rotating postal strike." *Globe & Mail*, 19 November.

McCartin, J.A. (2011) "The strike that busted unions." *The New York Times*, 2 August. Available at: https://www.nytimes.com/2011/08/03/opinion/reagan-vs-patco-the-strike-that-busted-unions.html.

McGrane, D. (2019) *The New NDP: Moderation, Modernization, and Political Marketing*. Vancouver: UBC Press.

McInnis, P. (2002) *Harnessing Labour Confrontation: Shaping the Postwar Settlement in Canada, 1943–1950*. Toronto: University of Toronto Press.

McInnis, P. (2012) "'Hothead troubles': Sixties-era wildcat strikes in Canada." In Campbell, L., Clément, D. and Kealey, G. (eds.) *Debating Dissent: Canada and the Sixties*. Toronto: University of Toronto Press.

McNally, D. (1993) *Against the Market: Political Economy, Market Socialism and the Marxist Critique*. New York: Verso Books.

McNally, D. (2003) "Beyond the false infinity of capital: Dialectics and self-mediation in Marx's theory of freedom." in Albritton, R. and Simoulidis, J. (eds) *New Dialectics and Political Economy*. New York: Palgrave Press.

Media Reform Coalition. (2016) *Jeremy Corbyn*. Available at: https://www.mediareform.org.uk/tag/jeremy-corbyn.

Medina, E. (2011) *Cybernetic Revolutionaries: Technology and Politics in Allende's Chile*. Cambridge, MA: MIT Press.

Meier, G. (1972) "Private foreign investment." In Dunning, J. (ed.) *International Investment*. Harmondsworth: Penguin Books.

Meiksins, P.F. (1989) "A critique of Wright's theory of contradictory class." In *The Debate on Classes*. London: Verso Books.

Melzer, N. (2019) "Demasking the torture of Julian Assange." *Medium.com*, 26 June. Available at: https://medium.com/@njmelzer/demasking-the-torture-of-julian -assange-b252ffdcb768.

Menon, A. and Bevington, M. (2018) "The economic cost of Brexit is unavoidable – but that doesn't mean it's not worth it." *The Conversation*, 29 November. Available at: https://theconversation.com/the-economic-cost-of-brexit-is-unavoidable-but-that-doesnt-mean-its-not-worth-it-107913.

Merkel, P.H. (1970) *Modern Comparative Politics*. Illinois: The Dryden Press.

Merrick, R. (2018) "Brexit: Leave 'very likely' won EU referendum due to illegal over-spending, says Oxford professor's evidence to High Court." *The Independent*, 5 December. Available at: https://www.independent.co.uk/news/uk/politics/vote-leave-referendum-overspending-high-court-brexit-legal-challenge-void-oxford-professor-a8668771.html.

Meslin, D. (2019) *Teardown: Rebuilding Democracy from the Ground Up*. Toronto: Penguin Books.

Meyer, D. (2020) " 'We will do this together': Germany will continue subsidizing work-ers' wages through the end of 2021." *Fortune*, 26 August. Available at: https://fortune.com/2020/08/26/germany-extends-kurzarbeit-pandemic-wage-support/.

Meyer-Larsen, W. (2000) *Germany, Inc.: The New German Juggernaut and its Challenge to World Business*. New York: John Wiley.

Miliband, R. (1969) *The State in Capitalist Society*. New York: Basic Books.

Miliband, R. (1970) "The capitalist state: Reply to Poulantzas." *New Left Review* 59: 53–60.

Miliband, R. (1973) "Poulantzas and the capitalist state." *New Left Review* 82: 83–92.

Miliband, R. (2009 [1961]) *Parliamentary Socialism*. London: Merlin Press.

Miliband, R., Liebman, M., Saville, J. and Panitch, L. (eds.) (1986) *Socialist Register 1985/ 86: Social Democracy and After*. London: Merlin Press.

Millar, F.D. (1980) "Shapes of power: The Ontario Labour Relations Board, 1944–1950." Phd Thesis, York University.

Mills, C.W. (1956) *The Power Elite*. Oxford: Oxford University Press.

Mills, T. (2016) *The BBC: Myth of a Public Service*. London: Verso Books.

Mills, T. (2017) "Democracy and public broadcasting." In Panitch, L. and Albo, G. (eds.) *Socialist Register 2018: Rethinking Democracy*. London: Merlin Press.

Mills, T. (2019) "The BBC's fabled impartiality was only ever an elite consensus." *The Guardian*, 24 November. Available at: https://www.theguardian.com/commentis-free/2019/nov/24/bbc-impartiality-elite-consensus-crisis-legitimacy.

Milton, J. (2020) "Oshawa could be the engine of a Green New Deal in Canada." *The Bullet*, 4 March. Available at: https://socialistproject.ca/2020/03/oshawa-could-be-the-engine-of-a-green-new-deal-in-canada/.

Mirowski, P. (2013) *Never Let a Serious Crisis Go to Waste: How Neoliberalism Survived the Financial Meltdown*. London/New York: Verso Books.

Mitchell, T. (1991) "The limits of the state: Beyond statist approaches and their critics." *American Political Science Review* 85(1): 77–96.

Mitchell, T. (1999) "Society, economy and the state effect." In Sharma, A. and Gupta, A. (eds.) *The Anthropology of the State*. Oxford: Blackwell.

Moore Jr., B. (1966) *Social Origins of Dictatorship and Democracy: Lord and Peasant in the Making of the Modern World*. Boston, Beacon Press.

Morais, L. and Saad Filho, A. (2012) "Neo-developmentalism and the challenges of economic policy-making under Dilma Rousseff." *Critical Sociology* 38(6): 789–98.

Morgan, N. (2020) "Nicky Morgan's speech on the future of media and broadcasting." Department for Digital, Culture, Media and Sport. Available at: https://www.gov.uk/government/speeches/nicky-morgans-speech-on-the-future-of-media-and-broadcasting.

Morozov, E. (2019) "Digital socialism? The calculation debate in the age of big data." *New Left Review* 116. Available at: https://newleftreview.org/issues/II116/articles/evgeny-morozov-digital-socialism.

Morris, W. (1889) "Bellamy's looking backward." *Commonweal*, 21 June. Available at: https://www.marxists.org/archive/morris/works/1889/commonweal/06-bellamy.htm.

Morton, D. (2007) *Working People*, 5th Edition. Montreal: McGill-Queen's University Press.

Moschonas, G. (2002) *In the Name of Social Democracy: The Great Transformation – From 1945 to the Present*. London: Verso Books.

Mulhall, J. (2019) "Modernising and mainstreaming: The contemporary British far right." Commission for Countering Extremism. Available at: https://www.gov.uk/government/publications/modernising-and-mainstreaming-the-contemporary-british-far-right.

Mulhern, F. (1984) "Towards 2000: Or news from you-know-where." *New Left Review* 148: 5–30.

Münkler, H. and Münkler, M. (2019). *Abschied vom Abstieg. Eine Agenda für Deutschland*. Berlin: Rowohlt.

Murray, R. (1971) "The internationalization of capital and the nation state." *New Left Review* 67: 84–109.

Nachtwey, O. (2016) *Die Abstiegsgesellschaft*. Berlin: Suhrkamp Verlag.

Nardelli, A. (2015) "How the UK civil service has changed in 10 charts." *The Guardian*, 19 November. Available at: https://www.theguardian.com/politics/2015/nov/19/how-the-uk-civil-service-has-changed-in-10-charts.

Naylor, R.T. (1975) *The History of Canadian Business, 1867–1914 Volume II: Industrial Development*. Toronto: Lorimer.

Neilson, C. Humphries, J. and Ulyssea, G. (2020) "Information frictions and access to the Paycheck Protection Program." NBER Working Paper 27624. Available at: http://www.nber.org/papers/w27624.

Neiuwbeerta, P. and Ultee, W. (1999) Class voting in Western industrialized countries, 1945–1990: Systematizing and testing explanations." *European Journal of Political Research* 35: 123–160.

Neumann, S. (1956) *Modern Political Parties*. Chicago: University of Chicago Press.

Nickelsburg, M. (2019) The app that helped Alexandria Ocasio-Cortez get elected is spreading to progressive campaigns across the country. *GeekWire*, 24 January. Available at: https://www.geekwire.com/2019/app-helped-alexandria-ocasio-cortez-get-elected-spreading-progressive-campaigns-across-country/.

Niven, D. (2004) "The mobilization solution? Face-to-face contact and voter turnout in a municipal election." *The Journal of Politics* 66(3): 868–884.

Nordlinger, E.A. (1981) *On the Autonomy of the Democratic State*. Cambridge, Mass.: Harvard University Press.

Nunn, A. (2018) *The Candidate*. New York: OR Books.

O'Connor, J. (1973) *The Fiscal Crisis of the State*. New York: St. Martin's Press.

O'Leary, J. (2019) "Poverty in the UK: A guide to the facts and figures." *Full Fact*, 27 September. Available at: https://fullfact.org/economy/poverty-uk-guide-facts-and-figures/.

O'Toole, F. (2018) *Heroic Failure: Brexit and the Politics of Pain*. London: Head of Zeus.

Oesch, D. (2008) "The changing shape of class voting." *European Societies* 10(3): 329–355.

Ofcom (2019) *News Consumption in the UK: 2019*. Available at: https://www.ofcom.org.uk/__data/assets/pdf_file/0027/157914/uk-news-consumption-2019-report.pdf.

Offe, C. (1975) "The theory of the capitalist state and the problem of policy formation." In Lindberg, L. (ed.) *Stress and Contradiction in Modern Capitalism*. Lexington, Mass., D.C. Heath.

Offe, C. (1980) "The separation of form and content in liberal democratic politics." *Studies in Political Economy* 3: 5–16.

Offe, C. (1984) *Contradictions of the Welfare State*. Cambridge, Mass., M.I.T. Press.

Oficina Nacional de Crédito Público (2010) "Deuda pública del Estado Argentino: datos al 30-06-2010." Buenos Aires: Ministerio de Economía. Available at: http://www.mecon.gov.ar/finanzas/sfinan/documentos/informe_deuda_publica_30-06-10.pdf.

Oguz, S. (2015) "Rethinking globalization as internationalization of capital: Implications for understanding state restructuring." *Science & Society* 79(3): 336–62.

Ohmae, K. (1990) *The End of the National State*. New York: Free Press.

Okun, A.M. (1975) *Efficiency and Equality: The Big Tradeoff*. Washington, D.C.: Brookings Institution.

Ollman, B. (ed.) (1998) *Market Socialism: The Debate Among Socialists*. New York: Routledge Press.

Öniş, Z. (1998) *State and Market: The Political Economy of Turkey in Comparative Perspective*. Istanbul: Bogazici University Press.

Opportunity Insights (2020) *Opportunity Insights Economic Tracker.* Available at: https://www.tracktherecovery.org/.

Ormrod, R.P. (2006) "A critique of the Lees-Marshment market-oriented party model." *Politics* 26(2): 110–118.

Orren, K. and Skowronek, S. (1986) "Editor's preface." *Studies in American Political Development* 1: vii-viii.

Palloix, C. (1975) "The internationalization of capital and the circuit of social capital." In Radice, H. (ed.) *International Firms and Modern Imperialism.* London: Penguin Books.

Palloix, C. (1977) "The self-expansion of capital on a world scale." *Review of Radical Political Economics* 9(2): 3–17.

Palmer, B.D. (1987) "Labour protest and organization in nineteenth-century Canada, 1820–1890." *Labour/Le Travail* 20: 61–83.

Palmer, B.D. (1992) *Working Class Experience: Rethinking the History of Canadian Labour, 1800–1991.* Toronto: McClelland and Stewart.

Palmer, B.D. (2009) *Canada's 1960s: The Ironies of Identity in a Rebellious Era.* Toronto: University of Toronto Press.

Palmer, B.D. (2017) "Leo Panitch: Political passions and socialist sobriety." *Studies in Political Economy* 98(3): 324–332.

Panebianco, A. (1988) *Political Parties: Organization and Power.* Cambridge: Cambridge University Press.

Pangle, T.L. (1988) *The Spirit of Modern Republicanism: The Moral Vision of the American Founders and the Philosophy of Locke.* Chicago: University of Chicago Press.

Panitch, L. (1976) *Social Democracy and Industrial Militancy: The Labour Party, the Trade Unions and Incomes Policy, 1945–1974.* Cambridge: Cambridge University Press.

Panitch, L. (ed.) (1977a) *The Canadian State: Political Economy and Political Power.* Toronto: University of Toronto Press.

Panitch, L. (1977b) "The role and nature of the Canadian state." In *The Canadian State: Political Economy and Political Power.* Toronto: University of Toronto Press.

Panitch, L. (1981) "Dependency and class in Canadian political economy." *Studies in Political Economy* 6: 7–34.

Panitch, L. (1985) *Working-class Politics in Crisis: Essays on Labour and the State.* London: Verso.

Panitch, L. (1986a) *Working Class Politics in Crisis: Essays on Labour and the State.* London: Verso Books.

Panitch, L. (1986b) "The impasse of social democratic politics." In Miliband, R., Saville, J., Liebman, M. and Panitch, L. (eds.) *Socialist Register, 1985–1986.* London: Merlin Press.

Panitch, L. (1986c) "The state and the future of socialism." In *Working Class Politics in Crisis: Essays on Labour and the State.* London: Verso Books.

Panitch, L. (1992) "The NDP in power: Illusion and reality." *Studies in Political Economy* 37(1): 173–188.

362 REFERENCES

Panitch, L. (1993) "A different kind of state?" In Albo, G. Langille, D. and Panitch, L.
(eds.) A Different Kind of State? Popular Power and Democratic Administration.
Toronto: Oxford University Press.

Panitch, L. (1994) "Globalisation and the state." In Miliband, R. and Panitch, L. (eds.)
Socialist Register 1994: Between Globalism and Nationalism. New York: Monthly
Review Press.

Panitch, L. (1996) "Rethinking the role of the state." In Mittelman, J. (ed.) Globalization:
Critical Reflections. Boulder, CO: Lynn Rienner.

Panitch, L. (2000a) "Reflections on a strategy for labour." In Panitch, L. and Leys, C.
(eds.) Socialist Register 2001: Working Classes, Global Realities. London: Merlin Press.

Panitch, L. (2000b) "The new imperial state." New Left Review 2: 5–20.

Panitch, L. (2001) Renewing Socialism: Democracy, Strategy and Imagination. Colorado:
Westview Press.

Panitch, L. (2002) "The impoverishment of state theory." In Aronowitz, S. and Bratsis,
P. (eds.) Paradigm Lost: Revising State Theory. Minneapolis: University of Minnesota
Press.

Panitch, L. (2010) Giovanni Arrighi in Beijing: An alternative to capitalism?" Historical
Materialism 18(1): 74–87.

Panitch, L. (2013) "An exemplary intellectual." In Ehrlich, N, Marks, L. and Yuval-
Davis, N. (eds.) The Work of Avishai Ehrlich: Political Sociologist, Activist and Public
Intellectual. Newcastle: Cambridge Scholars Publishers.

Panitch, L. (2014) "Repensando o marxismo e o imperialismo para o século XXI."
Tensões mundiais, Fortaleza 10(18–19): 91–101.

Panitch, L. (2015) "BRICS, the G20 and American empire." In Bond, P. and Garcia, A.
(eds.) BRICS: An Anti-Capitalist Critique. Johannesburg: Jacana Media.

Panitch, L. (2016) "On revolutionary optimism of the intellect." in Panitch, L. and Albo,
G. (eds.) Socialist Register 2017: Rethinking Revolution. London: Merlin Press.

Panitch, L. (2018) "Democratizing the party and the state: Transcending the limits of
the left." In Gray, P.C. (ed.) From the Streets to the State: Changing the World by Taking
Power. Albany: State University of New York Press.

Panitch, L. (2019) "Ralph Miliband's masterpiece at 50." Jacobin, 16 June. Available
at: https://www.jacobinmag.com/2019/06/ralph-miliband-state-capitalist-society.

Panitch, L. and Albo, G. (eds.) (2014) Socialist Register 2015: Transforming Classes.
London: Merlin Press.

Panitch, L. and Albo, G. (eds.) (2016) Rethinking Revolution: Socialist Register 2017.
London: Merlin Press.

Panitch, L., Albo, G. and Chibber, V. (eds.) (2011) Socialist Register 2012: The Crisis and
the Left. London: The Merlin Press.

Panitch, L., Albo, G. and Chibber, V. (eds.) (2013) Socialist Register 2014: Registering
Class. London: Merlin Press.

Panitch, L. and Gindin, S. (2000) "Transcending pessimism, rekindling socialist imagination." In Panitch, L. and Leys, C. (eds.) *Socialist Register 2000: Necessary and Unnecessary Utopias*. London: Merlin Press.

Panitch, L. and Gindin, S. (2002) "Gems and baubles in Empire." *Historical Materialism* 10(2): 17–43.

Panitch, L. and Gindin, S. (2004a) "American imperialism and Euro-capitalism: The making of neoliberal globalization." *Studies in Political Economy* 71(1): 7–38.

Panitch, L. and Gindin, S. (2004b) "Global capitalism and American empire." In Panitch, L. and Leys, C. (eds.) *Socialist Register 2004: The New Imperial Challenge*. London: Merlin Press.

Panitch, L. and Gindin, S. (2004c) "Finance and American empire." In Panitch, L. and Leys, C. (eds.) *Socialist Register 2005: The Empire Reloaded*. London: Merlin Press.

Panitch, L. and Gindin, S. (2005a) "Euro-capitalism and American empire." In Coates, D. (ed.) *Varieties of Capitalism, Varieties of Approaches*. London: Macmillan-Palgrave.

Panitch, L. and Gindin, S. (2005b) "Superintending global capital." *New Left Review* 35: 101–123.

Panitch, L. and Gindin, S. (2006a) "Bringing the working class in: Michael Lebowitz's Beyond 'Capital'." *Historical Materialism* 14(2): 113–34.

Panitch, L. and Gindin, S. (2006b) "Capitalismo global e o império norte-americano." In Panitch, L. and Leys, C. (eds.) *Socialist Register 2004: El Nuevo Desafío Imperial*. Buenos Aires: CLACSO.

Panitch, L. and Gindin, S. (2012) *The Making of Global Capitalism: The Political Economy of American Empire*. New York: Verso Books.

Panitch, L. and Gindin, S. (2013) "The integration of China into global capitalism." *International Critical Thought* 2: 146–158.

Panitch, L. and Gindin, S. (2015) "Marxist theory and strategy: Getting somewhere better." *Historical Materialism* 23(2): 3–22.

Panitch, L. and Gindin, S. (2016) "Class, party, and the challenge of state transformation." In Panitch, L. and Albo, G. (eds.) *Socialist Register 2017: Rethinking Revolution*. London: Merlin Press.

Panitch, L. and Gindin, S. (2018a) *The Socialist Challenge Today*. London: Merlin Press.

Panitch, L. and Gindin, S. (2018b) "Trumping the empire." In Panitch, L. and Albo, G. (eds.) *Socialist Register 2019: A World Turned Upside Down?* London: Merlin Press.

Panitch, L., Gindin, S. and Maher, S. (2020) *The Socialist Challenge Today: Syriza, Corbyn, Sanders*. Chicago: Haymarket Books.

Panitch, L. and Konings, M. (eds.) (2009) *American Empire and the Political Economy of Global Finance*. Houndsmill, Basingtoke: Palgrave Macmillan.

Panitch L., Konings, M., Gindin, S. and Aquanno, S. (2009) "The political economy of the subprime crisis." In Panitch, L. and Konings, M. (eds.) *American Empire and the Political Economy of Global Finance*. Basingstoke: Palgrave Macmillan.

Panitch, L. and Leys, C. (1997) *The End of Parliamentary Socialism: From New Left to New Labour*. London: Verso Books.

Panitch, L. and Leys, C. (2001) *The End of Parliamentary Socialism: From New Left to New Labour*, 2nd edition. London: Verso Books.

Panitch, L. and Leys, C. (2020) *Searching for Socialism: The Project of the Labour New Left from Benn to Corbyn*. London: Verso Books.

Panitch, L. and Swartz, D. (1984) "Towards permanent exceptionalism: Coercion and consent in Canadian industrial relations." *Labour/Le Travail* 13: 133–157.

Panitch, L. and Swartz, D. (1988) *The Assault on Trade Union Freedoms: From Consent to Coercion Revisited*. Toronto: Garamond.

Panitch, L. and Swartz, D. (2003) *From Consent to Coercion: The Assault on Trade Union Freedoms*. Toronto: Garamond.

Pareto, V. (1966) *Sociological Writings*. Edited by S.E. Finer and translated by D. Mirfin. New York: Frederick A. Praeger.

Parker, G. (2019) "Boris Johnson weighs three potential Brexit scenarios." *Financial Times*, 2 October. Available at: https://www.ft.com/content/e81bd39e-e455-11e9-9743-db5a370481bc.

Parnaby, A. (2006) "'The best men that ever worked the lumber': Aboriginal longshoremen on Burrard Inlet, BC, 1863–1939." *Canadian Historical Review* 87(1): 1–15.

Parrot, J.C. (2005) *My Union, My Life: Jean-Claude Parrot and the Canadian Union of Postal Workers*. Halifax: 2005.

Patroni, V. (2018) "Uncertain transitions." In Posner, P.W., Patroni, V. and Mayer, J.F. (eds.) *Labor Politics in Latin America: Democracy and Worker Organization in the Neoliberal Era*. Gainesville: University of Florida Press.

Peck, J. and Tickell, A. (2002) "Neoliberalizing space." *Antipode* 34(3): 380–404.

Pedwell, T. (2018) "Postal union to fight back-to-work bill: Vote on speeding legislation through House of Commons may happen before weekend." *Globe & Mail*, 23 November.

Penney, J. (2017) "Social media and citizen participation in 'official and 'unofficial' electoral promotion: A structural analysis of the 2016 Bernie Sanders digital campaign." *Journal of Communication* 67(3): 402–23.

Perez, C. (2002) *Technological Revolutions and Financial Capital*. London: Edward Elgar.

Perez, C. (2004) "Technological revolutions, paradigm shifts and socio-institutional change." In Reinert, E. (ed.) *Globalization, Economic Development and Inequality: An Alternative Perspective*. Cheltenham: Edward Elgar.

Pérez Roig, D. (2012) "Los hidrocarburos no convencionales en el escenario energético argentino." *Theomai* 25: 113–27.

Pettit, P. (1997) *Republicanism: A Theory of Freedom and Government*. Oxford: Oxford University Press.

Phillips, L. and Rozworski, M. (2019) *The People's Republic of Wal-Mart: How the World's Biggest Corporations are Laying the Foundation for Socialism*. New York: Verso Books.

Philo, G., Berry, M., Schlosberg, J., Lerman, A. and Miller, D. (2019) *Bad News for Labour: Antisemitism, the party and public belief*. London: Pluto Press.

Pidcock, L. (2020) "A letter to the movement." *Tribune*, 6 February. Available at: https://tribunemag.co.uk/2020/02/letter-to-the-movement.

Pilon, D. (2015) "Researching voter turnout and the electoral subaltern: Utilizing 'class' as identity. *Studies in Political Economy* 96: 69–91.

Pilon, D. (2019) "A reconnaissance of everyday working class ideology in British Columbia." In Laycock, D. (ed.) *Political Ideologies in Parties, Policy, and Civil Society*. Vancouver, UBC Press.

Piva, A. (2018) "La épica de un país ordenado. En torno a la caracterización del gobierno de Cambiemos." *Revista Intersecciones: Teoría y crítica social*. Available at: https://www.intersecciones.com.ar/2018/12/18/la-epica-de-un-pais-ordenado-en-torno-a-la-caracterizacion-del-gobierno-cambiemos/.

Piva, A., and Mosquera, M. (2019) "¿La emergencia de un nuevo ciclo político? Notas para la caracterización de la situación política." *Revista Intersecciones: Teoría y crítica social*. Available at: https://www.intersecciones.com.ar/2019/07/20/la-emergencia-de-un-nuevo-ciclo-politico-notas-para-la-caracterizacion-de-la-situacion-politica/.

Piven, F.F. and Cloward, R.A. (1982) *The New Class War: Reagan's Attack on the Welfare State and Its Consequences*. New York: Pantheon Books.

Pocock, J.G.A. (1975) *The Machiavellian Moment: Florentine Political Thought and the Atlantic Republican Tradition*. Princeton: Princeton University Press.

Poggi, G. (1990) *The State: Its Nature, Development, and Prospects*. Stanford: Stanford University Press.

Polanyi, K. (1944) *The Great Transformation*. New York: Farrar & Rinehart.

Pontusson, J. and Rueda, D. (2010) "The politics of inequality: voter mobilization and left parties in advanced industrial states." *Comparative Political Studies* 43(6): 675–705.

Poulantzas, N. (1969) "The problem of the capitalist state." *New Left Review* 58: 67–78.

Poulantzas, N. (1973) *Political Power and Social Classes*. London: New Left Books.

Poulantzas, N. (1974a) *Fascism and Dictatorship*. London: Verso Books.

Poulantzas, N. (1974b) "The internationalization of capitalist relations and the nation state." In *Classes in Contemporary Capitalism*. London: New Left Books.

Poulantzas, N. (1975) *Classes in contemporary capitalism*. London: New Left Books.

Poulantzas, N. (1976a) "The capitalist state: A reply to Miliband and Laclau." *New Left Review* 95: 63–83.

Poulantzas, N. (1976b) *Crisis of the Dictatorships*. London: Verso Books.

Poulantzas, N. (1977) *Poder Político e Classes Sociais*. São Paulo: Martins Fontes.

Poulantzas, N. (1978a) *As Classes Sociais no Capitalismo Hoje*. Rio de Janeiro: Zahar.

Poulantzas, N. (1978b) *Staatstheorie*. Hamburg: VSA-Verlag.

Poulantzas, N. (1978c) *State, Power, Socialism*. London: New Left Books.

Poulantzas, N. (2008) "The political crisis and the crisis of the state." In James, M. (ed.) *The Poulantzas Reader: Marxism, Law, and the State*. London: Verso Books.

Pramuk, J. (2020) "Bernie Sanders raises mammoth $46.5 million in February, announces TV ad buys in nine states." *CNBC*, 1 March. Available at: https://www.cnbc.com/2020/03/01/bernie-sanders-announces-february-fundraising-and-2020-primary-ad-buys.html.

Price, M. (2017) *Engagement Organizing: The Old Art and the New Science of Winning Campaigns*. Toronto: On Point Press.

Professional Institute of the Public Service of Canada v. Northwest Territories (Commissioner), [1990] 2 S.C.R. 367.

Przeworksi, A. and Sprague, J. (1986) *Paper Stones: A History of Electoral Socialism*. Chicago: University of Chicago Press.

PSAC v. Canada, [1987] 1 S.C.R. 424.

Radice, H. (1975) *International Firms and Modern Imperialism*. London: Penguin Books.

Radice, H. (1984) "The national economy: A Keynesian myth?" *Capital and Class* 8(1): 111–140.

Radice, H. (2013) "Utopian socialism and the Marxist critique of political economy." Paper presented at the Utopian Studies Society (Europe) International Conference, July.

Rakovsky, C. (1928) "The 'professional dangers' of power." *Bulletin of the Opposition*, August. Available at: https://www.marxists.org/archive/rakovsky/1928/08/prodan-ger.htm.

Ramírez Gallegos, F. (2016) "Political change, state autonomy, and post-neoliberalism in Ecuador, 2007–2012." *Latin American Perspectives* 43(1): 143–157.

Reference re Public Service Employee Relations Act (Alta.), [1987] 1 S.C.R. 313.

Republic National Committee (2020) "Resolution regarding the Republican Party platform." Available at: https://prod-cdn-static.gop.com/docs/Resolution_Platform_2020.pdf.

Republican Party Platforms (1972) "Republican Party platform of 1972." Online by G. Peters and J.T. Wooley, *The American Presidency Project*. Available at: https://www.presidency.ucsb.edu/documents/republican-party-platform-1972.

Reuters Staff (2019) "Former PM Blair says Britain is a mess." *Reuters*, 25 November. Available at: https://uk.reuters.com/article/uk-britain-election-blair-highlights/highlights-former-pm-blair-says-britain-is-a-mess-idUKKBN1XZ0XY.

Richardson, B. (2016) "Corbynmania: Citizen-consumers and the case for an alternative political marketing." *Journal of Customer Behaviour* 15(3): 283–297.

Riddell, C. (2004) "Union certification success under voting versus card-check procedures: Evidence from British Columbia, 1978–1998." *Industrial and Labor Relations Review* 57(4): 493–517.

Ries, C. (2019) "Bernie Sanders is running an unprecedented campaign." *Common Dreams*, 2 May. Available at: https://www.commondreams.org/views/2019/05/02/bernie-sanders-running-unprecedented-campaign.

Robertson, M. (2020) "Left economics from below? Defending the Programme after Corbyn." *New Socialist*, 25 August. Available at: http://newsocialist.org.uk/left-economics-below-defending-programme-after-corbyn/.

Robinson, I. (1993) *North American Free Trade As If Democracy Mattered*. Ottawa: Canadian Centre for Policy Alternatives.

Robinson, W.I. (1996) *Promoting Polyarchy: Globalization, US Intervention, and Hegemony*. Cambridge, England: Cambridge University Press.

Robinson, W.I. (2001) "Social theory and globalization: The rise of a transnational state." *Theory and Society* 30(2): 157–200.

Robinson, W.I. (2004) *Theory of Global Capitalism: Production, Class, and State in a Transnational World*. Baltimore: Johns Hopkins University Press.

Robinson, W.I. (2005) "Global capitalism: The new transnationalism and the folly of conventional thinking." *Science & Society* 69(3): 316–328.

Robinson, W.I. and Harris, J. (2000) "Towards a global ruling class? Globalization and the transnational capitalist class." *Science & Society* 64(1): 11–54.

Rojas, R. (2018) "The Latin American left shifting tides." *Catalyst* 2(2).

Rosenbluth, F. and Shapiro, I. (2018) *Responsible Parties: Saving Democracy from Itself*. New Haven: Yale University Press.

Ross, S. and Russell, J. (2018) " 'Caterpillar hates unions more than it loves profits': The electro-motive closure and the dilemmas of union strategy." *Labour/Le Travail* 81: 53–85.

Rothbard, M. (1991) "The end of socialism and the calculation debate revisited." *Review of Austrian Economics* 5(2): 51–76.

Rowthorn, B. (1971) "Imperialism in the seventies – Unity or rivalry?" *New Left Review* 69: 31–54.

Rutter, J. (2020) "Boris Johnson's imperial premiership." *UK in a Changing Europe*, 6 July. Available at: https://ukandeu.ac.uk/boris-johnsons-imperial-premiership/.

RWDSU v. Dolphin Delivery, [1986] 2 S.C.R. 573.

RWDSU v. Saskatchewan, [1987] 1 S.C.R. 460.

Sainsbury, D. (1990) "Party strategies and the electoral trade-off of class-based parties: A critique and application of the 'dilemma of electoral socialism'." *European Journal of Political Research*,18(1): 29–50.

Sandel, M.J. (1998) *Democracy's Discontent: America in Search of a Public Philosophy*. Cambridge: Harvard University Press.

Sanders, M.E. (1999) *Farmers, Workers, and the American State, 1877–1917*. Chicago: University of Chicago Press.

San Francisco Bay Area Kapitalistate Group (1977) "Political parties and capitalist development." *Kapitalistate*. 6: 7–38.

Sangster, J. (2004) " 'We no longer respect the law': The Tilco Strike, labour injunctions, and the state." *Labour/Le Travail* 54: 47–88.

Saraiva, C. Donnan, S. Pickert, R. (2020) "Thousands of $600 checks never made it to unemployed Americans." *Bloomberg*, 27 July. Available at: https://www .bloomberg.com/news/articles/2020-07-27/with-600-checks-expiring-some -americans-never-got-their-money.

Saros, D. (2014) *Information Technology and Socialist Construction: The End of Capital and the Transition to Socialism*. Abingdon and New York: Routledge Press.

Saskatchewan Federation of Labour v Saskatchewan, [2015] 1 SCR 245.

Savage, L. and Smith, C. (2017) *Unions in Court: Organized Labour and the Charter of Rights and Freedoms*. Vancouver: UBC Press.

Schmitter, P.C. and Lehmbruch, G. (eds) (1979) *Trends Toward Corporatist Intermediation*. Beverly Hills: Sage Publications.

Schorr, M. (2012) "Argentina: ¿nuevo modelo o viento de cola? Una caracterización en clave comparativa." *Nueva Sociedad* 237: 114–27.

Scruggs, L. and Allan, J.P. (2006) "The material consequences of welfare states: Benefit generosity and absolute poverty in 16 OECD countries." *Comparative Political Studies* 39(7): 880–904.

Secretaría de Finanzas. (2010) "Deuda pública del estado argentino. Datos al 30–09–2010." Ministerio de Economía y Finanzas Públicas. Available at: http://www. mecon.gov.ar/finanzas/sfinan/documentos/informe_deuda_publica_30-09-10.pdf.

Seymour R. (2015) "UKIP and the crisis of Britain." In Panitch, L. and Albo, G. (eds.) *Socialist Register 2016: The Politics of the Right*. London: Merlin Press.

Seymour R. (2019) "Nigel Farage is the most dangerous man in Britain." *The New York Times*, 28 May.

Shenker, J. (2019) *Now We Have Your Attention: The new politics of the people*. London: The Bodley Head.

Sim, S. (2001) *Post-Marxism: An Intellectual History*. London and New York: Routledge Press.

Simpson, A. (2014) "Inside New Labour's rolling coup: the Blair supremacy." *Red Pepper*, 1 December. Available at: https://www.redpepper.org.uk/inside-new-labours-rolling-coup-the-blair-supremacy/.

Skeggs, B., Thumim, N. and Wood, H. (2008) " 'Oh goodness, I am watching reality TV': How methods make class in audience research." *European Journal of Cultural Studies* 11(1): 5–24.

Sklair, L. (2001) *The Transnational Capitalist Class*. Oxford: Blackwell.

Skocpol, T. (1973) "A critical review of Barrington Moore's *Social Origins of Dictatorship and Democracy*." *Politics & Society* 4: 1–34.

Skocpol, T. (1979) *States and Social Revolution*. Cambridge: Cambridge University Press.

Skocpol, T. (1980) "Political response to capitalist crisis: Neo-Marxist theories of the state and the case of the New Deal." *Politics and Society* 10: 155–201.

Skocpol, T. (1985) "Bringing the state back in: strategies of analysis in current research." In Evans, P., Rueschemeyer, D. and Skocpol, T. (eds.) *Bringing the State Back In.* Cambridge: Cambridge University Press, 1985.

Skocpol, T. (1987) "The dead end of metatheory: Review of *Powers of Theory: Capitalism, the State, and Democracy* by Robert R. Alford and Roger Friedland." *Contemporary Sociology* 16: 10–12.

Skocpol, T. and Amenta, E. (1986) "States and social policies." *Annual Review of Sociology* 12: 131–57.

Skowronek, S. (1982) *Building a New American State: The Expansion of National Administrative Capacities, 1877–1920.* Cambridge: Cambridge University Press.

Slinn, S. (2004) "An empirical analysis of the effects of the change from card-check to mandatory vote certification." *Canadian Labour and Employment Law Journal* 11: 258–301.

Smith, A. (1999 [1776]) *The Wealth of Nations,* Books 1–3. London: Penguin Books.

Smith, C. (2012) " 'We didn't want to totally break the law,': Industrial legality, the Pepsi Strike, and workers' collective rights in Canada." *Labour/Le Travail* 74: 89–121.

Smith, C. (2017) "Freedom of association and the political economy of rights: The collective freedoms of workers after *SFL v. Saskatchewan.*" *Studies in Political Economy* 98: 124–150.

Smith, C. (2020) "Political economy and the Canadian working class: Conflict, crisis and change." In Whiteside, H. (ed.) *Canadian Political Economy.* Toronto: University of Toronto Press.

Smith, C. (2021) "Class struggle from above: The Canadian state, industrial legality, and (the never-ending usage of) back-to-work legislation." *Labour/Le Travail* 86: 109–123.

Smith, M. (2019) "Most Conservative members would see party destroyed to achieve Brexit." *YouGov,* 18 June. Available at: https://yougov.co.uk/topics/politics/articles-reports/2019/06/18/most-conservative-members-would-see-party-destroye.

Starblanket, T. (2018) *Suffer the Little Children: Genocide, Indigenous Nations, and the Canadian State.* Atlanta: Clarity Press.

Stepan, A.C. (1978) *State and Society: Peru in Comparative Perspective.* Princeton: Princeton University Press.

Stiglitz, J. (2001) "Information and the change in the paradigm in economics." Prize lecture, December 8. Available at: https://www.nobelprize.org/uploads/2018/06/stiglitz-lecture.pdf.

Strange, S. (1996) *The Retreat of the State: The Diffusion of Power in the World Economy.* New York: Cambridge University Press.

Streeck, W. (2017) *How Will Capitalism End?* London: Verso Books.

Swartz, D. and Warskett, R. (2012) "Canadian labour and the crisis of solidarity." In Ross, S. and Savage, L. (eds.) *Rethinking the Politics of Labour in Canada.* Halifax: Fernwood.

"Symposium: Introduction to the Symposium on the State." 2017. *Studies in Political Economy* 98(2): 175–76.

Tabb, W.K. (2009) "Globalization today: At the borders of class and state theory." *Science & Society* 73(1): 34–53.

Task Force on Labour Relations (Woods Commission) (1968) *Canadian Industrial Relations.* Ottawa: Ministry of Supply and Services.

Taylor, F.M. (1929) "The guidance of production in a socialist state." *The American Economic Review* 19(1): 1–8.

The Canadian Railway Employees' Monthly (1950a) "Five day, forty-hour week written into Canadian law by militant railway unions," September.

The Canadian Railway Employees' Monthly (1950b) "President's message to all members of the brotherhood on strike, August 22–30, 1950," September.

Therborn, G. (1978) *What Does the Ruling Class Do When it Rules?* London: New Left Books.

Thomas, P. (2009) *The Gramscian Moment: Philosophy, Hegemony, and Marxism.* Leiden and Boston: Brill.

Toffler, A. (1981) *The Third Wave.* London: Pan Books Ltd.

Tooze, A. (2018) *Crashed: How a decade of financial crisis changed the world.* London: Allen Lane.

Toronto Star (1950a) "Concessions by unions 11th-hour offer by railways fruitless," 22 August.

Toronto Star (1950b) "Starve within a week, 29,000 in Timmins fear ration gasoline now," 22 August.

Toronto Star (1950c) "10,000 miners facing layoff in Sudbury area," 22 August.

Toronto Star (1950d) "Order M.P.'s flown to Ottawa by R.C.A.F. for strike session," 22 August.

Toronto Star (1950e) "Arbitration by law binding on both sides said St. Laurent plan," 22 August.

Tossutti, L. (2019) "Engaging youths across the education divide: Is there a role for social capital?" *Canadian Journal of Political Science* 52: 501–520.

Touraine, A. (1971) *The Post-Industrial Society, Tomorrow's Social History: Classes, Conflicts and Culture in Programmed Society.* Translated by F.X. Mayhew. New York: Random House.

Tracy, R. (2020) "Mnuchin Calls for forgiving PPP loans to smallest businesses." *Wall Street Journal,* 17 July. Available at: https://www.wsj.com/articles/mnuchin-suggests-automatic-forgiveness-of-paycheck-protection-program-loans-11595000522.

Trump, D. (2019). "Remarks at the Turning Point U.S.A. Student Action Summit in West Palm Beach, Florida." 31 December.

Tsoukalas, K. (1999) "Globalization and 'the Executive Committee': Reflections on the contemporary state." In Panitch, L. and Leys, C. (eds.) *Socialist Register 1999: Global Capitalism Versus Democracy.* New York: Monthly Review Press.

Tucker, E. (1991) " 'That indefinite area of toleration': Criminal conspiracy and trade unions in Ontario, 1833–1877." *Labour/Le Travail* 27: 14–51.

Tucker, E. (2010) *"Hersees of Woodstock Ltd. v. Goldstein*: How a small town case made it big." In Fudge, J. and Tucker, E. (eds.) *Work on Trial: Canadian Labour Law Struggles.* Toronto: Irwin.

Tucker, E. and Fudge, J. (1996) "Forging responsible unions: Metal workers and the rise of the labour injunction in Canada." *Labour/Le Travail* 37: 81–120.

UE News (1950) "New law threatens all: Official back-to-work order sets strike-breaking pace rouses all unionists," *UE New* 9, 1 September.

United Nurses of Alberta v. Alberta (Attorney General), [1992] 1 S.C.R. 901.

United States Census Bureau (no date) *Household Pulse Survey Data Tables.* Available at: https://www.census.gov/programs-surveys/household-pulse-survey/data.html.

United States. Congress. Senate. (1976) *Final report of the Select Committee to Study Governmental Operations with Respect to Intelligence Activities, United States Senate: together with additional, supplemental, and separate views.* Washington, D.C.: Government Printing Office.

US Bureau of Labor Statistics (no date) *Work Stoppages.* Available at: https://www.bls. gov/wsp/.

van der Pijl, K. (1998) *Transnational Classes and International Relations.* London: Routledge Press.

van der Waal, J., Achterberg, P. and Houtman, D. (2007) "Class is not dead – it has been buried alive: Class voting and cultural voting in postwar western societies (1956–1990)." *Politics and Society* 35(3): 403–426.

Vernon, R. (1971) *Sovereignty at Bay.* Harmondsworth: Penguin Books.

Vizard, S. (2015) "What marketers should take away from Jeremy Corbyn's Labour leadership win." *Marketing Week,* 14 September. Available at: https://www.marketingweek.com/what-marketers-should-take-away-from-jeremy-corbyns-labour-leadership-win/.

Vogl, J. (2014) *The Specter of Capital.* Stanford: Stanford University Press.

Waddell, B. (2001) *The War Against the New Deal.* DeKalb: Northern Illinois University Press.

Wade, R. (1996) "Globalization and its limits: Reports of the death of the national economy are greatly exaggerated." In Berger, S. and Dore, R. (eds.) *National Diversity and Global Capitalism.* Ithaca: Cornell University Press.

Wahl, P. (2019) *Gilets Jaunes. Anatomie einer ungewöhnlichen sozialen Bewegung.* Köln: Neue Kleine Bibliothek.

Wain, Y., Sidhu, S., Vassilev, G., Mubarak, S., Martin, T. and Wignall, J. (2018) "Trends in self-employment in the UK." *Office for National Statistics.* Available at: https://www.ons.gov.uk/employmentandlabourmarket/peopleinwork/employmentandemployeetypes/articles/trendsinselfemploymentintheuk/2018-02-07.

Wainwright, H. (1982) *The Lucas Plan: A New Trade Unionism in the Making.* London: Alison and Busby.

Wainwright, H. (1994) *Arguments for a New Left: Answering the Free-Market Right.* Oxford: Blackwell.

Wainwright, H. (2007) *Reclaim the State: Experiments in Popular Democracy.* London: Seagull.

Wainwright, H. (2020a) "Swords into ploughshares; planes into ventilators parts." *Red Pepper.* Available at: https://www.redpepper.org.uk/swords-into-ploughshares/.

Wainwright, H. (2020b) "Former chief scientist blasts government coronavirus response." *Red Pepper.* Available at: https://www.redpepper.org.uk/top-scientist-blasts-government-covid-response/.

Walker, P. (2018) "Tory members 'a breed apart' from other main parties, study finds." *The Guardian,* 4 January. Available at: https://www.theguardian.com/politics/2018/jan/04/tory-members-a-breed-apart-from-other-main-parties-study-finds.

Wallerstein, I. (1979) *The Capitalist World-Economy.* Cambridge: Cambridge University Press.

Wallerstein, I. (1980) *The World Capitalist System II: Mercantilism and the Consolidation of the European World Economy, 1600-1750.* New York: Academic Press.

Wallerstein, I. (1982) *The Modern World-System, vol. II: Mercantilism and the Consolidation of the European World-Economy, 1600–1750.* New York: Academic Press.

Warren, B. (1975 [1971]) "How international is capital?" in Radice, H. (ed.) *International Firms and Modern Imperialism.* London: Penguin Books.

Warren, J. and Carlisle, K. (2005) *On the Side of the People: A History of Labour in Saskatchewan.* Toronto: Coteau Books.

Wearden, G. (2019) "Ex-top civil servant: Hammond was right to query no-deal backers." *The Guardian,* 29 September. Available at: https://www.theguardian.com/politics/2019/sep/29/ex-top-civil-servant-hammond-was-right-to-query-no-deal-backers.

Webber, J. (2019) "Mercado mundial, desarrollo desigual y patrones de acumulación: La política económica de la Izquierda Latinoamericana." In Gaudichaud, F, Webber, J., and Modonessi, M. (eds.) *Los Gobiernos Progresistas Latinoamericanos Del Siglo XXI. Ensayos de Interpretación Histórica.* Mexico: Universidad Nacional Autónoma de México.

Weber, M. (1946) "Politics as a vocation." In Gerth, H.H. and Mills, C.W. (eds) *From Max Weber: Essays in Sociology.* Oxford: Oxford University Press.

Weber, S.H. (2004) *The Success of Open Source.* Cambridge, MA: Harvard University Press.

Weinstein, J. (1968) *The Corporate Ideal in the Liberal State: 1900–1918.* Boston: Beacon Press.

Weiss, L. (1997) "Globalization and the myth of the powerless state." *New Left Review* 225: 3–27.

Weiß, V. (2017) *Die autoritäre Revolte. Die Neue Rechte und der Untergang des Abendlandes.* Stuttgart: Klett-Cotta.

Wells, D. (1995) "Origins of Canada's Wagner Model of industrial relations: The United Auto Workers in Canada and the suppression of rank-and-file unionism, 1936–1953." *Canadian Journal of Sociology* 20: 193–224.

Wesley, J.J. and Moyes, M. (2014) "Selling social democracy: Branding the political left in Canada." In Marland, A. Giasson, T. and Small, T.A. (eds.) *Political Communication in Canada: Meet the Press and Tweet the Rest.* Vancouver: UBC Press.

Wetherly, P. (2008) 'Can capitalists use the state to serve their general interest?'. In Wetherly, P. Barrow, C.W. and Burnham, P. (eds.) *Class, Power and the State in Capitalist Society: Essays on Ralph Miliband.* New York: Palgrave Press.

Wetherly, P., Barrow, C.W. and Burnham, P. (eds.) (2008) *Class, Power and the State in Capitalist Society: Essays on Ralph Miliband.* New York: Palgrave Press.

Wheatcroft, G. (2020) "The opportunist triumphant." *New York Review of Books,* 16 January.

Whitaker, R. (1977) "Images of the state in Canada." In Panitch, L. (ed.) *The Canadian State: Political Economy and Political Power.* Toronto: University of Toronto Press.

White, H. (2016) "In Contempt? Witnesses before select committees." *Institute for Government,* 18 April. Available at: https://www.instituteforgovernment.org.uk/blog/contempt-witnesses-select-committees.

Whitty, G. (2001) "Education, social class and social exclusion." *Journal of Education Policy* 16(4): 287–295.

Wile, R. (2014) "The true story of how McDonald's conquered France." *Business Insider,* 22 August. Available at: http://www.businessinsider.com/how-mcdonalds-conquered-france-2014-8.

Wilenius, P. (2004) "Enemies within: Thatcher and the unions." *BBC Report,* March. Available at: http://large.stanford.edu/publications/coal/references/miners/wilenius/

Williams, R. (1989) *Resources of Hope: Culture, Democracy, Socialism.* London: Verso Books.

Willman, D. (2020) "CDC coronavirus test kits were likely contaminated, federal review confirms." *The Washington Post,* 20 June. Available at: https://www.washingtonpost.com/investigations/cdc-coronavirus-test-kits-were-likely-contaminated-federal-review-confirms/2020/06/20/1ceb4e16-b2ef-11ea-8f56-63f38c990077_story.html.

Winders, B. (1999) "The roller coaster of class conflict: Class segments, mass mobilization, and voter turnout in the U.S., 1840–1996." *Social Forces* 77(3): 833–862.

Wood, E.M. (1986) *The Retreat from Class.* London: Verso Books.

Wood, E. (1995) *Democracy Against Capitalism: Renewing Historical Materialism.* Cambridge: Cambridge University Press.

Wood, E. (2003) *Empire of Capital.* London: Verso Books.

Work and Pensions Committee (2019) "Letter from Chair, Frank Field to Secretary of State, Amber Rudd." 28 February, In: House of Commons Work and Pensions

Committee, Correspondence. Available at: https://www.parliament.uk/business/committees/committees-a-z/commons-select/work-and-pensions-committee/inquiries/parliament-2017/inquiry19/.

World Economic Forum (2020) *The Global Risks Report 2020*. Geneva: World Economic Forum.

Wright, E.O. (1985). *Classes*. London: Verso Books.

Wright, E.O. (2010) *Envisioning Real Utopias*. London: Verso Books.

Wright, E.O. (2015) *Understanding Class*. London: Verso Books.

Wriston, W. (1992) *Twilight of Sovereignty: How the Information Revolution is Transforming the World*. New York: Scribner's.

Wylde, C. (2018) "Twenty-first century developmental states? Argentina under the Kirchners." *Third World Quarterly* 39(6): 1115–1132.

Yates, M.D. (ed.) (2007) *More Unequal: Aspects of Class in the United States*. New York: Monthly Review Press.

Zucker, L.G. (1987) "Institutional theories of organization." *Annual Review of Sociology* 13: 443–63.

Index

www.ingramcontent.com/pod-product-compliance
Lightning Source LLC
Chambersburg PA
CBHW070900030426
42336CB00014BA/2269